FIFTH EDITION

PERSONNEL ADMINISTRATION IN EDUCATION

A Management Approach

Ronald W. Rebore, Sr.
St. Louis University

Allyn and Bacon

Boston • London • Toronto • Sydney • Tokyo • Singapore

*As a service-rendering institution, the school will be successful
in direct proportion to the quality of its employees.*

To Sandy, Ron, and Lisa

Senior Editor: Raymond Short
Vice President and Publisher, Education: Nancy Forsyth
Editorial Assistant: Karin Huang
Marketing Manager: Kris Farnsworth
Editorial Production Service: Chestnut Hill Enterprises, Inc.
Manufacturing Buyer: Megan Cochran
Cover Administrator: Linda Knowles

Library of Congress Cataloging-in-Publication Data

Rebore, Ronald W.
    Personnel administration in education : a management approach /
Ronald W. Rebore, Sr. — 5th ed.
        p.   cm.
    Includes bibliographical references and index.
    ISBN 0-205-26912-5 (alk. paper)
    1. School personnel management—United States.   I. Title.
LB2831.58.R43   1998
371.2'01'0973—dc21   97-16286
                                                                    CIP

Printed in the United States of America
10   9   8   7   6   5   4   3   02   01   00   99   98

CONTENTS

PREFACE

The evolving culture of our contemporary society continues to have an ongoing and profound effect on the practice of school personnel management. The aspects of this effect are reflected in the fifth edition of *Personnel Administration in Education.*

A significant example of this evolving culture is set forth in the section on total quality management of the personnel function. This type of management strategy has enriched private business and industry for a number of years. The tenets of this strategy are now appearing in school district administration offices and, in this book, are explicated in relation to the personnel management function.

The U.S. Congress enacted *The Americans with Disabilities Act of 1990,* which is *the most comprehensive legislation ever passed protecting the rights of individuals with disabilities.* Furthermore, *The Civil Rights Act of 1991* has the potential of costing violators punitive damages through the decisions of jury trials. In 1993, Congress also passed the *Family and Medical Leave Act,* which gives eligible employees the right to leave employment under certain circumstances. Alcohol and controlled substances testing has been mandated for particular occupations, such as school bus drivers, by the *Omnibus Transportation Employee Testing Act of 1991.*

The mobilization of military reserves and National Guard units into active duty in 1990 as a consequence of Operation Desert Storm prompted most school personnel managers to investigate the responsibilities that school districts have toward those employees called-up for duty in the armed services.

Sexual harassment in the workplace has gained the attention of school district personnel across the nation as the media have presented coverage of the consequences of this inappropriate and illegal behavior. The issues of human immunodeficiency virus (HIV), acquired immune deficiency syndrome (AIDS), and AIDS related complex (ARC) challenge the ability of school personnel administrators to meet the humane needs and legal requirements of those staff members so infected while addressing the concerns of coworkers, parents, and the public at large.

The phenomenon of collaborative bargaining as an alternative to the traditional model of negotiations has also become more prevalent in school districts.

Health risks in the workplace, an issue that is related to the ever-increasing cost of Workers' Compensation, is seriously affecting school district budgets. Likewise, the costs of fringe benefits continue to rise, prompting managed health care as an alternative to traditional medical and hospital insurance programs.

The ethical responsibilities of school personnel administrators has become a national concern over the honesty of employees in all levels of government, including public education.

The underlying root cause of the "reform" movement is the level of accountability or lack thereof in public schools. Taxpayers in general and parents in particular believe that they are not receiving their proper entitlement. A large number of tax levy elections continue to fail because of this perception. The problem of accountability is a "people" problem and, thus, is a personnel administration problem.

It is evident that school district administration parallels that of corporations and other organizations in our American society. Fiscal management, curriculum development, physical plant management, employee supervision, and personnel administration have become specialties that require educationally sophisticated administrators.

The fifth edition of *Personnel Administration in Education: A Management Approach* continues to set forth information relative to personnel administration that has surfaced since the publication of the fourth edition. This information and accompanying analysis is significant and will have a profound effect on personnel administration. Thus, this edition explicates the following: the *Health Insurance Portability and Accountability Act of 1996;* the *Small Business Job Protection Act of 1996;* procuring health care and related insurance; health care program coverages; a glossary of health care terms and acronyms; a job description for the director of employee benefits; medical savings accounts; recruiting on the internet; enhanced procedures for terminating the employment of staff members; genetic testing and the *Americans With Disabilities Act of 1990;* in addition to other updating of materials and the selected bibliographies.

Personnel Administration in Education should be of interest to three categories of individuals: first, professors of educational administration who have the instructional responsibility of teaching courses in personnel administration; second, practicing central-office administrators and building principals who want to become more familiar with the field of human resource management; and last, school board members and superintendents who may be searching for a model in order to establish a central-office, human resource administrative position.

Chapter 1 establishes the rationale and organizational structure that support effective human resource administration. Chapters 2 through 5 are concerned with the acquisition of personnel, and Chapters 6 through 9 deal with personnel retention. Each of these chapters addresses a major dimension of the entire personnel management function and identifies the processes, procedures, and techniques necessary to carry out these dimensions. This orientation to personnel administration is the reason for the subtitle of the book, *A Management Approach.* Finally, Chapter 10 considers the legal, ethical, and policy implications of personnel administration.

At this point, I would like to sincerely thank my colleagues teaching at universities and their students who reviewed *Personnel Administration in Education* and made valuable suggestions for its improvement. I continue to incorporate as many of their suggestions as possible.

R. W. R.

1

ORGANIZATIONAL DIMENSIONS

THE STRUCTURAL FRAMEWORK OF PUBLIC EDUCATION

Philosophical Imperatives

The system of free and universal elementary and secondary education in the United States is one of its unique and distinguishing characteristics. It is generally considered to be our greatest safeguard of freedom and the best guarantee for the economic and social welfare of our citizens.

The school as an institution receives its mandate from the society it serves. It is, however, only one of many institutions. The government, family, and church also play a role in our society.

These institutions have complementary purposes. Each in its own right provides for the advancement of society in general and the individual citizen in particular. The educational programs of the school would be ineffective without the support of government, the family, and the church. A hallmark, however, of modern-day society and these institutions is change. This is dramatically pointed out by the National School Public Relations Association.

> Calculators, cable television, microcomputers, video discs, satellites, teleconferencing—the list of new technologies arriving on the scene almost daily is growing and becoming more important to our lives. Only a decade ago, the idea of computers being as common in the home as the television was looked upon as an idea as far-fetched as man walking on the moon was in the middle of this century.
>
> No one will deny that the . . . (present) is the age of technology, an age as dramatic as the industrial revolution in its capacity to change the way we live. Students today will have their future, and much of their present, dominated by electronic wizardry. And unless they have an understanding of and the ability to use the new technology, they will be as illiterate as persons who cannot read or write.[1]

---

[1]National School Public Relations Association, "New Challenge for Schools: Age of Information," *Education USA,* 24, no. 19 (January 4, 1982), p. 141.

This statement focuses on communicative and technological advancement, but in the complexity of any given society, infinite streams of change occur simultaneously. The family, church, school, and government with all their subcomponents are not static institutions but rather evolving entities.

Change is not only continual but also accelerative. This is further complicated by the fact that changes occur unevenly. Technology may be undergoing mutations faster than it is possible to change educational programs that can make this new knowledge available, which in turn leaves students years behind in learning about new advances.

Our perception of reality and how this relates to societal and individual needs determines the content of our educational programs. Although fundamental principles such as individual freedom, individual responsibility, and democratic government must be continuously taught in our schools, the accelerating rate of change in areas such as technology demands that our schools be flexible enough to adjust to new developments and conditions. Education cannot be static in the dynamic milieu of reality.

At various times in the history of our nation, educators, professional organizations, local governments, and the federal government have formally stated the goals and purposes of American education. Three of the most influential reports on the goals of American education are *Ten Imperative Needs,* issued in 1954 by the National Education Association, *Four Dimensions of the Task of the School,* developed in 1960 by the Midwest Administration Center; and *Imperatives in Education,* promulgated in 1966 by the American Association of School Administrators. There is a great degree of similarity among these declarations. All are concerned in some way with promoting family life, personal health and growth, intellectual development, creative talent, proper use of leisure time, vocational preparation, social responsibility, and human relations skills. In themselves these reports are hardly subject to improvement and should be studied by all who are concerned with education. However, the goals elucidated in these reports must be understood within the context of continual evolution.

More recently the National Education Association Center for Innovation established a Mastery in Learning Consortium. The goal of this effort is to enable students to achieve "mastery in learning" and faculty members "mastery in teaching" by creating learning communities committed to comprehensive organizational change. Another example is the New Standards Project which was established by the National Center on Education and the Economy. The goal of this project is to establish national standards and performance-based assessments in mathematics, science, English, language arts, and history.

Responsibilities of Federal and State Government

Carrying out these objectives of American education is the responsibility of the individual states. The U.S. Constitution is conspicuous in its omission of any provision or specific reference to education. The Tenth Amendment to the Constitution, ratified in 1791, states that "the powers not delegated to the United States by the Constitution, nor prohibited by it to the States, are reserved to the States respectively, or to the people." Thus, education has consistently been considered a state function.

Experience shows, however, that the federal government has been involved; in fact, its involvement has been extensive. Through the legislative branch, Congress provides funds that support special services and programs in local school districts. Through the U.S. Office of Education, the executive branch of the government exercises authority over educational matters. The creation of a cabinet-level Department of Education exemplifies the extent of this involvement. The many Supreme Court decisions affecting Education testify to the influence of the judicial branch of the federal government on our schools.

The National School Boards Association issued a publication in 1982, entitled *The Federal Role in Education: A Foundation for the Future,* that sets forth an analysis of why the federal government becomes involved with public education. The following summarizes the major issues that have fostered federal involvement:

Economy

The connection between public education and the nation's economic well-being is now stronger than ever before. New technologies are quickly changing the work place. Federal assistance is needed to identify national labor market trends and to develop career awareness in order to meet the needs of the nation's changing work force.

Poverty

Poverty is an ever-increasing national problem. In 1980, 29.3 million people, or 13 percent of the U.S. population, were under the poverty line. The path out of poverty for millions of disadvantaged students is compensatory education. According to the author, the need for a strong federal role in educational solutions is as great as ever because of the magnitude of the problem, the human cost of ignoring the problem, and the historical movement of poor people across state lines.

Defense

As weapons and support systems become more technological, the military needs more trained workers. The armed forces currently spend over $12 billion per year on human resource training programs; in many cases to teach fundamental technical skills to relatively short-term employees. These fundamentals could be taught in the public schools if appropriate programs were supported.

Civil rights

Although much racial discrimination in education was eliminated during the 1960s, federal data collection and enforcement are still needed today to maintain this progress. Education plays a central role in attaining the benefits of a democratic society. Therefore, Congress performs a legitimate function when it identifies and corrects cases of discrimination based on race, sex, handicapping condition, or English deficiency.[2]

An example of influence exerted upon education by President Ronald Reagan's administration was the report by the National Commission on Education, *A Nation at Risk: The Imperative for Educational Reform* which was issued in 1983.

The commission's recommendations are based upon the following assumptions. First, everyone has the capability to learn. Second, everyone is born with the desire to learn,

---

[2]Educational Research Service, "Federal Role in Education," *ERS Bulletin,* 10, no. 2 (October 1982). p. 4.

which can be nurtured through formal education. Third, a solid high school education is within everyone's reach. Fourth, lifelong learning will help people to develop the skills necessary for new careers and for citizenship.

President George Bush released a long-range plan for achieving national educational goals on April 18, 1991 that was titled, *America 2000: An Education Strategy*. The following national goals were established in this plan:

1. By the year 2000, all children in the United States will start school ready to learn;
2. By the year 2000, the high school graduation rate will increase to at least 90 percent;
3. By the year 2000, U.S. students will leave grades four, eight, and twelve having demonstrated competency in challenging subject matter including English, mathematics, science, history, and geography; and every teacher in the United States will ensure that all students learn to use their minds well, so that they may be prepared for responsible citizenship, further learning, and productive employment in our modern economy;
4. By the year 2000, U.S. students will be first in the world in science and mathematics achievement;
5. By the year 2000, every adult American will be literate and will possess the knowledge and skills necessary to compete in a global economy and exercise the rights and responsibilities of citizenship;
6. By the year 2000, every school in America will be free of drugs and violence and will offer a disciplined environment conducive to learning.

The U.S. Secretary of Education, Richard W. Riley, stated in a speech at the 1993 National School Boards Association's Convention that there are three "overarching principles" in President Clinton's administration: 1. improving teaching and learning; 2. creating opportunity and responsibility in the school; 3. building partnerships with other agencies.[3]

In an ever-shrinking world and nation, the goals of U.S. education cannot be left solely to the discretion of the states. This involvement of the federal government, however, should not supplant the jurisdiction of state governments but rather should complement and enrich their efforts.

The authority of the states to create and govern public schools is embodied in the state constitutions and exercised through the state legislatures. All state legislatures have delegated certain aspects of this authority to local units, boards of education. To insure some control over local units, state legislatures have established minimum educational program requirements and teacher certification requirements and have provided state funds to help finance education.

The administrative arm of most state legislatures is a *State Department of Education,* which is usually governed by a board and administered by a commissioner or state superintendent, Figure 1–1 visualizes the relationship between the state and local boards of education.

The National Council of Chief State School Officers has properly emphasized the state's educational responsibility and the state's relationship to local and federal agencies.

---

[3]National School Boards Association, "Riley Advocates 'Goals 2000' Legislation," *School Board News,* 13, no. 6 (April 1993), p. 5.

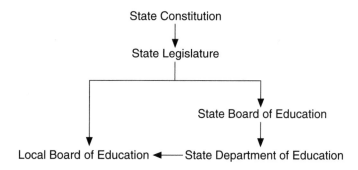

FIGURE 1–1   Jurisdictional Flow Chart

The following quotation from the Council has historical significance because it has been invoked many times to explain the responsibility of the state.

Our system of constitutional government makes the states responsible for the organization and administration of public education and for general supervision of nonpublic schools. Each state has in practice delegated authority to organize and operate schools to various types of local administrative units of its own creation (Boards of Education). Within its general unity, our system of education leaves room for diversified programs among states and local administrative units.

Local, state and federal governments all have a vital interest in education. Each can contribute most effectively only if there is appropriate allocation of responsibility among them and only if relations among them are properly defined. Initiative and responsibility must be encouraged in the local units which operate most of the schools. The states must insure organization, financial support and effective administration of education programs of suitable quality and make certain these programs are available to every child. The federal government has an obligation to provide supplementary assistance to the states in accord with the national interest in universal education.

Local school boards and other state education authorities represent the public in the administration of education. Working with their professional staffs, these authorities are responsible for carefully planned programs of education and for obtaining the participation of the people in planning the kinds of schools and education they need and want.[4]

Responsibilities of the Board of Education

School districts are perhaps the most democratically controlled of any agency of government. The citizens of a local community elect school board members, who are charged with

[4]The National Council of Chief State School Officers, *Our System of Education* (Washington, D.C.: The National Council of Chief State School Officers, 1950), pp. 5–6.

formulating policies for the governance and administration of the schools. State departments of education exercise some regulatory authority, assuring that a minimum educational program is provided in every school district, but the citizens of the local district maintain control of the schools through locally elected boards.

As the duties and responsibilities of school boards are presented, it is essential to keep in mind that education is a state function. The courts have consistently upheld this principle. By virtue of the authority delegated to school boards from each state legislature, boards represent the state, even though the members are locally elected. Board members, as individuals, exercise no authority outside a legally constituted meeting. Policies can be agreed upon only in an official meeting, and individual members cannot commit the board to any definite action except as authorized by the board at a legal meeting.

In exercising their authority to govern schools, boards of education should carefully formulate and adopt policy statements. This very difficult task cannot be successfully accomplished without guidance from the professional educational staff and, at times, an attorney. Board policies must not conflict with the U.S. Constitution, federal law, and federal court decisions. In like manner, policies must not conflict with the appropriate state constitution, state statutes, or state court decisions. Regulations issued by a state department of education should be considered by a board in creating policies but may be ignored. However, penalties such as loss of state aid make it impractical for a school board to create policies in conflict with such regulations. Local traditions, opinions, and goals also should be taken into consideration because policies objectionable to the local community will weaken citizen support. There are many more influences in our contemporary society that affect board decisions today than were present even five years ago. Figure 1–2 illustrates some of these influences on policy formulation.

Some advantages for developing policies have been outlined in *The School and Community Relations* and may serve as a rationale for school boards.

- Policy facilitates the orientation of new board members regarding relations between the school and the community.
- Policy facilitates a similar orientation for new employees—both professional and non-professional—in the school system.
- Policy acquaints the public with the position of the school and encourages citizen involvement in educational affairs.

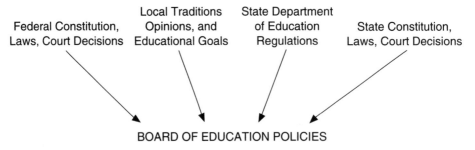

FIGURE 1–2

- Policy provides a reasonable guarantee that there will be consistency and continuity in the decisions that are made under it.
- Policy informs superintendents what they may expect from the board and what the board may expect from them.
- Policy creates the need for developing a detailed program in order to implement it.
- Policy provides a legal reason for the allocation of funds and facilities in order to make the policy work.
- Policy establishes an essential division between policymaking and policy administration.[5]

School board policies should not be confused with administrative rules and regulations, which constitute the detailed manner by which policies are implemented. Rules and regulations delineate who does what, when, and where. In fact, many rules and regulations may be required to implement one policy.

A properly conceived and phrased board of education policy has the following characteristics:

- It is stated in broad, general terms, but in terms that are clear enough to allow for executive direction and interpretation.
- It reveals the philosophy of the board of education as members understand the desires of the community.
- It provides purpose and rationale for the subject about which a policy is being made.
- It suggests how the matter is to be carried out.
- It is never executive in substance or tone.
- It covers situations that are likely to occur repeatedly.
- It is always subject to review by the board, with the objective of improvement in accordance with changing conditions.

Likewise, the policy should

- Provide support and authority for all school programs and activities.
- Be brief, clear, concise, and complete.
- Be stable even during personnel changes.
- Have adequate provisions for review and amendment.[6]

After the board of education establishes its policies, it is the responsibility of the superintendent of schools and his or her staff to establish administrative processes and procedures that implement the board policies.

The policies of a school board are usually incorporated into a manual in order to be easily consulted by administrators, teachers, and citizens.

---

[5]Donald R. Gallagher, Don Bagin, Leslie W. Kindred, *The School and Community Relations,* 6th ed. (Needham Heights, MA: Allyn and Bacon, 1997), p. 37.

[6]Missouri School Board Association, *A Manual for Missouri School Board Members* (Columbia, Mo.: The Association, 1981), p. H–3.

There are four popular formats used in writing policies. The most common format is the resolution style, on which the school board votes to take action. Equal Employment Opportunity and Affirmative Action Policies are usually adopted in this resolution style. A second format sets forth the rationale for the policy and establishes broad goals. The third style incorporates an identification of who is responsible for implementing the policy. This is a common practice in formulating policies that address a specific function, such as collective bargaining. The policy might identify the "Director of Employee Relations" as the chief negotiator for the school board and establish the confines within which he or she will function. A fourth format is used when the school board wishes to eliminate possible misunderstanding about how the policy is to be implemented. This type of style, therefore, incorporates administrative rules and regulations.

THE ADMINISTRATIVE PROCESS

Theoretical Considerations

Administration is an indispensable component of all institutions in organized society; yet, it is often taken for granted.

The need for administration has been evident whenever there was a task to be performed by two or more people. Many ancient records of significant events describe administrative activities. From building the pyramids in Egypt to supervising medieval feudal domains to governing colonies in distant hemispheres—all have demanded a degree of administrative skill and understanding of the administrative process.

Our understanding of the nature of administration has also evolved. The earliest concepts centered around the "action" model. Administrators were those who took charge of an activity and accomplished a task. The formal study of administration is a recent phenomenon that has found its most fertile climate in the business world, where much study is devoted to the effective execution of managerial leadership roles.

The need for the formal study of administration in public education grew out of the increased complexity of urban school districts. The illusion that anyone with a good general education could become an effective administrator was quickly shattered during the urbanization period.

Administration is the social process of managing human, financial, and material resources toward the fulfillment of a mission. The school administrator fulfills these requisites by developing and establishing administrative processes, procedures, and techniques that harness human, financial, and material energies. The importance of administrative leadership stems from its potential for converting these energies within an organization to the fulfillment of educational objectives.

This definition also views administration as an executive activity, distinct from policy making. Administration is primarily concerned with the implementation, not the making, of policy. More specifically, the administration of a district is responsible for carrying out the policies of the board of education.

The systems approach to administration has gained steadily in popularity ever since President Johnson mandated its implementation in federal agencies, and the outcry for accountability in the public sector advanced its use. In the systems approach the school is viewed as a network of interrelated subsystems. Emphasis is given to formulating short- and long-range objectives that can be translated into operational activities that are implemented and evaluated.

The approach followed in this book focuses on the personnel function as a function. Thus, administration is viewed as an all-encompassing process composed of various functions. Three of the most critical functions in a school system are personnel administration, instructional programs administration, and support services administration. Support services here include transportation, food service, and financial administration. Each of these functions has goals that are implemented through administrative processes, procedures, and techniques—which are collectively referred to as *management*. This book, of course, centers on the personnel function and its management.

Functions are carried out by administrators within a given organizational framework. The remaining portion of this section delineates and clarifies the role of the superintendent of schools and major central office administrators.

The Organization of Central Office

Historically and, in most states, by statutory mandate, school boards have delegated the responsibility for implementing policies to a chief executive officer, the superintendent of schools. The superintendent assumes full control of all operations. As school districts grow in size and complexity, it becomes necessary to develop specialized functions, and the central-office staff comes into being. However, all employees, professional and other, ultimately report to the superintendent and are subordinate to him or her. The superintendent is the only employee who deals with the board of education on a regular and direct basis.

The superintendent's role description falls into the following three major categories:

Chief Advisor

The superintendent is the main consultant and advisor to the school board on all matters concerning the school district. The superintendent is expected to contribute to the board's deliberations by furnishing reports, information, and recommendations, both upon request of the board and upon self-directed initiative.

A list of the superintendent's duties and functions as the board's chief advisor includes the following:

1. Formulate and recommend personnel policies necessary for the efficient functioning of the school staff.
2. Provide information to the school board on vital matters pertaining to the school system.
3. Prepare and submit to the board a preliminary budget.
4. Recommend all candidates for employment. (The board may reject specific candidates recommended, but all personnel should be employed only on the superintendent's recommendation.)
5. Submit an annual report to the board on the operations of the school system.

✗ Executive Officer

Once a policy decision has been established by the board of education it becomes the responsibility of the executive officer of the board and the district's staff to execute that decision. The administration should implement board policies via rules and regulations. As the chief executive officer of the district, the superintendent sets the tone for the entire system. In performing this function the duties and responsibilities of the superintendent are to

1. Carry out policies and regulations established by the board. (In matters not specifically covered by board policies, the superintendent should take appropriate action and report the action to the board not later than the next meeting.)
2. Prepare regulations and instruct school employees as may be necessary to make effective the policies of the board.
3. Direct all purchases and expenditures in accordance with the policies of the board.
4. Formulate and administer a program of supervision for the schools.
5. Develop a program of maintenance and improvement or expansion of buildings and site.

✗ Educational Leader

The superintendent's leadership role should be exercised not only with other professional educators within the district but with regional, state, and national professional educators, organizations, and agencies.

As the educational leader within the community, the superintendent will be called upon to keep the public informed as to the activities, achievements, needs, and directions of the school system.

The superintendent should exercise a leadership role with the board by keeping the members informed of new trends in education and their implications for the local district.

A leadership role must also be assumed among the staff members of the school district. Without the support and understanding of the employees, the goals and objectives set by the district cannot be achieved.[7]

Two ongoing trends in school administration and particularly in the superintendency emphasize (1) management techniques rather than instructional leadership; and (2) the administrative team approach to central office and building level management. In most districts the administrative team is a cluster of similarly educated administrators who amplify the efforts of the superintendent.[8] Each administrator usually has the title of deputy, associate, or assistant superintendent. In most school districts, personnel having the title of

---

[7]Iowa Association of School Boards, *The Iowa School Board Member: A Guide to Better Boardmanship* (Des Moines, Iowa, 1980), pp. 37–40.

[8]See the American Association of School Administrators, *Profiles of the Administrative Team* (Arlington, Va: The Association, 1971), p. 11.

director or coordinator are not members of the administrative team, but rather support personnel to the team.

Formal designation of membership on the administrative team is appointment to the superintendent's cabinet, which is a strategy-planning and decision-making body. The heads of personnel administration, instructional programs administration, and support services administration are typically included in the cabinet.

This formal organization of the superintendent's cabinet is not meant to imply that the superintendent should confine the "team" effort only to the highest levels of school-district administration. Rather, the establishment of a cabinet is an attempt to share the strategy-planning process with key administrators. The issues and problems facing school districts are so far-reaching today that the superintendent must have continual and effective counsel in making decisions.

Because there is a need in all school districts to identify various echelons in the administrative organization, it is recommended that the title of director or coordinator be attached to administrative positions reporting to an assistant superintendent in charge of a particular function. Although it is in no way meant to be all-inclusive, Figure 1–3 represents a possible central-office organization that incorporates a line authority from superintendent to assistant superintendents (cabinet positions) to directors and coordinators. The number of central-office administrators listed suggests that this could be the organizational structure for a school district with a student population between fifteen and twenty thousand. Please note that the director of affirmative action and director of community relations report directly to the superintendent, which is a common practice.

HUMAN RESOURCE ADMINISTRATION

The Personnel Function

In every school district people must be recruited, selected, placed, appraised, and compensated, whether this is performed by a central personnel office or assigned to various administrators within the school district.

The goals of the personnel function are basically the same in all school systems—to hire, retain, develop, and motivate personnel in order to achieve the objectives of the school district, to assist individual members of the staff to reach the highest possible levels of achievement, and to maximize the career development of personnel.

These goals must be implemented through the following dimensions of the personnel function:

- *Human Resource Planning*   Establishing a master plan of long- and short-range personnel requirements is a necessary ingredient in the school district's curricular and fiscal planning processes.
- *Recruitment of Personnel*   Quality personnel, of course, are essential for the delivery of effective educational services to children, youth, and adults.
- *Selection of Personnel*   The long- and short-range human resource requirements are implemented through selection techniques and processes.

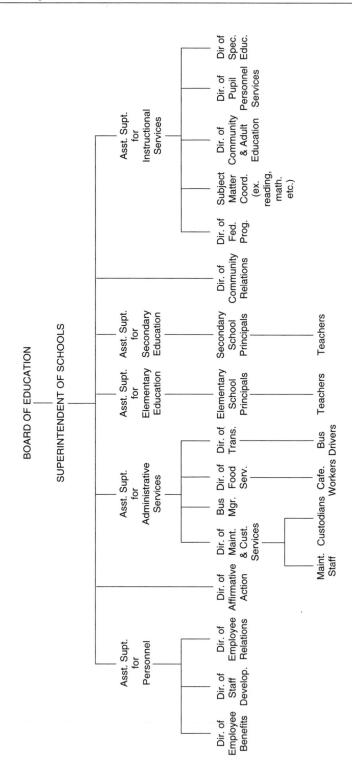

FIGURE 1–3

- *Placement and Induction of Personnel*   Through appropriate planning, new personnel and the school district accommodate each other's goals.
- *Staff Development*   Development programs help personnel meet school district objectives and also provide individuals with the opportunity for personal and professional growth.
- *Appraisal of Personnel*   Processes and techniques for appraisal help the individual grow professionally and help the school district attain its objectives.
- *Compensation of Personnel*   Establishing programs that reward quality performance helps to motivate personnel.
- *Collective Negotiations*   The negotiating process gives personnel an opportunity to participate in matters that affect their professional and personal welfare.

Unfortunately, many school districts still see the personnel function only as the hiring of competent teachers. These eight dimensions of the personnel function are not discrete, isolated entities, but rather, integral aspects of the same function. Each of the next eight chapters addresses one of these dimensions. Administrative processes, procedures and techniques for accomplishing the personnel function are reviewed. Also, major issues that significantly influence the administration of personnel are addressed.

Personnel Administrators

Many school districts have seen the need in recent times to delegate a major share of the personnel function to a specialized central-office unit. In this type of organization, an assistant superintendent (or personnel director) administers the personnel function and aids the superintendent in solving personnel problems. Personnel administrator is usually a staff position that exists to service line administrators. Line positions include the assistant superintendents for secondary education and elementary education, administrators of certain support services, and building principals. These administrators have been granted authority to make decisions in the supervisory process as it relates to staff, faculty, and students.

The personnel function has an impact on the continual staffing of positions, which in turn directly affects the quality of educational programs, but it also has a significant effect on the budget. Approximately 80 percent of all school district expenditures are for salaries and benefits. Inefficiency in the personnel function can potentially cost the taxpayer unnecessarily large sums of money.

Boards of education and administrators are seldom fully aware of the pervasive effect their personnel decisions have on the planning process. Every position within a school system generates a series of decisions as to the type of work to be performed, the qualities needed for its proper performance, and its economic value. A variety of actions are required for the proper recruiting, selecting, inducting, developing, and appraising of personnel. Policies and procedures also must be established regarding academic freedom, tenure, health, grievances, leaves of absences, and retirement. In all but the very smallest districts the movement of personnel into and out of a school district requires the attention of personnel specialists.

The number of strikes by public school teachers has remained relatively constant over the last ten years. Salaries, fringe benefits, and working conditions constitute the major issues that may lead to an impasse at the table and result in a strike. Education, however, is a relative newcomer to the negotiations process.

Collective negotiation is traditionally a personnel function and correctly belongs under the jurisdiction of the assistant superintendent for personnel. Because of the magnitude of the issues involved with this process, most school districts should consider establishing the position of director of employee relations. The American Association of School Administrators sponsored the publication of a monograph in 1974 entitled "Helping Administrators Negotiate," with the prophetic subtitle, "A Profile of the Emerging Management Position of Director of Employee Relations in the Administrative Structure of a School System."

The knowledge explosion and the constantly changing social milieu have also produced a major issue in the area of personnel administration. In the past, staff development was viewed primarily from the in-service training model, which concentrated on providing a few workshops on instructional materials. The last quarter century, however, has ushered in federal legislation and litigation that have more clearly defined the rights of racial minorities, women, students, and the handicapped. This, coupled with the deluge of new instructional technologies, the differing attitudes of the new professionals entering teaching, and the changing values of our society as manifested by parents and students, have created a need for an ongoing staff development program for administrators and teachers alike. This function is so specialized that, like collective negotiations, it also requires the attention of a personnel specialist, the director of staff development.

The avalanche of federal legislation and litigation concerning minority rights has made it necessary to establish a central-office administrative position, usually entitled *director of affirmative action*. Most federal legislation contains an equal opportunity clause, which in turn dictates the organization of a detailed program for carrying out the intent of the law in all phases of the personnel function. This organized program is more commonly called "affirmative action." Chapter 2 presents a complete explanation of all major civil rights legislation and the concept of affirmative action. A unique feature of this administrative position in the organizational structure of a school district is the fact that the director of affirmative action usually reports directly to the superintendent of schools. This provides integrity in the school district's compliance with civil rights legislation because the director is thus protected from the influences of other administrators.

The escalating cost of health care is an issue facing every school district that provides health care and related fringe benefits to employees. Most school districts have undertaken drastic measures in an attempt to control costs which has eventuated in what is commonly referred to as "managed care." Along with the many innovations underway is the need to hire personnel staff members who not only have experience but also academic credentials in health care management. Further, the rising cost of workers' compensation reinforces the need to hire personnel staff members who also have experience and understand the nuances of risk management. Most school district use the title, *director of employee benefits,* to designate that staff member who is responsible for managing the employee benefits and workers' compensation programs. The administrator, of course, reports to the Assistant Superintendent for personnel.

The accompanying job descriptions for the five major personnel specialists are meant only to be a guide (see Exhibit 1–1). Each individual district must decide on the exact specifications for these positions.

EXHIBIT 1–1

Job Description for the Assistant Superintendent for Personnel

Job Summary

The assistant superintendent for personnel is responsible for managing the school district's human resource program. This includes the establishment and maintenance of effective two-way communications between the various organizational levels; and the formulation, recommendation, and administration of the school district's human resource policies.

Organizational Relationships

The assistant superintendent has a line relationship with the superintendent of schools and reports directly to him or her. He or she serves as the superintendent's chief advisor on human resource matters and has a staff relationship with other administrative personnel. The assistant superintendent for personnel has a line relationship with his or her immediate staff, which includes the director of staff development, the director of employee benefits, and the director of employee relations. These administrators report directly to the assistant superintendent.

Organizational Tasks

The assistant superintendent for personnel is directly responsible for establishing administrative processes, procedures, and techniques for human resource planning, recruitment of staff, selection of personnel, the placement and induction of personnel, staff appraisal and compensation programs. He or she is further responsible for supervising the director of staff development, the director of employee benefits, and the director of employee relations.

Job Qualifications

In terms of education and experience, the assistant superintendent for personnel should possess

- Appropriate state administrator certification.
- A doctorate in educational administration.
- Formal course work in the areas of curriculum, finance, school law, personnel administration, and collective negotiations.

- Classroom teaching experience and five years as a building level administrator.

Job Description for the Director of Employee Relations

Job Summary

The director of employee relations is responsible for the administration of the school district's management-employee relations program. This includes establishing and maintaining effective two-way communications between the various organizational levels; formulating, recommending, and administering school district management-employee relations policies; and administering the collective negotiations process.

Organizational Relationships

The director of employee relations has a line relationship with the assistant superintendent for personnel and reports directly to him or her. He or she serves as the assistant superintendent's chief advisor on employee relations. He or she has a staff relationship with other administrative personnel. The director of employee relations has a cooperative-professional relationship with nonadministrative personnel with whom he or she negotiates. Of course, the director has a line relationship with his or her immediate staff and they report directly to the director.

Organizational Tasks

In preparing for negotiations, the director of employee relations shall

- Develop negotiations strategies for management.
- Prepare proposals and counterproposals for management.
- Analyze and evaluate employee proposals, and advise management accordingly.
- Know state laws and court decisions relevant to professional negotiations.
- Secure input from all administrative personnel prior to developing management's proposals.

Continued

EXHIBIT 1–1   *Continued*

In at-the-table negotiations, the director of employee relations shall

- Serve as the chief negotiator for the school district.
- Direct the school district's negotiations team.
- Keep administrative personnel informed during negotiations.
- Draft negotiated agreements reached with unions.
- Maintain records of proposals and counterproposals presented by all parties during negotiations.

In administering the negotiated agreement, the director of employee relations shall

- Serve as the school district's chief advisor in the interpretation of adopted agreements.
- Serve as the school district's chief advisor in all grievance matters.
- Consult with principals and other supervisors concerning their understanding of and compliance with the adopted agreements.
- Initiate management's grievances and mediation activities.

Job Qualifications

In terms of education and experience, the director of employee relations should possess

- Appropriate state administrator certification.
- Master's degree (minimum).
- Formal course work in the areas of educational administration with exposure to courses in curriculum, finance, school law, collective negotiations, and personnel administration.
- Classroom teaching experience and at least two years as a building principal.

Job Description for the Director of Staff Development

Job Summary

The director of staff development is responsible for the management of the school district's staff development program. This includes the establishment and maintenance of effective two-way communications between the various organizational levels; and

the formulation, recommendation, and administration of the school district's staff development policies.

Organizational Relationships

The director of staff development has a line relationship with the assistant superintendent for personnel and reports directly to the assistant superintendent. He or she serves as the assistant superintendent's chief advisor on staff development matters. The director of staff development has a staff relationship with other administrative personnel and has a cooperative–professional relationship with nonadministrative personnel with whom he or she works. The director has a line relationship with his or her immediate staff and they report directly to him or her.

Organizational Tasks

In planning and implementing a staff development program, the director shall

- Establish and implement ongoing needs-assessment techniques with all personnel.
- Analyze and evaluate assessment instruments.
- Secure input from administrative personnel concerning the most desirable time and place for program presentation.
- Evaluate program presentations.

Job Qualifications

In terms of education and experience, the director of staff development should possess

- Master's degree (minimum).
- Formal course work in the areas of testing and measurement, statistics, curriculum, and supervision.
- A minimum of two years professional experience as a teacher or building administrator.

Job Description for the Director of Affirmative Action

Job Summary

The director of affirmative action is responsible for administering the school district's affirmative action program. This includes establishing and maintain-

Continued

EXHIBIT 1–1 *Continued*

ing effective two-way communications between organizational levels; formulating, recommending, and administering the school district's affirmative action policies.

Organizational Relationships

The director of affirmative action has a line relationship to the superintendent of schools and reports directly to the superintendent. He or she serves as the superintendent's chief advisor on affirmative action matters. The director of affirmative action has a staff relationship with other administrative personnel and has a cooperative–professional relationship with nonadministrative personnel with whom he or she works. Of course, the director has a line relationship with his or her immediate staff and they report directly to the director.

Organizational Tasks

The director of affirmative action is responsible for the following tasks:

- Studying affirmative action problems and suggesting solutions to the superintendent, if possible.
- Using school district data in reviewing the qualifications of all employees, with particular emphasis on minorities and women, as the data relate to fair employment practices.
- Developing and updating goals and timetables for correcting identifiable deficiencies.
- Advising the superintendent on recruitment of minorities and women for those classified and certificated positions in which they may be falling short of the district's affirmative action goals.
- Assuming the role of compliance officer and making all contacts with state and federal agencies.
- Reviewing all job announcements, job descriptions, and selection criteria to ensure compliance with affirmative action requirements.
- Briefing the superintendent on the nature, purpose, and intent of all laws, executive orders, policies, regulations, and reports of external agencies that affect the school district's affirmative action program.

- Helping district administrators investigate formal complaints of alleged discrimination relating to fair employment practices and recommending corrective measures to the superintendent.
- Maintaining liaison with local, state, and federal agencies and with organizations concerned with promoting fair employment practices.
- Representing the school district at meetings, conferences, and other gatherings pertaining to the affirmative action program.
- Working with appropriate individuals and agencies in ascertaining correct population characteristic data for the district.
- Compiling an annual report to the superintendent on the progress of the school district's affirmative action program.

Job Qualifications

In terms of education and experience, the director of affirmative action should possess

- Master's degree (minimum).
- Formal course work in the areas of educational administration with exposure to school law, collective negotiations, and personnel administration.
- Classroom teaching experience, two years as a building principal, and two years as a central office administrator.

Personal abilities and characteristics are universal for all administrators. The superintendent, assistant superintendents, directors, and building principals must have good human relations skills; they must possess good writing skills; they must work well with details; and, to use a term from the business community, they must be self-starters.

Job Description for the Director of Employee Benefits

Job Summary

The director of employee benefits is responsible for the management of the school district's fringe benefits program. This includes the establishment and maintenance of effective two-way communication

Continued

EXHIBIT 1–1 *Continued*

between the various organizational levels; and the formulation, recommendation, and administration of the school district's employee benefits policies.

Organizational Relationships

The director of employee benefits has a line relationship with the assistant superintendent for personnel and reports directly to him or her. He or she serves as the assistant superintendent's chief advisor on employee benefits, and has a staff relationship with other administrative personnel. The director of employee benefits has a cooperative–professional relationship with nonadministrative personnel with whom he or she works. Of course, the director has a line relationship with his or her immediate staff and they report directly to him or her.

Organizational Tasks

In planning and implementing the employee benefits program, the director shall

- Establish and implement ongoing monitoring techniques to evaluate the cost effectiveness and efficient management of the benefits program.
- Establish and chair the employee benefits committee which is charged with reviewing employee fringe benefits, making suggestions for improving benefits, making suggestions for containing costs, reviewing specifications for bidding benefits insurance, reviewing the analysis of bids, and annually making recommendations to the superintendent of schools.
- Collaborate with personnel from the procurement department in developing specifications for bidding benefits insurance.
- Develop, implement, and evaluate an annual survey of employee perceptions concerning the scope and effectiveness of the fringe benefits program.
- Serve as the liaison between the district and those companies providing health care and related insurance.

- Develop informational materials and provide presentations to employees about the district's fringe benefits program.

In planning and implementing the workers compensation program, the director shall

- Establish and implement ongoing monitoring techniques to evaluate the cost effectiveness and efficient management of the workers compensation program.
- Establish and chair the employee safety committee which is charged with reviewing safety rules and procedures, making suggestions for improving safety rules and procedures, reviewing specifications for bidding workers compensation insurance, reviewing the analysis of bids, and annually making recommendations to the superintendent of schools.
- Collaborate with personnel from the procurement department in developing specifications for bidding workers compensation insurance.
- Develop, implement, and evaluate an annual safety audit.
- Serve as the liaison between the district and the company providing workers compensation insurance.
- Develop informational materials concerning safety on the job and provide safety training to employees.

Job Qualifications

In terms of education and experience, the director of employee benefits should possess

- Bachelor's Degree (minimum).
- Formal course work in the areas of personnel administration, fringe benefits management, risk management, insurance management, workers compensation.
- Three years experience in at least one of the following areas: personnel administration, fringe benefits management, risk management, insurance management, or workers compensation management.

Source: All five job descriptions were modeled on the job description for the Director of Employee Relations in the *American Association of School Administrators,* "Helping Administrators Negotiate" Arlington, Va.: The Association, 1974).

⋆ Total Quality Management (TQM)

A management strategy known as "total quality management (TQM)," originated in post-World War II Japan and was developed by a United States citizen named W. Edwards Deming. This strategy helped Japan rebuild its industrial and commercial enterprises to a point that outreached its pre-war status. Indeed, Japan has become an economic giant!

In 1980 an American television special focused on the role that Deming played in Japan's economic resurrection. From that time forward, W. Edwards Deming has exerted a tremendous influence on the pursuit of quality by private business and industry in the United States.

The tenets of this book on personnel administration have not been developed from the principles promulgated by Deming but they are certainly complementary to his approach. There continues to be a strong emphasis in the private sector for corporations to adopt Deming's approach and there appears to be serious movement in public education along these same lines. Thus, Appendix A, "Total Quality Management Of The Personnel Function," elucidates how Deming's principles can be applied specifically to personnel administration.

Also, it is important to note the concern that chief executive officers in private business and industry have to find ways of measuring the quality of their corporation's performance. This has lead to the establishment of the Malcolm Baldrige National Quality Award program. Named for the former Commerce Secretary, Malcolm Baldrige, the United States Congress established this award in 1987. The purpose of the award is to recognize U.S. companies that practice and promote quality.[9]

The award program is administered by the American Society for Quality Control. Funding for the award comes from two sources, the applicants' fees and private contributions. Companies applying for the award must undergo an extensive evaluation by an independent team of public and private sector examiners who are experts in quality control. These examiners conduct on-site visitations and review the thirty-two-page application form.

A maximum of two awards are given each year. There are three categories of companies qualified to submit applications: manufacturing companies, service companies, and small businesses. The companies who win the award are required to promote the award program and are required to share the approaches that they employ on total quality management.

⋆ SUMMARY ⋆

Our system of free and universal public education is unique to U.S. society. The school as an institution receives its mandate from the society it serves. Change is an integral part of this society. The content of our educational programs must address the fundamental principles of individual freedom, individual responsibility, and democratic government but must also retain the flexibility to meet new developments and conditions.

[9]Ellen Freeman Roth, "Wins of Change," *World: The Magazine for Decision Makers,* 25 (1991), p. 12.

Implementing society's educational objectives is the responsibility of the individual states. The state's authority to create and govern public schools is embodied in the state constitution, and it exercises this authority through the state legislature. The administrative arm of the state legislature is the Department of Education, which is usually governed by a board and administered by a commissioner or state superintendent. The legislature also delegates authority to local units, boards of education. However, the state maintains some control over the local boards by establishing minimum educational program requirements and teacher certification requirements, and by providing funds to help finance education.

The federal government has increased its influence on education through congressional acts that provide funds for special programs, through the regulations of the U.S. Department of Education, and through Supreme Court decisions. However, the federal government's power and influence are still considerably adjunct to state authority in education.

School districts are perhaps the most democratically controlled agencies of government. Citizens of a local community elect school board members, who adopt policies for the governance and administration of the schools. The implementation of board policies is the responsibility of the administrative staff.

Administration is the process of managing human, financial, and material resources to accomplish an educational mission formulated as policies by the board of education. Therefore, administration is an executive rather than a policy-making activity. Its various functions include personnel administration, instructional programs administration, and support services administration. Each of these functions has objectives that are implemented through administrative processes, procedures, and techniques.

Functions are performed by administrators within a given organizational structure. The superintendent, as the chief executive officer of the school board, has full control of all school operations. These operations are so complex that his or her efforts must be amplified by a central-office administrative team. This team is usually composed of assistant superintendents who administer the major functions of the school system. These assistant superintendents form a cabinet that helps the superintendent formulate strategies and shares in the decision-making process. Directors and coordinators perform administrative tasks that support the major functions of the district. They report directly to assistant superintendents.

Every school system performs a personnel function whether it is accomplished by a central-office unit or assigned to various administrators within the system. The goals of the personnel function are to achieve the objectives of the school district and to help individual staff members maximize their potentials and develop their professional careers. These goals are implemented through human resource planning, recruitment, selection, placement and induction, staff development, appraisal, compensation, and collective negotiations.

All but the very smallest school districts should delegate the personnel function to an assistant superintendent. The complexity of this function in our schools and the great impact it has on total school operations necessitate the hiring of this personnel specialist.

Collective negotiation has also created a need in most school districts for another specialist, the director of employee relations, who reports to the assistant superintendent for personnel and who is charged with managing the negotiations process.

The knowledge explosion, increased federal legislation and litigation, and the changing attitudes of parents, students, and educators have necessitated an ongoing staff development program for administrators and teachers. Like collective negotiation, this area is so specialized that most districts should consider establishing the position of director of staff development, who also reports to the assistant superintendent for personnel.

The avalanche of federal legislation and litigation also has mandated the creation of a central-office administrative position, director of affirmative action. Each federal legislation requires that a detailed compliance program be established under the direction of an administrator who will be free from the influence of other administrators. Thus, the director of affirmative action should report directly to the superintendent of schools.

The escalating cost of health care, the need to implement managed care, and the rising cost of workers' compensation has reinforced the need for school districts to establish the position of *director of employee benefits*. The administrator reports to the assistant superintendent for personnel.

APPENDIX A: "TOTAL QUALITY MANAGEMENT" OF THE PERSONNEL FUNCTION

In post-World War II Japan, an American named W. Edwards Deming introduced the theory and application of "total quality management"(TQM) to the Japanese with outstanding results. Today, Japan occupies a prominent position among the leading industrial/business nations. It is true that the economy in Japan now suffers from the same pitfalls that plague the United States and the other industrial/business nations, but Japan's rapid rise from devastation is worthy of note and study. Deming's approach was the catalyst for this success.

In private business and industry, the first concept concerning quality management was introduced during the late 1970s. It was labelled "quality circles" and called for groups of employees to meet and discuss how improvements could be made within their areas of responsibility. Supervisors and managers were unprepared for this innovation in most companies and the technique quickly vanished. However, the major thrust in business and industry of the total quality management approach occurred during the 1980s and is still gaining momentum throughout the country.

In education, the total quality management approach is just beginning to take hold in some school districts and is certain to continue throughout the 1990s. This phenomenon is appearing not only in the management aspect of school districts but also in the instructional sphere.

This section will discuss how Deming's fourteen principles can be applied to the management of human resources. These principles were elucidated in Deming's 1986 book, *Out of the Crisis.*

1. *Create constancy of purpose toward improvement of product and service.* Too often personnel administrators are entangled in the problems of daily operations to the point at which they lose sight of the overall vision that should drive the personnel function. The dimensions of this function cannot be put into practice without a plan. This plan should be part of a master plan for the entire school district. Today such a plan is often termed a *strategic plan.* The superintendent and his or her cabinet usually take responsibility for initiating the development of the strategic plan.

Personnel administrators, of course, should have the major responsibility for developing that part of the strategic plan that deals with personnel management.

2. *Adopt the new philosophy.* The new philosophy is a belief that all staff members can and should contribute not only to the development of the strategic plan but also to the implementation of the plan. The emphasis is on collaboration rather than on coercion. The assistant superintendent for personnel along with the directors of employee relations, staff development, and affirmative action should assume the leadership in developing the processes, procedures, and techniques for implementing the eight dimensions of the personnel function; but interviewers, direct compensation specialists, and secretaries along with all other staff members should also be intricately involved in this development.

The involvement enhances the self-esteem of staff members and certainly provides valuable insight into how processes, procedures, and techniques should be carried out. For example, receiving applications and other credentials from applicants for an advertised position may be the major responsibility of a secretary. Who would know more than that secretary about how this procedure should be improved? However, this secretary may also have valuable insight about other dimensions of the personnel function as well as about the overall mission of the school district and the personnel function.

3. *Cease dependence on inspection to achieve quality.* Staff members are the only people who can properly assess and improve the quality of service. Individuals outside the school district lack the insight and experience that is necessary to make substantial improvements. The major ingredient, however, is ownership! Employees must perceive that they are valued members of the school district community and, in particular, must perceive that they are appreciated as providers of service to that dimension of the personnel function for which they are responsible.

4. *End the practice of awarding business on the basis of price tag.* The application of this principle for school district employees is better understood in relation to intrinsic and extrinsic rewards. Chapter 8, *Rewards,* provides a clear explanation of this principle. Once again, ownership of responsibilities by employees is the major factor in shifting away from the idea that a person works just to have the financial means for living. Public recognition and rewards for outstanding performance are good ways to demonstrate that employees are valued and that their contributions to the personnel function are appreciated.

5. *Improve constantly and forever the system of production and service, to improve quality and productivity.* Improvement must be built into the design of the processes, procedures, and techniques used in the personnel function. Thus, evaluation must be a component in every dimension of personnel management. For example, in the selection process, a follow-up interview with the new employee about his or her perceptions of the process might reveal where improvements need to be made.

It is also important to communicate to staff members that self-improvement in performing their responsibilities is an expectation. Chapter 7, *Appraisal,* sets forth nuances that support this principle.

6. *Institute training on the job.* With all the advances in technology and with the research that is constantly being conducted in the behavioral sciences, an employee can never state that he or she knows all there is to know about personnel management in general or about his or her area of responsibility in particular. Chapter 5, *Placement and Induction,* and Chapter 6, *Staff Development,* also address the necessity of this principle.

7. *Institute leadership.* This principle applies not only to the assistant superintendent for personnel and the other personnel administrators but it also applies to all staff members who have personnel responsibilities. Leadership in this context means that staff members should continually search for more effective ways of performing not only a given job but also for more effective ways of carrying out the entire personnel function with all of its dimensions. Thus, every staff member is an integral part of the whole and when one person falls short of quality performance, then the entire personnel function is adversely affected. In like manner, when one person excels in performance, the entire personnel function is enhanced.

8. *Drive out fear.* When staff members feel secure in their jobs, they are more likely to perform their duties at a higher degree of quality. Fear is definitely a motivator but it does not lead to constructive behavior. Rather, it makes people defensive and much more cautious about taking risks. Quality performance occurs when staff members take a stand about ideas that they believe will enhance the personnel function. Security allows staff members to make mistakes which, in turn, will become learning experiences that will help employees to acquire new insight and more effective skills.

9. *Break down barriers between departments.* Collaboration between administrators and other staff members will produce a higher quality of service. Thus, when employees perceive themselves as members of the "team" working alongside administrators to solve problems, the results are almost always effective. Communication between staff members becomes less guarded and a new atmosphere emerges which focuses on providing higher quality service.

10. *Eliminate slogans, exhortations, and targets.* The personnel function should be driven by goals rather than slogans, exhortations, and job targets. These tend to give the impression that employees must "measure up" to the levels set by the slogans and exhortations. However, effective change in the behavior of staff members usually takes place because of internal motivation rather than from external coercion. Goal setting thus becomes a collaborative process between personnel administrators and other staff members.

11. *Eliminate management by numerical quotas.* There is nothing more dehumanizing to staff members than reducing their performance to statistics. In large school districts, for example, where there is a high turnover of employees, those responsible for the selection of new staff members will probably be placed under significant pressure to "fill the slots." Trying to quickly fill vacant positions by eliminating time-consuming steps in the selection process will only replace one problem with another. The risk significantly increases of selecting a person who might become a problem employee. The termination of a staff member is much more difficult and much more costly than hiring the right person.

(12.) Remove barriers that prevent job managers and workers from taking pride in their workmanship. Generally speaking, everyone wants to do a good job. Personnel administrators should strive to remove obstacles that prevent other personnel staff members from quality performance. Outdated or insufficient equipment is a good example of a barrier that affects performance. However, even more important than the physical work environment is the attitude of staff members. If administrators do not encourage staff members to be creative and resourceful, they will not venture into the unknown. Rather, they will perform their assigned tasks from a status quo perspective.

(13.) Institute a vigorous program of education and self-improvement. "Nothing remains the same. If you do not progress, then you will regress." Most people have heard similar statements which have become part of our commonly held beliefs about the state of our existence. The reason they have the status of "commonly held," is that they are usually accurate statements. Thus, the personnel function is constantly in danger of becoming mediocre if staff members are not given the opportunity to develop their skills, learn new skills, and receive updated information.

Of course, there is a variety of models for providing in-service training such as seminars, workshops, mentoring, and college or university credit courses. This investment in employees will certainly have a long-term positive effect upon the school district and the personnel function.

(14.) Put everybody in the company to work to accomplish the transformation. The type of change described herein requires not only the commitment of the assistant superintendent for personnel but also commitment from every personnel staff member. It must be supported at all levels within the organization because top-level personnel administrators cannot effect this change by themselves.

It is also important for all staff members, administrators, directors, specialists, secretaries, and so on, to understand that change never ends. It is the constant condition of every human organization. Likewise it is important to accept the idea that change will produce mistakes but such mistakes will provide valuable information upon which the future can be built.

SELECTED BIBLIOGRAPHY

Carver, John. *Boards That Make a Difference.* San Francisco: Jossey-Bass Publishers, 1990.

Drucker, Peter F. *Managing for the Future: The 1990s and Beyond.* New York: Nal-Dutton, 1992.

Finkelstein, S., "Power in Top Management Teams: Dimensions, Measurement, and Validation," *Academy of Management Journal,* 35 (1992), pp. 505–538.

Harris, Ben M., Kenneth E. McIntyre, Vance C. Littleton, and Daniel Long, *Personnel Administration in Education: Leadership for Instructional Improvement* (2nd ed.). Rockleigh, N.J.: Allyn and Bacon, 1985.

Johnson, James H., *Total Quality Management in Education,* Eugene, Oregon: Oregon School Study Council, 1993.

McLeod, Willis B., Brenda A. Spencer, and Leon T. Hairston, "Towards a System of Total Quality Management: Applying The Deming Approach to the Education Setting." *Spectrum: Journal of School Research and Information.* 10, no. 2 (Spring 1992), pp. 34–42.

Morphet, Edgar L., Roe L. Johns, and Theodore L. Reller. *Educational Organization and Administration: Concepts, Practices, and Issues* (4th ed.). Englewood Cliffs, N.J.: Prentice-Hall, 1982.

National School Boards Association, *The Federal Role in Education: A Foundation for the Future.* Washington, D.C.: The Association, 1982.

Owens, Robert G., *Organizational Behavior in Education* (2nd ed.). Englewood Cliffs, N.J.: Prentice-Hall, 1981.

Rebore, Ronald W., *Educational Administration: A Management Approach.* Englewood Cliffs, N.J.: Prentice-Hall, 1985.

Scheer, Wilbert E., *People Policies: Successful Personnel Management.* Chicago, Ill.: Pluribus Press, 1984.

Schein, E. H. *Organizational Culture and Leadership,* 2nd ed. San Francisco: Jossey-Bass Publishers, 1992.

Schuster, Frederick E., *Human Resource Management* (2nd ed.). Englewood Cliffs, N.J.; Reston Publishing Company, 1985.

Scott, Dow, Diane Deadrick, and Stephen Taylor, "The Evolution of Personnel Research," Personnel Journal (August 1983), pp. 624–25.

Sergiovanni, Thomas J., Martin Burlingame, Fred D. Coombs, and Paul W. Thurston, *Educational Governance and Administration.* Englewood Cliffs, N.J.: Prentice-Hall, 1980.

Short, Paula M., John T. Greer. *Leadership in Empowered Schools: Themes from Innovative Efforts.* Upper Saddle River, New Jersey: Merrill/Prentice-Hall, Inc., 1997.

Strauss, George and Leonard R. Sayles, *Personnel: The Human Problems of Management.* Englewood Cliffs, N.J.: Prentice-Hall, 1980.

The Commission on Excellence in Education, *A Nation at Risk: The Imperative for Educational Reform.* Washington, D.C.: U.S. Government Printing Office, 1984.

Wilson, Richard B. and Mike Schmoker, "Quest for Quality," *The Executive Educator,* 14, no. 1 (January 1992), pp. 18–23.

Yukl, Gary. *Leadership in Organizations.* Englewood Cliffs, New Jersey: Prentice-Hall, Inc., 1994.

2

HUMAN RESOURCE PLANNING

Planning is a process common to all human experience. Before embarking on a journey an individual must understand where he or she is, know where he or she wants to go, and decide how best to get there. In an elementary form this exemplifies the essence of the process even as it is applied in educational organizations.

Through the process of human resource planning, a school district ensures that it has the right number of people, with the right skills, in the right place, and at the right time and that these people are capable of effectively carrying out those tasks that will aid the organization in achieving its objectives. If a school district is to achieve its objectives, it needs financial resources, physical resources, and people. Too often the people are taken for granted, and yet they are the force that directly affects the main objective of a school district—to educate children. Human resource planning thus translates the organization's objectives into people requirements.

In some school districts long- and short-range objectives are couched in ambiguous language and often known only by certain central-office administrators. This makes it difficult to involve building principals in the hiring process when unexpected vacancies occur, when replacements are needed because of natural attrition, or when new programs must be staffed.

Human resource planning, as a process, ensures the smooth development of an organization. "We assess where we are; we assess where we are going; we consider the implications of these objectives on future demands and the future supply of human resources; and we attempt to match demand and supply so as to make them compatible with the achievement of the organization's future needs."[1]

ASSESSING HUMAN RESOURCE NEEDS

The process of assessing human resource needs has four aspects. First, human resource inventories must be developed to analyze the various tasks necessary to meet the school dis-

[1]Stephen P. Robbins, *Personnel: The Management of Human Resources,* 2nd ed. (Englewood Cliffs, N.J.: Prentice-Hall, 1982), p. 76.

trict's objectives; these tasks are then matched against the skills of current employees. Second, enrollment projections must be developed for a five-year period. The extreme mobility of the American population has made this aspect increasingly important over the past twenty-five years. Third, the overall objectives of the school district must be reviewed within the context of changing needs. At a time when school district budgets are tight, all but the wealthiest districts must establish priorities in meeting objectives. Fourth, human resource inventories, enrollment projections, and school district's objectives must be organized into a human resource forecast, which becomes the mandate of the personnel department.

Implementing this human resource mandate becomes more complex, however, when viewed in the light of compliance with federal legislation, and in some districts when staff reductions are brought on by decreasing enrollment. Because both issues have had such a tremendous impact on the personnel function, they have been given particular emphasis in this chapter.

Human resource planning is sometimes understood only within the confines of the instructional program. However, for every two teachers there is usually one classified employee. The contemporary school district employs not only teachers and administrators but also cooks, custodians, maintenance personnel, secretaries, computer programmers, telephone switchboard operators, warehouse personnel, distribution truck drivers, and other specialists who are often considered by the average citizen to be employed only in the private business sector.

❊ Human Resource Inventories

Human resource planning begins with the development of a profile indicating the status of current human resources. This profile is generated through forms completed by employees, verified by supervisors, and finally sent to the personnel department. This form should include name of employee, age, date employed with the school district, sex, job title, place of employment within the district, education and/or training along with the dates when completed, special skills, and, for instructional personnel, certification.

A human resource profile for each job classification is then developed from the forms completed by the employees. The profile lists all relevant information for each job classification.

From a planning perspective, this information is valuable not only in determining what skills are available but also in developing new instructional programs and support services. The human resource profile also helps personnel administrators as they carry out other personnel tasks such as recruitment and staff development. For example, the length of time since an individual received his training or education helps the director of staff development plan appropriate programs.

The profile also provides crucial information for identifying weaknesses in the school district's ability to meet its objectives. For example, reviewing data under the "date employed" section will help the administration analyze such problems as staff turnover and job dissatisfaction. The "age of employee" information helps administrators formulate strategies for recruitment by identifying those individuals approaching retirement age. Accurate data are essential to every aspect of the personnel process and human resource profiles are an effective method of presenting such information.

✻*Enrollment Prediction*

Because educational institutions are service organizations, enrollment prediction is an essential aspect of human resource planning. Unless a school system makes an effort to predict declines or increases in the number of students to be served, it may unexpectedly experience half-filled classrooms and a surplus of teachers or overcrowded classrooms and a shortage of teachers.

The major question to be answered by an enrollment prediction is, How many children are expected to attend a particular school over the next five to ten years? Many methods can be used to forecast enrollments; among the most popular is the "percentage of retention" or "cohort-survival" technique. This method is predicated on birth rates and the historical retention of students (see Figure 2–1). However, another method is available that highlights enrollment trends before the statistical time required by the former technique has elapsed. The Keough Indicator Survey Scale uses social, financial, and residential factors for critical analysis of a school and community. The following discussion of enrollment prediction and brief explanation of the most common techniques in use are taken from a handbook published by the American Association of School Administrators (AASA).[2]

Commonly Asked Questions about Enrollment Prediction

1. *What simple prediction method is the most reliable today?* There is no "most reliable" prediction method. The best insurance is to use a variety of techniques to check and double-check each other. The Keough Indicator Survey Scale (KISS) should be used to begin any analysis (see Exhibit 2–1).

2. *Why will there be a continuing enrollment decline in view of the fact that the number of women of child-bearing age has increased?* The important factor is not the number of women of child-bearing age (15–44 years), but whether or not these women, in actuality, bear children. The number of women has increased but the number of births has declined. . . .

3. *What is a demographic survey?* A demographic survey of the school district includes a thorough census of the population determining who the people are, their living conditions, how many there are, how they intend to use the land, their length of residency, the number of children per household by ages and grades, and the various kinds of dwelling units found in the district.

4. *What are the advantages of a demographic survey?* By combining the information from a demographic survey with in-and-out migration rates, school attrition rates, and the number of live births, it is possible to make enrollment projections beyond the conventional linear model. This type of information gives the forecaster the tools with which to project more accurately by "feeling the pulse" of the district.

5. *What are the disadvantages of a demographic survey?* The two major disadvantages are costs and the time limitation on the utility of the data. The major costs will be for the personnel involved in planning, organizing, and administering the survey, processing the data and analyzing the results. Additional costs will include computer time and supplies. In regard to the time limitation on the utility of the data, unless supplemental surveys are

---

[2]American Association of School Administrators, *Declining Enrollment: What to Do,* Vol. II, AASA Executive Handbook Series (Arlington, Va.: The Association, 1974), pp. 8, 9.

Instructions

I   1. Fill in birth rate
     2. Fill in 1st Grade Enrollment
     3. Do necessary calculations to find average ratio

II   1. Fill in birth rate
     2. Multiply by Average Ratio

III   1. Fill in enrollment data
     2. Do necessary calculations to find retention ratio
     3. Fill in Projected 1st Grade Enrollment from II into appropriate columns of III.
     4. Multiply enrollment for a specific year and class by the retention ratio for the *next* class. Result is the predicted enrollment for that year, next class.
     5. Complete Chart

ENROLLMENT PREDICTION CHARTS
I

Birth Rate		1st Grade Enrollment		Enrollment Ratio of Birth Rate
1985		1991–92		
1986		1992–93		
1987		1993–94		
1988		1994–95		
1989		1995–96		
			Total of Ratios	
			Divide by 5	
			Average Ratio	

II

Birth Rate		X Average Ratio –	Projected 1st Grade Enrollment	For years
1990				1996–97
1991				1997–98
1992				1998–99
1993				1999–2000
1994				2000–2001

FIGURE 2–1 Cohort-Survival Technique

III

Year	Enrollment by Grade											
	1	2	3	4	5	6	7	8	9	10	11	12
1985–86												
1986–87												
1987–88												
1988–89												
1989–90												
Total by Grade												
Divide by 5												
Divide Grades	$\frac{2}{1}$	$\frac{3}{2}$	$\frac{4}{3}$	$\frac{5}{4}$	$\frac{6}{5}$	$\frac{7}{6}$	$\frac{8}{7}$	$\frac{9}{8}$	$\frac{10}{9}$	$\frac{11}{10}$	$\frac{12}{11}$	
Retention Ratio												

PROJECTED ENROLLMENT	Year	1	2	3	4	5	6	7	8	9	10	11	12
	1996–97												
	1997–98												
	1998–99												
	1999–2000												
	2000–2001												
	2001–2002												
	2002–2003												
	2003–2004												
	2004–2005												
	2005–2006												

FIGURE 2–1   Continued

EXHIBIT 2–1   Keough Indicator Survey Scale

INDICATORS:

1. Few (or no) problems with elementary school classes that are beyond your district's maximum class size guidelines. Are the days when extra students forced your schools to create classes on the auditorium stage, in halls, cafeteria, and gym just so many memories?
2. Evidence that elementary class size in your district is quietly slipping from 35 to 30 down to 23 or 20.
3. Statistics that show a consistent decline (over two or three years) in the number of students at certain grade levels within some elementary schools. Are there, for example, considerably fewer fourth graders than seventh graders in your district, with gradual decline in the classes between?
4. Indications that school officials are concerned about preschool census figures that usually are considered quite reliable. You may begin to hear about alternatives (computerizing the census process, conducting a mail census, telephone surveys) to traditional census-taking methods. The list of alternatives gets longer as the indications of enrollment declines become more ominous.
5. Feedback from local realtors that reveals a marked decrease in the influx of families with preschool children and of young marrieds.
6. Requests from elementary school administrators who want to convert unused classrooms into resource centers and special help areas. Such requests often reflect the frustrations of administrators who have lived with crowded or overcrowded buildings and who now envision empty classrooms in their school buildings.
7. Clamoring for school tax relief because, the taxpayers say, decreasing numbers of students should warrant a lower school budget. Wrestling with this simplistic argument will provide you with yet another experience in boardmanship.

If any of these seven indicators of enrollment decline seem suspiciously familiar to you, ask your board to answer the following eight questions. If the board comes up with Yes answers to the first three questions and No answers to questions four through eight, your next district project might well be the development of a contingency plan to prepare citizens for the often severe shock of school closings and consolidations.

1. Is your community close to a metropolitan area and did your community develop and grow as a result of population expansion in that metropolitan area?
2. Is your community one with expensive houses that continue to escalate in price disproportionately to general real estate values?
3. Does your community contain a high percentage of professional people or older people whose homes fulfill their lifetime needs and whose children are now in (or have been through) the local schools?
4. Even if your community has a highly reputed school system, will that good reputation draw in young families in spite of high-priced houses?
5. Does your community have a high level of mobility, with families moving in and out? (And who's moving in—families with children or retirees?)
6. Does your community contain pockets of middle-income housing that will attract young couples and families with small children?
7. Is there still land available in your community for future residential development?
8. Have service organizations (YMCA, YWCA, community clubs for children, religious groups) been maintaining an emphasis on programs for children of elementary school age? (If not, is the decreasing emphasis because of diminishing numbers of children to be served?)

Source: AASA, *Declining Enrollment,* pp. 45–47.

conducted the lifetime of demographic data usually does not exceed five years. This time limitation may be considerably less in a rapidly changing community.

6. *What kind of district would benefit most from a demographic survey?* In districts where enrollments are significantly fluctuating or are changing in a nonlinear fashion, the benefits gained through a demographic survey will probably offset the cost involved.

7. *What specific outside community factors should be taken into consideration when evaluating enrollment projections?* Transportation, movement of industry (in-out), change in zoning regulations, change in subdivisions regulations, change in government or military installations (opening or closing), urban renewal, subdivision of large land holdings (farms, estates), highway systems.

8. *Will the Keough Indicator Survey Scale (KISS) predict enrollment figures?* The Keough Indicator Survey Scale (KISS) is an informal instrument designed to help administrators pinpoint community factors that have slowly developed in shrinking enrollment communities. It will predict trends; it will not yield numerical figures.

Reviewing School District Objectives

The future objectives of a school district determine future human resource needs. The number and mix of employees are determined by the types of services called for by organizational objectives. Establishing objectives is the prerogative of the board of education. The board, however, must rely on the advice of the school administration as it establishes objectives that will best meet the educational needs of the community.

The review of current objectives in light of future educational needs is a cooperative task. In a district operating under the organizational structure presented in Chapter 1, the assistant superintendents for secondary education, elementary education, and instructional services would have the primary responsibility for determining future objectives. The assistant superintendent for personnel would develop a human resource forecast to meet the projected objectives developed by the three other assistant superintendents. The assistant superintendent for administrative services would then translate the objectives and human resource needs into a fiscal plan. The superintendent of schools is charged with prioritizing the objectives and recommending them to the school board for approval.

This review of objectives is not a one-time task but rather a continual process. The objectives, however, should be established for at least a five-year period and if the need occurs, could be revised into a new five-year plan each year. Thus a set of objectives is always in effect for a set period of time.

Human Resource Forecasting

When the objectives have been reviewed and an overall human resource forecast has been established, a more explicit projection of future human resource needs must be developed. There are five commonly accepted methods for computing future needs.[3]

1. *Expert Estimate:* Those staff members in the school district most familiar with employment requirements use their experience and judgment to estimate future needs.

---

[3]Bruce Coleman, "An Integrated System for Manpower Planning," *Business Horizons,* October 1970, pp. 89–95.

2. *Historical Comparison:* By this method, past trends are projected into the future.

3. *Task Analysis:* Each person in each type of position is studied to determine demand. This method is sometimes effective in uncovering specific quality shortages within a school system.

4. *Correlation:* Human resource requirements fluctuate in relation to such variables as decreasing enrollment, fiscal resources, and new programs. A correlation of these variables can be statistically formulated.

5. *Modeling:* This usually refers to decision-making models. However, it may be broadened to include reviewing the programs in other school systems, and how they are organized, in order to formulate a model for staffing.

Whatever method or combination of methods are used, the human resource inventories on current employees can provide data about the age, sex, education, certification, and types of positions within the school district.

The Supply of Human Resources

An increase in a school system's supply of human resources can come from two sources, newly hired employees and individuals returning from absences such as maternity, military, and sabbatical leaves. Both types of increases are relatively easy to incorporate into a human resource forecast because hiring is controlled and leaves are usually for set periods of time.

Decreases in a school system's supply of human resources, however, are more difficult to predict. Deaths, voluntary resignations, and dismissals are unpredictable except in the broadest sense, as through statistical averaging. However, some decreases, such as sabbatical leaves, can be controlled; and others, such as retirements, are easier to predict.

The available labor force has a significant effect on human resource forecasting. Graduates from high schools, colleges, and universities continually replenish the supply of labor necessary to carry out the mandate of public education. In recent years, however, educational organizations have experienced a decrease in the number of applicants for mathematics and science teaching positions because of the higher wages and advancement opportunities available in private business and industry.

A major source of employees other than recent graduates includes older individuals, particularly women reentering the work force and seeking full-time or part-time employment, either to supplement family income or, in many cases, to provide the primary income for the family. Divorce rates and the high cost of living are key factors contributing to the number of women reentering the labor force.

Matching Needs with Supply

A final activity in human resource forecasting is to match the school district's future human resource needs with current supply. This will pinpoint shortages, highlight areas of potential overstaffing, and identify the number of individuals who must be recruited from the labor force to satisfy future needs.

In the final analysis, human resource planning ensures that we have the right number and mix of people to meet the school district's future needs as determined by its future objectives.

REDUCTION IN FORCE

A persistent problem facing metropolitan areas is decreasing pupil enrollments, which has led to a surplus of teachers in some school districts. Declining enrollments have particular significance in the human resource planning process and have caused the initiation in some districts of a procedure commonly referred to as reduction in force, or RIF. Excess employees are usually placed on involuntary leave according to a seniority system, which follows the principle of "last in, first out." Retained employees may be transferred within the school system to balance a particular staff or faculty. Such changes are certain to create anxiety among individuals who have become accustomed to the atmosphere and procedures of a particular school. Because many school districts have hired minorities only within the last decade, the use of seniority-based reduction procedures usually means that minority employees are among the first to go. Court-mandated desegregation and the legislative demand for affirmative action call for the introduction of alternatives to RIF whenever possible in such school districts.

Alternatives to Reduction in Force (RIF)

Two of the most successful alternatives to RIF have been early retirement incentive programs (see Exhibit 2–2) and retaining individuals for positions that will become vacant through attrition or will be created because of program development.

Teacher negotiations have centered in recent years on the job security issue, and many contracts now call for teachers in excess areas to be transferred to other positions (see Exhibit 2–3), hired as permanent substitutes, or retrained for new assignments at school district expense.

The Role of the Principal

A key person in human resource planning is the building principal. He or she is usually the first to spot dwindling enrollments. The principal, of course, can provide the central-office staff with up-to-date and projected enrollment figures, with projected maintenance and capital improvement costs, and with projected staffing needs.

The principal also has front-line contact with staff members, students, and parents. Therefore, he or she should be responsible for preparing teachers with possible job loss and for easing the concerns of parents and students. To perform these tasks effectively, the principal must become an integral part of the human resource planning process—being relied upon for data and input. In like manner, he or she must be constantly kept informed of central-office decisions before such decisions are announced to the staff and public.

Commonly Asked Questions about Reduction in Force[4]

1. What specific steps should be used by the assistant superintendent for personnel in matters of RIF?[5]

---

[4]AASA, *Declining Enrollment*, pp. 31–34.

[5]Seniority, alone, is not the only consideration in many states. Staff members holding certificates in other areas and considered competent in those areas may supersede senior teachers in those areas. Check state and local laws.

EXHIBIT 2–2   Early Retirement Incentive Programs (Pasadena Unified School District)

The Pasadena Early Retirement Incentive Program was designed to help solve the problem of declining enrollments and to save the district money by encouraging those at the maximum salary to retire early.

The specific components of the program are as follows:

1. The person must have served satisfactorily for a minimum of ten years with the Pasadena Unified School District.
2. The person must be currently earning $11,194 or more. (People on leave or on part-time assignments would not be eligible.)
3. The person must be 50 years of age or older.
4. The person selecting the program will serve a maximum of twenty days per year at activities mutually agreed upon. These activities vary with the individual but in general include:
   a. Demonstration teaching.
   b. Working on staff development and in-service programs.
   c. Helping with testing programs.
   d. Compiling test data as it relates to Reading and Math Profiles.
   e. Orienting and providing aid to new teachers.
   f. Designing and producing programs for the closed circuit TV station.
   g. Updating curriculum guides and other learning materials. (Substitute teaching was not included.)
5. The person selecting Early Retirement will be on a contract as a Consultant for a period of five years or to age 65, whichever comes first.
6. The person will be eligible to maintain the Medical Insurance Plan currently held. (These are Ross Loos and Blue Cross, but do not include Vision or Dental Programs available to district employees.)
7. The annual compensation for Consultants under this program will range from $2,500 to $4,000, based upon the following schedule.

AMOUNT PRESENTLY EARNED	EARLY RETIREMENT INCENTIVE PLAN
$11,194–11,619	$2,500
11,620–12,045	2,600
12,046–12,805	2,750
12,806–13,565	3,000
13,566–14,325	3,250
14,326–15,085	3,500
15,086–15,839	3,750
15,840 or over	4,000

Source: AASA, *Declining Enrollment,* pp. 52–53. Modified for this presentation.

- Rank employees in order of seniority.
- Consult with legal counsel for specific wording of written notices to ensure that all the legal technicalities and notification deadlines will be met.
- It is usually considerate to include some less formal message within the body of the letter.
- Hold a preliminary meeting with possibly affected teachers.
- Issue letters informing teachers that they may be excessed within the coming year (registered mail).
- Issue letters informing teachers that they will be excessed (registered mail).

EXHIBIT 2–3   Bedford, Massachusetts, Public Schools

OFFICE OF THE SUPERINTENDENT OF SCHOOLS

Transfers and Position Placement

This notice deals specifically with faculty members in elementary classroom teaching situations; because of its importance, however, this notice is being sent to all staff members. This morning it was my distinct displeasure to announce to twelve staff members that their services would not be required during the next school year DUE TO THE DECLINE IN THE NUMBER OF TEACHING POSITIONS AT THE ELEMENTARY SCHOOL LEVEL.

This situation has been generated not only by the decline in elementary enrollment but also by the past practice of granting Leaves of Absence.

At the present time there are no known retirements for this June nor have any staff members other than first year personnel expressed any plans for leaving the system's employment.

The system is at a point where twelve "first year" staff members have received dismissal letters in accord with the legal requirements that such letters be sent and received by April 15. It is my hope that further developments might alleviate the circumstances of the dismissals mentioned above.

Steps to Be Taken

1. Any elementary staff members who desire transfers during the next school year should state their interest to the Superintendent's Office in writing within the next ten days (before April 25).

2. In the absence of transfer requests it may be necessary to transfer "involuntarily" tenured staff members. This process must take place, if necessary, prior to May 15.

3. The above steps are specified in Article 12 of the School Committee/Teacher Association contract. When these steps have been taken, administrative decisions will be required to fill the balance of openings. It is my hope that such openings may be filled with qualified personnel from among those who have been "excessed."

While meeting with the excessed teachers this morning, I pointed out to them that the Superintendent's Office will lend as much support as possible to any efforts they make in seeking other employment. At this time, I would urge all staff members who are anticipating retirement, family relocation, or any other cause for cessation or disruption of employment to be in touch with me. Such information, if made available to me, will help to ease some of the anxieties which our younger colleagues are experiencing at this point.

Known Openings for Staff Members Eligible for Transfer

Page School:	Grade 3, Grade 5, Grade 6
Lane School:	Grade 3 (2)
Center School:	Grade 5
Davis School:	Grade 5, Grade 6 (2)

Source: AASA, *Declining Enrollment,* pp. 52–53. Modified for this presentation.

2. *What if two or more teachers were employed at the same time?* In this case some districts have held drawings to establish seniority. If a lottery is to be used, the following guidelines are suggested:

- Hold drawing early in school year.
- Conduct drawing with an auditor and teacher organization representative present to witness the proceedings.

• Do not allow teachers to personally draw numbers from the lottery (this causes unnecessary anxiety).

• Request witnesses to sign consent statement upon completion of drawing.

3. *What is an alternative to RIF?* ERIP [Early Retirement Incentive Program]? In today's tight-money market, there are just so many times the district can financially afford to reduce the teacher/pupil ratio. The only other alternative is to bring in more students. Some of the outlying suburban districts of Boston have opted to bus inner city children. This is one of the country's few voluntary metropolitan integration plans. Inner city children are transported to participating school districts, which accept them on a space available basis.

4. *What can a district do to help well qualified excessed teachers?* Many districts send listings of the teachers they are laying off along with their qualifications and recommendations to neighboring districts.

5. *What are alternatives to administrator RIF?* Some districts have used excessed building administrators in one- or two-year consultant positions. In one district, an excessed administrator was reassigned as a RIF coordinator.

6. *What is the role of the principal in school closings?* Elementary school principals are often the least used but probably most valuable resource of the district. Principals frequently operate on the "outer fringes" of central office, so most teachers do not regard them as "the administration"; likewise, they are not considered part of the teaching ranks by central office, so most chief administrators do not regard them as "the teachers." The unique position held is that of middle manager and, therefore, acceptable to everybody. Usually principals know and enjoy good relationships with parents and the community—frequently a much closer contact than any other person in the district. Remember, superintendents may come and go, but the elementary principal always stays. All these make the elementary principal of unparalleled value in community/school relations—especially in school closings.

7. *What can the superintendent do to help elementary principals during school closing efforts?*

• Principals should be fully briefed as to the needs of the district years before a school closing is a reality, and continually briefed as events unfold.

• Principals should be provided with a direct channel for input and play an integral role in the planning. They both want and need to be involved in the decision-making process.

• They will need to be sensitized to the emotional/psychological concerns of teachers and community.

• They will need special "briefing sessions" if they are going to be responsible for conducting coffee hours in the community or public meetings at school.

• They will need to be given support materials (newsletters, questionnaires) if they are to act effectively in the community.

8. *What suggestions can be offered to plan for RIF?*

• A moratorium on leave policies will reduce the number of teachers returning to claim positions vacated at higher enrollment levels. Offer only one or two year termination contracts to new teachers (some states prohibit this policy).

- Institute ERIP.
- Institute staffing needs studies before going into contract negotiations that may call for job security items in the new contract.
- Prepare the community and staff for possible teacher reduction.
- Request that teachers planning to retire or leave the district file such intention at least a year in advance whenever possible.

9. *What can subject area supervisors do to provide for program continuity?*

- Some districts have required student program record cards for each student in the district. These cards list the materials the child has used and the progress achieved. When the child moves to a new school the program card will move with him.
- Every attempt should be made to move materials and teachers to the same new school as the child.
- Feed-in transitional programs should be instituted when similar reading or math programs do not exist in the new school.

10. *What specific guidelines for inventory should be instituted?* New inventory forms should be developed. These forms should provide for other than simple numbers recording—columns for outdated materials slated for disposal, columns for ultimate destination of materials. In addition, guidelines indicating what constitutes school material and what can be termed teacher-held material need to be clearly delineated. This is a highly charged item for teachers. When teachers have used the same textbook manual for years, when they have written in the margins, when they have scribbled in little teaching notes to themselves, they come to regard these materials as "theirs." They will not give them up to be packed in a box and carried off to a new school. While these materials belong to the district, they are a part of the basic teaching resources without which the teachers feel they cannot teach effectively. To avoid the separation of teacher and "special" materials a Special Inventory Form should be provided. The materials listed on this form can be kept by the teacher, but recorded for inventory/purchasing needs.

11. *How can school districts keep job security from becoming a negotiations issue?* Keeping difficult issues off the negotiations table is the responsibility of the school district negotiator. Be the negotiator an outside attorney, a professional negotiator, a school administrator, or a member of the school board, the main function will be to determine those items which are considered nonnegotiable. Items dealing with control over the school system operations are essentially the domain of the school board and administration. More and more, however, any and all items that are related to the operations of schools are becoming negotiable. A firm position in this particular matter of job security, along with community understanding, will be necessary.

12. *How can school districts prepare for the possible "public outcry" that will accompany the release of young staff who are well liked by parents?* Only an

extensive public information program, one which keeps all citizens notified of the circumstances involved, will guarantee that a school district will enjoy a sympathetic ear from its community when younger staff members are forced out of their positions.

FEDERAL INFLUENCES ON HUMAN RESOURCE PLANNING

A hallmark of our contemporary American society is the avalanche of federal legislation and court decisions delineating and more clearly defining civil rights. The term *civil rights* is somewhat misunderstood and is most often applied to the constitutional rights of racial minority groups. However, it correctly refers to those constitutional and legislative rights that are inalienable and applicable to all citizens. The human resource forecast should provide direction for the recruitment and selection processes. In so doing, this forecast must not violate the civil rights of job applicants or lead the school district into an indefensible position.

What follows is an explanation of major federal legislation, executive orders, and court decisions that should provide direction in the implementation phase of a human resource forecast. It is not meant to be exhaustive because the legislative and judicial processes are organic in nature; therefore, modifications and change will undoubtedly occur. The underlying concept of equality, however, has timeless application.

As prelude to this information, the important concept of *affirmative action* must be clearly understood because it is a requirement incorporated or implied in civil rights legislation and executive orders.

Affirmative Action

Definition

The sometimes-quoted cliche, "There can be justice for none if there is not justice for all," captures the intent of civil rights legislation. Affirmative action programs are detailed, result-oriented programs, which, when carried out in good faith, result in compliance with the equal opportunity clauses found in most legislation and executive orders.[6] Affirmative action, therefore, is not a law within itself but rather an objective reached by following a set of guidelines that insure compliance with legislation and executive orders. Thus, an organization does not "violate" affirmative action; it violates the law.

Brief History of Affirmative Action

Although the term *affirmative action* is of recent origin, the concept of an employer taking specific steps to utilize fully and to treat equally minority groups can be traced to President Franklin D. Roosevelt's Executive Order 8802, issued in June 1941. This executive order, which had the force of law, established a policy of equal employment opportunity in regard to defense contracts. President Roosevelt issued a new order in 1943 extending

---

[6]"Labor Law Reports—Employment Practices," *Office of Federal Contract Compliance Manual,* 2nd ed., Report 86, No. 580, July 3, 1975 (New York: Commerce Clearing House), foreword.

the order to all government contractors and for the first time mandating that all contracts contain a clause specifically forbidding discrimination.

In 1953 President Dwight D. Eisenhower issued Executive Order 10479, which established the Government Contract Compliance Committee. This committee received complaints of discrimination against government contractors, but had no power to enforce its guidelines.

The period of voluntary compliance ended in 1961 when President John F. Kennedy issued Executive Order 10925. This order established the President's Committee on Equal Employment Opportunity and gave it the authority to make and enforce its own rules by imposing sanctions and penalties against noncomplying contractors. Government contractors were required to have nondiscrimination clauses covering race, color, creed, and national origin.

In September 1965 President Lyndon B. Johnson issued the very important Executive Order 11246, which gave the secretary of labor jurisdiction over contract compliance and created the Office of Federal Contract Compliance, thereby replacing the Committee on Equal Employment Opportunity. Every federal contract was required to have a seven-point equal opportunity clause, by which a contractor agreed not to discriminate against anyone in hiring and during employment on the basis of race, color, creed, or national origin. Further, the contractor also had to agree in writing to take affirmative action measures in hiring. President Johnson's Executive Order 11375 in 1967 amended Executive Order 11246 by adding sex and religion to the list of protected categories.

The secretary of labor issued Chapter 60 of Title 41 of the Code of Federal Regulations for the purpose of implementing Executive Order 11375. The secretary delegated enforcement authority to the Office of Federal Contract Compliance (OFCC), which reports to the assistant secretary of the Employment Standards Administration.

The Office of Federal Contract Compliance provides leadership in the area of nondiscrimination by government contractors and also coordinates matters relating to Title VII of the 1964 Civil Rights Act, as amended, with the Equal Employment Opportunity Commission (EEOC) and the Department of Justice.

The EEOC was established by Title VII of the Civil Rights Act to investigate alleged discrimination based on race, color, religion, sex, or national origin. The EEOC was greatly strengthened in 1972 by the passage of the Equal Employment Opportunity Act. It extended coverage to all private employers of fifteen or more persons, all educational institutions, all state and local governments, public and private employment agencies, labor unions with fifteen or more members, and joint labor-management committees for apprenticeships and training. This act also gave the Commission the power to bring litigation against an organization that engages in discriminatory practices.

Equal Employment Opportunity Commission (EEUC)

A major failing of many school administrators is their lack of understanding about EEOC and its influence on human resource administration. From time to time this five-member commission has established affirmative action guidelines that, if adopted by school districts, can minimize liability when claims of discrimination occur. To further aid employers, on December 11, 1978, the EEOC adopted additional guidelines that can be used to avoid liability arising out of claims of "reverse discrimination" that result from affirmative action aimed at providing employment opportunities for women and racial and ethnic minorities. The following compilation from several sources will provide a framework for affirmative action compliance.

Eight steps have emerged from federal guidelines:[7]

First, each board of education should issue a written policy covering equal employment opportunity and affirmative action to be enforced by its chief executive officer, the superintendent. Commitments that should be included in the policy are a determination to recruit, hire, and promote for all job classifications without regard to race, creed, national origins, sex, or age (except where sex or age is a bona fide occupational qualification); a determination to base decisions concerning employment solely on individual qualifications as related to the requirements of the position; and a determination to insure that all personnel matters such as compensation, benefits, transfers, layoffs, returns from layoffs, and continuing education will be administered without regard to race, creed, national origin, sex, or age.

Second, the superintendent should appoint a top level official to be directly responsible for implementing the program. This official usually has the title *Director of Affirmative Action*. He or she should be responsible for developing policy statements and affirmative action programs. In addition, he or she should initiate internal and external communications, assist other administrators in the identification of problem areas, design and implement auditing and reporting systems, serve as a liaison between the district and enforcement agencies, and keep the superintendent informed of the latest developments in the area of equal opportunities.

Third, a school district should disseminate information about its affirmative action program both internally and externally. The board policy should be publicized through all internal channels, such as at meetings and on bulletin boards. External dissemination might take the form of brochures advertising the district; written notification to recruitment sources; clauses in purchase orders, leases, contracts; and written notification to minority organizations, community agencies, and community leaders.

Step four begins with a survey and analysis of minority and female employees by school and job classification. The percentage and number of minority and female employees currently employed in each major job classification should be compared to their presence in the relevant labor market—that is, the area in which you can reasonably expect to recruit. This will determine "underutilization," defined as having fewer minorities or women in a particular job category or school than could be reasonably expected; and "concentration," defined as more of a particular group in a job category or school than would reasonably be expected. A survey also should be conducted to identify those females and minorities who have the credentials to handle other jobs. Such employees can be transferred to these positions, if necessary.

With this information, the school district's administration should proceed to step five, developing measurable and remedial goals on a timetable. Once long-range goals have been established, specific and numerical targets can be developed for the hiring, training,

---

[7]The eight steps are a composite of those found in the Equal Employment Opportunity Commission's *Affirmative Action*, Vol. I (Washington, D.C.: Government Printing Office, 1974), pp. 18–64.

transferring, and promoting of personnel to reach goals within the established time frame. During this step the causes of underutilization should be identified.

Step six calls for developing and implementing specific programs to eliminate discriminatory barriers. This is the heart of an affirmative action program and must be discussed under several subheadings, which topics also will be further expanded in subsequent chapters. All persons involved in every aspect of the hiring process must be trained to use objective standards that support affirmative action goals. Recruitment procedures for each job category must be analyzed and reviewed to identify and eliminate discriminatory barriers. Recruitment procedures should include contacting educational institutions and community action organizations that represent minorities.

Reviewing the selection process to ensure that job requirements and hiring practices contribute to the attainment of affirmative action goals is a vital part of step six. This includes making certain that job qualifications and selection standards do not screen out minorities, unless the qualifications can be significantly related to job performance and no alternate nondiscriminatory standards can be developed.

Upward mobility systems such as promotions, transfers, and continuing education play an important role in fulfilling step six. Through careful record keeping, existing barriers may be identified and specific remedial programs initiated. These programs might include providing training for targeted minorities and women who are currently qualified for upward mobility, and providing more extensive training for those who are not yet qualified.

Wage and salary structures, benefits, and conditions of employment are other areas of investigation. Title VII of the 1964 Civil Rights Act and the Equal Pay Act require fiscal parity for jobs of equal skill and responsibility. All fringe benefits such as medical, hospital, and life insurance must be equally applied to personnel performing similar functions. Even in instances where states had "protective laws" barring women from hard or dangerous work, the courts generally found that the equal employment requirements of Title VII superseded these state laws. Courts have also barred compulsory "maternity leave" and the discharge of pregnant teachers.

Under affirmative action guidelines, the criteria for deciding when a person will be terminated, demoted, disciplined, laid off, or recalled should be the same for all employees. Seemingly neutral practices should be reexamined to see if they have a disparate effect on minority groups. Special considerations, such as job transfers and career counseling, should be given to minorities who have been laid off because of legitimate seniority systems.

Step seven is to establish internal auditing and reporting systems to monitor and evaluate progress in meeting the goals of the affirmative action program. Quarterly reports based on the data already outlined should be available to all administrators, enabling them to see how the program is working and where improvement is needed. The issue of keeping records on current employees and applicants by gender, race, or national origin is a very sensitive issue. Such record keeping has been used in the past as a discriminatory device, and some states have outlawed the practice. However, in certain litigation these records have been used as evidence of discriminatory practices. The data could even be demanded by enforcement agencies, and it is necessary for affirmative action record keeping. The EEOC suggests that such information be coded and kept separate from personnel files.[8]

---

[8]See Equal Employment Opportunities Commission's *Affirmative Action,* p. 60.

Developing supportive district and community programs is the last step in an affirmative action program. This may include developing support services for recruiting minority and female employees and encouraging current employees to further their education in order to qualify for promotions.

The EEOC Administrative Process

Alleged discrimination charges can be filed with any of EEOC's district offices. The Equal Employment Opportunity Commission received an average of six thousand charges each month. The following outlines the administrative process involved with an allegation of employment discrimination.[9]

The Charge of Discrimination.　A charge can be filed by any person, by others on behalf of that person, or by any of the EEOC commissioners. This charge must be filed within one hundred and eighty days from when the alleged discriminatory act occurred. In those states that have an employment discrimination law, the time may be extended to three hundred days. EEOC must first refer the charge to the appropriate state agency. The Equal Employment Opportunity Commission begins its investigation after the state agency concludes its procedures or after sixty days from the date of referral by EEOC to the state agency, whichever occurs first.

Some discriminatory practices are considered to be "continuing violations." A failure to promote because of a discriminatory system of promotions is an example of a continuing violation because it occurs each day the practice is followed. However, when an individual is denied employment because of discrimination, this constitutes a specific violation that occurred on a particular date. A continuing violation arises over a lengthy period of time. The time limit for filing a charge involving a continuing violation is one hundred eighty days after the cessation of the discriminatory practice. Therefore, as long as a practice continues, there is no time limit for filing a charge.

If an individual is subject to a collective bargaining agreement and believes that he or she has been discriminated against, he or she may follow the grievance procedures set out in the master contract. This procedure in no way alters the time period during which a charge must be filed.

Investigation of the Discrimination Charge.　It usually takes eighteen months after a charge is filed for an investigation to begin. The EEOC will demand broad access to an employer's records. An employer may object to the subpoena of records on the following grounds: the information is privileged, the compilation of information would be excessively burdensome, or the information sought is irrelevant to the charges.

The Determination.　When the investigation has been completed, the EEOC will make a determination concerning the discrimination charges. This determination will take one of two forms: "reasonable cause," which means that the charge is meritorious and both parties (employer and charging party) are invited to conciliate the case; or "no cause," which

---

[9]Dennis G. Collins, "Equal Employment Opportunity Act," *Journal of Missouri Bar,* October–November 1978, pp. 467–474.

means that the charge has no merit. If the charging party continues to believe that discrimination occurred, the court system is the next avenue of recourse.

The Process of Conciliation.   This process begins when the employer or his authorized representative meets with the staff of EEOC at one of the district offices to explore methods of conciliation. The usual methods employed are listed below.

1. The employer and charging party may agree to a "conciliation agreement." The terms of this agreement are designed to eliminate the discriminatory practice and may include provisions such as: back pay; reinstatement of the charging party if he or she was terminated; establishing goals and a timetable for hiring and promoting minorities. EEOC negotiates approximately seven thousand conciliation agreements each year, recovering millions of dollars for employees who have experienced discrimination.

2. With the concurrence of EEOC, the employer may extend an offer to the charging party. If the charging party rejects the offer, EEOC issues a "right to sue" notice, which gives the charging party ninety days to bring legal action against the employer.

3. The employer and charging party may agree to a settlement for a single individual. However, if the investigation by EEOC reveals a discriminatory practice against a class of persons such as females or handicapped persons and if the employer along with EEOC is unable to reach an agreement on a class determination, such is considered a "failure of conciliation," and the case is referred to the litigation division of the Equal Employment Opportunity Commission.

4. If the employer, charging party, and EEOC are unable to reach an agreement, this also is considered a "failure of conciliation" and referral is made to the litigation division.

The Litigation Division.   When conciliation fails, the litigation division evaluates the case to determine if there is a significant legal issue involved or if the case could have a significant impact on systematic patterns of discrimination. If one or both of these conditions exist, EEOC will most likely bring a lawsuit against the alleged discriminating employer.

The vast majority of lawsuits filed in federal courts, however, are instigated by private individuals pursuing their claims of discrimination or are class action suits filed by a group of citizens. The prerequisites to filing an individual claim of discrimination in federal court are: the charge was filed first with EEOC within the required time, EEOC issues a "right to sue" letter, and the charging party filed suit within ninety days from receipt of the letter.

A "right to sue" letter is usually issued by EEOC under three circumstances: (1) when a charge of discrimination is determined to have a "no cause" status by EEOC, which allows the charging party to appeal through the courts; (2) when the litigation division of EEOC rejects a case for legal action; (3) when EEOC enters into a conciliation agreement with an employer that does not include the charging party's claim.

If a federal court rules in favor of the charging party, it may grant any award it deems equitable. Injunctive remedies, on the other hand, require an employer to do something such as modifying a promotional policy that does not follow affirmative action guidelines and discriminates against minorities. In an individual case of discrimination when back pay is involved, the court may award back pay to the discriminate for a period of up to two years prior to the date when the charge was filed with EEOC.

Bona Fide Occupational Qualification

Discrimination by sex, religion, or national origin is allowed by the Equal Employment Opportunity Act under one condition, stated in the law as follows:

> Notwithstanding any other provision of this title, (1) it shall not be an unlawful employment practice for an employer to hire and employ employees, for an employment agency to classify, or refer for employment any individual, for a labor organization to classify its membership or to classify or refer for employment any individual, or for an employer, labor organization, or joint labor management committee controlling apprenticeship or other training or retraining programs to admit or employ any individual in any such program, on the basis of his religion, sex, or national origin in those certain instances where religion, sex, or national origin is a bona fide occupational qualification reasonably necessary to the normal operation of that particular business or enterprise, and (2) it shall not be an unlawful employment practice for a school, college, university, or other educational institution or institution of learning to hire and employ employees of a particular religion if such school, college, university, or other educational institution or institution of learning is, in whole or in substantial part, owned, supported, controlled, or managed by a particular religion or by a particular religious corporation, association, or society, or if the curriculum of such school, college, university, or other educational institution or institution of learning is directed toward the propagation of a particular religion.[10]

Therefore, a school district's personnel administrator has the right to specify a female for the position of swimming instructor when part of the job description includes supervising the locker room used by female students. In like manner, a Lutheran school official may hire only those applicants who profess the Lutheran creed because the mission of the school is to propagate that particular faith.

In certain school districts the national origin of teachers is extremely important. If in a particular school district over 30 percent of its student population has Spanish surnames, being of Hispanic origin could be a bona fide job qualification for certain teaching positions in that school system.

Judicial Review of Affirmative Action

Court decisions have further modified affirmative action regulations. Although the courts will continue to refine the interpretation of the Civil Rights Act and the Equal Employment Opportunity Act, certain basic conclusions have emerged and provide direction to school districts in their efforts to construct and implement an affirmative action program.[11]

First, discrimination has been broadly defined, in most cases including a class of individuals rather than a single person. Where discrimination has been found by the courts

---

[10]*The Equal Employment Opportunity Act of 1972* (Washington, D.C.: U.S. Government Printing Office, 1972), p. 4.

[11]Equal Employment Opportunity Commission, *Affirmative Action,* pp. 4–12.

to exist, remediation must be applied to all members of the class to which the individual complainant belongs.

Second, it is not the intent but rather the consequences of employment practices that determine if discrimination exists.

Third, even when an employment practice is neutral in text and impartially administered, if it has a disparaging effect upon members of a protected class (those groups covered by a law) or if it perpetuates the effects of prior discriminatory practices, it constitutes unlawful discrimination.

Fourth, statistics that show a disproportionate number of minorities or females in a job classification relative to their presence in the work force constitutes evidence of discriminatory practices. When such statistics exist, the employer must show that this is not the result of overt or institutional discrimination.

Fifth, for an employer to justify any practice or policy that creates a disparaging effect on a protected class, he must demonstrate a "compelling business necessity." The courts have interpreted this in a very narrow sense to mean that no alternative nondiscriminatory practice can achieve the required result.

Finally, court-ordered remedies not only open the doors to equal employment opportunity but also require employers to "make whole" and "restore the rightful economic status" of all those in the affected class. In practice, courts have ordered fundamental changes in almost every aspect of employment.

Two U.S. Supreme Court decisions have had an indirect effect upon affirmative action programs in school districts. The first case, *Regents of the University of California* v. *Bakke,* was decided in 1978 and dealt with admission quotas to a medical school. The second, *United Steelworkers* v. *Brian F. Weber,* also decided in 1979, dealt with a voluntary race-conscious affirmative action plan in private industry. Both cases addressed the issue of reverse discrimination.

✷Civil Rights Act, 1991

The passage of this new civil rights legislation along with the Americans with Disabilities Act of 1990 set school districts on a new path for the 1990s. This is particularly true with regards to the Civil Rights Act of 1991. The law extends punitive damages and jury trials for the first time to employees who have been discriminated against because of their race, national origin, gender, disability, or religion. School districts must be vigilant in developing and carrying out proper procedures for the selection, disciplining, and termination of employees.[12]

There are two significant procedural changes. First, the law allows compensatory and punitive damages. Prior to passage of this law and with few exceptions, plaintiffs could receive remedies limited to lost pay and benefits, reinstatement, and attorney fees. Now plaintiffs can receive "compensatory damages," for emotional pain, inconvenience, and mental anguish. Further, if the plaintiff can prove that the employer acted with "malice" or with "reckless indifference," he or she may be awarded punitive damages. The customary

[12]Joann S. Lublin, "Rights Law to Spur Shifts in Promotions," *Wall Street Journal,* 30 December 1991, sec. 2, p. B1.

remedies of receiving lost pay and benefits, reinstatement, and attorney fees are still available in addition to compensatory and punitive damages.

The major consideration for superintendents, assistant superintendents, and school board members is that they can be named as co-defendants in an action brought against a school district under the Civil Rights Act of 1991. The reason for this is that punitive damages cannot be levied against a school district because it is a governmental agency but punitive damages can be levied against individuals such as administrators and school board members.

Limits on the amount of compensatory and punitive damages have been established as follows:

- Plaintiffs may be awarded damages up to $50,000 if the school district has at least 15 but not more than 99 employees.
- Plaintiffs may be awarded damages up to $100,000 if the school district has between 100 and 200 employees.
- Plaintiffs may be awarded damages up to $200,000 if the school district has between 200 and 500 employees.
- Plaintiffs may be awarded damages up to $300,000 if the school district has more than 500 employees.

There are two exceptions to these limits. For age discrimination the limit is twice the amount of lost pay and benefits, and for race discrimination there is no limit. There is another liability for a school district that has not been available in the past in relation to damages. A plaintiff who prevails may also recover the cost of expert witness fees.

The second significant procedural change involves the right of a complainant to receive a jury trial in an employment discrimination case in which compensatory and/or punitive damages are being sought. Jury trials were seldom allowed in employment discrimination cases prior to this law. The major consideration concerning this issue is not only the unpredictability of juries but also the perceived bias of juries against employers.

Because of this law there is also a significant substantive change in the way in which the school personnel function is managed. The Civil Rights Act of 1991 overruled several U.S. Supreme Court decisions which appeared to be pro employer. Under the new law, in a discrimination case, the burden of proof is clearly placed on the school district to justify an employment practice that taken at face value is neutral but which results in discrimination against a protected class.[13]

Equality for the Handicapped

Title V of the Rehabilitation Act of 1973 contains five sections, four of which relate to affirmative action for handicapped individuals and one of which deals with voluntary actions, remedial actions, and evaluation criteria for compliance with the law. The congressional intent of the Rehabilitation Act is identical to the intent of other civil rights legislation, such as the Civil Rights Act (covering discrimination based on race, sex, religion, or national

[13]*Education USA,* 35, no. 18 (1993), 5.

EXHIBIT 2–4   Board of Education Policy on Equal Employment Opportunity and Affirmative Action

The following sample policy has been developed to illustrate more clearly how school districts can comply with the intent of federal legislation and litigation set forth in this chapter.

The board of education recognizes that implementation of its responsibility to provide an effective educational program depends on the full and effective utilization of qualified employees regardless of race, age, sex, color, religion, national origin, creed, or ancestry.

The board directs that its employment and personnel policies guarantee equal opportunity for everyone. Discrimination has no place in any component of this school system. Therefore, all matters relating to recruitment, selection, placement, compensation, benefits, educational opportunities, promotion, termination, and working conditions shall be free from discriminatory practices.

The board of education further initiates an affirmative action program to be in compliance with Title VII of the Civil Rights Act of 1964 and the Equal Employment Opportunity Act of 1972. This program shall insure minority and female proportional representation and participation in all employment opportunities; that civil rights will not be violated, abridged, or denied; that recruitment and selection criteria will be unbiased; that information relative to employment and promotional opportunities will be disseminated on an equal basis; and finally, that every employee has a right to file an internal or external complaint of discrimination and to obtain redress therefrom based on the finding of facts substantiating the complaint.

The following school district administrators are responsible for the effective implementation of the affirmative action program.

Superintendent of Schools. As the chief executive officer of the school system, the superintendent is directly responsible for exercising a leadership role in formulating and implementing procedures that are in keeping with this policy.

Director of Affirmative Action. Under the supervision of the superintendent, the director is responsible for the administration of the affirmative action program.

---

origin) and Title IX of the Educational Amendments (covering discrimination based on sex). However, the U.S. Department of Health, Education and Welfare (HEW) emphasized in the Federal Register promulgating the Rehabilitation Act that it contains a fundamental difference:

> The premise of both Title VII (Civil Rights Act) and Title IX (Educational Amendments) is that there is no inherent difference of equalities between the general public and the persons protected by these statutes and, therefore, there should be no differential treatment in the administration of federal programs. Section 504 (Rehabilitation Act), on the other hand is far more complex. Handicapped persons may require different treatment in order to be afforded equal access, and identical treatment may, in fact, constitute discrimination. The problem of establishing general rules as to when different treatment is prohibited or required is compounded by the diversity of existing handicaps and the differing degree to which particular persons may be affected.[14]

[14]Department of Health, Education, and Welfare, "Nondiscrimination on the Basis of Handicap," *Federal Register,* vol. 41, no. 96 (May 17, 1976).

Subpart B of Section 504 of the Rehabilitation Act specifically refers to employment practices. It prohibits recipients of federal financial assistance from discriminating against qualified handicapped individuals in recruitment, hiring, compensation, job assignment/ classification, and fringe benefits. Employers are further required to provide reasonable work environment accommodations for qualified handicapped applicants or employees unless they can demonstrate that such accommodations would impose an undue hardship. The law applies to all state, intermediate, and local educational agencies. Finally, any agency that receives assistance under the Education of the Handicapped Act must take positive steps to employ and promote qualified handicapped persons into programs assisted under this Act.

Reasonable Accommodation

The requirement that employers make "reasonable accommodations" in the work environment for handicapped applicants and employees has created a great deal of confusion. Reasonable accommodations include providing employee facilities that are readily accessible to and usable by handicapped persons; taking action such as restructuring jobs, modifying work schedules, modifying and/or acquiring special equipment or devices, and providing readers.

In order to determine whether an accommodation imposes an undue hardship on an employer, the following factors should be considered: first, the size of the agency or company with respect to the number of employees; second, the number and type of facilities available; third, the size of the employer's budget; fourth, the composition of the work force; and finally, the nature and type of accommodation needed.

If an employer believes that reasonable accommodations would impose a hardship, the burden of proof rests with the employer.

Employment Criteria

The U.S. Department of Health and Human Services (formerly HEW) in concert with the guidelines on selection procedures developed by the Equal Employment Opportunity Commission prohibits the use of any employment test or other criteria that screens out or discriminates against handicapped persons unless the test or selection criteria is proven to be job related. Therefore, in selecting and administering tests to an applicant or employee with a handicap, the test results must accurately reflect the individual's job skills or other factors the test purports to measure rather than the person's impaired sensory, manual, or speaking skills, except when these skills are required for successful job performance.

The term *test* includes measures of general intelligence, mental ability, learning ability, specific intellectual ability, mechanical and clerical aptitudes, dexterity and coordination, knowledge, proficiency, attitudes, personality, and temperament. Formal techniques of assessing job suitability that yield qualifying criteria include specific personal history and background data, specific educational or work history, scored interviews, and scored application forms.

School district administrators must realize that they may be called on to present evidence concerning the validity and reliability of the testing procedures they use in selection and promotion processes. Casual techniques, of course, are very difficult to defend.

✱ Preemployment Inquiries

Subpart B of Section 504 of the Rehabilitation Act specifies that recipients of federal financial assistance should take (a) remedial action to correct past discrimination, (b) voluntary action to overcome the limited participation of handicapped individuals, (c) affirmative action to employ the handicapped. An employer may use preemployment inquiries to determine progress in complying with the Rehabilitation Act. Subpart B also contains the following provision: An employer must state on all preemployment written questionnaires or, if no written questionnaire is used, must tell applicants that preemployment information is being requested for the purpose of implementing remedial, voluntary, or affirmative action programs; the employer must state that the information is being requested on a voluntary basis, that it will be kept confidential, and that refusal to provide such information will not subject the applicant or employee to any adverse treatment.

Nothing in Subpart B prohibits an employer from making employment conditional on the results of a medical examination prior to the assumption of duties by a handicapped person. However, this condition can be applied only if all entering employees are required to have a medical examination and only if the results of such examinations are used in accordance with appropriate remedial, voluntary, and affirmative action programs.

The medical information collected must be maintained on separate forms from other employment data and must be accorded the same confidentiality as medical records. This information may be used by supervisors and managers to determine the restrictions in the duties of handicapped employees and to determine necessary accommodations. First aid and safety personnel may also use this information when emergencies occur. Finally, government officials may have access to such information when investigating an employer's compliance with the Rehabilitation Act.

✱ Organizational Action Required

Although Subpart B of Section 504 does not require school districts to develop an affirmative action program for the handicapped, it does require three types of organizational activities: remedial action, voluntary action, and self-evaluation. The Office of Civil Rights investigates allegations of discrimination by school districts against the handicapped and the director of the office can require remedial action if discrimination is confirmed against handicapped persons who are currently employed, who are no longer employed in the district but were when the discrimination occurred, or who would have been employed in the district had the discrimination not occurred.

In addition, school districts may take voluntary measures to alleviate discrimination. Such measures usually begin with the construction of a self-evaluation procedure. Paragraph 87.4 of the Federal Register outlines the self-evaluation requirements as follows:

> Within one year of the effective date of publishing Section 504 regulations (May 4, 1977), local school districts must: (a) evaluate, with the assistance of handicapped individuals and organizations, current district policies and practices that do not meet Section 504 requirements, (b) modify such district policies and practices, and (c) take appropriate remedial steps to eliminate the effects of any discrimination that resulted from adherence to such policies and practices.

Furthermore,

a local school district that employs fifteen or more persons must, for at least three years following completion of the self-evaluation, maintain on file and make available for public inspection: (a) a list of the interested individuals consulted, (b) a description of areas examined and any problems identified, and (c) a description of any modifications made and of any remedial steps taken.[15]

Table 2–1 schematically presents the necessary components for planning, conducting, and analyzing a self-evaluation procedure.

⚹ The Americans With Disabilities Act, 1990

President George Bush signed into law the *Americans with Disabilities Act* (ADA) on July 26, 1990. This is the most comprehensive legislation ever passed protecting the rights of individuals with disabilities. Within the first eleven months after its passage, the Equal Employment Opportunity Commission received 11,760 discrimination complaints which represented about 15 percent of that agency's caseload. During that same period aggrieved persons collected over 11 million dollars in awards.[16] From a practical perspective, however, ADA is an extension of the Rehabilitation Act of 1973. This extension pertains to the private sector and to those local and state governmental agencies that receive no federal monies. Because almost every school district in the nation receives some federal financial assistance, either directly or indirectly, which is the threshold requiring adherence to the Rehabilitation Act, school districts in compliance with the Rehabilitation Act will have little difficulty complying with the ADA.

There are five titles to ADA. All of them except Title IV have some impact upon school districts. Title IV pertains to telecommunications companies.

TABLE 2–1   Conceptual Components for a Self-Evaluation Model

Phase I	Develop policy statements, goals, and objectives.
Phase II	Appoint a self-evaluation coordinator and define this individual's responsibilities.
Phase III	Develop a self-evaluation design.
Phase IV	Implement the self-evaluation design.
Phase V	Analyze staffing procedures and practices.
Phase VI	Modify procedures and practices.
Phase VII	Monitor and evaluate these procedures and practices.

Adapted from Richard Clelland, *Section 504: Civil Rights for the Handicapped* (Arlington, Va.: American Association of School Administrators, 1978), p. 28.

[15]Dept. of HEW, *Nondiscrimination.*

[16]*Wall Street Journal,* 27 July 1993, sec. 1, p. A1.

⊁*Title I*

This title regulates employment practices and took effect on July 26, 1992 for school districts.

⊁*Title II*

All services, programs, and activities of state and local governmental agencies are subject to Title II even if they are provided by a contractor. This title took effect on January 26, 1992 and includes all activities involving all public contact as part of ongoing operations. Thus, classroom instruction and pupil transportation are affected. Even though Title II includes employment practices, the Department of Justice has decided that Equal Employment Opportunity regulations governing Title I are sufficient for Title II.

⊁*Title III*

This title also took effect on January 26, 1992. It pertains to public accommodations and applies only to the private sector. School districts are not covered by Title III as such. However, if a school district contracts with a private company to provide pupil transportation or food service as examples, the district must ensure that the private company is operating in compliance with Title III. This compliance issue is usually set forth as a section in the contract between the district and the company providing the service.

⊁ *Title IV*

This title took effect on July 26, 1993 and requires telecommunication companies to provide telecommunication relay services for people with hearing or speech disabilities.

⊁*Title V*

This title contains a number of provisions. The most important for school districts involves the relationship of ADA to other laws. It states, for example, that the "highest standard" applies whether that standard is ADA, the Rehabilitation Act, a state law, or even a local ordinance. It also prohibits retaliation against persons seeking redress under the ADA and allows the court to award attorney fees to the prevailing parties.[17]

⊁ *Jurisdiction and Scope of ADA*

Under the jurisdiction of the Equal Employment Opportunity Commission, the ADA covered all school districts with 25 or more employees after July 26, 1992 and all districts with 15 or more employees after July 26, 1994. However, under the jurisdiction of the Department of Justice, discrimination is prohibited by school districts regardless of the number of employees after January 26, 1992.[18]

Because both the Department of Justice and the Equal Employment Opportunity Commission have been given jurisdiction for the enforcement of ADA, coordination between these two agencies is necessary. Further, because the Department of Labor has jurisdiction

---

[17]National School Boards Association, "Americans with Disabilities Act," *Updating School Board Policies,* 23, no. 4 (May 1992), pp. 1–2.

[18]U.S. Equal Employment Opportunity Commission, *The Americans with Disabilities Act: Your Responsibilities as an Employer.* Washington, D.C.: The Commission, 1991, p. 1.

in cases involving discrimination and affirmative action under the Rehabilitation Act of 1973, coordination between this agency and the Department of Justice and the Equal Employment Opportunity Commission is not only necessary but also critical.

Under ADA it is unlawful to discriminate in all personnel functions including:

recruitment
selection
promotion
training
staff development
rewards including direct and indirect compensation
reduction in force
termination
placement
leave
voluntary fringe benefits

Who Is Protected by ADA?

Title I sets forth who is qualified to be protected by ADA. Essentially, under ADA a person is disabled if he or she has a physical or mental impairment that substantially limits a major life activity. ADA also protects individuals who have a record of a substantially limiting impairment, and people who are regarded as having a substantially limiting impairment.

The terms "physical or mental impairment" in this definition include cerebral palsy, muscular dystrophy, multiple sclerosis, AIDS, HIV infection, emotional illness, drug addiction, alcoholism, and dyslexia, etc. However, such conditions as a person's height, weight, or muscle tone, if these are within normal ranges, do not qualify under these terms. Further, the color of hair or eyes, being pregnant, or having served a sentence in prison are not examples of a "physical or mental impairment." When determining if a person has a protected disability, the decision must be made without regard to mitigating measures such as medication and assistive or prosthetic devices.

The term "major life activity" means an activity that an average person can perform with little or no difficulty. Thus, hearing, seeing, speaking, breathing, performing manual tasks, walking, caring for oneself, learning, or working are major life activities. The Equal Employment Opportunity Commission takes into account three factors when determining if a disability substantially limits these major types of life activities: (1) the nature and severity of the impairment; (2) its duration or expected duration; (3) the actual or expected permanent long-term impact resulting from it. Thus, a broken limb, influenza, or a tonsillectomy are not disabilities.[19]

The term "record of impairment" refers to a disability for which an individual no longer receives treatment. Therefore, people who have a history of heart disease, mental illness, drug disease, or alcoholism are also protected by this law.

---

[19]Equal Employment Opportunity Commission, Final Rule, "Equal Employment Opportunity for Individuals with Disabilities," *Federal Register* (26 July 1991) vol. 56, no. 144, p. 35735.

The term "regarded as impaired" is meant to indicate those individuals who are not physically or mentally impaired but who are regarded as impaired as a result of fear or stereotyping. This definition applies to people about whom there is unsubstantiated concern regarding productivity, safety, insurance, liability, attendance, cost of accommodation, accessibility, workers' compensation costs, or acceptance by co-workers.[20]

In March, 1995, the Equal Employment Opportunity Commission issued an interpretation of the Americans With Disabilities Act setting forth that the law protects people from employment discrimination who are healthy but who carry abnormal genes. More and more people are taking advantage of new genetic tests that can identify a person's predisposition to diseases such as Alzheimer's, heart, and certain types of cancer. This information allows individuals to access preventive measures and early treatment; it is also helpful in predicting what disease genes can be passed on to their children. If the results of these tests are known by potential employers, some of them might discriminate against those applicants who carry abnormal genes, in order to avoid future lost days from work and higher employer-paid health care premiums. Further, such information might tempt an employer to fire an employee for the same reason.[21]

The Selection Process Under ADA

An applicant for a position in a school district who is also protected by ADA must otherwise qualify for the job. The term "otherwise qualify" means that the applicant can perform the essential functions of the job with or without reasonable accommodation.

Therefore, the applicant must satisfy job requirements for educational background, employment experience, skills, licenses, and other qualification standards that are job-related. Further, the person must be able to perform those tasks that are essential to the job either with or without reasonable accommodation.

The school district can still hire the best qualified applicant and it does not impose any affirmative action obligations.

Determining what are essential functions is critical to not discriminating against a qualified candidate who has a disability under ADA. This determination about essential functions must be made before carrying out certain processes of the personnel function. This is certainly true in relation to initiating the selection process which includes developing a job description and advertising the position. A number of factors should be considered in determining if the function is essential:

1. The actual work experience of present and/or past employees in the job;
2. The time needed to perform a function;
3. The terms of a collective bargaining agreement;
4. The consequences of not requiring that an employee perform a function;
5. The degree of expertise or skill required to perform the function;
6. The number of other employees available to perform the function or among whom the performance of the function can be distributed;
7. Whether the reason the position exists is to perform that function.[22]

---

[20]National School Boards Association, 23, no. 4, p. 3.

[21]*St. Louis Post-Dispatch,* "Health Carriers of Bad Genes Protected," 9 April 1995, p. A8.

[22]Equal Employment Opportunity Commission, Final Rule, p. 35735.

Reasonable accommodation may be defined as any change or adjustment to the job or the work environment which will permit a qualified person with a disability to participate in the selection process, to perform the essential functions of a job, and to enjoy benefits and privileges of employment equal to those enjoyed by employees without disabilities. Therefore, reasonable accommodation may include:

1. Acquiring or modifying equipment or devices;
2. Job restructuring;
3. Part-time or modified work schedules;
4. Adjusting or modifying examinations, training materials or policies;
5. Providing readers and interpreters;
6. Making the workplace readily accessible to and usable to people with disabilities.[23]

The reasonable accommodation requirement also applies to employees who become disabled after employment with the district. All of the above with the addition of *reassignment to another position* must be considered for the employee who becomes disabled.

In determining what accommodations may be necessary, the Equal Employment Opportunity Commission recommends the following approach.

First, determine the essential functions of the job.

Second, consult with the individual who has the disability in order to determine the individual's precise limitations and how they may be overcome.

Third, also with the individual's assistance identify potential accommodations and assess their effectiveness.

Fourth, after considering the preferences of the individual with the disability, implement the accommodation most appropriate for the individual and the employer. It is important to understand that ADA does not require selection of the best accommodation as long as the accommodation selected provides an equal opportunity to perform the job.

Examples of equipment which may be a reasonable accommodation include telecommunications devices, special computer software to enlarge or convert print documents to spoken words, telephone headsets, speaker phones, and adaptive light switches.

Undue Hardship

It is not necessary to provide a reasonable accommodation if this would cause an undue hardship on the school district. This means that the accommodation would be unduly costly, extensive, substantial, disruptive, or would fundamentally alter the nature of operation of the school district. Factors which can be considered in making this determination of undue hardship are the cost of the accommodation, the size of the school district, the financial resources of the district, and the nature or structure of the district's operations.

If a particular accommodation would be an undue hardship, the school district staff must try to identify another accommodation which will not pose a hardship. Further, if the hardship is caused by the lack of financial resources, the school district must attempt to find funding from an outside source such as a vocational rehabilitation agency. The applicant or employee must also be given the opportunity to provide the accommodation or pay for a portion of the accommodation that constitutes an undue hardship.[24]

[23]*Ibid.,* pp. 35735–35736.

[24]U.S. Equal Employment Opportunity Commission, pp. 5–6.

Accessibility

Title II contains the provisions of ADA relating to accessibility. ADA required school districts to conduct a self-evaluation by January 26, 1993. Most school districts will have a self-evaluation on file which complied with Section 504 of the Rehabilitation Act of 1973. Thus, the school district should have included in that evaluation only those policies and practices which were not covered in the previous self-evaluation. The self-evaluation should provide an opportunity for input from interested individuals, from individuals with disabilities, and from organizations representing people with disabilities. Each school district is to maintain a file that is open to inspection by the public which includes the names of the interested persons consulted, a description of the areas examined, the problems identified, and a description of any modifications made.[25]

School districts were also required to maintain on file a transition plan open to inspection by the public which set forth the structural changes to facilities that were to be undertaken in order to achieve program accessibility. This should have included a time schedule for taking corrective action and the name of the school district official responsible for implementing the plan.

ADA also required school districts to appoint a staff member responsible for investigating complaints regarding noncompliance and a procedure for the prompt and equitable resolution of complaints.

Damages for Noncompliance with ADA

Hiring, reinstatement, back pay, and injunctive relief are some of the remedies that are possible under ADA. The list has been expanded by the Civil Rights Act of 1991 to include damages such as future pecuniary losses, inconvenience, mental anguish, and emotional pain subject to specific dollar limitations. Punitive damages may not be awarded against a school district under ADA.[26]

AIDS and Discrimination

There is no topic or issue that has focused the attention and concern of so many people during the last five years as the disease of AIDS (Acquired Immune Deficiency Syndrome). Without going into a long discussion of the medical aspects of the disease, it is sufficient for this treatment to state that the disease can be transmitted to others and that it is always fatal.

The hysteria over this disease caused Dr. C. Everett Koop, the surgeon general, to send an explanatory brochure to all the households in the U.S. All health officials are in agreement about the manner in which the disease may be transmitted. Sexual contact with an infected person and the sharing of drug needles or syringes are the most common ways that the disease is transmitted.

Health officials are also in agreement that the disease cannot be transmitted by casual contact with an infected person. In fact, ordinary and casual contact between family members where a member had AIDS verified that the disease cannot be transmitted this way.

---

[25]National School Boards Association, "American with Disabilities Act," *Updating School Board Policies,* 23, no. 5 (June 1992), pp. 3–4.

[26]National School Boards Association, 23, no. 4, p. 2.

The hysteria continues to exist, however, and has caused concern in the workplace, which has resulted in discriminatory practices by some individuals, companies, agencies, and organizations. A significant development occurred in 1987 that has been helpful in dealing with discrimination against people infected with the AIDS virus. In *School Board of Nassau* v. *Arline,* the U.S. Supreme Court ruled that an infectious disease could constitute a handicap under Section 504 of the Rehabilitation Act of 1973. In this case the infectious disease was tuberculosis. However, in that same year a federal district circuit court of appeals in California applied the *Arline* decision to a case involving an Orange County teacher with AIDS. The court ordered the school district to reinstate the teacher to his previous duties.[27]

A further development occurred in 1988, when the U.S. Justice Department reversed its earlier position on AIDS and declared that fear of contagion by itself does not permit federal agencies and federally assisted employers to fire or discriminate against workers infected with the virus.

This legal opinion is binding on school boards, federal agencies, government contractors, managers of federally subsidized housing projects, and other organizations receiving federal contracts or financial assistance. The opinion emphasized that each situation must be determined on a case-by-case basis in order to decide if an infected person poses a direct threat to the health of others in the workplace.

The Rehabilitation Act of 1973 requires an employer to make "reasonable accommodations" for people with disabilities, which now includes AIDS. The accommodations must be made if the person with AIDS can still perform the essential requirements of his or her job.

If an employer can demonstrate that making such accommodations would pose an undue hardship, then the company, agency, or organization can be excused. However, the regulations governing undue hardship are very stringent.

A situation in which the reasonable accommodation regulation probably would not apply is in the case of a school bus driver who has advanced symptoms of the disease. The effects of AIDS on the central nervous system would preclude that person from continuing to drive a school bus.

It is extremely important to protect the privacy of individuals who have AIDS. Medical information on employees is confidential.

This fact is clearly set forth in *Gammel* v. *United States* (1984). In this case the U.S. government wanted to review the medical records of a federal employee, Mr. Gammel. The U.S. contended that Gammel was a potential health risk to the general public and reviewing his medical records would provide the necessary information in order to suitably assign him where he would not be a threat to the public.

Gammel's attorney argued that the Fourteenth Amendment of the United States Constitution protects the privacy rights of citizens and the release of medical information would violate this Amendment unless there was proof that a clear and present danger to public safety, in fact, existed. The U.S. government failed to establish such proof and therefore, the Federal District Court ruled in favor of Gammel.

---

[27]Sally Banks Zakariya, "What if AIDS Comes on Staff?" *The Executive Educator,* 9, no. 4 (April 1987), pp. 21–22.

EXHIBIT 2–5   Sample AIDS Policy

The board of education is committed to providing a school environment free from health risks for all students and staff members. This policy has been developed utilizing information from the federal Center for Disease Control. In particular it has been written to protect the rights of school personnel who are infected with the Human Immunodeficiency Virus (HIV) which causes Acquired Immune Deficiency Syndrome (AIDS), which, in turn, can cause AIDS Related Complex (ARC).

Further, the development of this policy has been guided by medical information which has documented that the HIV virus cannot be transmitted by casual person-to-person contact.

Thus, the Board of Education sets forth the following provisions.

- Each case of HIV, AIDS, or ARC will be evaluated on an individual basis.
- The administration will provide an ongoing program of education on the subject of HIV, AIDS, and ARC to students, staff, and the community.
- Employees who have been diagnosed as infected with HIV, AIDS, or ARC are encouraged to report this to the superintendent of schools accompanied by a written statement from a licensed physician which reports on the employee's medical condition and capability of continuing in his or her present position.
- This medical information will be confidential to the superintendent of schools. The superintendent will share this information with other employees only on a "need to know" basis which determination will be made in consultation with the infected employee. Those staff members so informed will also be instructed by the superintendent on the legal and policy provisions that require this information to be confidential.
- The employee shall continue in his or her position unless a deterioration in the employee's health significantly interferes with the performance of his or her job responsibilities. The employee's physician may also determine that the employee's job responsibilities pose a threat to his or her health. In either situation, a reasonable effort will be made to place the employee in another position.
- The employee is guaranteed all the protections and safeguards that other employees have according to law and board of education policy.

Therefore, if the personnel records of public school districts contain medical information about employees, these records are confidential. The only reason for revealing the contents of such records would be the existence of a clear and present danger to public health or safety.

There is also an area of concern in relation to the rights of co-workers of AIDS infected employees. This issue has been addressed in a private sector federal court case, *Whirlpool* v. *Marshall* (1988). Basically, the case reaffirmed that the best available medical information does not consider casual contact with an AIDS infected person to be a health risk. The contact in schools between staff members and, in fact, between staff members and students can be classified as casual and thus there is no risk of contracting AIDS. School district personnel policies and procedures must reflect this position.

In summary, case law clearly upholds the employment and privacy rights of persons with AIDS, with ARC, and with an HIV positive test. Further, case law upholds these same rights for persons suspected of being infected. It is imperative that the assistant superintendent for personnel insure that discrimination does not occur in school district practices against persons with AIDS or with the above mentioned AIDS related conditions. A potential area for serious discrimination exists in life, medical, and hospitalization insurance programs.

Vietnam Era Veterans Readjustment Assistance Act

This Act was passed by Congress in 1974. School districts receiving $10,000 or more in federal funds must take affirmative action to hire disabled veterans of all wars, and all veterans of the Vietnam era. This Act defines a disabled veteran as a person who has a 30 percent or more disability rating from the Veterans Administration, or who was discharged or released from active duty for a service connected disability.

Mobilization of Military Reserves and National Guard into Active Duty

On August 22, 1990, President George Bush ordered the mobilization of U.S. military reserves and national guard units into active duty. This was the first mobilization in twenty years. It activated approximately 40,000 troops. This mobilization, of course, was necessary in order to support the then forthcoming war in the Persian Gulf against Iraq. The war was named Desert Storm.

When the employee enters active military service he or she is immediately covered by the military health care system. Dependents of the employee are eligible to be covered by the Civilian Health and Medical Program of the Uniformed Services (CHAMPUS) under certain conditions. The most significant condition is the length of time that the employee will be on active duty. If the mobilization is for less than thirty days, dependents cannot be enrolled in CHAMPUS. However, if the mobilization is extended, CHAMPUS coverage will begin on the thirty-first days of active duty. If the mobilization is for more than thirty days at the outset, coverage begins from the first day of active duty. Dependents must receive health care from military health facilities or receive permission to go to a civilian facility.

Reservists and National Guard members are covered under the provisions of the Veteran's Reemployment Act of 1940 which also was amended in 1986. This act obliges the school district to give reservists and National Guard members time off from their civilian jobs to participate in military training and active duty. Also, the act protects them from termination and discrimination because of their military obligations. Further, the reservist or National Guard member is covered by an "escalator principle" which means that he or she will continue to accrue seniority, fringe benefits, and salary increases. Thus, if other employees in the same job category as the reservist or National Guard member received an increase in salary and/or additional fringe benefits, he or she will receive the same salary increase and/or fringe benefits when he or she returns to work. However, if there was a reduction in fringe benefits or salary for all the members of the job category, the same reductions will apply to the reservist or National Guard member upon his or her return.

Upon his or her release from military training or active duty, the reservist or National Guard member has ninety days to apply for reinstatement into his or her prior held position. If the prior held position is not available, he or she must be offered a position of like status or the job that is nearest in duties to the one he or she left.

In regard to health care benefits, the employer cannot impose a pre-existing exclusion or waiting period before reinsuring the reservist or National Guard member.

✗ *The Omnibus Transportation Employee Testing Act, 1991*

On October 28, 1991 President Bush signed into law The Omnibus Transportation Employee Testing Act which required the Secretary of Transportation to promulgate regulations for alcohol and controlled substances testing for persons in safety-sensitive positions including motor carriers. Implementation for districts with 50 or more employees was done in 1994. For districts with fewer than 50 employees, implementation began in early 1995.[28]

Regulations have been established that require school bus drivers and drivers of private motor carriers of passengers to submit to controlled-substance testing.

Other regulations require school districts to conduct pre-employment, post-accident, random, reasonable suspicion, and return-to-duty testing. School districts must publish the board of education policy concerning this law and must publish implementation procedures which should include the action that the school district will take if a bus driver is found to be in violation of this law.

School districts must also develop procedures for the collection, shipment, and accessioning of urine specimens. The Department of Transportation requires urine samples to be analyzed by laboratories certified by the Department of Health and Human Services' National Institute on Drug Abuse. Laboratories are required to report the analysis to a medical review officer who contacts the bus driver concerning the results of the testing and who reports the results to the school district. Of course, these reports are confidential. The school district administrator responsible for determining if a reasonable suspicion exists to require a bus driver to undergo testing must receive at least 60 minutes of training on the physical, behavioral, speech, and performance indicators of probable controlled substance abuse. Finally, a bus driver who has violated this law must receive information from the school district concerning resources that are available for helping the bus driver with his or her drug abuse problem.

✗*Family and Medical Leave Act, 1993*[29]

President Clinton signed into law the Family and Medical Leave Act (P.L. 103–3) on February 5, 1993. The fundamental purpose of this act is to provide eligible employees as defined by section 3(e) of the Fair Labor Standards Act with the right to take twelve weeks of unpaid leave per year in connection with certain circumstances.

An employee may invoke this law in conjunction with the following:

1. The birth and first-year care of a child. This includes paternity leave.
2. The adoption or foster parent placement of a child. The entitlement ends when the child reaches age one or the twelve-week period ends.

---

[28]Jim Wright, "School Districts Must Plan in 1993–94 Budget Costs for Drug Testing Employees," *School Bus Fleet* (February/March 1993), p. 48.

[29]U.S. Congress, *Family and Medical Leave Act.* Washington, D.C.: U.S. Government Printing Office, 1993.

3. The illness of an employee's spouse, child, or parent. This includes a step-child, foster child, a child over eighteen years of age incapable of self care, and a step-parent.

4. The employee's own illness. This means a serious health condition that may result from not only illness but also injury, impairment, physical or mental condition. This may involve inpatient care or any incapacity requiring absence from work for more than three days and which involves continuing treatment by a health care provider. Also, this refers to any treatment for prenatal care.

The law became effective on August 5, 1993. However, in those school districts which have a collective bargaining agreement with one or more bargaining units, the law became effective upon the termination of the master contract or on February 5, 1994 whichever occurred earlier. Because this is a labor law, the United States Department of Labor is the federal agency responsible for the development of implementation regulations.

All employees of private elementary and secondary schools and all employees of public school districts are covered by this law. In business and industry, a company must employ fifty or more people to be subject to the mandates of the law.

Eligibility under this law means that an employee must have worked for the school district at least twelve months. The employment may have been consecutive or non-consecutive. Also, the employee must have worked at least 1,250 hours during the year preceding the leave. Thus, many part-time employees will not be eligible. There is also an exemption which could apply to the superintendent of schools and many other administrators. This exemption allows a board of education to deny the request for leave of an employee whose salary falls within the highest 10 percent category. The reason for the exclusion is that the absence of such an employee may cause substantial and grievous economic injury to the school district.

A school district may use a number of methods to calculate the twelve-month period during which twelve weeks of leave may be requested. For example, the district policy may be the calendar year, twelve months forward from the date that an employee returned from a leave, or any fixed twelve-month period. When both spouses are employees of the same school district, the combined amount of leave for birth, adoption, and family illness may be limited to twelve weeks. Obviously, this restriction does not apply to personal illness.

There are special regulations pertaining to "intermittent leave," "reduced leave schedule," and "leave near the end of an academic term." This provision applies to teachers and does not include teacher assistants and aides unless their principal job is actual teaching. Counselors, psychologists, curriculum specialists, and support staff such as cafeteria, maintenance, and transportation employees are not covered by the special regulations.

Thus, a teacher may take intermittent leave which means a period of time from one hour to several weeks. A person being treated with chemotherapy is an example of such a situation. However, if a teacher will be absent more than 20 percent of the total number of working days during the period of the leave which is considered a reduced leave schedule, a school district may require the teacher to take leave for a particular duration which must not be longer than the duration of the treatment. An alternative approach for a school district is to transfer the teacher to a different assignment on a temporary basis. The teacher must receive equivalent pay and benefits. For example, a school district could assign the teacher to a full-time substitute teacher position.

In regards to leave near the end of an academic year, a school district may require a teacher to continue on leave until the end of the term if the leave begins more than five weeks but continues into three weeks before the end of the term. Further, the school district may require the teacher to continue leave until the end of the term unless the leave is for the teacher's own serious health condition under two conditions: (1) if the leave begins with five or fewer weeks before the end of the semester but lasts for more than two weeks and ends during the two-week period before the end of the term; (2) if the leave begins during the three-week period before the end of the semester and will last for more than five days.

If the employee has prior knowledge about the need for a leave, he or she is required to give thirty days verbal or written notice. When the employee does not have prior knowledge about the need for a leave, notice must be given as soon as is practicable which may be interpreted as two working days.

The school district may require the employee to first use accrued paid leave such as sick, personal, or vacation leave. The district must continue to pay health plan premiums for the employee during the period of leave and this period must be treated as continued service for purposes of vesting and eligibility to participate in retirement plans. However, the employee is not entitled to accrue additional benefits during the period of unpaid leave such as additional paid sick leave.

The school district may require certification from the employee's health care provider or the family member's health care provider concerning the date when the condition began, its duration, the necessity for leave, and the employee's inability to perform his or her job functions. A second opinion from a health care provider can be required by the school district at its own expense; and a third opinion can be obtained on the same condition with this opinion binding.

Upon return from leave, an employee is entitled to the same position or an equivalent position as when leave commenced, with the same salary, benefits, and working conditions. The district may require a certification from the employee's health care provider stating that the employee is able to resume work. School districts must not only inform employees about the provisions of this act but also policies and procedures for invoking this act must be in writing and be provided to the employee prior to taking leave in order for the district to enforce the act.

Complaints by employees can be initiated with the U.S. Department of Labor. The Department may conduct an administrative investigation or may file suit in court. Thus, federal record keeping requirements and investigations will be consistent with the Fair Labor Standards Act. The statute of limitations is two years except in cases where willful violation is alleged which carries a three-year limitation. A school district that violates this law may be subject to the following damages: (1) Lost wages and benefits; (2) all other costs other than wages which an employee may have incurred as a result of the violation. The other costs usually include attorney and witness fees, but could also include, as an example, reimbursement for professional nursing care up to a sum equal to twelve weeks of wages if the employee's leave was denied.

⚹ *Equality for Women*

The French writer Stendhal believed that granting women equality would be the surest sign of civilization and would double the intellectual power of the human race. Although he wrote over one hundred years ago, equality for women continues to be a significant issue in our society.

In educational organizations the question of equal employment opportunity for women traditionally applies to a specific job classification—administration. It is clear to all observers that women are well represented in teaching, custodial, food service, and bus driving positions. Skilled trade positions (carpenters, electricians, and plumbers) in most school districts, however, are dominated by males, as are industrial arts teaching positions. In such situations, the norms of affirmative action previously outlined in this chapter are applicable. The critical issue, however, is the need to have women better represented in administrative ranks.

Why are there so few female administrators? Many researchers have put forth various theories. One such study argues that the causes are increased salary levels for teachers, which attracted more men, who were subsequently promoted to administrative positions; entry of male veterans into education after World War II and the Korean War, which also led to their eventual entry into administration; the executive image projected for administrators in the 1950s and 1960s, which attracted more men; and myths of male superiority.[30]

The legal mandate of equal employment opportunity for women emanates primarily from two federal laws: Title IX of the Education Amendments of 1972, which prohibits sex discrimination in educational programs or activities, including employment, when the school district is receiving federal financial assistance; and, of course, Title VII of the Civil Rights Act of 1964, as amended in 1972, which prohibits discrimination on the basis of sex as well as religion, national origin, race, or color.

In February 1992 the U.S. Supreme Court issued a unanimous opinion in connection with a lawsuit, *Franklin v. Gwinnett County Public Schools,* which upheld unlimited punitive and compensatory damages for victims of gender discrimination under Title IX of the Education Amendments of 1972. This is a landmark decision. Prior to this a female employee who believed that she had been discriminated against could seek only back pay in addition to the injunctive and declaratory relief otherwise available.

Potential Areas of Employment Discrimination Concerning Women

As a general rule school districts—and all employers—are prohibited from establishing job qualifications that are derived from female stereotyping. The courts have uniformly required employers to prove that any sex restriction is indeed a bona fide occupational qualification.

Some of the most common forms of discrimination against females in the business-industrial community are even less defensible in educational organizations. For example, females have been denied employment because of height and weight limitations. In such situations a woman, who is capable of performing the job-related tasks, has clearly established case law precedent to bring the employer to court. However, it still occurs that an exceptionally talented woman may not be hired for an administrative position because she is a "nice and petite" person who does not measure up to the image of a strong leader.

The Equal Employment Opportunity Commission prohibits discrimination against women for the following reasons: because of their marital status, because they are

---

[30]John and Gail McLure, "The Case of the Vanishing Woman: Implications for the Preparation of Women in Educational Administration," *UCEA Review,* XVI (September 1974), p. 6.

pregnant, because they are not the principal wage earner in a family, or because they have preschool age children.

The preferences of customers and clientele are not bona fide occupational qualifications. Thus, the preference of parents and even students for male principals and administrators in a given school district does not permit the district to discriminate against females seeking administrative positions.

Maternity as a Particular Form of Discrimination

On October 31, 1978, President Carter signed into law a pregnancy disability amendment (PL 95–555) to Title VII of the Civil Rights Act of 1964. The law had the effect of eliminating unequal treatment for pregnant women in all employment-related situations. The EEOC issued guidelines for implementing this law, indicating that it is discriminatory for an employer to refuse to hire, train, assign, or promote a woman solely because she is pregnant; to require maternity leave for a predetermined time period; to dismiss a woman because she is pregnant; to deny reemployment to a woman who has been on maternity leave; to deny seniority credit to a woman who has been on maternity leave; and to deny disability or medical benefits to a woman for disability or illness unrelated to but occurring during pregnancy, childbirth, or recovery from childbirth.

Recruitment and Selection

To insure that discrimination against women does not occur in employment, as a first step, the school district's leadership should review recruitment and selection procedures. The following specific actions will minimize the potential for discriminating:

1. Use women as recruiters and interviewers.
2. Develop a list of women for potential promotion from within the school district.
3. Encourage female employees to apply for available administrative positions.
4. When recruiting outside the school district, contact for referrals such organizations as the American Association of University Women (AAUW), the National Council of Administrative Women in Education (NCAWE), the National Organization for Women (NOW), and minority employment agencies.
5. Include female representatives on selection committees.
6. Remove such title designations as Mr., Mrs., Miss, and Ms. from application forms.
7. When interviewing female applicants, ask only questions that are related to the abilities needed for job performance.
8. Review and evaluate the entire selection process to assure that job descriptions, selection criteria, and data-gathering instruments (such as paper-pencil tests and job applications) are job-related and do not screen out women.

Promotion and Training

Positive steps also must be taken to overcome patterns of inequality that have become traditional in some school districts. Among the most effective procedures are the following:

1. Publicize all promotional opportunities.
2. Seek out capable women and assign them administrative tasks when possible, giving them the experience to move into administrative positions.

(3.) Examine procedures for promotion to eliminate all facets except those that present a fair assessment of the employee's ability and record.

(4.) Recommend women for administrative internship and in-service programs.

⭐ *Sexual Harassment*[31]

In 1980 the Equal Employment Opportunity Commission declared sexual harassment to be a violation of Title VII of the Civil Rights Act of 1964. Basically there are two types of sexual harassment, *quid pro quo* discrimination and hostile environment discrimination. The first type is obvious. *Quid pro quo* discrimination occurs when an employment or personnel decision is based upon an applicant's or employee's submission to or rejection of unwelcome sexual conduct. Thus, a *quid pro quo* personnel decision occurs when employment opportunities or fringe benefits are granted because of an employee's submission to the employer's or supervisor's sexual advances.

Hostile environment discrimination occurs when unwelcome sexual conduct interferes with the employee's job performance. The standard for deciding environmental discrimination is if the sexual conduct substantially affected the job performance of a reasonable person. Factors to consider in investigating hostile environment discrimination are: was the conduct physical, verbal, or both; the frequency of the conduct; the position of the harasser, co-worker or supervisors; if other employees were involved in the conduct; if there was more than one person against whom the conduct was directed; and was the conduct hostile or patently hostile.

It is also important to investigate if the sexual conduct was unwelcome. Did the person alleging sexual harassment indicate by his or her conduct that the sexual advances were unwelcome? In making this determination, the timing of the protest and whether a prior consensual relationship existed with the alleged harasser are significant factors.

School districts are liable for the actions of their administrators and supervisors when these individuals act as the "agent" for the school district at the time of the harassment. For *quid pro quo* discrimination, the administrator or supervisor is always acting as the agent of the school district. For hostile environment discrimination, the school district is liable if the district knew or should have known of the sexual harassment of the supervisor.

For co-workers who sexually harass their colleagues, the school district is liable if the agents, administrators and supervisors, knew or should have known about the harassment. When sexual conduct becomes known, the appropriate administrator or supervisor must act to remedy the situation.

It is also the responsibility of the administrators and supervisors to take appropriate action to protect employees in the workplace against sexual harassment by non-employees. This responsibility is present when school district agents knew or should have known about the harassment.

In order for a school district to demonstrate to employees and the general public that sexual harassment will not be tolerated, the board of education should adopt a policy prohibiting such conduct and administrative procedures should be developed to effectively

---

[31]Equal Employment Opportunity Commission, *Guidelines on Sexual Harassment in the Workplace.* (Washington, D.C.: U.S. Government Printing Office, 1991).

deal with allegations. Further, all employees should be required to participate in a staff development program about the issue of sexual harassment.

The board of education policy should set forth the commitment of the school district to deal with sexual harassment in an expeditious and effective manner. Administrative procedures to implement the policy should set forth the complaint process and should include the filling out of a complaint form which must be signed by the complainant. The appropriate personnel administrator should inform all the parties of their rights. Both the complaint and the investigation should be kept confidential. The procedures also should contain a timeline for completion of the investigation. The policy and procedures must be communicated to all staff members.

A staff development program about sexual harassment for all employees should contain the following components: an explanation of the board policy and administrative procedures; specific examples of sexual harassment; myths about sexual harassment; the distinction between welcome, consensual, and illegal sexual harassment. Administrator and supervisor staff development should include the above but also should stress the importance of protecting the complainant against retaliation. Exhibit 2–6 is a sample board of education policy on sexual harassment.

Policy of Nondiscrimination on the Basis of Sex

Good intentions by school administrators to remedy past practices of discrimination against women and to prevent future practices are not sufficient. The only defensible course of action is for the superintendent of schools to recommend a policy for adoption by the board of education. This would complement the school district's affirmative action policy and would provide the assurance required by law. The American Association of School Administrators has published a sample policy which is intended to be a guide for local boards of education in their policy formulation efforts. While the entire sample policy includes sections dealing with educational programs, facilities, and services, the part reprinted here deals only with employment activities (see Exhibit 2–7).

The Equal Pay Act

The U.S. Congress enacted in 1963 the Equal Pay Act, which requires employers to pay males and females the same salary or wage for equal work. This act is part of the Fair Labor Standards Act and protects employees who work for an employer engaged in an enterprise affected by interstate commerce. The interpretation of interstate commerce was broadly defined by the court in *Usery* v. *Columbia University,* 568 F. 2d 953 (2d cir. 1977). In addition, the interpretation of equal work has been broadly defined to mean *substantially* equal and thus, strict equality of jobs is not required. Thus, this Act requires equal pay for jobs that demand equal skill, effort, and responsibility, and that are carried out under similar working conditions. However, if salaries or wages are contingent upon a seniority system, a merit system, a system that measures pay by production quantity or quality, or factors other than sex, this Act does not apply.

An example of a court case involving the Equal Pay Act is *EEOC* v. *Madison Community Unit School District Number 12,* 818 F. 2d 577 (7th Cir. 1987). In this case, a female who coached girls' track and tennis was paid substantially less than the males who

---

EXHIBIT 2–6   Sample Sexual Harassment Policy

The board of education is committed to providing a work environment free from sexual harassment by administrators, supervisors, co-workers, and non-employees.

It is a violation of this policy for the above-named categories of employees and non-employees to engage in sexual harassment by making unwelcome sexual advances, unwelcome requests for sexual favors, and by other unwelcome verbal or physical conduct of a sexual nature.

It is a violation of this policy for an administrator or supervisor to make a decision affecting the employment of an individual on the basis of that person's submission to or rejection of sexual conduct. If an administrator or supervisor offers an opportunity or fringe benefit to an employee on the basis of that person's submission to or rejection of sexual conduct, it also is a violation of this policy.

Conduct of a sexual nature that unreasonably interferes with a person's job performance will be considered sexual harassment.

It is the duty of each administrator and supervisor to monitor his or her area of responsibility for the purpose of maintaining an environment free from sexual harassment. Further, it is the duty of each administrator and supervisor to protect an employee who files a complaint of sexual harassment from retaliation.

An employee or former applicant for employment who believes that he or she has been a victim of sexual harassment should file a complaint with the director of affirmative action as soon as possible after the incident. If the director of affirmative action is the alleged harasser, the complaint should be filed with the superintendent of schools. If the superintendent is the alleged harasser, the board of education should receive the complaint.

When the complaint is received, the director of affirmative action should initiate an investigation as soon as possible. If the complainant requests an investigator of the same gender and if the director of affirmative action is not of the same gender, another person of the same gender as the complainant will be appointed by the director to conduct the investigation. After the investigation, a report of the findings will be presented to the complainant, the alleged harasser, and the superintendent of schools. Both the investigation and the report are to be considered confidential. An employee who is found to be in violation of this policy will be subject to disciplinary action up to and including termination of employment with the school district.

It is the responsibility of the superintendent of schools to cause the development of administrative procedures to implement this policy; to cause the initiation of a staff development program concerning sexual harassment in the workplace, this policy, and administrative procedures. This program must be offered to every employee.

---

coached the boys' track and tennis at the same school. In addition, a female assistant coach of the girls' basketball team was paid less than a male assistant coach of the boys' track team; still another female coach was paid less for coaching girls' basketball, softball, and volleyball than a male coaching boys' basketball, baseball, and soccer. Finally, an assistant coach of the girls' track team was paid less than the assistant coach of the boys' track team.

The Equal Employment Opportunity Commission filed a lawsuit against the school district, stating that the inequities violated the Equal Pay Act. The U.S. district court ruled in favor of the EEOC but the school district appealed to the U.S. Court of Appeals, Seventh Circuit. This Court affirmed the district court's decision in the following situations: boys' and girls' track, boys' and girls' tennis, boys' baseball and girls' softball. However,

EXHIBIT 2–7   District Employment Activities

This policy applies to all aspects of the district's employment programs, including but not limited to, recruitment, advertising, the process of application for employment, promotion, granting of tenure, termination, layoffs, wages, job assignments, leaves of absence of all types, fringe benefits, training programs, employer-sponsored programs, social or recreational programs, and any other term, condition, or privilege of employment. Specifically, the following personnel employment practices are prohibited:

a. *Tests*. Administration of any test or other criteria that has a disproportionately adverse effect on persons on the basis of sex unless it is a valid predictor of job success and alternative tests or criteria are unavailable.

b. *Recruitment*. Recruitment of employees from entities that furnish as applicants only or predominantly members of one sex, if such action has the effect of discriminating on the basis of sex.

c. *Compensation*. Establishment of rates of pay on the basis of sex.

d. *Job Classification*. Classification of jobs as being for males or females.

e. *Fringe Benefits*. Provision of fringe benefits on the basis of sex; all fringe benefit plans must treat males and females equally.

f. *Marital and Parental Status*. Any action based on marital or parental status; pregnancies are considered temporary disabilities for all job-related purposes and shall be accorded the same treatment by the district as are all other temporary disabilities. No inquiry shall be made by the district in job applications as to the marriage status of an applicant, including whether such applicant is "Miss or Mrs." But, inquiry may be made as to the sex of a job applicant for employment if it is made of all applicants and is not a basis for discrimination.

g. *Employment Advertising*. Any expression of preference, limitation, or specification based on sex, unless sex is a bona fide occupational qualification for the particular job in question.

Policy enforcement   To ensure compliance with this policy, the superintendent shall

1. Designate a member of the administrative staff
   a. to coordinate efforts of the district to comply with this policy;
   b. to develop and ensure the maintenance of a filing system to keep all records required under this policy;
   c. to investigate all complaints of this policy;
   d. to administer the grievance procedure established in this policy; and
   e. to develop affirmative action programs, as appropriate.
2. Provide for the publication of this policy on an ongoing basis to students, parents, employees, prospective employees, and district employee unions or organizations, such publication to include the name, office address, and telephone number of the compliance administrator designated pursuant to this policy.

Grievance procedure   Any employee of this district who believes he or she has been discriminated against, denied a benefit, or excluded from participation in any district activity, on the basis of sex in violation of this policy, may file a written complaint with the compliance administrator designated by this policy. The compliance administrator shall cause the review of the written complaint to be conducted and the written response mailed to the complainant within ten working days after receipt of the written complaint. A copy of the written complaint and the compliance administrator's response shall be provided each member of the Board of Education. If the complainant is not satisfied with such response, he or she may submit a written appeal to the Board of Education, indicating with particularity the nature of disagreement with the response and his or her reasons underlying such disagreement.

Continued

EXHIBIT 2–7   *Continued*

The Board of Education shall consider the appeal at its next regularly scheduled Board meeting following receipt of the appeal.

The Board of Education shall permit the complainant to address the Board in public or closed session, as appropriate and lawful, concerning his or her complaint and shall provide the complainant with its written decision in the matter as expeditiously as possible following completion of the meeting.

Evaluation   The Superintendent shall present a report to the Board of Education in a public meeting on or about July 21, 1976, and in a public meeting to be held on or about the anniversary of that date each year thereafter, describing the district's compliance with this policy during the previous year, which report can be the basis of an evaluation of the effectiveness of this policy by the Board of Education and a determination as to whether or not additional affirmative action is necessary in light of all the facts.

Source: Sample Policy for the Sex Equality in Education (Arlington, Va.: American Association of School Administartors, 1977), modified for this chapter.

the Court of Appeals reversed the district court's decision in comparing boys' soccer to girls' volleyball, boys' soccer to girls' basketball, and boys' track to girls' basketball. The Court stated that these situations did not require equal skill, effort, and responsibility.[32]

There is another aspect to the equal pay issue. When a school district has a performance-based evaluation system that is used to determine the salaries and wages of employees, the Equal Pay Act does not apply. However, in all organizations employees tend to compare their salaries and wages with those of coworkers, and compare how productive these coworkers are in comparison with themselves. The effects of this situation for school administration can be serious. It is a situation that will only fester if it is ignored. The best approach is to reemphasize the relationship between performance and reward; it is also important to reiterate that the performance-based evaluation process is the vehicle for determining the level of performance and the amount of reward.

Obviously, if a school district does not have an effective evaluation process, a merit-based reward program cannot be initiated. Performance and reward are two aspects of the same process—They go hand-in-hand![33]

Equality by Age

The Age Discrimination in Employment Act of 1967, as amended, is taking on ever-increasing importance for personnel administrators. This act was passed by Congress to promote the employment of the older worker based on ability rather than age by prohibiting arbitrary discrimination. Also, under this act the Department of Labor has consistently sponsored informational and educational programs on the needs and abilities of the older

---

[32]Data Research, Inc., *Deskbook Encyclopedia of American School Law* (Rosemount, Minnesota: Data Research, 1989), pp. 216–218.

[33]"Incentive Pay Plans Full of Problems . . . ," *Education USA,* 28, no. 32 (April 7, 1986), p. 248.

worker. The "Statement of Findings and Purpose" in the Age Discrimination in Employment Act sets forth a rationale for its passage that is a true reflection of current societal trends towards older workers:

Sec. 2.(a) The Congress hereby finds and declares that

(1) in the face of rising productivity and affluence, older workers find themselves disadvantaged in their efforts to retain employment, and especially to regain employment when displaced from jobs;

(2) the setting of arbitrary age limits regardless of potential for job performance has become a common practice, and certain otherwise desirable practices may work to the disadvantage of older persons;

(3) the incidence of unemployment, especially long-term unemployment with resultant deterioration of skill, morale, and employer acceptability is, relative to the younger ages, high among older workers; their numbers are great and growing; and their employment problems grave;

(4) the existence in industries affecting commerce of arbitrary discrimination in employment burdens commerce and the free flow of goods in commerce.

⤬ Provisions of the Age Discrimination in Employment Act

The law protects individuals who are at least forty years of age but less than seventy. It applies to private employers of twenty or more persons, and to federal, state, and local governmental units regardless of the number of persons employed. The law also applies to employment agencies and labor organizations having twenty-five or more members in an industry affecting interstate commerce. The law does not apply to elected officials or their appointees.

It is against the law for an employer to refuse to hire or otherwise discriminate against any person as to compensation, terms, conditions, or privileges of employment because of age; to limit, segregate, or classify employees so as to deprive any individual of employment opportunities or adversely affect that individual's status as an employee because of age. It is against the law for an employment agency to refuse to refer for employment or otherwise discriminate against an individual because of age, or to classify and refer anyone for employment on the basis of age. It is against the law for a labor union to discriminate against anyone because of age by excluding or expelling that person from membership; to limit, segregate, or classify its members on the basis of age; to refuse to refer anyone for employment so as to result in a deprivation or limitation of employment opportunity or otherwise adversely affect an individual's status as an employee because of age; or to cause or attempt to cause an employer to discriminate against an individual because of age.

Furthermore, the provisions of the Age Discrimination in Employment Act prohibit an employer, employment agency, or labor union from discriminating against a person for opposing a practice that is unlawful because of this act, discriminating against a person making a charge, assisting or participating in any investigation, proceeding, or litigation under this act; publishing a notice of an employment vacancy that indicates a preference, limitation, or specification based on age.

⭑ *Exceptions to the Age Discrimination in Employment Act*

The prohibitions of this act do not apply if age is a bona fide occupational qualification reasonably necessary to the normal performance of a given task. Therefore, test pilot positions might be filled with individuals no older than forty-five, because accurate and quick reflexes are necessary to the safe flying of experimental aircraft. However, it would be difficult to justify age as a bona fide occupational qualification in education institutions.

The prohibitions of the Age Discrimination in Employment Act do not apply when an individual is discharged or disciplined for good cause, and when the terms of a new or existing employee seniority or benefits program differentiates by reason of age. However, no employee benefits plan can be used as an excuse for failing to hire an individual because of age.

⭒ *Enforcement of the Age Discrimination in Employment Act*

The administration of this act passed from the Department of Labor to the Equal Employment Opportunity Commission on July 1, 1979. At that time the average number of complaints had reached five thousand annually. The EEOC can conduct investigations, issue rules and regulations to administer the law, and enforce the provisions of the law through the courts when voluntary compliance cannot be obtained.

Conclusion

This section has dealt with four major federal influences on the human resource planning process. Although affirmative action and the legislation on equality for the handicapped, women, and individuals by age represent central trends in personnel administration, these are by no means the only federal considerations that affect personnel processes.

The following laws enacted by Congress in the nineteenth and twentieth centuries constitute a significant part of the national public employment policy that directly and indirectly affects the employment policies of public and private educational institutions. They should be studied by all personnel administrators.

1883	Pendleton Act (Civil Service Commission)
1931	Davis-Bacon Act
1932	Anti-Injunction Act
1935	National Labor Relations Act
1935	Social Security Act
1936	Walsh-Healey Public Contracts Act
1938	Fair Labor Standards Act
1947	Labor-Management Relations Act
1959	Labor-Management Reporting and Disclosure Act
1962	Work House Act
1967	Reemployment of Veterans Act
1968	Garnishment Provisions, Consumer Credit Protection Act
1974	Employee Retirement Income Security Act
1986	Immigration Reform and Control Act
1990	Immigration Act

In addition, it must be kept in mind that various states and cities have enacted statutes and ordinances that also exert significant influence on personnel administration.

Finally, Chapter 2 includes three appendices: (A) Steps in Developing an Affirmative Action Program; (B) Summary Facts Concerning Job Discrimination; and (C) Steps in Filing a Charge of Job Discrimination. These provide summary data that further clarify how federal legislation impinges on personnel management.

SUMMARY

Planning is a process common to all human experience. It encompasses an understanding of the present condition, future objectives, and methods for reaching these objectives.

Human resource planning as a process in personnel management is undertaken to ensure that a school district has the right number of people, with the right skills, in the right place, and at the right time.

The first step in the human resource planning process is to assess human resource needs, which includes the following four aspects: developing human resource inventories, developing a five-year enrollment projection, developing school district objectives, and developing a human resource forecast.

One of the most pressing problems facing metropolitan areas, one with a particular significance in human resource planning, is declining pupil enrollments. Two of the most successful alternatives to reduction in a work force have been early retirement incentive programs and the retraining of individuals for positions that will become vacant through attrition or will be created through program development.

A hallmark of our contemporary American society is the avalanche of federal legislation and court decisions, which in turn have had a definite influence on the human resource planning process. Incorporated or implied in all civil rights legislation is the important concept of affirmative action. Affirmative action is not a law within itself but rather an objective reached by following a set of guidelines that ensure compliance with legislation and executive orders.

The Equal Employment Opportunity Commission was established by Title VII of the Civil Rights Act to investigate alleged discrimination in employment practices based on race, color, religion, sex, or national origin. This five-member commission has also established, from time to time, affirmative action guidelines.

Alleged discrimination charges can be filed with any of EEOC's district offices. The administrative process includes an individual's filing of a charge, investigation of the charge, determination of the charge, and the process of conciliation.

Limited discrimination is allowed by the Equal Employment Opportunity Act under one condition: when there is a bona fide occupational qualification mandating the employing of an individual of a particular sex, religious affiliation, or national origin. Therefore, a school district personnel administrator has the right to employ a female rather than a male for the position of swimming instructor when the job description includes supervising the locker room used by female students.

The Civil Rights Act of 1991 is landmark legislation because it extends punitive damages and jury trials for the first time to employees who have been discriminated against because of their race, national origin, gender, disability, or religion.

The Rehabilitation Act of 1973 prohibits recipients of federal financial assistance from discriminating against qualified handicapped individuals in recruitment, hiring, compensation, job assignment/classification, and in those fringe benefits provided. Employers are further required to provide reasonable accommodations for qualified handicapped employees. The Vietnam Era Veterans Readjustment Assistance Act of 1974 requires affirmative action to hire disabled veterans of all wars and all veterans of the Vietnam era.

The Americans with Disabilities Act of 1990 is also landmark legislation because it is the most comprehensive legislation ever passed protecting the rights of individuals with disabilities. There are five titles to ADA and all of them except Title IV have some impact upon school districts.

On August 22, 1990 President George Bush ordered the mobilization of U.S. military reserves and national guard units into active duty. This triggered several issues concerning the health care of dependents and the reentry of reservists and members of the national guard into the workplace.

On October 28, 1991 President Bush signed into law the Omnibus Transportation Employee Testing Act which required the Secretary of Transportation to promulgate regulations for alcohol and controlled substances testing for persons in safety-sensitive positions including school bus drivers.

President Clinton signed into law the Family and Medical Leave Act on February 5, 1993. The fundamental purpose of this act is to provide eligible employees with the right to take unpaid leave in connection with certain circumstances.

' Equality in employment opportunity for women is a central issue in personnel management. The legal mandate of equal opportunity for women emanates primarily from two federal laws: Title IX of the Education Amendments of 1972, which prohibits sex discrimination in educational programs or activities, including employment, when the school district is receiving federal financial assistance; and, of course, Title VII of the Civil Rights Act of 1964, as amended in 1972. In addition, President Carter in 1978 signed into law a pregnancy disability amendment to the Civil Rights Act. This law had the effect of eliminating unequal treatment of pregnant women in all employment-related situations.

Since 1980 the Equal Employment Opportunity Commission has considered sexual harassment to be a violation of Title VII of the Civil Rights Act of 1964. The issue of sexual harassment in the workplace has gained national attention and will continue to be a concern in school districts across the nation.

The Equal Pay Act of 1963 requires employers to pay males and females the same salary or wage for equal work.

The Age Discrimination in Employment Act of 1967, as amended, promotes the employment of the older worker by prohibiting arbitrary discrimination based on age.

Because of their importance, only major federal influences in the human resource planning process have been presented in this chapter in detail. However, personnel administrators must also become familiar with all legislation that protects employment opportunity rights.

APPENDIX A*
STEPS IN DEVELOPING AN AFFIRMATIVE ACTION PROGRAM

- Establish a strong company policy and commitment.
- Assign responsibility and authority for the program to a top company official.
- Analyze present work force to identify jobs, departments, and units where minorities and females are underutilized.
- Set specific, measurable, attainable hiring and promotion goals, with target dates, in each area of underutilization.
- Make every manager and supervisor responsible and accountable for helping to meet these goals.
- Reevaluate job descriptions and hiring criteria to assure that they reflect actual job needs.
- Find minorities and females who qualify or who can become qualified to fulfill goals.
- Review and revise all employment procedures to assure that they do not have a discriminatory effect and that they help attain the goals.
- Focus on getting minorities and females into upward mobility and relevant training pipelines especially where they have not had previous access.
- Develop systems to monitor and measure progress on a continued basis. If results are not satisfactory in meeting goals, find out why, and make necessary changes.

APPENDIX B
SUMMARY FACTS CONCERNING JOB DISCRIMINATION

Title VII of the 1964 Civil Rights Act, as amended, provides that an individual cannot be denied a job or fair treatment on a job because of

- Race
- Color
- Religion
- Sex
- National Origin

The act established the Equal Employment Opportunity Commission (EEOC) to insure that these rights are protected.

If an individual believes that he or she has been discriminated against in the workplace by any of the groups below, he or she may file a charge of discrimination with the EEOC.

- Private employer of fifteen or more persons
- State and local government

Source: U.S. Equal Employment Opportunity Commission, *Affirmative Action and Equal Employment* (Washington, D.C.: U.S. Government Printing Office, 1974), p. 3.

- Public and private educational institutions
- Public and private employment agencies
- Labor unions with fifteen or more members
- Joint labor-management committees for apprenticeship and training programs

Also a charge may be filed by another person or by a group if the person alleging the discrimination gives his or her permission to these other parties.

The EEOC does not cover discrimination because of

- Citizenship
- Political affiliation
- Sexual life style

It also does not cover job discrimination by federal government agencies, government-owned corporations, Indian tribes, or by small private employers with fewer than fifteen workers.

If a person wishes to file a charge of job discrimination, he or she must do so promptly—within 180 days from the time the discrimination took place.

An employer is prohibited by law from harassing or bothering an individual in any unfair manner because he or she filed a charge, assisted in an investigation, or opposed unlawful employment practices.

APPENDIX C
STEPS IN FILING A CHARGE OF JOB DISCRIMINATION

To file a charge of job discrimination, an individual must

- Visit the nearest EEOC District Office or mail in a "Charge of Discrimination" form. If a form cannot be obtained, a written statement may be sent identifying all parties and clearly describing what act(s) of discrimination took place.
- Be interviewed by an intake officer of the commission at the district office or be interviewed by telephone if an in-person interview is impossible.
- Provide information, including records and names of witnesses to the discrimination.
- Swear or affirm, under oath, to the charge of discrimination, or make a declaration under penalty of perjury.

As the charging party, an individual must

- Cooperate with the commission.
- Attend fact-finding conferences and other meetings when scheduled.
- Inform the commission of changes in his or her address, telephone number, and other such information.
- Contact the commission if he or she wishes to withdraw the charge.

After a charge is filed

- The employer, union, employment agency, or labor-management committee named in the charge will be notified.
- In many states, the charge may be referred for remedy to a state or local fair employment practices agency for 60 days (120 days if the agency is new).
- The commission may require the person making the charge to attend a fact-finding conference in order to establish facts, define issues, and determine a basis for negotiating a settlement.
- If settlement efforts are unsuccessful, the commission may investigate to determine the merits of the charge.
- After the investigation, the commission will issue a letter of determination on the merits of the charge.

SELECTED BIBLIOGRAPHY

"Affirmative Viewpoints," *Education USA,* 28, no. 11 (November 1985), p. 81.

Americans with Disabilities Act. (1990), P. L. 101–336, 42 U.S.C., 12101 et seq.

Arnold, Jean B., "Family Leave: It's the Law," *The American School Board Journal,* 180, no. 10 (October 1993), pp. 31–34.

Breck, William, "Suit Yourself with Strategic Planning," *The School Administrator,* 8, no. 46 (September 1989), pp. 14–16.

Clay, Katherine, Sara Lake, and Karen Tremain, *How to Build a Strategic Plan: A Step-by-Step Guide for School Managers.* San Carlos, Calif.: Ventures for Public Awareness, 1989.

Cohan, Audrey, Mary Ann Hergenrother, Yolanda M. Johnson, Laurie S. Mandel, and Janice Sawyer. *Sexual Harassment and Sexual Abuse: A Handbook for Teachers and Administrators.* Thousand Oaks, California: Corwin Press, Inc., 1996.

Collier, Beverly H., "Halting Sexual Harassment," *The Executive Educator,* 11, no. 11 (November 1989), pp. 28–33.

Equal Employment Opportunities Commission and the U.S. Department of Justice. (1991). *Americans with Disabilities Act Handbook.* (EEOC Publication No. BK-19). Washington, D.C.: U.S. Government Printing Office.

Gittins, Naomi E., and Jim Walsh, *Sexual Harassment in the Schools: Preventing and Defending Against Claims.* Alexandria, Virginia: National School Boards Association, 1991.

Gupton, Sandra Lee, and Gloria Appelt Slick. *Highly Successful Women Administrators: The Inside Stories of How They Got There.* Thousand Oaks, California: Corwin Press Inc., 1996.

Hayes, James L., "Affirmative Action in the 1980's: What Can We Expect?" *Management Review,* 70 (May 1981), 4–7.

"Job Discrimination," *Federal Regulations of Employment Service,* Supplement to Binder 1, September 1978, p. 12. Rochester, N.Y.: Lawyers Co-Operative Publishing Co., 1978.

Lavelle, Marianne, "Defiance Can Backfire in Sexual Harassment Cases," *The National Law Journal* (17 June 1996), pp. B1, B2.

Lewis, John F., Susan C. Hastings, and Anne C. Morgan, *Sexual Harassment in Education.* Topeka, Kansas: National Organization on Legal Problems in Education, 1993.

McDowell, Douglas S., Jeffrey A. Norris, and Lorence L. Kessler (Eds.), *Basic EEO Resource Manual: Practical Guidance for EEO Professionals and Attorneys.* Washington, D.C.: National Foundation for the Study of Employment Policy, 1988.

Mauro, Tony, "How the EEOC is Reaching Out to Employers," *Nation's Business* (August 1984), pp. 25–26.

Miron, Louis F. *Resisting Discrimination: Affirmative Strategies for Principals and Teachers.* Thousand Oaks, California: Corwin Press, Inc., 1996.

Polansky, Harvey B., "Early Retirement Incentive Plans," *School Business Affairs,* 56, no. 12 (December 1990), pp. 26–30.

Stephens, Charles E. (Ed.), *Enrollment Projections.* Bloomington, Ind.: Phi Delta Kappa, 1989.

Templer, Andrew J., and James M. Tolliver, "Affirmative Action—Making it Effective in the Public Sector," *Public Personnel Management Journal,* 12 (Summer 1983), pp. 175–181.

U.S. Congress, Senate Committee on Labor and Public Welfare, *The Equal Employment Opportunity Act of 1972,* p. 3. Committee Report, 92nd Congress, 2nd session, March 1972. Washington, D.C.: U.S. Government Printing Office, 1972.

U.S. Equal Employment Opportunity Commission, *Affirmative Action and Equal Employment,* Vols. I & II. Washington, D.C.: U.S. Government Printing Office, 1974.

Walters, Ronald, "The Politics of Affirmative Action," *The Western Journal of Black Studies,* 6 (Fall 1982), pp. 175–181.

Weast, Jerry D., "Strategic Planning Based on Comprehensive Data," *Spectrum: Journal of School Research and Information,* 7, no. 3 (Summer 1989), pp. 3–7.

Wirtz, Thomas J. and Anne Kiefer, "Community-Based Strategic Planning," *Spectrum: Journal of School Research and Information,* 6, no. 3 (Summer 1988), pp. 3–9.

Wright, Jim. "Ready to Meet New Drug Test Requirements?" *School and College* (March 1994), pp. 13–19.

Zakariya, Sally Banks, "What To Do If Someone On Your Staff Has AIDS," *The Executive Educator,* 9, no. 4 (April 1987), pp. 19–21.

3

RECRUITMENT

After the human resource planning process identifies current and future staffing needs, the next step is to recruit personnel. In the 1970s many school districts experienced a rather dramatic decrease in pupil enrollment. This phenomenon forced districts to lay off large numbers of teachers, which affected the number of college students entering schools of education. Young people interested in teaching anticipated a rather dismal job market upon completion of their education and thus changed their career goals. This situation was compounded by the large number of teachers who retired in the 1980s and by the many teacher defections to the business community.

Now, school districts across the country are suffering the effects of the past decade. There is a shortage of teachers, particularly in large metropolitan school districts. In fact, the National Center for Educational Statistics has predicted a significant shortage of teachers reaching far into the 1990s.

There is a particular concern in urban school districts where African American and Hispanic student populations continue to grow yearly. Demographers predict that this trend will gain momentum and will last well into the next century. Hispanic student growth will eventually overtake the growth in African American students. There is no corresponding increase in the percent of African American and Hispanic teachers and administrators.[1]

Obviously this situation places an immediate and long term responsibility on personnel administrators to develop strategies for recruiting minority employees.[2]

Therefore, the recruitment process has never been more important to school districts as they search for the best people available to help achieve the mission of each district, educating children and young people. This is the major thrust of every recruitment program—not to hire just to fill a position, but rather to acquire the number and type of people necessary for the present and future success of the school district. Affirmative action

---

[1]Sarah Lubman, "Efforts to Hire Minority Educators Aim to Narrow Student-Teacher Ethnic Gap," *Wall Street Journal,* 7 September 1993, sec. B, pp. B1, B9.

[2]Donald J. Fielder, "Wanted, Minority Teachers," *The Executive Educator,* 15, no. 5 (May 1993), pp. 33–34.

requirements, future staffing needs, and dual certification are issues that impinge on recruitment programs. It is a mistake to assume that the correct mix of people will be available to fill vacancies without making a concerted effort to find the most qualified individuals to fill specific human resource needs.

Recruitment as a process also entails discovering potential applicants for anticipated vacancies. This perspective on the recruitment process depends to a great extent on the size of the school district. An urban or metropolitan school district will engage, of course, in recruiting potential applicants more often than smaller suburban districts. Many other variables influence the extent of recruiting activities. First, the employment conditions in a community where the school district is located will affect recruitment. For example, the existence of a university with a school of education located near the district will probably ensure sufficient applicants for entry-level teaching positions. In like manner, the labor pool in a metropolitan area will have many skilled carpenters, electricians, and plumbers.

A second set of variables affecting recruitment include working conditions, salary levels, and fringe benefits provided by a school district. These affect employee turnover and, therefore, the need to engage in recruitment activities. Districts experiencing a rapid increase in pupil population, and hence a need for increased staff, will look upon recruitment as a major personnel priority.

Finally, even school districts experiencing decreasing enrollment and reduction in the work force may need to engage in recruitment activities from time to time, because certain vacancies will require special skills that current employees lack. Industrial arts is a case in point. A school district may find that teachers who are already employed and scheduled to be placed on involuntary leave cannot be transferred to fill a vacancy in industrial arts because they lack the required certification.

Recruitment, therefore, should be common to all school districts. Private business and industry has for many years capitalized on this process to fill vacancies with exceptional individuals. The idea of "stealing" proven employees from another company has become an acceptable practice, considered perfectly legitimate if no coercion or illegal pressures are brought to bear on a potential employee. Private industry recognizes that talent and skills are scarce commodities. School districts, too, are ethically bound to find the most talented and skilled people available to achieve their mandate of educating children. In practice, this requires them to develop employment conditions, salary levels, and benefits that will attract the best applicants while remaining within the fiscal constraints of the school district.

The private sector's practice of overtly contacting and recruiting individuals who meet a given set of job requirements and encouraging them to become applicants should be emulated by school districts. It is recruitment in its purest form.

CONSTRAINTS ON RECRUITMENT

Affirmative Action

Many school districts make a practice of promoting already hired employees into supervisory or administrative positions. A school bus driver could advance to dispatcher and on from there to route supervisor and eventually become director of transportation. A classroom teacher may become a department chairperson and, if certificated as an administrator, an assistant principal with eventual promotion into the principalship. This is, of course, a legitimate practice with many advantages for building morale within the school district.

Employees who recognize that the district provides them with an opportunity to advance their careers through promotion to positions of greater responsibility are more likely to make a long-term commitment to the school district. In like manner, employees should also be made aware of the link between job performance and promotion. This places a responsibility on the administration to develop procedures that ensure promotion opportunities for those who have demonstrated on the job that they are capable of handling higher-level tasks. The appraisal process is the vehicle for documenting the quality of such performance.

Chapter 2 presented in detail the affirmative action and equal employment opportunity requirements mandated by various civil rights legislation. This legislation basically prohibits discrimination in recruitment because of race, age, handicap, military service, color, religion, sex, pregnancy, and national origin. The concept of equality in opportunity, however, must eventuate in a set of recruitment procedures.

Internal promotion as a practice does not nullify affirmative action requirements. The only exceptions to such requirements are those situations in which sex, not being handicapped, etc., constitute bona fide occupational qualifications. Thus, a school district may discriminate against a teacher's aid who has an orthopedic handicap by promoting another aid to a gymnastics teaching position when the ability to demonstrate routines is part of the job description.

Except for bona fide occupational qualifications, a district must establish promotion procedures that clearly do not discriminate against minorities and protected groups of employees. A district can demonstrate equal opportunity by advertising promotional opportunities, establishing promotion criteria, and offering equal access to career advancement training programs. No position should be filled without giving all qualified employees an opportunity to apply. This may be accomplished by publishing promotion opportunities on bulletin boards or in a district publication such as a newsletter. Whatever the method, it must be clear that all qualified employees have been informed of the opening and have been given an opportunity to apply.

Promotion criteria should include the level of current job performance, qualifications and skills, and job knowledge. Affirmative action does not require the promoting of unqualified employees; it does require that all qualified individuals be given an equal opportunity. Finally, minority employees should be encouraged to participate in educational and training programs that will enhance their knowledge and skills, thus providing them with the qualifications necessary to apply for promotions.

The size of a school district usually determines not only the extent of internal recruitment for promotion but also the extent of external recruitment. In a small school district it may happen that no one currently employed is qualified for an administrative or supervisory opening. Thus, external recruitment is the only available avenue for filling the vacancy.

Affirmative action and equal employment opportunity must be a major consideration in developing and implementing recruitment practices and procedures. The days should be gone when a person can be hired simply because he or she is someone's friend or relative. Physical appearance and the interviewer's "hunch" are also no longer acceptable criteria for hiring or promoting an individual.

The Reputation and Policies of the School District

A second possible constraint on recruiting candidates for a position emanates from the school district itself. Prospective candidates may not be interested in pursuing a job opportunity in a particular school district because of that district's image in the community. For example, a district that offers an inferior curriculum, that is understaffed, or that lacks support services will find it difficult to attract the best people in education.

The policies of the board of education and the administrative processes and procedures of the district are also important considerations to most candidates. These are the criteria by which the quality of the work environment may be measured. If, for example, a school district lacks a well-defined and effective appraisal process, the prospective candidate will have little confidence in the district's ability to evaluate adequately his or her future performance, which in turn may affect his or her salary increases.

The Position to Be Filled

A third constraint in recruiting for a position centers around the attractiveness of the job itself. A position that is viewed as anxiety-laden or that lacks promotion potential may not interest the best people.

The most common situation that falls within this category is the succession problem. Following either a very successful person or a person who was a failure will be difficult. If the person who previously held the position was exceptionally capable, a successor may find the expectations of the school board, parents, students, and even colleagues to be beyond anyone's capabilities. Following someone who failed in a position will probably be easier. However, the responsibilities of the job may have been neglected to the point where chaos and disorganization reign. A person brought in to restore order may make other employees anxious if they have become accustomed to a lack of supervision.

Salary and Fringe Benefits

The best people for a job will become candidates only if the financial rewards are in keeping with the responsibilities of the position. Education is a service enterprise and, as such, the major priority must be attracting highly qualified employees. A significant difference between school districts and private business and industry centers on the manner in which salaries and fringe benefits are ascribed to a particular position. In the private sector, recruiters may negotiate compensation with candidates. This practice helps to attract highly qualified individuals for less desirable positions. In school districts the salary for a position is usually fixed on a salary schedule, and the fringe benefits are universally applied to all employees in a certain category. This makes the recruitment of highly skilled candidates a very difficult task, particularly if the job is undesirable or if the district has a poor image.

The exceptions to this rule are the central-office administrative positions at the superintendent and assistant superintendent levels. In recruiting candidates for such positions, both salary and fringe benefits are usually negotiable.

A THEORY OF OCCUPATIONAL CHOICE

Although the focus of personnel administration is on the theory and practice of this function from an organizational perspective, in recruitment it is important to understand those factors that influence the career choices of prospective candidates. Further, recruitment as a practice is more effective if it is based on a vocational development theory.

Many theories of vocational development have become classics and are widely applied in the practice of vocational guidance. Eli Ginzberg, Donald Super, Anne Roe, and David Tiedeman are only a few of the researchers who have helped to advance the field of vocational guidance. This section will not do justice to the intricacies of these and other theories but will provide an overview that may be used in formulating recruitment strategies.

First, people have different interests, abilities, and personalities that, nevertheless, will qualify each person for many different occupations. In fact, experience verifies that an individual will probably change his or her entire occupational field at least three times during his or her working lifetime. When recruiting people for a particular position, the recruiter should understand how ability, interest, and personality interface in various occupations. For example, the successful high school journalism teacher may be a good candidate for the position of public relations director. Both occupations require the ability to communicate ideas, both require an interest in writing, and both require a person capable of relating to other people on a professional level. There are also links between guidance counseling and personnel administration, between the principalship and central-office administration. The essence of this observation is that the recruitment of candidates for a particular position must not be limited only to individuals who already perform similar tasks.

Second, occupational preferences, competencies, and the self-image of people will change with time and experience, making personal adjustment a continuous process. It is therefore unwise to assume that current employees are probably not interested in changing occupations within the organization. An internal search for potential applicants often reveals that many employees are interested in alternative positions.

Third, both life and work satisfaction depend on how well an individual can utilize his or her abilities and find adequate outlets for his or her interests, personality traits, and values. A high turnover of people in a certain position should clue a personnel administrator to reevaluate the responsibilities of the position to ascertain the accuracy of the job description. This reevaluation should then provide a clearer profile of the type of individual who will be successful in the job. It is obviously important to link the interest, abilities, and personality traits of potential candidates to how such individual characteristics will be challenged in the position. For example, a particular middle school principalship located in an urban ghetto may require a self-motivated individual who feels comfortable in an environment laced with a constant demand to handle students who are chronic behavioral problems, while at the same time supervising a highly unionized teaching staff. Not every applicant will have the personal characteristics necessary to be successful in this situation.

Fourth, the process of occupational choice is influenced by employment variables such as salary, fringe benefits, location, opportunity for advancement, and the nature of the work to be performed.[3] The importance of these variables will differ from one applicant to the next. In recruitment it is important from the very start to present this information to every candidate in an extremely clear format. Sometimes, an individual is so intent on finding an alternative to his or her present employment that he or she initially tends to overlook these variables. However, when an employment offer is made, these factors become very apparent, which may result in a refusal by the candidate after a search that has cost the school district considerable time and money.

Finally, vocational development is essentially a compromise between personal characteristics, such as interests and abilities, and external factors, such as the type of work to be performed. The effectiveness of this compromise is tested out through role playing, whether this be in fantasy, simulation, or in the actual work environment. The emergence of assessment centers gives testimony to this principle. Basically, the assessment center is a product of the business community; it is primarily used to set up career paths for already-hired employees. At such a center, a group of highly trained psychologists assesses the capabilities of an employee, matching his or her potential to the requirements of various positions within the corporation. A career path is then planned that will allow the employee to experience various levels of responsibility in different locations. As he or she demonstrates success at each level, the employee is advanced to a higher level along the path. Thus, an individual who has been hired as an employee in the customer complaint department may be placed, after an assessment, in the sales division, eventually moved on to assistant regional sales manager, then promoted to sales manager, and finally advanced to vice-president for the sales division.

The implication is that job success is the only true measure of how effective the recruitment process has been. This implication is often overlooked, and many school districts never evaluate their recruitment procedures through a follow-up study on the success of those who were hired.

METHODS OF RECRUITMENT

It can be demonstrated from experience that certain recruiting methods produce the best candidates for particular job vacancies. Consequently, before initiating the recruitment process, each job vacancy should be analyzed to ascertain what method will be most effective. For example, an advertisement for a business manager's position appearing in the classified section of *School Business Affairs* will most likely reach individuals with the required qualifications. An advertisement in a local newspaper will probably produce few, if any, qualified candidates. In like manner, a recruiter who visits students at a four-year teacher education college in search of candidates for a high school principal's position requiring a minimum of a master's degree in educational administration is looking in the wrong place.

---

[3]See Stephen P. Robbins, *Personnel: The Management of Human Resources,* 2nd ed. (Englewood Cliffs, N.J.: Prentice-Hall, 1982), pp. 98–99.

✳ *Internal Search*

In the private sector, most corporations find it advantageous to train their own employees for all positions beyond the lowest level. As mentioned, promotion from within has definite advantages, particularly in creating high morale among employees. The second and most obvious benefit to promoting from within is that supervisors have greater knowledge about a person already on the payroll than about an unknown applicant. The selection process discussed in the following chapter helps to minimize the danger of making the wrong choice. However, first-hand information about an employee's performance is the best basis on which that person can be promoted.

Educational organizations have not traditionally promoted from within because of the minimal number of job categories found in most school districts. Classroom teachers, principals, cooks, custodians, bus drivers, and a superintendent of schools continue to constitute the breadth of differentiation in staffing in rural and very small suburban school districts.

School districts located in metropolitan areas offer such a multitude of services that promotion from within is a possibility even for teaching positions. Teacher aids and substitute teachers can be promoted into full-time teaching positions when vacancies occur. Similarly, most large school districts have some classroom teachers who are qualified to become principals. The same situation occurs in support areas such as transportation, food service, and maintenance. Theoretically, a cook can be promoted into a commodities purchasing position and on to director of food services.

There are a few disadvantages to rigidly following a system of promoting from within. First, mediocre personnel in the school district may be promoted while excellent individuals in the community are not considered. Second, affirmative action requirements may dictate searching for personnel outside the organization. Finally, there is the possible danger of inbreeding. New ideas and methods are not only a welcomed change; they are absolutely necessary when the personnel in a school district appear content with the status quo.

The observations and performance evaluations of supervisors and principals are sources of information available to personnel administrators as they analyze a promotion-from-within policy.

It is a standard operating procedure in many school districts to post job vacancies on bulletin boards, in newsletters, or in special publications issued from the personnel office. This allows current employees to apply for positions or to notify friends, relatives, and associates about vacancies. The assumption here is that current employees should not be overlooked, but that a policy limiting all promotions to those presently employed is not the most beneficial approach for a school district.

Large urban school districts like Philadelphia are using an approach unique to school districts but which the business community has been using for some years. Many of these districts are having difficulty recruiting teachers particularly in science and mathematics. Through grants from private foundations such as the DeWitt Wallace-Reader's Digest Fund, these districts are offering to pay a portion of the costs for staff members to acquire a college degree in order to hire them to fill teacher vacancies. Teacher assistants have been targeted as a group of staff members who are more likely to take advantage of this kind of program.

⭐ *Referrals*

Current employees are perhaps the best source of referrals when a vacancy occurs. There are a number of reasons for this observation. The most significant reason is that employees will not usually recommend someone unless they believe that the referred person will do a good job, since their reputations as recommenders are at stake.

A quality control on referrals from current employees is the job performance of the recommender and his or her satisfaction with the school district as a whole. A recommendation from an employee with inferior performance or from an employee who is constantly complaining about the policies and procedures of the district should be carefully reviewed.

The employee recommending a friend may also confuse friendship with potential job success. It is not uncommon for people to want friends in the workplace, both for social and economic reasons. An employee, for example, may want to share a ride to work with a friend who lives in the same neighborhood.

Referrals from teachers and principals, however, often reflect professional rather than social contact. Membership in professional organizations such as the National Association of Secondary School Principals or the National Education Association is one way in which people become acquainted with the competencies of colleagues. Consequently, such referrals may be more credible than referrals based only on social contact.

A school district should establish a policy and procedures that will encourage employees to recommend people for job vacancies. A common practice is for the employee to provide the personnel department with the name or names of potential candidates. The personnel department can then send letters to the referred individuals, stating that they have been recommended to become candidates and inviting them to submit an application for the job.

It should be noted that the invitation is extended to become a "candidate"; a personnel administrator must be very careful not to give the referred person the impression that the job is being offered.

⭐ *Employment Agencies*

Employment agencies fall into two categories; public or state agencies and private agencies. For all practical purposes, teachers and administrators have made limited use of employment agencies in their searching for professional positions. This is not the case for support personnel such as custodians, bus drivers, and cafeteria workers.

A public employment service was established in 1933 as a federal–state partnership. It was created not only to help individuals find suitable employment but also to help employers find qualified workers. All fifty states have a state employment service agency, with branch offices strategically located throughout each state. The U.S. Training and Employment Service supervises these agencies. The agencies provide services to those receiving unemployment benefits; benefits are available only to people who are registered with the state employment agency. Although state employment agencies are happy to list individuals with extensive training and highly developed skills, most people with such qualifications go to private agencies. Consequently, employers have not found it advantageous to list job vacancies requiring significant qualifications with state agencies. This situation may improve, however, because the U.S. Training and Employment Service is in the process of implementing a nationwide job bank with listings from throughout the country. All public employment service agencies can be connected to this job bank. Nevertheless, it is foolish for a school district not to list all vacancies with the appropriate state employment service agency because of the possibility that the right employee may be registered. The financial outlay for such a listing is negligible, requiring nothing more than the cost of postage.

Private employment agencies, of course, charge a fee for their services. This fee may be charged to either the employer or employee, or shared by both. The fee arrangement is usually dictated by the supply-and-demand principle. When applicants are abundant, potential employees are usually required to absorb the fee. When applicants are scarce, the employers pay the fee.

Another major difference between public and private employment agencies is in the scope of services provided. Private agencies not only advertise and screen applicants for a job but also provide a guarantee against unsatisfactory performance for a specified period of time, usually six to twelve months. If a particular employee does not work out, the agency will place him elsewhere and find the company another without a fee.

Some private employment agencies specialize in helping to fill executive positions, a practice commonly referred to as "head-hunting." Through nationwide contacts and through extensive investigation of each potential executive's credentials, these agencies are able to recommend candidates for executive management positions, usually in private business and industry. They charge a rather high fee for this service, usually a percentage of the executive's first-year salary; 30 percent of a salary in excess of $100,000 is not uncommon.

While most school districts do not engage the services of private employment agencies in searching for potential candidates to fill school executive positions, a growing trend in this direction can be seen, particularly in relation to the position of superintendent of schools. This trend is reflected in the consulting services offered by the American School Board Association and such state organizations as the Illinois Association of School Boards. These associations offer basically the same type of services as the private employment agencies in searching for school superintendents. The fee, however, is not as high as that charged by the private agencies, usually ranging between $5,000 and $25,000, depending on the time and expenses incurred during the search.

Further, in recent years private consulting firms have begun to specialize in the recruitment of potential candidates for vacant superintendencies. Like other private agencies, they have nationwide contacts, advertise the position, and screen potential candidates.

This is certainly a healthy trend in education, but it carries with it a potential danger. Associations and private consulting agencies may develop a list of favored candidates who are continually recommended for positions; in turn, it could become difficult for even qualified individuals to "break into" the inner circle of favored candidates.

Colleges and Universities

Most educational institutions offer placement services not only to recent graduates but also to former graduates. The most important service available in these placement departments is the maintaining of a personal file containing references, transcripts, and other pertinent documents. Thus, each time an individual leaves a position, he may request his supervisor and other colleagues to send letters of reference to his placement service. This, in turn, will alleviate the burden of requesting former employers and colleagues to write reference letters each time an application is made for a different job. The placement service simply duplicates the references and sends them to prospective employers on the request of the graduate.

In terms of recruiting, listing vacancies with college and university placement services will not only reach recent graduates but also individuals with extensive experience who still use the service as a receptacle for employment references. Because teachers and administrators seeking jobs in school districts seldom use private or public employment agencies, college and university placement services are the best sources for finding potential candidates for professional positions.

Professional Organizations

In the private sector, professional organizations and labor unions provide placement services for their members. These organizations either publish a roster of job vacancies or notify individual members concerning potential jobs. This is generally not true of professional organizations in education. They usually list job vacancies in the classified section of their publications. They do not operate placement services, per se. In fact, having a classified section advertising jobs in a professional publication is common only to those organizations representing a specialty in educational administration. Professional education administration organizations include the American Association of School Personnel Administrators (AASPA), Association for Supervision and Curriculum Development (ASCD), Association of School Business Officials (ASBO), Council of Educational Facility Planners International (CEFPI), National Association of Elementary School Principals (NAESP), National Association of Pupil Personnel Administrators (NAPPA), National Association of Secondary School Principals (NASSP), National School Boards Association (NSBA), and National School Public Relations Association (NSPRA).

The American Association of School Administrators (AASA) is an exception. It publishes a listing of vacancies nationwide covering the following categories: the superintendency, the assistant superintendency, central-office positions, administrative positions in higher education, and professorships of educational administration. AASA's *Job Bulletin* is mailed to all members of this professional organization.

Recruiting on the Internet

Both job seekers and personnel departments in school districts are discovering the benefits of *on-line* recruiting. This approach has already begun to transform the recruiting process and, from all indications, it will continue to gain acceptance as a legitimate method of recruiting employees.

School districts are designing *home pages* which provide potential employees access to information about school districts such as: salary and fringe benefits information, student-teacher ratios, financial solvency, employee turnover, student discipline, etc. A potential employee can also access information about the application process an even send a resume via e-mail directly to a school district.

Of course, there are school districts experiencing difficulties which will prevent them from recruiting through the internet. For example, a district with substandard salaries and fringe benefits probably will not provide such information which, in turn, will discourage seasoned job seekers from considering school districts that neglect to include such information.

When a school district has a unexpected vacancy, recruiting on the internet could provide a pool of applicants in the shortest period of time. In addition there are companies and organizations which provide its members with a job posting site on the internet. This allows a job seeker to post copy of his or her resume on the site and allows school district recruiters the ability to search the resume bank on a daily or weekly basis in order to find suitable candidates for job vacancies. This is a compelling reason to use this recruitment tool. The greatest advantage, however, to recruiting through the internet is the ability to reach as many potential applicants as possible in the most cost effective manner. If this method gains acceptance among job seekers, it could reduce postage costs and may even eventuate in a reduction in the number of staff members needed to manage the recruitment process in school districts.

Other Sources for Recruitment

There are two other avenues for obtaining potential job applicants: unsolicited or walk-in applicants and minority media resources. Although affirmative action requirements usually dictate advertising most positions, the walk-in applicant can be a good candidate. Most unsolicited applicants contact the school district either by mail, by telephone, or in person. It is important to inform such individuals of the potential for employment with the district and to present them with an application to be filled out. If a vacancy occurs that fits an applicant's qualifications, that individual should then be contacted and invited to activate his or her application by written notification.

Every metropolitan area has minority populations that are serviced by media resources that can be used in recruiting minorities. For example, in the southwestern United States, there are many local radio stations that are directed to the Mexican–American population. Advertising vacancies on these radio stations can be a valuable method of recruiting.

ADVERTISING POSITION VACANCIES

When a school district wishes to communicate that it has a vacancy, it usually develops a formal advertisement. This advertisement can be used to implement the various methods of recruitment.

The Content and Style of an Advertisement

The content of an advertisement is determined by the job description and criteria that will be used in selecting the most qualified candidate for the position. The procedures used in determining and writing job descriptions along with the method of developing selection criteria will be addressed in Chapter 4.

To be effective, an advertisement must accurately reflect the major responsibilities of the position and the minimum qualifications to become a candidate. This is no easy task, because the advertisement must also be brief if it is to appear in a newspaper, newsletter, or professional publication. Appendix B contains sample advertisements that may be used as models in writing vacancy notices and that reflect some factors that should be taken into consideration.

The sample ads are modeled after those found in newspapers. The first two advertise vacancies in educational organizations, a school district and a college of education at a state university. The following five advertise vacancies in private business and industry. The most striking difference between the two types of advertisements is usually the format. Educational organizations traditionally begin by giving the name of the organization, then the title of the position along with very specific and quantitative requirements.

For example, the first advertisement in Appendix B states:

GOODVILLE SCHOOL DISTRICT, SPECIAL EDUCATION POSITIONS
AVAILABLE, Instructor for the severely handicapped.

Further, it states that the positions require a B.S. degree in special education, certification (licensing) to work with the severely handicapped, with preference given to applicants who have teaching experience.

Advertisements for positions in private business and industry usually begin by giving the title of the job and then information about the company along with detailed and subjective requirements. The advertisement for "Training Executive" in Appendix B states that the desired candidate should be high-powered and a seasoned professional with seven years experience in professional training. Only two of the advertisements for the private sector, "Direct Compensation Specialist" and "Personnel Planning and Research Senior Specialist," do not emphasize subjective qualifications. However, it is interesting to note that these two are also the only ones for positions in the private sector that are not blind ads. A blind ad is one with no identification of the company; interested persons are asked to reply to a newspaper box number or a post office box number. These two ads place greater emphasis on the company and the responsibilities of the position. Large corporations with a national reputation seldom use blind advertisements when they are seeking to fill a position that is currently unoccupied.

School districts usually identify their districts and list objective rather than subjective requirements. These are desirable practices. Candidates should know the name and location of the educational organization since this may determine the level of interest they have in the position and, in turn, may limit the number of applicants to those who are seriously interested in the job. Subjective requirements for a job are better evaluated through the selection process. Individuals are seldom good judges of their subjective qualifications, and many could be falsely encouraged or discouraged from applying for a position if subjective qualifications are listed in the advertisement. The practice of giving information about the organization and listing the job title first will effectively attract the attention of those individuals who are most qualified for the position.

A final note about the advertisements for educational organizations in Appendix B: these two models illustrate a very common but sometimes misleading technique. Each ad contains a number of vacancies, which might imply that the organization has a high turnover of employees and, further, might suggest that selection will not be a very discriminating process because of the number of applicants for numerous positions. It might be more appropriate for a school district to place fewer vacancies in any one advertisement and, when possible, to advertise each position by itself.

Recruitment Brochures

Appendix A contains samples of a special type of advertisement, the recruitment brochure. These brochures are usually mailed to individuals who have indicated an interest in an advertised position. The brochure provides potential candidates with extensive information, enabling them to better ascertain if they wish to apply for the job and also if they possess the minimum requirements. The recruitment brochure is obviously much more extensive in content and scope than the normal advertisement.

The format for such brochures will vary, but certain information is usually provided. The most important information to communicate includes the announcement of the vacancy, the procedure for applying, a description of the qualifications that the successful candidate must possess, information about the community served by the school or school district, and data about the school and/or school district, which normally includes financial, personnel, and curriculum information.

Appendix A contains two models of recruitment brochures for the positions of superintendent of schools and high school principal. Such brochures are normally used when recruiting candidates for school executive positions.

Brochures are certainly a valuable recruitment tool and should be used as much as possible for all vacancies in a school district. A general information brochure containing data about the community and school district could be used when recruiting for teachers and support personnel. The tailored special-position brochure could be reserved for executive educational positions. This approach would help to hold down the cost of printing a special brochure for the more commonly occurring vacancies in a school district.

SUMMARY

After the human resource planning process identifies current and future staffing needs, the next step is to recruit qualified personnel. However, certain constraints on recruitment must be taken into consideration. Affirmative action requirements, the reputation and policies of a school district, the enormous responsibilities of positions in education, the salary and fringe benefits offered in certain school districts—all have an influence on how a district will implement the recruitment process.

To carry out a recruitment program effectively, personnel administrators must have a good understanding of vocational development theory. The following principles are common to many theories and can be used to formulate recruitment strategies. First, people have different interests, abilities, and personalities, which will qualify them for a number of occupations. Second, the occupational preferences, competencies, and the self-image of people will change with time and experience, making personal adjustment a continuous process. Third, both life and work satisfaction depend on how well individuals can utilize their abilities and find outlets for their interests, personality traits, and values. Fourth, the process of occupational choice is influenced by employment variables such as salary, fringe benefits, location, the opportunity for advancement, and the nature of the work to be performed. Finally, vocational development is essentially a compromise between personal characteristics such as interests and abilities, and external factors such as the type of work to be performed.

Experience shows that certain recruiting methods produce the best applicants for particular job vacancies. Therefore, before initiating the recruitment process, administrators should analyze each job vacancy to ascertain what method will be most effective. The most common methods include internal search, referrals, contacting employment agencies, advertising vacancies with college and university placement services, advertising on the Internet, advertising in newspapers and in the publications of professional organizations, following up on unsolicited applications, and contacting community organizations that promote the interests of minority groups.

When a school district wishes to communicate that it has a vacancy, it usually produces a formal advertisement. The content of an advertisement is dictated by the job description and criteria to be used in selecting the most qualified candidate for the position. An effective advertisement must accurately reflect the major responsibilities of the position and the minimum qualifications an individual must possess to become a candidate for the job.

In terms of content and style, the most effective advertisement will include the title of the position, information about the school district, information on how to apply, and desired qualifications for candidates. Listing subjective qualifications and using "blind ads" are generally not appropriate. It is also more effective for a school district to place only a few vacancies in a given advertisement and, when possible, to advertise each position by itself.

A special type of advertisement is the recruitment brochure. Its purpose is to provide potential candidates with enough information to allow them to determine if they wish to apply for the job and if they possess the necessary requirements. The brochure should include the announcement of the vacancy, the procedure for applying, a description of the qualifications that the successful candidate must possess, information about the community served by the school or school district, and financial, personnel, and curricular data about the school and/or school district.

General information brochures containing data about the community and school district could be used when recruiting teachers and support personnel. The more extensive brochure is commonly reserved for recruiting school executives. The cost of printing such brochures for each vacancy would be prohibitive.

✳ *APPENDIX A*
MODEL RECRUITMENT BROCHURES FOR THE POSITIONS OF
SUPERINTENDENT OF SCHOOLS AND HIGH SCHOOL PRINCIPAL

POSITION AVAILABLE

SUPERINTENDENT OF SCHOOLS
GOODVILLE SCHOOL DISTRICT

An Equal Opportunity and
Affirmative Action Employer

ANNOUNCEMENT OF VACANCY

The Board of Education of Goodville School District is seeking a superintendent of schools.

The salary of the superintendent selected will be determined by his* professional preparation and by his successful experience in educational administration, as well as by other qualifications.

Professional assistance for the initial screening of applicants has been secured, which is a special consultant committee consisting of:

- A superintendent from a neighboring school district
- Dean of the School of Education, Goodville University

All letters of application, nominations, inquiries, credentials, and copies of legal proof of administrative qualifications should be mailed to the President of the Goodville School Board.

To receive consideration, applicants must do the following by January 1:

1. Submit a formal letter of application indicating a desire to be a candidate for the position.
2. Send up-to-date confidential credentials from his university, up-to-date resume, and a listing of his educational accomplishments by title.
3. Legal proof or other evidence showing qualification to be a superintendent.

THE PERSON NEEDED

The Board of Education of the Goodville School District and the community it serves are committed to the continuing development of quality schools. They are seeking a person who has had successful administrative experience as a superintendent, or in a central-office position with comparable responsibilities. The superintendent they are seeking should have a thorough understanding of and interest in public school education; a concern for the welfare and motivation of students is of prime importance. By his experience, knowledge, and stature, he must reflect credit upon himself and the district he serves.

Continued

The superintendent selected must be skilled in providing educational leadership; he must be a goals-oriented educator with proven success in the continuing development of teamwork among the administrative/teaching staff, board of education, and community.

Although no candidate can be expected to meet all qualifications fully, preference will be given to candidates with capabilities and/or potential as follows:

- Successful experience in financial management, budgeting, and fiscal responsibility, with the ability to evaluate the financial status of the district and establish a management plan based on projected revenues and future curriculum programs.
- In the area of human relations, the ability to work with the public, students, and staff, thus leading to good school personnel management. This aspect also includes evaluation of and in-service training for staff.
- An "educational manager" who delegates responsibility, yet maintains accountability through the management–team concept.
- Ability to exercise leadership and decision making in selection and implementation of educational priorities—a person with a realistic and responsible educational philosophy.
- The ability to objectively select, evaluate, assign, and realign staff.
- Willingness to help formulate, review, and effectively carry out board policies; and to communicate and relate openly and honestly with the board of education, keeping members informed on issues, proposals, and developments within the district.
- Ability to maintain desired student behavioral patterns.
- Successful administrative experience in a comparable district.
- A strong academic background in and an ability to evaluate and plan curriculum and programs while constantly keeping in mind the present and future financial status of the district.
- Skillful educational leadership in the development of long- and short-range district goals and objectives—a "management type" educational leader.

THE COMMUNITY

The Goodville School District is currently serving the educational needs of nearly 20,000 residents in a geographic area of great growth potential. It covers 80 square miles—one of the largest school districts in the state.

The district is highly diverse and is rich in cultural background and life styles. Approximately 30 percent of the residents live in a rural setting, with the remaining 70 percent located in suburban communities. Our district is enriched by a broad range of ethnic and racial compositions.

As Goodville is located just 25 miles south of a major metropolitan area, many of our residents can conveniently commute to work to and from the city.

Local employment continues to be enhanced with the growth of many industrial parks.

As a microcosm of life styles and cultures, the school district encourages unique opportunities in community living and education.

It is a district of parks, forest preserves, churches, schools, shopping centers, and excellent recreational facilities. We are served by three local newspapers, in addition to a large daily

Continued

newspaper and a local radio station. Goodville State University is located in our district, and many other colleges and universities are within an hour's drive.

THE SCHOOLS

The Goodville School District enrolls more than 5600 pupils in K–12. Additionally, the district offers services in preschool education, special education, and adult education. Currently there are six K–6 elementary schools; two junior high schools, 7–9; and one high school fully accredited and recognized. The school system is supported by approximately 361 certificated staff members and 171 support personnel.

Concern and support for the teaching of basic skills has been equally recognized by the school board and administrative staff. However, many innovative services and programs are provided to teachers, parents, and students. An alternative education program for secondary students is recognized as the finest in the county. Additionally, great steps have been taken toward identification of pupils' learning styles and the proper mode of instruction to enhance these styles.

Bilingual programs, special education, teacher in-service, and parent workshops have led state trends.

Extracurricular activities have always been a vital part of the educational program. The district prides itself on its athletic programs and band/orchestra activities for both boys and girls.

PHILOSOPHY OF THE BOARD OF EDUCATION

Policy-making Body

The Board of Education is primarily a policy-making body and shall maintain an administration to operate the schools efficiently with the funds available, shall constantly strive to improve all aspects of the school system, and shall keep the public well informed about educational issues.

Education of the Child

The Board believes that the education of each child in the district is the heart of the entire school operation and that administration, business management, building management, and all other services should be appraised in terms of their contributions to the progress of instruction. It shall be the goal of the Board to offer each child the opportunity to develop his or her educational potentialities to the maximum. It shall be the intention of the Board of Education to provide for equality of educational opportunity for all children regardless of sex, race, color, creed, or national origin.

STAFF

Administration:	1	Superintendent
	2	Assistant Superintendents
	5	Directors

Continued

	9	Principals
	7	Assistant Principals
	6	Curriculum Coordinators
	1	Business Manager/Treasurer
Staff:	314	Classroom Teachers
	14	Counselors
	12	Learning Resource Specialists
	16	Special Education Specialists
	8	Nurses
	5	Speech Correctionists
	30	Paraprofessionals
	43	Secretarial/Clerical Personnel
	40	Custodial/Maintenance Personnel
	30	Bus Drivers
	20	Cafeteria Workers
Student Composition:	730	Black, Non-Hispanic
	152	Hispanic
	32	Asian or Pacific Islander
	9	American Indian or Alaskan Native
	4,677	White, Non-Hispanic
	5,600	Total Enrollment

FINANCIAL DATA

Assessed Value	$280,000,000.00
TAX RATE	4.50
Bonded Indebtedness	10,000,000.00
BUDGET EXPENDITURES	20,000,000.00

Note: Use of the masculine gender in this brochure is simply a matter of convenience. All qualified persons, regardless of sex, are eligible to apply for this position.

Announcing a Vacancy

PRINCIPAL OF THOMAS JEFFERSON HIGH SCHOOL

THE COMMUNITY

Goodville is primarily a suburban residential community with easy access to the metropolitan area, as well as to all major shopping centers. Parochial schools, both elementary and secondary, are located within the school district's boundaries.

There are many active parent organizations working on behalf of the students, all of which foster a close relationship between the schools and the parents in the community.

The Chamber of Commerce functions as a viable catalyst for the business community.

The Goodville School District has one of the highest tax bases in the county.

Continued

THE PRINCIPAL

The Goodville School District is seeking qualified applicants for the position of principal for Thomas Jefferson High School.

The following qualifications and leadership abilities will be taken into consideration in the selection process:

- Good interpersonal relations skills
- Skill in all types of communications
- Ability to generate support and enthusiasm among students, faculty, and the community for the total educational program, including extracurricular activities
- Proven ability to formulate and implement both short- and long-range objectives
- Experience in the evaluation process of both staff and programs
- Certification as a secondary school administrator
- Classroom teaching experience for five years
- Educational administrative experience for three years

THE SCHOOL DISTRICT

The Goodville School District was organized in 1875. Education in Goodville encompasses the entire community. Starting with the preschooler, aged 3–5, there are tuition-sponsored programs in early childhood education. Evening courses are offered to adults in a continuing education program.

The total district enrollment is about 5,500 students. There are four elementary schools, one middle school, and one high school. The district employs approximately 300 professional educators and 100 support employees.

The Board of Education is composed of six members, each elected for a three-year term. The district's budget is $20 million and the average per pupil expenditure is approximately $3,600.

THE HIGH SCHOOL

Thomas Jefferson High School has an enrollment of 2,000 students and a staff of 98 full- and part-time certificated professionals. The school is fully accredited by the North Central Association of Colleges and Secondary Schools.

Approximately 68 percent of the graduating class goes on to college. This requires a comprehensive offering of courses, which currently numbers approximately 150.

The High School campus is located on a twenty-four acre site. Built in several stages, the school was completed in 1972 when a major addition provided much-needed classrooms and expanded physical education and drama facilities.

THE STAFF

"Experienced and highly qualified" best describes the high school faculty. Approximately 65 percent have more than fifteen years teaching experience; 60 percent have taught fifteen years or more in the high school; 75 percent of the faculty members have a master's degree or better.

Salaries are paid according to placement on an adopted schedule that recognizes experience and education. Fringe benefits include a unique plan for staff sick leave, personal leave, major medical insurance, dental insurance, term life insurance, and excellent retirement benefits.

Administrators with a twelve month contract receive one month's vacation.

APPENDIX B
MODEL NEWSPAPER ADVERTISEMENTS

GOODVILLE SCHOOL DISTRICT
SPECIAL EDUCATION POSITIONS AVAILABLE

Instructor for the severely handicapped   Requirements are BS degree in Special Education and certification in SH: teaching experience preferred.

Educational examiner   Requires MA degree and certification in one or more special education areas. Knowledge of and/or experience in psychometric administration and interpretation are desirable. Expertise in assessment of functional abilities, social adaptation, and perceptual and language skills are mandatory. Previous experience in either diagnostics or educational programming would be highly beneficial.

Speech/language/hearing pathologists   Openings include Language classroom instructors; Speech/Language pathologists. Requirements are MA degree, eligibility for state certification; Certificate of Clinical Competence from the American Speech-Language-Hearing Association and classroom experience preferred. Part-time positions are also available requiring MA degree and state certification in Speech Correction. Hours are 4–6, Monday thru Thursday.

Interpreter for the deaf   Requires a minimum of 64 college hours, Expressive Interpreter Certificate (NRID), knowledge of different sign systems, and experience with handicapped students.

Excellent fringe benefits. For application call or write

Goodville School District
Director of Personnel

An Equal Opportunity and Affirmative Action Employer

GOODVILLE STATE UNIVERSITY

Goodville State University is a regional multipurpose institution enrolling 9,000 students. It is located in Goodville, a community with a population of 37,000 located 120 miles south of a major metropolitan area.

Educational administration & foundations   Associate or Assistant Professor to coordinate Specialist Degree Program, teach graduate and undergraduate courses, including Methods of Research and one or more of the following: Educational Finance, Secondary School Administration, or Foundations of Education. Experience with state financial accounting systems and familiarity with schools in or similar to the Southeast state region desired. Doctorate in educational administration or educational leadership required. Five years' experience including district-level administration required.

Continued

Educational administration & foundations Assistant Professor to teach graduate and undergraduate courses, including Methods of Research and one or more of the following: Educational Finance, Secondary School Administration, Secondary School Supervision, or Foundations of Education. Advise graduate and undergraduate students. Doctorate in educational administration or educational leadership desired; doctorate in directly related field considered. Five years' experience in educational administration required. Experience in urban school administration, multicultural programs, or secondary administration desired.

Reading education Assistant Professor or Instructor to teach undergraduate and graduate courses including developmental, secondary, and remedial reading, and graduate reading practicum. Competency in assessment techniques required. Advise graduate and undergraduate students. Doctorate in reading preferred; active doctoral candidate in reading considered. Five years' experience including elementary or secondary classroom teaching required. College teaching preferred.

University schools faculty positions The University School is a K–12 instructional program for 340 students that functions as an integral part of the Department of Education and the teacher education program. All positions require strong classroom skills and a special interest in working with teacher education programs.

Applications Applicants are required to have their placement file forwarded immediately. Completed application, current resume, and transcripts should be mailed by February 1 to

Dean
School of Education
Goodville University

PERSONNEL DIRECTOR

A large well-established company which is a leader in its field, with its corporate offices conveniently located in the Midwest, is seeking a Personnel Director. This individual will have the complete responsibility for directing the personnel function involving such activities as benefits administration, wage and salary administration, training, selection, employee relations, and EEOC.

The ideal candidate will have 4–6 years experience, be degreed (preferably in personnel administration) with previous supervisory experience. Good planning and organizing skills are essential, as well as the ability to communicate effectively.

This highly visible position on our corporate staff offers an excellent compensation and benefits package in addition to professional and personnel growth opportunities.

Apply in complete confidence, send resume and salary requirements to

Metro Daily Newspaper
Box 325

Equal Opportunity and Affirmative Action Employer

DIRECT COMPENSATION SPECIALIST

We're Energene, the pace-setting $4 billion energy-based company that's increasing America's energy options. Our activities are diverse—natural gas, LNG, propane, coal and petrochemicals. Our operations extend from Alaska to the Gulf of Mexico, in Canada and in the continental United States, on-shore and off-shore. Our operations range from transmission and exploration to managing large petrochemical complexes. Rapid expansion of our alternative energy programs has generated superlative career opportunities.

As our Direct Compensation Specialist, you will be responsible for developing annual proposals for structure increases in the corporation's basic exempt salary schedule and the schedule covering corporate executives. You will be working with our operating companies regarding the design of base salary and incentive plans as well as recommending new and/or innovative forms of compensation.

You will need at least two years experience in salary plan design and administration. Some experience in foreign and executive compensation is desirable. You should possess a good knowledge of job evaluation, salary survey techniques and salary structure design along with government wage laws and related regulations.

To explore this excellent opportunity, please send your resume, including salary history in complete confidence to

Director of Personnel
Energene Corporation

An Equal Opportunity and Affirmative Action Employer

PERSONNEL PLANNING & RESEARCH SENIOR SPECIALIST

As part of our company's commitment to effectively selecting and developing its employees, the company has launched an extensive approach to selection, career path planning, and employee development. Due to the success of the initial work in this area, an experienced Personnel Planning and Research Specialist is needed to join a team of talented professionals to assist in development and implementation of these processes.

The successful candidate will have had significant experience with test validation; design and administration of assessment centers; design, administration, and interpretation of organizational diagnostic instruments; career path planning; and succession planning. Experience in the design and development of courses would

Continued

be a plus. This is a unique opportunity to design and install selection and development systems for an industry leader whose senior management fully supports the effort. The successful candidate will have a master's degree in the behavioral sciences, preferably a Ph.D., and experience in the industrial application of selection/development programs.

We offer an excellent salary and complete company-paid fringe benefits, including a dental plan. Interested and qualified applicants should send a resume, including education and income history, in confidence to

Director of Personnel
Krantex Industries

An Equal Opportunity and Affirmative Action Employer

Training Executive
WHAT HAVE YOU DONE
FOR YOURSELF LATELY?

Your time and energy is being spent on training other managers for successful careers. You do it well. You've seen others succeed because of your efforts and talents. Now ask yourself a few questions. Within your present organizational structure, are there opportunities for your own career success? Are you being taken for granted? Are you with a corporation that's totally committed to the training function? If you're uncomfortable with your answers–it's time to do something for yourself. Think about joining a multi-billion dollar corporation that is structured for personal growth and individual recognition. We believe we are such a corporation.

SELF ACTUALIZATION
EGO-STATUS
BELONGINGNESS
SAFETY
BASIC

A HIERARCHY OF NEEDS

The individual we're looking for is a high-powered, seasoned professional who currently holds a responsible managment position within the Training function of a large corporation. Candidate's responsibilities must have included the design, implementation and presentation of effective Management Development and/or Sales Management Training programs. A minimum of 7 years professional training experience is preferred, ideally with emphasis in middle to upper management training programs.

Our training complex is located in the Midwest, and is considered one of the most sophisticated in the country. Along with the opportunity for personal career development, we offer an excellent compensation plan, plus complete benefits including relocation expenses. For prompt and confidential consideration, send a letter or resume, including salary history to:

Daily Newspaper
Box 530

An Equal Opportunity and
Affirmative Action Employer

LABOR RELATIONS

A Goodville Corporation is seeking a Manager of Labor Relations. We are a world leader in the institutional furniture industry, with a major commitment in open office systems furniture, entertainment and transportation seating.

This is an outstanding opportunity for a personnel generalist who enjoys labor relations and wishes to concentrate in that field. Must have minimum five years experience, including contract interpretation. The successful candidate should be aggressive and yet objective; creative, mature, well-organized, and a person of integrity. Communication skills are a must as is some exposure to safety and training. We offer a professional atmosphere and a secure future.

This highly valuable position offers an attractive salary, equitable relocation assistance, and excellent benefits. Qualified candidates should submit resume and salary history in confidence to

Metro Daily Newspaper
Box 645

An Equal Opportunity and Affirmative Action Employer

SELECTED BIBLIOGRAPHY

A Quality Work Force: America's Key to the Next Century. Denver, Colo.: Education Commission of the States, 1989.

Beckham, Joseph, *Legal Aspects of Employee Assessment and Selection in Public Schools.* Topeka, Kans.: National Organization on Legal Problems of Education, 1985.

Building a Quality Workforce. Washington, D.C.: Office of Public Affairs, Employment and Training Administration, U.S. Department of Labor, 1988.

Darling-Hammon, Linda, *Beyond the Commission Reports; The Coming Crisis in Teaching,* Santa Monica, Calif.: The Rand Corporation, 1984.

Fielder, Donald J., "Wanted: Minority Teachers," *The Executive Educator,* 15, no. 5 (May 1993), pp. 33–34.

Goldstein, William, *Recruiting Superior Teachers: The Interview Process.* Bloomington, Ind.: Phi Delta Kappa Education Foundation, 1986.

Gordon, June A., "Why Students of Color are not Entering Teaching: Reflections from Minority Teachers," *Journal of Teacher Education,* 45, no. 53 (November–December 1994), pp. 346–353.

Hammond, Doug and Gary Blakey, "School Bus Drivers: Recruitment & Training," *School Business Affairs,* 57, no. 4 (April 1991), pp. 26–30.

Jensen, Mary Cihak, *Recruiting and Selecting the Most Capable Teachers.* Eugene, Oreg.: Oregon School Study Council, University of Oregon, 1986.

U.S. Department of Education, *Teacher Attrition and Migration.* Washington D.C.: OERI/Education Information Branch, 1993.

Witty, Elaine P., *Teacher Recruitment and Retention.* West Haven, Conn.; NEA Professional Library, 1990.

4

SELECTION

The objective of the selection process is to hire individuals who will be successful on the job. Self-evident as this purpose may appear, its implementation requires a rather thorough process. The cost of selecting employees is a major expenditure for most school districts. If the process does not produce effective employees, the cost to the district is often incalculable because of inadequate performance, because of the expense connected with the termination process, and because of the expense involved in hiring new employees.

The minimum cost in hiring any new employee has been calculated at $1,000; it can cost as much as $25,000 to hire a superintendent of schools. In selecting an individual for most positions in a school district, the costs include advertising the position; printing and mailing applications; and personnel time required to review applications, to interview candidates, and to check references. This presupposes that many routine tasks, such as writing job descriptions, and establishing proper selection criteria, have already been accomplished. Training and orienting new employees is an additional cost directly related to the hiring process but often overlooked. Therefore, selecting individuals who will be successful and will remain with the school district for a reasonable period of time is an extremely important personnel process, not only significant in fulfilling the district's mandate to educate children but also affecting the financial condition of the school district.

A selection decision may result in four possible outcomes: two are correct decisions and two are errors. The correct decisions occur when the individual hired proves to be successful on the job or when a rejected applicant would have performed inadequately if hired. In both instances the selection process has met the objective of hiring the most appropriate candidate. The process has failed when a rejected candidate could have performed successfully on the job or when the individual hired performs inadequately.[1]

The selection process, therefore, should be implemented through a series of activities that will minimize the chances of hiring individuals who are inadequate performers. Exhibit 4–1 sets forth these activities in a sequence that will serve as a model throughout this chapter.

[1]See Stephen P. Robbins, *Personnel: The Management of Human Resources,* 2nd ed. (Englewood Cliffs, N.J.: Prentice-Hall, 1982), p. 122.

EXHIBIT 4–1   Steps in the Selection Process

1. Write the job description.
2. Establish the selection criteria.
3. Write the vacancy announcement and advertise the position.
4. Receive applications.
5. Select the candidates to be interviewed.

6. Interview candidates.
7. Check references and credentials.
8. Select the best candidate.
9. Implement the job offer and acceptance.
10. Notify unsuccessful candidates.

STEPS IN THE SELECTION PROCESS

Writing the Job Description

A written job description is the end product of a process that is commonly referred to as "job analysis." This process gathers information about the position: what an employee does; why he or she performs certain tasks; how he or she does the job; what skills, education, or training are required to perform the job; the relationship the job has to other jobs; what physical demands and environmental conditions affect the job. This information also is relevant to human resource forecasting, to creating job evaluation instruments, and in determining compensation programs.[2]

A number of recognized techniques can be used in job analysis. These include:

1. *Observation.* The person conducting the analysis directly observes the employee as he or she is performing his or her job.
2. *Individual Interviews.* Certain employees are extensively interviewed and the analyzed results from a number of these interviews are combined into the job analysis.
3. *Group Interviews.* This technique is similar to individual interviews except that a number of employees are interviewed at the same time.
4. *Job Questionnaire.* Employees check or rate tasks which they perform from a pre-established list of possible job tasks.
5. *Consulting.* Expert consultants are employed to describe specific tasks that should be performed by a certain category of employees.
6. *Supervisor Analysis.* Those who supervise certain categories of employees are consulted on the tasks which are appropriate to the job classification under study.
7. *Diary Method.* Certain employees are required to maintain a diary of their daily activities for a given period of time.[3]

---

[2]George B. Redfern, "Using Job Descriptions as an Administrative Tool," *Spectrum,* Winter 1984, p. 21.

[3]Robbins, *Personnel,* p. 79.

The seven methods described above are not meant to be used in isolation from each other. They are complementary techniques that will result in a superior job analysis if used in combination with each other. Of course, not all techniques will be required for each analysis. However, certain techniques are more appropriate to particular classifications of jobs. The first three methods would probably be more effective in analyzing the jobs of classified employees. Techniques four, five, and seven would be beneficial in analyzing the tasks common to professional positions. Number six would always be helpful in analyzing both professional and classified jobs.

The job analysis is, as previously mentioned, the vehicle for obtaining the necessary data to write a job description. The job description is an outline providing specific details concerning a job and the minimum qualifications necessary to perform it successfully.

No one format for writing a job description can be universally acclaimed as most effective in each and every circumstance. However, certain elements should be common to most job descriptions. These include the title of the job, duties that must be performed, the authority and responsibilities accompanying the job, and specific qualifications necessary to successful performance of the job.

Appendix A provides two sample job descriptions that are models of a particular style appropriate for school district positions. Note that the titles for these two positions are very specific. The first is a job description for a junior high school principal; and the second, for a high school biology teacher.

Each description begins with a summary of the job, outlining the overall responsibilities of the position. This is followed by a detailed explanation of specific job tasks and the relationship of the job to other positions in the organizational structure of the school district. At a time when legal rights and responsibilities are being emphasized by parents and employees, organizational relationships are extremely important and must be clearly explained to prospective employees. Finally, minimum job qualifications are listed as an integral part of the job description.

Job descriptions should be updated from time to time because working conditions will change with advances in technology and education. But it is absolutely critical to perform a job analysis and to revise the job description for a position each time it becomes vacant. This will affect the establishment of the selection criteria and will ensure that the individual being hired properly understands the responsibilities and duties of the job.

Establishing the Selection Criteria

The second step in the selection procedure is to establish the criteria against which the candidates will be evaluated to determine who will be offered the job. Selection criteria are very different from the job description, in that the selection criteria delineate those ideal characteristics that, if possessed by an individual to the fullest extent possible, would ensure the successful performance of the job. Obviously, no one person will possess all the characteristics to their fullest extent, and not all characteristics have equal importance in determining who is the best candidate.

The use of selection criteria also can become a method for quantifying the expert opinions of those who will be interviewing candidates. Without criteria, each interviewer is left to his own discretion in determining if an individual will be able to perform the job.

Quantifying the opinions of interviewers also provides data to show that the best candidate was offered the position, thus demonstrating that the school district is an affirmative action and equal opportunity employer. The candidate with the highest score should be offered the position first; if he or she does not accept, then the candidate receiving the next highest score should be offered the position, and so on.

It is a generally accepted practice in personnel management for the personnel department to assume the responsibilities for organizing and conducting job analyses, for writing job descriptions, and for establishing the selection criteria used in filling a vacancy.

The timing for writing the job description and for developing the selection criteria is extremely important. Both tasks should be performed before a job vacancy is advertised and before applications are received, not only because the advertisement should be based on the description but also because it will demonstrate that the criteria were not prepared to favor a particular applicant.

Appendix B presents a sample of three sets of selection criteria, one for a high school English teacher and a second for a sixth-grade elementary school teacher; the third presents general criteria for an elementary school teacher in a self-contained classroom. Each criteria instrument has been constructed in such a way that particular characteristics may be rated and a final score obtained. The significant difference between the first two instruments and the third is the weighting that is designated on the general criteria instrument. The compatibility of an applicant's educational philosophy with the school district's policies and curriculum is of primary importance, as indicated on this third instrument. Professional preparation is second, personal characteristics third, and experience the least important. The assumption underlying this third selection instrument is that an individual will best meet the needs of the school district if he or she has the proper attitude and philosophy. Experience will enrich an individual's performance, but philosophy is necessary to direct the benefits obtained by the experience. In like manner, an individual will grow in the job if his or her educational values are in harmony with those of the school district.

Note too that this third instrument is less specific in describing desirable characteristics and leaves the interviewer with more discretion in making a judgment about the candidate's qualifications. For example, an individual with a Ph.D. in early childhood education may not be the most desirable candidate for a first-grade self-contained classroom position. That applicant would be overqualified for such a position, but would be in appropriate candidate for a position in a laboratory school attached to a university in which aspiring teachers observe instructional techniques. In this latter situation, the candidate with a Ph.D. would likely receive the maximum number of points in the "professional preparation" category.

The first two criteria instruments, for a high school English teacher and sixth-grade teacher, are rather detailed and more traditional in style and content. Each is divided into categories, delineating academic, personal, and experiential qualifications.

This method of evaluating candidates places a responsibility on each interviewer to make a discriminatory judgment concerning the qualifications of each individual. The interview itself will not be the only source of information used to fill out the selection criteria instrument. The application, placement papers, transcripts, and letters of reference also will be used by the interviewers in determining an individual's qualifications for the job.

Each interviewer will sign and turn in to the personnel department a selection criteria instrument for each person interviewed. The personnel department is then responsible for compiling the results.

Writing the Job Vacancy Announcement and Advertising the Position

Chapter 3 describes in detail the nuances of writing a job vacancy advertisement. The advertisement should be viewed as an integral part of the selection process. It is based on the job description and should provide potential candidates with sufficient information to make a decision on whether to apply for the position. Consequently, an advertisement must clearly identify the job title, major responsibilities of the job, the name and location of the school district, how to apply for the job, and the minimum qualifications to become a candidate.

It is the responsibility of the personnel department to write the advertisement and to publish it according to the recruitment policy of the school district. In providing information about how to apply for a position, the advertisement should include a deadline for receiving applications. It is a common practice to allow a two-week period for receiving applications for classified and teaching jobs. A month is the usual time period allotted to receiving applications for school executive positions. Of course, each individual situation will dictate the length of time allotted for the receiving of applications and may deviate from these usual time periods.

A common mistake made by some school administrators and inexperienced personnel administrators is not providing sufficient time to effectively implement the selection process. A hurried process may place the school district in an indefensible position in terms of affirmative action requirements and, in addition, may result in the hiring of the wrong person. In an average-size school district, with a personnel department or at least one central-office personnel administrator, two months will be a comfortable time period to carry out the selection process. This period begins with the publication of an advertisement and extends through to the time when a job offer is made.

Receiving Applications

A central-office staff member, usually a secretary, should be assigned to receive all the applications for a given job vacancy. As the applications are received, they should be dated and placed in a file folder designated for the applications. This will provide integrity to the process, and also will provide a method of monitoring the incoming applications for a particular vacancy.

Many applicants will request their college or university placement offices to send their transcripts and letters of reference to the school district. These documents must also be dated and attached to the appropriate applications.

After the deadline for receiving applications has been reached, a master list should be compiled with the names, addresses, and telephone numbers of those who have applied. The master list also should include by title the other documents that have been received in support of each application, such as transcripts and letters of reference. The entire folder of applications, support documents, and the master list can then be assigned and given to a personnel administrator, who will perform the initial screening of the applications.

Keeping applicants informed during the selection process will help to cut down on the number of inquiries that are normally received in the personnel department. One very effective method is to send a postcard to each applicant stating that his or her application has been received and listing a date by which individuals will be selected for interviews.

It is also important to notify immediately those who sent in applications after the deadline that they will not be considered for the position. A common practice is to accept those applications postmarked on the day of the deadline.

Some school districts and many colleges and universities have initiated the practice of receiving applications *until the position is filled.* Under this procedure individuals who sent their applications to the school district by the deadline are given first consideration. If a suitable candidate is not identified, then those individuals who sent their applications to the district before a later designated date, are considered for the position and so on until a suitable candidate is offered and accepts the position. This is an acceptable practice which can encourage qualified individuals to apply for positions even though they did not know about the positions in a timely manner.

At this point a procedure can be initiated that will help in evaluating the effectiveness of the school district's affirmative action program. The master list of applicants should be given to the administrator responsible for monitoring the affirmative action program. He or she can then send a letter to all those who have made application, asking them to identify if they belong to one or more minority groups listed on an enclosed form, and requesting them to mail the form back to the school district. Because the purpose of the selection process is to hire the best candidate, it is important to state in this letter that filling out the form will have no bearing on who is hired for the position. Consequently, the form should not be signed by the applicant and should not be sent to the personnel department but rather to the affirmative action officer.

Selecting the Candidates to Be Interviewed

Screening the applications is the fifth step in the selection process. It is initiated to identify those applicants who are to be interviewed for the position.

The application form should contain a statement requesting the applicant to have his placement papers, transcripts, and letters of reference sent to the personnel department. These documents along with the application form will provide the personnel administrator with sufficient information to evaluate each person against the selection criteria and against the minimum education and certification requirements.

The number of applicants to be interviewed will depend on the number of people who apply and on the nature of the position to be filled. If only five people apply for a vacancy and if each person meets the minimum qualifications, all five can be interviewed. This, of course, is not the norm except for those very few job classifications in which there is a shortage of qualified individuals, such as the field of industrial arts. On the average, between three and five applicants are selected to be interviewed for classified and teaching positions. For school executive positions, the average number interviewed is between five and ten applicants.

Interviewing the Candidates

Interviewing candidates is a responsibility shared between the personnel department and other school district employees. The individuals who will participate in the interviewing process will be determined by the position to be filled. It is important to include not only those who will supervise the new employee but also others who have expert knowledge about the duties to be performed by the successful candidate. For example, candidates for a high school biology teaching position should be interviewed by the high school principal, the chairperson of the biology department, a biology teacher, a personnel administrator, and the assistant superintendent for secondary education. In like manner, candidates for an elementary principal position should be interviewed by the superintendent of schools, the assistant superintendent for elementary education, an elementary school principal, and a personnel administrator.

This same process is also useful in hiring classified employees. Applicants for a custodial position can be interviewed by the head custodian in a building, the director of maintenance and custodial services, a custodian, and a personnel administrator. However, the importance of involving employees with experience and expert knowledge in the hiring of employees for lower-level positions is seldom recognized in most school districts.

Members of the interviewing committee will need assistance in learning the strategies of credentials evaluation and interviewing. A method that will hold down expenses and make maximum use of the skills learned through a staff development program is to select a group of teachers, department chairpersons, classified employees, and building principals who will participate in the selection process for a year's time. Each year a different group of employees can be selected and trained to participate in evaluating credentials and interviewing applicants.

How these individuals are selected to participate in the hiring process will depend on the size of the school district. Seniority in the school district, of course, in one of the most defensible methods for selecting participants, but it is also imperative to have individuals who represent all job categories and teaching disciplines. Thus, a maintenance staff member, bus driver, cafeteria worker, elementary school art teacher, mathematics teacher, science teacher, social studies teacher, and so on, will be needed and should be available.

Released time from work is the most effective way to involve staff members. Substitute teachers and temporary classified employees will be needed to fill in for individuals who will be interviewing candidates and evaluating credentials during the working day. The average turnover of employees during a year's period of time is usually between 5 and 10 percent. This means that a given employee will participate in the selection process only on particular occasions, probably no more than ten working days a year.

Some school executives, such as assistant superintendents, will be more involved in the process because of their line authority to so many categories of employees. The assistant superintendent for elementary education, for example, will interview candidates for all elementary teaching and administrative vacancies. Of course, the immediate supervisor for the position to be filled is always a member of the committee.

Definition of an Interview
Essentially, an interview is a conversation between two individuals set up to generate information about the person being interviewed or other matters that are familiar to the

respondent.[4] However, there are four characteristics of an interview that distinguish it from an ordinary conversation. First, an interview is a structured conversation with direction and a format; it has a beginning, middle, and conclusion. Second, the interview is conducted by an individual who is prepared to move it in a direction dictated by the occasion. Third, both parties to the interview understand its purpose, which can be accomplished only through cooperation. Finally, the nature of the interview is clearly defined and specified.[5]

Types of Interviews

There are two basic types of interviews, the standardized interview and the open-ended interview. The standardized interview is conducted by asking a set of questions established to help insure that the responses of the candidates can be readily compared. It is most effective in the initial interviewing of all candidates.

The open-ended interview encourages the candidate to talk freely and at length about topics introduced by the interviewer to suit the occasion. It is very helpful in the follow-up sessions with the finalists for the job.[6]

In both types of interviews, the objectives are basically the same. The interviewer is attempting to gather facts from the respondent; to learn about the respondent's opinions, beliefs, and attitudes; and to experience the respondent as a person.[7]

The Role of the Interviewer

The interviewer has extremely important responsibilities. Not only does he or she direct the interview by asking questions, but also he or she must record the respondent's answers and present the respondent with a favorable image of the school district. Through the interview process, the interviewer must evaluate and come to a conclusion about the suitability of each candidate. A selection criteria instrument will be used to quantify the observations of the interviewer, but ultimately the observations are subjective interpretations.

All interviews are more effective if they are conducted in a pleasant environment. This will help put the candidate at ease and will facilitate the kind of verbal exchange that gives the interviewer the most information about each candidate. The interviewer should find a room that allows the interview to be conducted without interruptions and should arrange the furniture in the room so as to have eye contact with the candidate during the session.

Legal Implications of Interviewing

Federal legislation and court decisions have had a significant impact on the types of questions that legally may be asked in an interview. For example, it was once common practice to ask a candidate if he or she had ever been arrested or spent time in jail. Because of a

---

[4]See Henry S. Dyer, *The Interview as a Measuring Device in Education* (New Jersey: ERIC Clearing House on Tests, Measurements, and Evaluations, 1976), p. 2.

[5]See Auren Uris, *The Executive Interviewer's Handbook* (Houston, Texas: Gulf Publishing Company, 1978), p. 2.

[6]Dyer, *The Interview,* p. 2.

[7]See Uris, *Interviewer's Handbook,* p. 4.

court case, *Gregory* v. *Litton Systems, Inc.,* school districts are now permitted to ask only about a candidate's record of criminal conviction.[8] Further, questions about sexual preference are prohibited under anti-discrimination laws.[9]

Below is a list of the more common inquiries that have legal implications:

1. *Name:* It is lawful to inquire if an applicant has worked under a different name or nickname in order to verify work or educational records; it is unlawful to ask questions in an attempt to discover the applicant's ancestry, lineage, or national origin.
2. *Age:* For a minor, requiring proof of age in the form of a work permit or certificate of age is lawful; it is unlawful to require adults to present a birth certificate or baptismal record to the district.
3. *Race:* To request information about distinguishing physical characteristics is legal; to ask the color of the applicant's skin, eyes, etc., is illegal if this indicates directly or indirectly race or color.
4. *Religion:* All inquiries are illegal.
5. *Sex:* Inquiries regarding sex are permissible only when a bona fide occupational qualification exists.
6. *Ethnic Background:* It is legal to ask which languages the applicant reads, writes, or speaks fluently; inquiries about the applicant's national origin are illegal.
7. *Marital and family status:* Questions to determine if a man or woman can meet specific work schedules are lawful; inquiries about being married, single, divorced, etc., are unlawful.
8. *Credit Rating:* All questions about charge accounts or credit rating are unlawful.
9. *Work Experience:* It is lawful to ask why an applicant wants to work for a particular company or institution; asking what kind of supervisor the applicant prefers is unlawful.
10. *Life style:* Asking about future career plans is lawful; asking an applicant if he/she drinks alcoholic beverages or takes drugs is unlawful.[10]

The Art of Questioning

The success of the entire interviewing process rests on the interviewer's skill in asking questions. It is a skill that is acquired through experience. However, a well-planned interview with a pre-established set of questions can be extremely useful to even the most experienced interviewer, and it is a necessity in the standardized interview. Appendix C lists sample questions that have proven useful in the interviewing process.

---

[8]See "New Rules for Interviewing Job Applicants: Schools Ignore Them at Their Peril," *American School Board Journal,* 164 (1977), p. 28.

[9]Junda Woo, "Job Interviews Pose Rising Risk to Employers," *Wall Street Journal,* sec. B, pp. B1, B5.

[10]Anna Nemesh, "The Interviewing Process," *Business Education Forum,* 33 (1979), pp. 19–20.

Group Interviewing

Some school districts prefer group interviewing, in which a number of staff members who are scheduled to interview a candidate jointly perform this task. Group interviewing can be very effective, and it certainly cuts down on the amount of time spent on this process. The dynamics described in this chapter are also applicable to the group interviewing method. However, to be effective, one staff member must serve as the group leader and take responsibility for directing the interview.

Checking References and Credentials

Credentials

Checking references and credentials, the seventh step in the selection process, has profound implications. A candidate's "credentials" include such items as a college or university transcript, administrator or teacher certification document, and a physician's verification of health. Transcripts and health verifications should not be accepted if they are presented to the personnel department by the applicant; rather, they should be mailed directly to the school district by the respective college or university and physician. It is important to inform a candidate that his or her file is not complete until these documents are received.

It is common and accepted practice to request the health verification from a candidate only if he or she is chosen for the position. However, a contract or formal employment should not be initiated until the health verification has been received in the personnel department. It is best to state on the application form that a health examination will be required as a condition of employment if a job offer is made.

An administrator or teacher certification document is usually issued by a state department of education and given directly to the individual. Although the candidate presents the certification document to the personnel department, it is still necessary to contact the issuing state in order to ascertain if the certification remains valid. When a certification is revoked, the actual document is not always returned by the individual to the state department of education.

If a person is applying for a teaching or administrative position in a state where he or she is not currently certificated, he or she is responsible for obtaining written verification from the state department of education that he or she has the qualifications to receive certification. For such positions, a contract should never be offered to a candidate in the absence of a certification document or verification letter.

Letters of Reference

Letters of reference are the most vulnerable part of this process. A personnel administrator must write, telephone, or contact in person those individuals who have sent in reference letters supporting an applicant. The application form should state that a minimum of three reference letters are required; they should be mailed directly to the personnel department; and they must include a reference letter from the applicant's current or last immediate supervisor.

Evaluating reference letters is a very difficult task. There are three basic types of references. First is the glowing letter, affirming in detail that the candidate is an excellent employee with tremendous potential. Second is the letter indicating that the applicant's performance has been inferior and that he or she would be the wrong person for the job. Third is the reference letter telling very little about the applicant and couched in vague language. However, reference letters often have hidden messages, and understanding the significance of these references requires the talent of a personnel administrator who is skilled in detecting discrepancies between the candidate's credentials, his or her interview performance, and the reference letters. Consider, for example, the candidate who performs rather poorly in the interview and has unimpressive credentials, but who has an excellent letter of reference from his immediate supervisor. This could be an individual who is not performing satisfactorily in his or her present position and whose supervisor would be happy to see him or her find another job.

Obviously, it is the responsibility of a personnel administrator to verify the reference letters of the candidates who have been interviewed. It is impossible and unnecessary to check every reference for each candidate. However, it would be very difficult to choose the best candidate from those interviewed without reference verification.

Criminal-Background Investigation

The risk of hiring a person who has a criminal record has created much concern for personnel administrators over the past five years. School districts have been sensitized to this possibility because of the news media notoriety given to educators who have been convicted of child molestation. This is probably the ultimate nightmare of every school administrator!

Criminal-background investigations are time-consuming and expensive, in addition to being controversial. The National Education Association has taken a position in opposition to fingerprinting as a condition of employment. The often heard criticism is that fingerprinting is an insult to teachers and their profession. Others proclaim that such a procedure is the least that can be done to make schools safe for kids.

Conducting criminal-background investigations and the extent of such investigations is usually dependent upon a mix of school district policy, state statutes, and the discretion of the interviewing personnel administrator.[11] The extent of the investigation is usually limited in most school districts to checking with the local and state police in order to ascertain if the potential employee has been convicted of a crime. If he or she is a teacher, it is also possible to check with the Teacher Identification Clearinghouse, which is maintained by the National Association of State Directors of Teacher Education and Certification (NASDTEC). This nationwide clearinghouse has a data base of all teachers who have been denied certification and whose certification has been revoked or suspended for moral reasons. The data are available only to states that have joined the Clearinghouse. Individual school districts can neither join the Clearinghouse nor directly obtain information from it. Only states may join.

---

[11]Sally Banks Zakariya, "How You Can Identify People Who Shouldn't Work with Kids," *The Executive Educator,* 10, no. 8 (August 1988), p. 17.

Those states that are members agree to list, by name, any known alias, date of birth, and social security number of those persons from whom certification has been withdrawn or withheld over the past fifteen years. The individual state certification officials are responsible for finding out why the action was taken. This can easily be accomplished by contacting the certification official in the state where this occurred.[12]

A school district wishing to check the fingerprints of an applicant against the files of the FBI can do this only if the state in which the school district is located has passed legislation authorizing this type of investigation. This legislation must also have the approval of the U.S. Attorney General's Office. Even then, the request must be processed by a law enforcement agency such as the state police, which then acts as the conduit through which the information is channeled to the school district.[13]

As a final note to this issue, it is good personnel administration practice to conduct criminal-background investigations. In fact, if the wrong person is hired because a criminal-background investigation was not conducted, the liability of the school district for the wrongs committed by this person could be staggering.

Unlawful Employment of Aliens
In 1986 the U.S. Congress passed the Immigration Reform and Control Act, which makes it unlawful to knowingly hire an unauthorized alien, to continue the employment of one who becomes an unauthorized alien, or to hire any individual without first verifying his or her employability and identity.

Selecting the Best Candidate

The personnel administrator responsible for implementing the selection process for a particular vacancy must organize all relevant data in such a manner that a choice may be made by the superintendent of schools. The data should include the rank ordering by scores against the selection criteria of those candidates who were interviewed, verified credentials and reference letters, and the application forms.

The superintendent then selects the candidate who appears best qualified. If this selection process is utilized, this will usually be the candidate who scored the highest against the selection criteria.

Implementing the Job Offer and Acceptance

Professional Positions
The superintendent of schools may wish to interview the candidate he or she selects for a position or may wish to interview the top two, three, or five candidates before making a final choice. When the final decision has been made, the selected candidate must be offered the job in a formal manner. If this individual accepts the offer, a contract must be

[12]"Check Here for Help on Background Checks," *The Executive Educator,* 10, no. 8 (August 1988), p. 21.

[13]Zakariya, "How You Can Identify People Who Shouldn't Work with Kids," p. 17.

approved by the board of education and signed by the finalist. Usually, a board of education will require the superintendent to make a recommendation of employment and will want an explanation of why this particular person was selected.

Classified Positions

The superintendent also may want to interview candidates for classified positions, but in most cases will accept the recommendation of the personnel department to hire the candidate with the highest score in relation to the selection criteria. The superintendent may make the job offer himself or delegate this to a personnel administrator. Once the candidate accepts the offer, employment may commence at a mutually acceptable time.

Notifying the Unsuccessful Candidates

The final step in the selection process is to notify all applicants that the position has been filled. This is initiated only after the offer of employment has been accepted by the selected candidate since there may be a need to offer the position to another candidate if the first refuses the offer. Good public relations also dictates that all applicants be notified when the job has been filled; they have expended some time and money in applying for the position.

PRINCIPLES OF CONSTRUCTING APPLICATION FORMS

The first task in applying for a position is filling out an application form, an often tedious task enjoyed by very few people. There are two major reasons why most people dislike these forms. First, some forms require information that seems irrelevant, and second, some forms allot too little space for filling in the required information.

Application forms are constructed in one of two basic formats. The first style emphasizes detailed and extensive factual information about the individual; little or no attention is given to the person's attitudes, opinions, and values. Conversely, the second style emphasizes the applicant's attitudes, opinions, and values and asks for less factual information.

Appendix D provides examples of both styles. The application for a teaching position and the one for a classified job are samples of the factual information style. A third application form, one for a high school principal's position, is a sample of the second, less factual, style.

These samples also demonstrate the types of style commonly used for particular positions. The style is dictated by the kind of information the district needs to elicit from the applicants. For teaching and classified positions, factual information about the applicants' personal characteristics, their work experience, their professional preparation, and supportive data such as references help the personnel department determine who should be interviewed.

For school executive positions, the minimum requirements are highly specialized and thus can be requested on an application in a relatively limited space. Applicants to be interviewed are best selected by evaluating a set of responses that give some indication of each person's attitudes, opinions, and values.

Contents of the Application Form

The basic principle in constructing application forms is: Only ask for information you need to know! Most information requested on applications falls under one of the following headings: personal data, education and/or professional preparation, experience, and references. Exhibit 4–2 lists types of information that is inappropriate on an application form either because it is irrelevant or because it is illegal under civil rights and labor legislation.

The physical layout of the application form should give an individual sufficient space to answer the questions and to provide the requested information. The kinds of information requested should also be grouped under headings to provide continuity. This helps the personnel department in analyzing the applications, and helps the individual providing the data.

A FINAL NOTE

Employment Tests

The business and industrial community uses two techniques in the selection process that are seldom used by school districts: employment tests and assessment centers. Intelligence, aptitude, ability, and interest tests can provide valuable data when selecting classified employees. Legal rulings, however, have significantly limited their use because tests must be clearly job-related to justify their administration.

EXHIBIT 4–2 Irrelevant or Inappropriate Information Asked on Some Application Forms

Maiden name
Marital status
Name of spouse
Occupation of spouse
Number and age of children
Physical handicaps
Arrest record ("Convictions" is appropriate)
Height and weight (unless these are bona fide occupational qualifications)
If applicant owns a home or rents
If applicant has relatives employed by the school district (A policy against hiring relatives of present employees is questionable.)
If the applicant has an automobile and a driver's license (unless this is a bona fide occupational qualification)
Where the applicant attended elementary and high school (Irrelevant on professional applications)
Religion
National origin
Race

Aptitude and ability tests are easiest to justify and can be used successfully for most classified jobs. In fact, it would be inappropriate to hire a person to train as a school bus mechanic who did not possess mechanical aptitude. In like manner, an applicant for a secretarial position must be administered a typing test to measure the person's skill in this necessary secretarial area. It should be remembered that testing has definite limitations and the results must be interpreted in relation to the interview, references, and other employment documents.

Assessment Center

Assessment centers are places where supervisors have an opportunity to observe candidates for a particular job. Assessment centers are used primarily for management positions. The candidates are taken through a series of simulations dealing with administrative problems of the type that will probably be encountered on the job. The simulations usually take the form of case evaluations or decision-making games.

Standard Oil, Sears and Roebuck, IBM, and the Social Security Administration developed assessment centers to be used not only as a means for selecting candidates for job vacancies but also as a means for evaluating individuals for promotion to positions of higher responsibility. Although the expense in establishing an assessment center will make it prohibitive in most school districts, large metropolitan districts could find the use of an assessment center extremely beneficial in selecting teachers to be promoted into the principalship and other administrative positions.

SUMMARY

The objective of the selection process is to hire individuals who will be successful on the job. The cost of this process is a major expenditure for most school districts, which includes advertising the position, printing and mailing applications, and personnel costs for interviewing candidates and checking references. The selection process should be implemented through a series of steps that will minimize the chances of hiring individuals who are inadequate performers. These steps are as follows:

1. *Writing the Job Description.* The job description is the end product of another process known as the "job analysis." This process gathers information about each job through observations, interviews, questionnaires, consulting, and the diary method. The job description outlines specific details of a position and establishes the minimum qualifications needed to perform the job successfully.

2. *Establishing the Selection Criteria.* Criteria instruments delineate those ideal characteristics that, if possessed by an individual to the fullest extent possible, will ensure the successful performance of the job. The selection criteria instrument can be used also to quantify the expert opinion of those who will be interviewing candidates.

3. *Writing the Job Vacancy Announcement and Advertising the Position.* The advertisement is based on the job description and provides interested individuals with sufficient information to decide if they wish to apply for the position. The advertisement must clearly identify the job title, major responsibilities, name and location of the school district, application procedure, and the minimum job qualifications.

4. *Receiving Applications.* A central-office staff member should be assigned to receive all applications for a given vacancy. As the applications are received, they should be dated and filed in a designated folder. This will provide integrity to the process and will establish a method of monitoring the progress toward filling the vacancy.

5. *Selecting the Candidates to be Interviewed.* The application form should contain a statement requesting the applicants to have their placement papers, transcripts, and letters of reference sent to the personnel department. The application should provide sufficient information to evaluate each person against the selection criteria and against the minimum requirements for the job. A selected group of applicants are then interviewed for the position.

6. *Interviewing the Candidates.* Interviewing candidates is a responsibility shared by the personnel department and other school district employees. It is important to include not only those who will supervise the new employee but also others who have expert knowledge about the duties which will be performed by the successful candidate. An interview is essentially a conversation between two or more individuals conducted to generate information about the candidate. Interviewing is a learned skill; it also has profound legal implications.

7. *Checking References and Credentials.* "Credentials" refers to such items as a college or university transcript, teaching certification, and a physician's verification of health. These credentials along with letters of reference, whenever possible, should be sent directly to the personnel department by the issuing source.

8. *Selecting the Best Candidate.* The personnel administrator who is responsible for implementing the selection process for a particular vacancy must organize all relevant data in such a manner that a choice may be made by the superintendent of schools.

9. *Implementing the Job Offer and Acceptance.* For professional positions, a contract must be approved by the board of education and signed by the finalist before this step is completed. For classified positions, once the candidate affirms that he will accept the offer, employment may commence at a mutually acceptable time.

10. *Notifying the Unsuccessful Candidates.* This step is initiated only after the offer of employment has been accepted by the candidate because there may be a need to offer the position to another individual if the first selected candidate refuses the offer.

The risk of hiring a person who has a criminal record has created much concern for personnel administrators over the past five years. Conducting criminal-background investigations and the extent of such investigations are usually dependent upon a mix of school district policy, state statutes, and the discretion of the interviewing personnel administrator. The extent of an investigation is usually limited in most school districts to checking with the local and state police in order to ascertain if the potential employee has been convicted of a crime. When the potential employee is a teacher, it is also possible to check with the Teacher Identification Clearinghouse if the school district is in a state that is a member of this organization. A school district wishing to check the fingerprints of an applicant against the files of the FBI can only do this if the state in which the district is located has passed legislation authorizing this type of investigation.

The first task in applying for a position is filling out the application form. There are two basic formats used in constructing applications. The first format emphasizes detailed factual information; the second emphasizes the applicant's attitudes, opinions, and values.

The basic principle in constructing application forms is, "Only ask for information you need to know!" The information requested on most applications falls under one of the following headings: personal data, education and/or professional preparation, experience, and references. The physical layout of the form should allot sufficient space for answering the questions and providing the requested information.

The business and industrial community uses two techniques as part of the selection process that are seldom used by school districts: employment tests and assessment centers. Aptitude and ability testing can be used successfully as part of the selection process for most classified jobs in school districts. In fact, they are necessary for some positions. Assessment centers are places where supervisors have an opportunity to observe candidates for a particular job. Candidates are taken through a series of simulations dealing with administrative problems, the kind of which will probably be encountered on the job. Large metropolitan school districts could find the use of an assessment center beneficial in selecting teachers to be promoted into the principalship and other administrative positions.

APPENDIX A
JOB DESCRIPTIONS

JOB DESCRIPTION FOR A
JUNIOR HIGH SCHOOL PRINCIPAL

Job Summary

The junior high school principal is responsible for the maintenance and continuation of a sound instructional program within his or her school building. This includes using leadership and communication skills in dealing with teachers, counselors, and other professional staff members, and with classified personnel, so as to develop a climate that promotes quality educational practices.

Organizational Relationship

The junior high school principal has a line relationship with the assistant superintendent for secondary education and the superintendent of schools. He or she is directly responsible to the assistant superintendent for secondary education. The junior high school principal also has a line relationship with the building staff, which includes the assistant principal, teachers, counselors, librarian, and all other certificated and classified personnel within the building complex.

Organizational Tasks

The junior high school principal is responsible for establishing administrative processes and procedures in the junior high school for the following areas: in-service training, curriculum planning, scheduling and grading, budget development, building and grounds maintenance, classroom instruction, consulting with individual pupils, parents, and staff members; and other duties assigned by the assistant superintendent for secondary education. He or she is directly responsible for supervising and evaluating the assistant principal, teachers, counselors, librarian, educational specialists, secretaries, and custodians within the building complex.

Job Qualifications

The junior high school principal should possess the following educational and professional qualifications:

- A master's degree in educational administration.
- A State Secondary School Principal's Certificate.
- Minimum of five years experience as a classroom teacher.
- Minimum of two years experience as an assistant principal.

JOB DESCRIPTION FOR A HIGH SCHOOL BIOLOGY TEACHER

Job Summary

The high school biology teacher is responsible for teaching five periods of Biology I per school day with one noninstructional period for planning, grading papers, and individual conferences with parents and students. Teaching biology includes following the general curricular program established by the science department and approved by the building principal. The biology teacher accepts responsibility for the academic success of students when he or she is given reasonable control over those factors that contribute to such outcomes. He or she is responsible directly to the building principal.

Instructional Tasks

The high school biology teacher is responsible for promoting an effective instructional program in the classroom. This can be accomplished as follows: by evaluating the strengths and weaknesses of the curricular program and instructional materials; helping develop, implement, and evaluate new ideas, methods, and techniques for teaching biology; assisting in departmental budget preparation to ensure the appropriateness of instructional supplies; recognizing that each student is an individual with different needs and abilities; utilizing a variety of instructional techniques; serving on textbook committees; maintaining effective discipline and high academic standards; accepting constructive criticism; and recognizing the need for continuous self-evaluation.

General Professional Duties

In addition to specific instructional tasks, the high school biology teacher is also expected to maintain professional standards, including: keeping up-to-date on biology research findings; serving on committees to advise on such nonacademic affairs as school discipline, honors awards, assemblies, etc.; serving on science curriculum committees; advising guidance personnel on matters relating to the science program; showing concern for the totality of the science program; and participating in local and national science, teaching, and civic associations.

Job Qualifications

The high school biology teacher should possess the following minimum educational and professional qualifications:

- A bachelor's degree with a major or minor in biological science.
- A State Secondary School Teaching Certificate in high school biology.

APPENDIX B
SELECTION CRITERIA

SELECTION CRITERIA FOR A HIGH SCHOOL ENGLISH TEACHER

Applicant's Name _____ Date _____

A check on the scale is an indication of initial judgment. It is assumed that other sources of information may alter the interviewer's judgment as to the applicant's suitability. 1 = Inferior; 5 = Superior

SELECTION CRITERIA

A. *Personal Characteristics and Qualifications*

	1	2	3	4	5
1. Personal appearance—neat, clean, etc.					
2. Poise/stability—knows self					
3. Ability to present ideas					
4. Voice projection					
5. Use of English language/speech					
6. Pleasant personality—not irritating					
7. Exemplifies leadership traits					
8. Demonstrates good judgment					
9. Interacts well in a group					
10. Shows signs of creativity					
11. Flexible—evidence of cooperation					

Subtotal _____

B. *Professional Characteristics and Qualifications*

	1	2	3	4	5
1. Knowledge of subject matter					
2. Educational philosophy compatible with district's philosophy					
3. Concern for student differences					
4. Enthusiasm for teaching					
5. Teaching methodology—shows variety					
6. Pupil control techniques					
7. Professional attitude					
8. Knowledgeable about English curriculum					
9. Willingness to sponsor extracurricular activities					
10. Undergraduate and/or graduate grades in English					

Continued

11. Classroom management techniques
12. Job-related hobbies and/or special talents
13. Overall undergraduate and/or graduate grade-point average
14. Knowledge of teaching/learning process

1	2	3	4	5

Subtotal _____

C. *Experience and Training*
1. Relevance of previous teaching experience
2. Scope of previous teaching experience
3. Relevance of student teaching
4. Appropriateness of participation in professional organizations
5. Relevance of nonprofessional work experience

1	2	3	4	5

Subtotal _____

Total Score _____

The following is a general appraisal of this individual's promise for future success as an English teacher in our school district.

Should not be considered; poor applicant	Endorse with reservations; inferior applicant	Should be considered; average applicant	Good first impression; strong applicant	Exceptional potential; outstanding applicant

Additional comments:

Interview began _____ **Interview ended** _____

_____
Interviewer

SELECTION CRITERIA FOR A SIXTH-GRADE TEACHING POSITION

ACADEMIC CRITERIA

1. Has appropriate college or university coursework and degree(s).
2. Has earned a grade point average in undergraduate and/or graduate courses that meets the acceptable standards of the district.
3. Demonstrates through an appropriate interview a working knowledge of the English language in verbal and written context.
4. Demonstrates an understanding and working knowledge of elementary mathematics skills that are compatible with the District's mathematics curriculum guide.

Continued

5. Demonstrates the skills necessary to teach reading in a manner compatible with the district's reading curriculum guide.
6. Has had some formal or informal training in music and has developed the skill to perform with a musical instrument.
7. Has completed courses in drama or participated in extracurricular dramatic performances, plays, or musical presentations during high school or college.

PERSONAL CRITERIA

8. Indicates a willingness to interact and communicate in a constructive fashion with district staff and community constituents.
9. Exhibits healthy, considerate, mature attitudes that would promote positive intra-staff and community relationships.
10. Dresses in a manner meeting the expectations of the school district and meets socially acceptable standards of hygiene and health care.
11. Is physically capable of actively participating with minimum proficiency in a sixth-grade outdoor experience that includes repelling, canoeing, spelunking, and ropes course participation.
12. Expresses a willingness to abide by and implement the district's policies as prescribed by the board of education.

EXPERIENTIAL CRITERIA

13. Has relevant past teaching experience.
14. Has relevant student teaching experience.
15. Has a record of participating in extracurricular activities during high school and/or college (Extracurricular being defined as any organized school approved activity).
16. If applicant has had teaching experience, has demonstrated an interest in ongoing self-improvement by participating in professional workshops, seminars, college/university courses, or other professional programs.

SELECTION CRITERIA GRID FOR A SIXTH-GRADE TEACHING POSITION

Name of Applicant _____ **Date of Interview** _____

	Academic Criteria							Personal Criteria					Experiential Criteria				Total Points
	1	2	3	4	5	6	7	8	9	10	11	12	13	14	15	16	
3																	

Continued

	Academic Criteria							Personal Criteria					Experiential Criteria				Total Points
	1	2	3	4	5	6	7	8	9	10	11	12	13	14	15	16	
2																	
1																	

3 is the highest possible score **Grand Total** _____

Additional comments:

_____
Interviewer

SELECTION CRITERIA FOR AN ELEMENTARY SCHOOL TEACHER, SELF-CONTAINED CLASSROOM

Applicant _____ **Date of Interview** _____ **Interviewer** _____

	Possible Points	Designated Points
1. Professional Preparation—Does the applicant hold the necessary and desired college preparation and state certification?	25	
2. Experience—Was the applicant's past teaching experience or student teaching experience successful?	10	

Continued

3. Personal Characteristics—Are the applicant's mannerism and dress appropriate to the standards of the school district?	15	
4. Educational Philosophy—Are the educational ideas and values of the applicant compatible with the school district's policies and curriculum?	50	

Comments:

APPENDIX C
INTERVIEWING QUESTIONS AND DISCUSSION STATEMENTS

Interviewing Questions and Discussion Statements*

1. What unique qualities do you possess that we should consider?
2. What do you know about our school district?
3. Will you tell me about your hobbies?
4. What clubs and activities would you be willing to sponsor?
5. Please share with me your thoughts on:

   - Traditional education
   - Open education
   - Team teaching
   - Nongradedness
   - Large-group instruction
   - Small-group instruction

6. How do you feel about thematic (unit) planning?
7. In what ways would you provide for differentiated assignments?
8. How would you provide for the individualization of instruction?
9. What are your thoughts about PTA and other community organizations?

*Questions compiled by C. John Brannon, Superintendent of South Side Area School District, Hookstown, Pennsylvania.

10. How many students can you adequately instruct at any given time?
11. What is your philosophy of education?
12. Please tell me about the methods of evaluation that you would use.
13. Why will our school district be better for having hired you?
14. Why would you like to teach in our school district?
15. Please give me your thoughts on some recent educational literature that impressed you.
16. How would you provide for a rich educational climate in your classroom?
17. What is your conception of the way an instructional materials center should function in a school?
18. How would you utilize the services of the guidance and counseling staff?
19. What is wholesome about American education today?
20. What should be improved in American education as it exists today?
21. Do you feel you know yourself? Your hopes? Aspirations? Long-range goals?
22. What is your philosophy of life?
23. How does your area of certification relate to the other disciplines?
24. Please tell me about the artifacts you would regularly use in your instruction.
25. What is your concept of the role of the administration in relation to teachers? To students?
26. As a teacher in our district what would be your role in our community?
27. Are you familiar with the works of any of the educational philosophers?
28. Can you conceptualize educational programs and buildings in the year 2000? What might they be like?
29. In what way does your discipline (area of certification) lend itself to outdoor education?
30. Are you familiar with differentiated staffing? How would you relate to that eventuality in our district if you were, teaching here?
31. Should students have any part in the evaluation of teachers? Why?
32. To what extent should students be involved in determining what should be taught and how it should be taught?
33. What constitutes an effective classroom? Study hall?
34. Are you familiar with the scientific method of investigation? To what extent should that method be utilized in your classroom?
35. How would you handle controversial issues as they come before your class?
36. Please react to the job description prepared for the position for which you are applying.
37. What are your plans for furthering your education?
38. What, in your opinion, are the best ways to communicate with parents?
39. Is it still applicable that teachers should be exemplary in the community? Why?
40. What rights and responsibilities do you feel students should assume?
41. Please evaluate this interview and tell me how you think it could be improved to better acquaint other candidates with our district and the position for which you are applying.

Questions for Hiring a Principal—The Archdiocese of Cincinnati Office for Catholic Schools*

I. Professional Attitudes
    A. What kind of professional responsibility would you want to give members of your faculty?
        1. Do you believe in delegating authority?
        2. Do you believe that there are some problems you must solve alone?
            a. What resources would you use?
            b. How would you inform
                (1) The faculty?
                (2) The parents?
                (3) The students?

II. Interpersonal relationships
    A. Do you feel you meet people easily?
    B. Do you feel you are verbally fluent, clearly communicating your ideas to people?
    C. Do you feel you are able to communicate your enthusiasm and convictions in order to persuade those you will lead?
    D. What do you expect of the parents of the students?
    E. What would you expect of this board?
    F. Can you tell us about the methods you might use to maintain and strengthen communications among
        1. Teachers?
        2. Parents?
        3. Students?
        4. School board?
        5. Clerical help?
        6. Community people?
        7. Maintenance people?

III. Acceptance of responsibility
    A. Describe any educational situation in which you have exercised a leadership role.
    B. Once you make a decision what steps do you take to implement your decision?
    C. Do you have any personal feelings about yourself, founded in some concrete experience, that might give us some idea of your organizational ability?
        1. Projects?
        2. Programs?
        3. Administration?

*Archdiocese of Cincinnati Office for Catholic Schools, "Questions for Hiring a Principal" (Cincinati: The Archdiocese, 1980.)

IV. Understanding and evaluation of teaching
   A. Tell us a little about how you recognize effective and ineffective teaching.
   B. What evaluation techniques might you use to judge the teaching of the faculty?
   C. What are some of your ideas on in-service training for
      1. Veteran teachers?
      2. Beginning teachers?
   D. In selecting teachers for your staff what would you look for?
V. Self-evaluation
   A. How would you evaluate your own performance?
   B. Would you allow your faculty to evaluate you? If so, how?
   C. How would you expect this board to evaluate you?
   D. What do you see as the purpose of evaluation?
VI. Professional Qualifications
   A. Level of professional training
      1. What degrees do you have?
      2. In what academic areas have your studies been concentrated?
      3. How long were you a teacher?
         a. At what grade levels?
         b. How long did you teach in each school?
         c. What was your reason for leaving?
      4. In what academic areas do you feel you are strongest and weakest?
      5. Why did you decide to move into administration?
      6. What administrative positions have you held?
      7. Do you have any special training we should know about?
      8. Do you have any plans for continuing your education?
      9. What professional educational groups do you belong to?
      10. (If currently a principal) Why are you leaving your present administrative position?
   B. Knowledge of Curriculum
      1. What courses have you taken in the area of curriculum development?
      2. Have you ever participated in or initiated a curriculum innovation?
      3. What instructional changes might you develop for our school in the next few years?
      4. What long-range changes do you see in education?
         a. Do you feel it is important to make long-range plans?
         b. What steps would be necessary to reach long-range plans?
         c. Would one of your priorities be such planning?
         d. How would you go about it?
   C. Understanding of educational psychology
      1. Have you had any training in educational psychology?
      2. What is your attitude toward student discipline?
      3. What do you see as the primary work of each teacher?

APPENDIX D
JOB APPLICATIONS

TEACHER'S APPLICATION
Goodville School District

For Office Use Only

Interview Date _____

Interviewer _____   Date _____

Position _____   Soc. Sec. No. _____

I. Personal Information:

Name _____
       Last   First   Middle

Date of birth _____   Age _____

Present Address _____   Phone _____
                   Street   City   State   Zip

Permanent Address _____   Phone _____
                   Street   City   State   Zip

General conditions of health _____

Are you willing to take a physical exam? _____

II. Professional Information:

List in order of preference, the subjects or grades you are prepared to teach:

1. _____ 2. _____ 3. _____

List the Teaching Certificates held: State Retirement No. _____

_____

List Teaching Certificates held (other States):

_____

Membership in professional organizations: _____

What co-curricular activities are you prepared to sponsor (secondary level)? _____

_____

III. Teaching Experience:

List experience in chronological order (starting with first position held), and account for each school year since you began teaching.

No. Yrs Exp.	Inclusive Dates		Name of School	Location City or County, State	Grades, Sub. or Position	Annual Salary	Name of Prin.	Present Address of Principal
	From	To						

Continued

Kindergarten _____ Years   Junior High _____ Years
Elementary _____ Years   Senior High _____ Years   Other _____ Years
Total Teaching Exp. _____ Years
Name of superintendent under whom you last taught _____

IV. Educational and Professional Training:

Total Number of Hours to Date _____ Undergraduate _____ Graduate _____
Major _____ Number of Major Hrs. _____ Minor _____ Number of Minor
Hrs. _____

	Name of Instit. Attended	State	Dates Attended		Time in Yrs. and Fractions of Yrs.	Graduation		Subjects	
			From	To		Date	Degree	Major	Minor
A. Undergraduate Work									
B. Graduate Work									
C. Additional Education									

D. For both secondary and elementary majors

Hours of Student Teaching	
Place of Student Teaching	
Name of Coop. Teacher	
Subject or Grade Level of Student Teaching	

V. Professional References:

Location of confidential placement file _____

It is the responsibility of the applicant to have his/her placement file and college/university transcripts sent to the school district.

Continued

Please list three people who have firsthand knowledge of your work performance. Have these individuals send letters of reference to the personnel department if references are not included in your placement file. One of the three reference letters must be from your current or last immediate supervisor.

Name	Official Position	Present Address

Signature: _____

Goodville School District

For Office Use Only

Date Rec'd _____
Interview Date _____
Starting Date _____
Position _____
School _____
Salary _____
Term. Date _____

CLASSIFIED APPLICATION FOR EMPLOYMENT

Position _____

PLEASE PRINT OR TYPE

Today's Date _____

PERSONAL INFORMATION

Name _____
      Last   First   Middle
Present address _____
            Street   City   State   Zip code
Phone _____ **Social Security No.** _____
Date of birth _____ **Place** _____
General condition of health _____
Are you willing to take a physical exam? _____

Continued

EDUCATION INFORMATION

Circle Highest Grade

Completed: 1 2 3 4 5 6 7 8 9 10 11 12 13 14 15 16

Name of school and location:	Dates of Attendance	Day or Night	Full- or Part-time	Type of Course(s)
Elem:	from _____ to _____	_____	_____	_____
Jr. High	from _____ to _____	_____	_____	_____
Sr. High	from _____ to _____	_____	_____	_____
College	from _____ to _____	_____	_____	_____

MILITARY SERVICE

Branch _____ From _____ To _____ Present Status _____

Highest rank _____ Duties _____

List any special training received in service _____

Type of discharge _____

EMPLOYMENT RECORD

List the most recent employment first and work back consecutively

From	To	Firm Name & Supervisor	Firm Address	Salary Beg.	Last	Position, Duties and Reason for Termination

List any experience, skills, or qualifications which you feel would especially fit you for work in our district: _____

Are you a member of the Non-Teacher Retirement System? _____

If Yes, give Retirement No. _____

GENERAL INFORMATION

When can you start work? _____ What wage or salary do you expect? _____

List civic organizations to which you belong and office(s) held within last three years:

_____

Have you ever been convicted of any violation of law other than a traffic violation? _____

If yes, give particulars of each conviction and state what disposition was made of each:

_____

Have three people with firsthand knowledge of your work performance send letters of reference to the personnel department. One of the three reference letters must be from your current or last immediate supervisor.

_____
                                                    Signature

APPLICATION FOR HIGH SCHOOL PRINCIPAL

PERSONAL INFORMATION

Date _____

Last Name	First	Middle

Business Address _____ Telephone_____

City _____ State _____ Zip Code _____

Home Address _____ Telephone _____

City _____ State _____ Zip Code _____

PRESENT POSITION _____

School's student enrollment _____ School's annual budget _____

Salary during current school year _____

PROFESSIONAL PREPARATION: Highest degree earned _____

Institution and Location	Major/Minor	Degree	Date Received
_____	_____	____	_____
_____	_____	____	_____

My confidential file can be acquired from:

Name of Institution: _____

Address: _____

_____

SUMMARY OF EXPERIENCE: List all experience in reverse chronological order. Please include both school and nonschool experience.

Institution and Location	Position	From/To	Years	Size/Unit	Highest Salary
_____	____	____	___	____	____
_____	____	____	___	____	____
_____	____	____	___	____	____
_____	____	____	___	____	____

Type of administrator certificate held _____

In which state(s) _____

QUESTIONS

The following questions are designed to help the interviewers know you as a person and as a professional. Your concise and candid responses are very important.

1. Why do (did) you want to become a high school principal?

2. What do (would) you consider to be your major strengths as an administrator?

3. In your previous experience, in what ways have you most influenced a school?

Continued

4. What basic problem-solving approaches or principles do (would) you use to deal with school issues?

5. What methods or approaches do (would) you use to bring about change in a school?

6. How do (would) you delegate responsibilities to others?

7. As a principal, what communication approaches or systems are (would be) most effective for you?

8. How do (will) you, as a principal, work most effectively with central-office administrators?

9. What about being a high school principal has been (will be) most rewarding to you?

_____

Signature

SELECTED BIBLIOGRAPHY

Al-Rubaiy, Kathleen, "Five Steps to Better Hiring," *The Executive Educator,* 15, no. 8 (August 1993), pp. 21–23.

Caliendo, Richard J., "Selecting Capable Teachers," *Spectrum: Journal of School Research and Information,* 2, no. 1 (Winter 1986), pp. 22–27.

Davis, Beverly Irby and Genevieve Brown, "Your Interview Image," *The Executive Educator,* 14, no. 6 (June 1992), pp. 22–24.

Ficklen, Ellen, "Inflated Resume, Deflated Career," *The Executive Educator,* 10, no. 6 (June 1988), pp. 22–23.

Finn, Jr., Chester E., "Pick Principals With Promise," *The Executive Educator,* 10, no. 6 (June 1988), pp. 20–22.

Gokey, William, "Hiring? Consider Expanded Interviews," *The Executive Educator,* 11, no. 3 (March 1989), pp. 27–28.

Goodale, James G., *The Fine Art of Interviewing.* Englewood Cliffs, N.J.: Prentice-Hall, 1982.

Kowalski, Theodore J., Phillip McDaniel, Andrew W. Place, and Ulrich C. Reitzug, "Factors that Principals Consider Most Important in Selecting New Teachers," *Spectrum: Journal of School Research and Information,* 10, no. 3 (Summer 1992), pp. 34–39.

Principal Selection Guide. Washington, D.C.: Superintendent of Documents, U.S. Government Printing Office, 1988.

Redfern, George B., "Using Job Descriptions as an Administrative Tool," *Spectrum: Journal of School Research and Information,* 2, no. 1 (Winter 1984), pp. 21–26.

"Selection of Principals More by Politics than Merit," *Education USA,* 26, no. 16 (December 1983), pp. 121–128.

Steller, Arthur W., "Chart a Course for Selecting New Principals," *Updating School Board Policies,* 15, no. 5 (May 1994), pp. 1–3.

Zakariya, Sally Banks, "Wanted: Criminal Background Checks," *The Executive Educator,* 10, no. 8 (August 1988), pp. 17–19.

5

PLACEMENT AND INDUCTION

After a person has been hired, the next two processes involve placing that individual in an assignment and orientating him or her to the school community. Both of these processes are covered in this chapter because they are interrelated; both also are continual processes because some staff members will be reassigned each year and thus will require a certain amount of induction. Placement and induction, therefore, should not be viewed as a one-time task but rather as an ongoing concern of the personnel department.

PLACEMENT

In all but the very smallest districts, a new employee should not be told that he or she has been hired only for a particular job in a specific school building. The selection process explicated in the previous chapter will result in the employment of an individual for a certain position. However, the employee must understand from the outset that the assignment can be changed, even immediately, if the administration deems such to be in the best interest of the school district.

Placement Policy

The sample placement policy given below specifies how placement could be handled by a school district:

> The placement of employees within the school system is the responsibility of the superintendent of schools. The superintendent may delegate the implementation of the placement process to other appropriate administrators, but he or she ultimately retains the responsibility for placement. In determining assignments, the wishes of the employee are taken into consideration if these do not conflict with the requirements of the district's programming, staff balancing, and the welfare of students. Other factors that will be taken into consideration in making

assignments are educational preparation and training, certification, experience, working relationships, and seniority with the school system.

A staffing survey form will be secured from each employee annually in February to assist in making assignment plans for the forthcoming school year.

Professional staffing assignments will be announced by April 1. Administrators affected by an assignment change will be notified of the change by the superintendent of schools. Teachers affected by a change in grade or subject assignment will be notified of the change by their respective building principals. Teachers affected by a building transfer will be notified of the transfer by an administrator from the personnel department.

Classified staffing assignments will be announced by May 1 and will become effective on July 1. Supervisors and managers affected by an assignment change will be notified of the change by the superintendent of schools or his designated representative. Other employees affected by a change in assignment will be notified by their immediate supervisors.

The board of education placement policy given above clearly specifies the role of the superintendent in assigning all staff members to particular positions within the school system. The planning required in making assignments is very complicated, demanding the full-time attention of at least one personnel administrator in most metropolitan school districts. The human resource planning inventories described in Chapter 2 could provide the personnel department with valuable information for making assignments. Of course, it is to the advantage of the school district to make assignments that are in harmony with the wishes of the employees. A significant cause of low morale, particularly among teachers, is the assigning of individuals to schools, grade levels, and subject areas that they find undesirable. Using the staffing survey is one method of minimizing discontent over reassignments. The survey instrument can be very simple in construction and very easy to fill out. Exhibit 5–1 is an example of an instrument that would provide the personnel department with information concerning the placement preferences of staff members.

The personnel department must also consider a number of circumstances in trying to fulfill the wishes of employees in making reassignments. Some of these circumstances include maternity leave, resignations, retirements, deaths, and terminations. In addition, the following variables must be taken into consideration: staff balancing, affirmative action requirements, the certification of professional employees, experience in an assignment, and working relationships.

For example, a teacher who is having difficulty accepting a certain principal's philosophy about how to handle children with behavioral problems might request reassignment to another school. The personnel department then would determine if another position is or will become available that requires the certification qualifications of the teacher. Further, an analysis must be made to determine if such a reassignment would upset the balance in either school between experienced and inexperienced teachers, male and female teachers, and minority representation.

The welfare of students and implementation of the school district's instructional program are other important considerations in making reassignments. An industrial arts teacher who is certificated also as a physical education teacher might be denied reassignment to the

---

EXHIBIT 5–1   Staffing Survey

Name _____

Present Job Position Assignment _____

Present Building Assignment _____

I wish to be considered for reassignment as follows:

Requested Job Position Assignment _____

Requested Building Assignment _____

I understand that reassignment requests will be reviewed but are not guaranteed and that all decisions will be based on seniority, availability, and will be made in accordance with the best interests of the school district.

_____
Signature

---

physical education department because of the scarcity in applicants for industrial arts positions or because he has taught only industrial arts throughout his fifteen-year career as a teacher.

When there are a number of requests for reassignment, seniority is a defensible criterion in making decisions only after the other variables have been considered. Those employees with the most seniority in the school district should be given the first choices in assignments; involuntary reassignments should be given to those employees with the least seniority. Involuntary reassignments are sometimes necessary because of unexpected vacancies.

Placement Grievance Procedure

If an employee has a concern regarding a permanent or temporary change in assignment, the following procedure must be observed: (1) The employee should initiate an interview with the administrator who processed the assignment change. (2) If agreement is not reached at this point, the employee may initiate an interview with the superintendent of schools and formally request a review of the reassignment; should the employee continue to be dissatisfied, he may resign his position with the school district.

The due process presented in this grievance procedure identifies the superintendent of schools as the ultimate authority in reviewing assignments within the school district. A grievance procedure is necessary to effectively operate the district and highlights the fact

---

EXHIBIT 5–2   Request for Assignment Review

Name _____

Present Job Assignment _____

Present Building Assignment _____

Job Reassignment _____

Building Reassignment _____

Please state in detail why you would like to have your assignment reviewed:

_____

_____

_____

_____

_____

_____

_____

_____

                                    _____
                                                    Signature

---

that an individual is employed in the district and not in a particular school or position. Exhibit 5–2 is an example of a form that can be used when reviewing an assignment that an employee finds undesirable.

INDUCTION

Induction is the process designed to acquaint newly employed individuals with the community, the school district, and with their colleagues. Reassigned employees need to be acquainted with their new school, program, and colleagues. Much of what this section covers is equally applicable to both newly employed and reassigned individuals. It is an administrative responsibility that is often neglected or loosely organized in many school districts. The industrial and business communities place a high priority on induction; they have recognized for many years the cause-and-effect relationship of this process to employee retention and job performance.

An effective induction program must have well-defined objectives that reflect the needs of new employees and the specific philosophy of the school system. Although the objectives of an induction program will vary among individual school districts, some universal objectives should be common to all programs:

1. To make the employee feel welcome and secure.
2. To help the employee become a member of the "team."
3. To inspire the employee towards excellence in performance.
4. To help the employee adjust to the work environment.
5. To provide information about the community, school systems, school building, faculty, and students.
6. To acquaint the individual with other employees with whom he will be associated.
7. To facilitate the opening of school each year.

These objectives support the ultimate purpose of an induction program, to promote quality education for children. The employee who is able to adjust in a reasonable period of time to a new position helps to accomplish this purpose.

Once the overall purpose and specific objectives are defined, the subsequent steps include deciding on the most effective method of implementation and the content of the program. Some school districts consider a one- or two-day orientation at the beginning of each school year to be sufficient. Other districts provide an ongoing induction program to orient new employees and reassigned employees. Certainly, an ongoing program is better able to meet the concerns of reassigned individuals in large school districts who will need information about their new school building, the faculty, the students, and the community it serves. The fallacy, as previously mentioned, is assuming that induction is a one-time task, only for new employees.

Induction programs fall into one of two major categories: informational and personal adjustment programs. Informational programs, in turn, are concerned with either initial material or updating information. Initial data consist primarily of information about the school system, the community it serves, and the particular school in which the employee will work. New employees, of course, are targeted for this type of program. Updating informational programs are geared to the employee who is reassigned; they concentrate on the particular school and community to which he or she has been reassigned.

Personal adjustment programs aim at helping the newly hired or reassigned employee interact with the principal, faculty, students, and parents of a particular school. With a classified employee, the emphasis will be on helping the individual interact with his or her supervisor and fellow workers as well as those administrators, faculty members, students, and parents with whom he or she will come into contact.

The following four sections deal with the content and methods of four induction programs. The first is most effective in orienting individuals to the school system; the second helps orient individuals to the community served by the school system and/or particular school. The third is designed to orient employees to the school to which they are assigned; the fourth is geared to orienting the employees to the people with whom they must establish a relationship.

The School District

The personnel department is responsible for implementing this part of the induction program. The main thrust of this program is to convey an understanding of the school system's policies and services and to identify system-wide personnel such as assistant superinten-dents, program directors, and coordinators.

All employees should receive a copy of the school board policies and a copy of the employee manuals that pertain to their specific job. They should be allowed time during the orientation sessions to become familiar with these policies and manuals. To be truly ef-fective, the program should also give the employees the opportunity to ask clarifying ques-tions about policies and procedures.

The employee benefits provided by the school district must be carefully explained to new employees. Major medical and hospitalization insurance applications, retirement forms, government payroll withholding forms, and other enrollment documents are gener-ally explained to new employees at the earliest possible time during the orientation process. Most insurance programs require a new employee to enroll a spouse and dependents within thirty days after commencing employment. If a spouse or dependent is enrolled after that time, he or she is usually required to take a physical examination, and the insurance com-pany may deny coverage because of a medical condition. For example, a newly employed teacher who does not enroll his wife in a medical insurance program within the thirty days grace period may be denied coverage for her because she has a heart condition. The most effective vehicle for conveying an understanding of policies, procedures, and services is the small-group seminar. In this format, five to ten employees are assigned to a personnel administrator who presents the material and instructs them about how to fill out all neces-sary forms. This is usually done within the first few days of employment. A meeting, break-fast, or luncheon could be held each year, during which the superintendent of schools, board members, and other central-office administrators and staff members are introduced to new employees. Such a special event is very effective in conveying to new employees the idea that they are important to the district.

The Community

Orientation to the community is also the responsibility of the personnel department. Em-ployees should be presented with information about the social, racial, cultural, ethnic, and religious makeup of the community. Specific topics to be covered should include occupa-tions, customs, clubs and organizations, church denominations, museums, libraries, col-leges or universities, and social services.

Orientation to the community usually begins during the selection process, particularly during the interview. Candidates are told about the community and questioned about how they would respond to its various publics if they were employed with the district.

A very effective way to begin the orientation process after selection is with a tour of the community conducted by the personnel department or, perhaps, the Chamber of Com-merce. Other methods include introducing new employees at club or organization meet-ings and inviting representatives from community resource services, such as libraries or museums, to address the new employees about their programs.

Orientation to the community does not end with the initial program; rather, a contin-uous updating should be provided by the personnel department. For example, as commu-nity service resources are improved or changed, this information should be brought to the attention of school staff members.

The School Building and Program

The building principal has the responsibility for orienting new teachers to a particular school. First and most important is introducing new teachers to all other employees, both professional and classified, who work in the building. Classified employees should be introduced by their immediate supervisors to both professional and other classified employees.

New employees must know in detail the layout of the building in which they will work. This is best accomplished by giving new employees a tour of the facility and, if it is a large school, presenting each person with a map.

Explaining administrative procedures is also the responsibility of the building principal. It is essential for new teachers to know how to complete attendance forms, where to obtain supplies and materials, how to requisition audio-visual equipment, and how the school schedule operates. An initial conference with the building principal, an assistant principal, or a department chairperson is one method of explaining these procedures to new staff members.

Orientating the new teacher to the instructional program is the responsibility of the building principal. Like administrative procedures, this may be delegated to an assistant principal or a department chairperson. At times explaining the instructional program might be a central-office task, especially when the school district has subject matter coordinators and a uniform curriculum in all the schools.

In some school districts a new teacher is assigned to an experienced teacher during the first year of employment. The new teacher will then have a definite person to call on when questions arise about the curriculum or building procedures. This has proven to be a successful technique because the experienced teacher does not pose a threat to the new teacher, whereas an administrator might.

Personal Adjustment

In line with the current research on the effectiveness of participatory decision making, establishing good working relationships among colleagues is viewed as most important if an organization is to achieve its objectives. In a service-rendering organization, such as a school district, that is even more crucial because good human relations is the basis for the effective delivery of services. Forming relationships with other staff members helps an employee to achieve satisfaction in his or her work. Nothing is less satisfying than being alienated from colleagues in an organization.

The responsibility for helping a new employee form meaningful relationships with other staff members rests with the individual's immediate supervisor or, if the new employee is a teacher, with the building principal.

A highly effective orientation method for new employees is to organize activities that give them the opportunity to socialize with other staff members. Many schools make a practice of serving refreshments and allotting a certain amount of time for personal interaction either before or after meetings. Christmas parties or dinners are also an effective means of enabling employees to meet each other on a social level, which can provide staff members with new insight about each other.

Service on faculty, school, and district committees is another way for employees to become acquainted with each other while providing the district with valuable assistance in carrying out projects. Textbook selection committees, energy conservation committees, and principals' advisory committees are common in many school districts and have proven to be very successful.

Finally, it is important for professional staff members to become affiliated with local, state, and national teacher and administrator organizations. These organizations not only provide an avenue for exchanging ideas but also are a source of current professional information. Their social activities certainly help the individual form relationships with professionals in other school districts.

A Final Note

Many new employees come from other states or, at least, have lived beyond the immediate vicinity of the school district. Although not a part of the formal induction program, helping the new employee relocate is a valuable service that the personnel department can provide. Relocation can be facilitated by making initial contacts with real estate agents for new employees and by chauffeuring them around the area, pointing out aspects of the neighborhoods reasonably close to their school and the district.

Evaluating the effectiveness of induction programs is an extremely important part of the induction process. Evaluation of the programs for professional employees is best accomplished by establishing an induction committee chaired by a personnel administrator and composed of teachers, principals, and supervisors. This committee should gather input from new teachers which can be used to make changes in the programs. This same procedure can be initiated to evaluate programs for classified employees, that is, by establishing a committee composed of classified staff members and supervisors to react to the suggestions and insights of new employees after their first year with the district.

THE INDUCTION OF FIRST-YEAR TEACHERS

An area of special concern is the induction of first-year teachers. Douglas Hunt, who directed a project on the induction of beginning teachers, summarized a common insight about the plight of these teachers which still holds true:

> The importance of the proper induction and orientation of new appointees cannot be overestimated. Too many potentially capable teachers, including many who have devoted years of preparation to their careers, resign their positions and give up teaching because of an unnecessarily unpleasant and frustrating initial experience in a school that lacks an effective comprehensive orientation program. The consequence is unfortunate, not only for the young teacher but also for society, which loses the valuable services of a trained teacher.[1]

---

[1]Jay E. Greene, *School Personnel Administration* (New York; Chilton Book Co., 1971), p. 214.

James Conant, the noted educator, was very vocal about this concern and had recommended a number of suggestions that he believed should be guaranteed by school boards to first-year teachers. They include

1. Limited teaching responsibility.

2. Aid in gathering instructional materials.

3. Advice of experienced teachers whose own loads are reduced so that they can work with the new teachers in their own classrooms.

4. Shifting to more experienced teachers those pupils who create problems beyond the ability of the novices to handle effectively.

5. Specialized instruction concerning the characteristics of the community, the neighborhood, and the students.[2]

The National Association of Secondary Principals (NASSP) considers induction to be a continuation of teacher education and further postulates that a significant amount of learning by the new teacher will take place during the induction process.[3] NASSP initiated a project to study the induction of first-year teachers, which basically elaborated on Conant's recommendations. The committee also developed a four-phase time period during which induction should occur. Phase I would begin during the summer months and would concentrate on orienting the new teachers to the school, school district, and community. Phase II, scheduled for the week before school opens, would emphasize procedures and identify support personnel. Phase III, during the first semester, would include daily meetings between a beginning teacher and a cooperating master teacher. They would review practical aspects of teaching, such as lesson planning, testing, grading, and disciplinary techniques. During the second semester, the final phase would emphasize a more theoretical approach to teaching. The new teacher would be encouraged to begin evaluating his or her performance and verbalizing his or her philosophy of education.

MENTORING AS AN INDUCTION STRATEGY FOR BEGINNING TEACHERS

The education reform movement, which formally began with the publication of *A Nation at Risk,* has resulted in the enacting of legislation in over sixteen states calling for the inclusion of *mentoring* as an induction strategy for newly hired teachers. These states have mentoring programs that differ one from the other to some degree. However, the basic concept is the same in all of the programs, which is the pairing of an experienced teacher with a beginning teacher in order to provide the beginning teacher with support and encouragement.

The experienced teacher can act as a role model for the beginning teacher and through coaching help the teacher develop his or her competencies, self-esteem, and sense of

---

[2]James Conant, *The Education of American Teachers,* cited in Douglas W. Hunt, "Guidelines for Principals." Project on the Induction of Beginning Teachers (Arlington, Va.: National Association for Secondary School Principals, 1969), p. 3.

[3]See Hunt, "Guidelines for Principals," pp. 3–8.

professionalism. In some school districts, the beginning teacher attends traditional orientation and induction programs. A mentor is assigned to each teacher, who then provides support throughout the entire year. In other school districts, beginning teachers are assigned to a group comprising other beginning teachers, the interaction of which is facilitated by a mentor.

It is important to clarify the role of the mentor to building principals and to the beginning teachers. This is especially true in relation to the issue of teacher evaluation. The mentor should not be an evaluator but rather someone who assists. Teacher evaluation should be the responsibility of administrators only.

The criteria for selecting mentors and the process for matching such mentors with beginning teachers are also important considerations. Research indicates that mentors are successful when they are older than the beginning teachers and when they are of the same gender.[4]

Other research sets forth the issues that confront beginning teachers and therefore reveals the kinds of competencies that mentors must possess. This is extremely helpful information in the mentor selection process. Beginning teachers need assistance from mentors in handling discipline problems, in classroom management, in lesson planning, in understanding the written and unwritten rules of the school, in developing socialization skills, and in developing techniques for handling parent conferences.[5]

Newly selected mentors will usually require some type of staff development in order to acquire or enhance certain skills. For example, programs to enhance supervision and coaching techniques or programs that update the mentors on instructional strategies can be most helpful.

The success of mentoring programs has not been significantly documented through research at this writing. However, preliminary observations seem to indicate that this is an effective first-year teacher induction technique.

MENTORING AS AN INDUCTION STRATEGY FOR BEGINNING ADMINISTRATORS

While mentoring programs for beginning teachers are becoming commonplace, mentoring programs for beginning administrators are rare, indeed! Ohio is an exception. This state plan mandates the following:

> Participation of currently employed, experienced administrators in the planning of the entry-year program.
> Provision of initial orientation for the new staff member, including an introduction to: the pupils and community; school policies, procedures and routines;

---

[4]C. Galvey-Hjornevik, "Mentoring Among Teachers: A Review of the Literature," *Journal of Teacher Education,* 37, (1986), pp. 6–11.

[5]T. Brzoska, *Mentor Teacher Handbook* (Vancouver, Wash.: Evergreen School District, 1987), p. 288.

courses of study; competency-based education programs; the layout and facilities of the assigned building(s); the nature of the entry-year program; and "additional information an entry-year person may need to be adequately prepared for a specific assignment."

Provision of ongoing assistance for the entry-year person differentiated to provide for professional needs related to his or her specific assignment.

Ongoing assistance in acquiring knowledge of the district curriculum, responsibilities for implementing that curriculum, and the instructional resources available for such implementation.

Assistance with management tasks identified as especially difficult.

Provision of a mentor for the entry-year administrator. The mentor must hold an administrative personnel certificate similar to that of the entry-year person.[6]

The Dayton City School District in Ohio expanded the state's requirements for mentors. The volunteer mentors must have between two to ten years of effective experience in their current positions or roles with Dayton Public Schools; be interested in working with relatively inexperienced administrators to assist them with their personal and professional improvement; be willing to share vulnerabilities, as well as experiences and strengths; serve as "friendly critics"; and make time in hectic schedules to serve as a helper.[7]

An evaluation of the program in Dayton after the initial year of the mandate brought forth the following conclusion:

> In summary, the experience with this program for school administrators has been very positive from the perspective of both the school district and the participating administrators. The program has done much to alleviate the natural feelings of anxiety that accompany the entry year for district school administrative personnel. For school districts that recognize the value of new administrative staff getting started on the right foot, such a program deserves consideration.[8]

Administrators who were mentors have indicated receiving many benefits as a result of their participation. Among these benefits are exposure to ideas from other school districts, learning about research, satisfaction from being a teacher again, and affirmation of their professional competence.[9]

---

[6]William R. Drury, "Entry-Year Administrator Induction: A State and Local School District Model," *Spectrum: Journal of School Research and Information,* 6, no. 1 (Winter 1988), p. 8.

[7]Drury, "Entry-Year Administrator Induction," p. 9.

[8]Drury, "Entry-Year Administrator Induction," p. 10.

[9]Marsha A. Playko and John C. Daresh, "Mentoring Programs for Aspiring Administrators: An Analysis of Benefits to Mentors," *Spectrum: Journal of School Research and Information,* 11, no. 3 (Summer 1993), pp. 14–15.

AN INDUCTION MODEL

The approach exemplified in Appendix A, Orientation Checklist for Newly Assigned Teachers, is based on induction models used in business and industry. This model attempts to deal with the major problems associated with induction through a series of one-on-one interviews, explanations, observations, and evaluative discussions. This model constitutes an expansion of the mentoring approach.

The new teacher encounters key staff members who can offer assistance in becoming acclimated to the total school community. This approach applies the "team management" concept to the induction process. Eight to ten people are selected to serve on the induction team based on their position, experience, and professional expertise. The most appropriate team in a high school would include the principal, an assistant principal, the new teacher's department chairperson, a guidance counselor, an audio-visual coordinator, the activities director, the athletic director, a student council advisor, a librarian, and a senior faculty member.

Each of these individuals will meet with the new teacher on at least two scheduled occasions during the academic year. The principal, assistant principal, and department chairperson individually will observe a class taught by the new teacher during the first semester. A conference is held one week prior to each observation in order to discuss the content of the lesson and the teaching techniques that will be used by the teacher. A post-observation conference between the teacher and observer is then held to review the teacher's performance.

The observer prepares a written critique of the class, including a mutually agreed on action plan for improving the teacher's performance. This report may describe points on which the teacher and observer disagree. The teacher receives a copy of the critique, which is filed with the building principal.

The guidance counselor, audio-visual coordinator, activities director, athletic director, student council advisor, librarian, and senior faculty member are selected to provide support to the new teacher. These professionals are valuable resource persons who are associated with different aspects of the school. Through discussions with these staff members, the new teacher is given the opportunity to seek advice and help in dealing with student-related problems and instructional concerns.

Appendix B, Induction Calendar, is an example of an instrument that can be used with the new teacher. It is a complete schedule of planned encounters with colleagues and supervisors. When the names of the various individuals are filled in, the new teacher can see the extent of the induction program, which, in turn, may alleviate some of his or her first-year teaching apprehension.

SUMMARY

After a person has been hired, the next two processes involve placing that individual in an assignment and orienting him to the school community.

The placement of employees within the school system is the responsibility of the superintendent of schools. The planning required in making assignments is a very complicated task, demanding the full-time attention of at least one personnel administrator in most metropolitan-area school districts. It is to the advantage of the school district to make assignments that are in harmony with the wishes of the employees. A staffing survey is one method of systematically gathering information on the placement preferences of employees.

Other variables that the personnel department must take into consideration in making assignments include staff balancing, certification requirements, experience, and working relationships. However, the welfare of students and implementation of the school district's instructional program are the most important considerations. When there are a number of requests for reassignment, seniority is a defensible criteria after these other variables are considered. A due process should be established to give employees the opportunity to have an assignment reviewed by the appropriate administrator.

Induction is the process designed to acquaint newly employed individuals with the school system and with other staff members. It is also the process for acquainting reassigned employees with their new school, program, and colleagues. An effective induction program must have well-defined objectives that will help the employee to feel welcome and secure, to become a member of the "team," to be inspired towards excellence in performance, to adjust to the work environment, and to become familiar with the school community.

Induction programs fall into one of two major categories: informational and personal adjustment programs. Informational programs are concerned with providing either initial material or updated information. Initial data consist primarily of information about the school system, the community it serves, and the school where the new employee will work. Updated informational programs are geared to the employee who is reassigned; they concentrate on a particular school and community. Personal adjustment programs are designed to help the newly hired or reassigned employee interact with the other people for whom and with whom he or she will work.

To orient new employees effectively to the school district, policies and services must be thoroughly explained and system-wide personnel identified. Orientation to the community must convey to employees a knowledge of the social, cultural, ethnic, racial, and religious makeup of the community. The occupations, customs, clubs and organizations, church denominations, museums, libraries, colleges and universities, and social services are also topics that should be covered in this program.

Orienting a new employee to a particular school begins with an introduction to the other staff members. A tour of the facility and an explanation of administrative procedures along with an orientation to the instructional program are also important aspects of this induction.

Personal adjustment orientation centers on encouraging new employees to establish working relationships with their colleagues. Organized activities such as faculty meetings, holiday parties or dinners, faculty and district committees, and membership in professional organizations provide new employees with the opportunity to establish desired relationships with other professionals.

Evaluating the effectiveness of the induction process is extremely important and will provide the necessary data for improving the programs.

An area of special concern centers on the induction of first-year teachers. Many potentially excellent teachers are lost to the education profession because they were not properly inducted. A number of suggestions and models have been developed. They all recognize the importance of giving first-year teachers time to consult with colleagues and providing them with feedback concerning their performance. Many school districts have developed mentoring programs not only for beginning teachers but also for entry-year administrators.

APPENDIX A*
ORIENTATION CHECKLIST FOR NEWLY ASSIGNED TEACHERS

ORIENTATION CHECKLIST FOR NEWLY ASSIGNED TEACHERS

School building: Questions concerning this
                                                    should be directed to:

NAME	POSITION	DEGREES	DEPT.	DATE OF EMPLOYMENT

The majority of new teachers begin their careers with an enthusiastic, sincere desire to be successful. Each looks not only to the principal but to various professional co-workers for information and instruction concerning his or her specific position, equipment, materials, and numerous regulations that apply to the teaching profession. Coupled with professional preparation, personal drive, and creativity, success or failure of a new member of the staff rests in large part on his or her interaction and cooperation with supervisors and fellow workers.

The checklist that follows has been devised as a minimum measure of the responsibilities that professional staff members have to newly hired teachers in their orientation and induction into the teaching profession in a specific system and locale.

TO BE DONE

WHO	WHEN	ACTION TO BE TAKEN	NOTES
Superintendent or Assistant Superintendent for Personnel	Date contract signed	1. Welcome to school district. 2. Discuss district regulations concerning length of school day, pay periods, job assignment. 3. Give out district handbook, which includes available information about fringe benefits, retirement, payroll deductions, etc.	
NAME	DATE	4. Present signed copy of contract and related information concerning Teachers Association Agreement.	
Principal	Preservice interview	1. Welcome to the school. 2. Give out and discuss: a copy of school philosophy, faculty handbook, student handbook (some topics, e.g., discipline).	
NAME	DATE		

Continued

*Adapted from the following: Ronald Gagnepoin, M. A., "Induction Schedule" (Unpublished research paper, St. Louis University, 1978.)

TO BE DONE			
WHO	**WHEN**	**ACTION TO BE TAKEN**	**NOTES**
		3. Discuss newly contracted teacher's resume and the manner in which the information in this document can help the teacher with students.	
		4. The school orientation-induction calendar is presented and explained (assistance offered, observations and critique discussions, interviews).	
		5. Introduce to assistant principal.	
Assistant Principal ———— NAME	Preservice Interview ———— DATE	1. Welcome to staff. 2. Discuss special administration procedures: reporting teacher or student absenteeism, policies on leaves of absence, workshops, instructional needs, etc. 3. Introduce the teacher to department chairperson, librarian, guidance counselor, student activities director, A-V coordinator, student council advisor, athletic director (all members of induction team).	
Department Chairperson ———— NAME	Inservice day through first week ———— DATE	1. Welcome the teacher to the department. 2. Introduce the teacher to other members of the department. 3. Discuss and explore topics of concern: departmental objectives, classroom methods, text(s) and workbook(s), experiences of person (travel, clubs, hobbies, etc.) 4. Review school/district policies concerning guest speakers, field trips, films and other materials, assignments of students. 5. Discuss lesson planning—what the teacher is going to do, or how it will be done; what the department chairperson expects to be done. 6. Discuss grading system and entire philosophy for evaluation of student progress within school system. 7. Discuss association memberships that are recommended for professional growth and development.	
Guidance Counselor ———— NAME	By end of second week ———— DATE	1. Reintroduce yourself and welcome the teacher. 2. Discuss general characteristics of the student body. 3. Explore services provided to students and the role that the teacher may play in directing students to counselors.	

Continued

TO BE DONE

WHO	WHEN	ACTION TO BE TAKEN	NOTES
		4. Explain academic advisement program and the role of the teacher. 5. Discuss the discipline/communication problems the teacher may be having with students.	
A-V Coordinator _____ NAME	By end of second week _____ DATE	1. Reintroduce yourself and explain the role of A-V coordinator. 2. Explain procedures for acquiring various pieces of equipment (usage, forms involved, time factors, etc.) along with how to set up and operate equipment; indicate common problems, appropriate action to correct, etc.; detail methods for obtaining required locations for use of hardware and equipment when applicable.	
Activities Director, Student Council Advisor, Athletic Director _____ NAMES	By end of second week _____ DATE	1. Reintroduce yourselves and explain areas of responsibility. 2. Explain the various types of activities currently available to the student body. 3. Discuss the procedures for organizing activities—district rules, State Athletic Association rules, etc. 4. Explain the financing of activities, how faculty members are compensated, and limits that exist concerning money. 5. Discuss the various rules established for use of school facilities outside the normal school day and explain the procedures that must be followed for club activities, fund raising, etc.	
Librarian _____ NAME	By end of second week _____ DATE	1. Reintroduce yourself and explain the role of the librarian. 2. Explain library procedures and services available to the teacher and students.	
Department Chairperson _____ NAME	By end of second week _____ DATE	1. Meet with the new teacher and discuss problems that may have occurred. 2. Establish observation date for following week. a) What will teacher be covering? b) What methods will be used? c) What particular item(s) would the teacher like the chairperson to pay special attention to during the class?	Observation Date _____ Period _____ Class _____ Level _____ Room _____

Continued

TO BE DONE

WHO	WHEN	ACTION TO BE TAKEN	NOTES
		3. By talking with the teacher, try to alleviate any fears he or she may have regarding the observation.	
		4. Inform principal of the date and period of the observation if a substitute teacher is needed to fill in for the chairperson.	
Department Chairperson NAME	After observation, during next planning period of new teacher DATE	1. Meet with the teacher and discuss observation. a) Very important to emphasize positive items especially those the teacher might not be aware of. b) Carefully discuss item(s) about which the teacher wanted feedback. c) Be certain to call attention to any negative items and suggest ways teacher might improve. Discuss thoroughly and try to c) work out an action plan on one or more items with the teacher. 2. Write up a report summarizing both the good and bad points, points of disagreement, and the action plan agreed on to remedy any weakness. 3. Give a copy of the report to the teacher and to the principal. 4. Discuss with the principal the need for further observation.	
Senior Faculty Member NAME	By end of third week DATE	1. Reintroduce yourself and reidentify your role for teacher. 2. Find out how the teacher is faring. Discuss experiences you have had that might help teacher to identify with you. 3. Answer those questions/problems you can and direct the teacher to particular people for more detailed answers to questions you are not able to answer.	
Principal NAME	By end of fourth week DATE	1. Meet with the teacher and discuss problems mentioned in department chairperson's report. Also, explore the success or failure the teacher has experienced in carrying out the action plan. 2. Establish observation date for following week. a) What will teacher be covering? b) What methods will be used? c) What particular item(s) would the teacher like the principal to pay special attention to during the class?	Observation Date _____ Period _____ (different from first) Class_____ Level _____ Room _____

Continued

TO BE DONE

WHO	WHEN	ACTION TO BE TAKEN	NOTES
		3. Make certain that you will not be observing the same period as during the first observation.	
A-V Coordinator NAME	By end of fourth week DATE	1. Meet with the teacher, reintroduce yourself if necessary; talk further with the teacher about equipment and if necessary, demonstrate use of equipment. 2. Suggest some equipment (if teacher has not yet used any equipment) that might facilitate his or her teaching. 3. Review procedure for getting and using equipment. Encourage the teacher to incorporate audiovisual techniques into classroom instruction.	
Principal NAME	After obser-vation, during next plan-ning period of teacher DATE	1. Meet with the teacher and discuss observation. a) Emphasize the teacher's positive points. b) Carefully review your observations on items that the teacher wanted feedback about. c) Discuss items mentioned by department chairperson. Carefully explore weak points of instruction and suggest further ways to improve. d) Update the action plan. 2. It is very important to avoid too authoritarian an approach in your discussion with the teacher. The teacher must be encouraged to develop his or her best style. 3. Write up a report summarizing improvements shown and areas still in need of improvement; include any points of disagreement and the updated action plan. 4. Give a copy of the report to the teacher and place a copy in his or her file. 5. Discuss your observation with department chair- person and jointly decide if chairperson should set up a future observation for seventh week.	
Librarian NAME	By end of sixth week DATE	1. Meet with the teacher in library, reintroduce yourself if necessary, and further explain available resources to the teacher. 2. Offer to suggest library assignments that he or she might use with his or her class.	

Continued

TO BE DONE

WHO	WHEN	ACTION TO BE TAKEN	NOTES
Guidance Counselor _____ NAME	By end of eighth week _____ DATE	1. Reintroduce yourself, if necessary, to the teacher when you meet and discuss problems that the teacher may be having with students. 2. Review the school's grading system with the teacher and listen to the teacher's views on grading. Give your views on how realistic or unrealistic you consider his or her ideas to be. 3. Discuss any problem situations the teacher may have encountered and how he or she handled or might have handled the situations. 4. Review available services that might help the teacher and his or her students.	

Activities Director, Student Council Advisor, Athletic Director
 	
_____
NAMES
	Tenth week
	
	_____
	DATE
		1. Explore what interest the new teacher has in sponsoring extracurricular activity.
		2. Review rules of the school concerning supervision of students participating in extracurricular activities and building usage by clubs.
		3. Offer the necessary help to the teacher if he or she wants to sponsor an extracurricular activity.
		  a) Explain how to request P.A. announcements.
		  b) Point out what bulletin boards may be used for the posting of meeting notices.
		  c) Introduce the teacher to available books and materials on sponsorship that might be of help to him or her.
		4. Discuss the interest of the teacher in coaching sports.	

Department chairperson _____ NAME	Eleventh week _____ DATE	1. Check on progress the teacher is making with action plan by talking with him or her during a planning period. Make other suggestions that might help the teacher. 2. Review the teacher's grading of students. Discuss student reactions to grades. If any problems surfaced, try to help the teacher plan a course of action to avoid future problems.	

Continued

TO BE DONE			
WHO	**WHEN**	**ACTION TO BE TAKEN**	**NOTES**
		3. Discuss the assignments, projects, and other work performed by students. Is too much or too little being demanded of pupils?	
Assistant Principal ———— NAME	Twelfth week ———— DATE	1. It is your function at this time to review with the teacher problems or concerns that you have as a member of the administration. a) Teacher arriving at school on time? b) Showing up for assigned duties on time? c) Administrative duties performed in a satisfactory manner? Any deadlines missed? Other problems? Any complaints against the teacher should be given to him or her in writing, and he or she should be given the opportunity to clarify and write a response to the complaints. It must be remembered that teachers and administrators can make mistakes. Education is a joint effort; sometimes new and experienced teachers forget this. 2. The next step is to set up with the teacher an observation date for the coming week. a) What material will be covered? b) What particular items of the teacher' action plan are most in need of observation? c) What new teaching techniques has the teacher tried? What success has he or she experienced with them? d) Have the other three observations, discussions, and action planning been of much help? Why? Why not?	Last Observation Date ——— Period ——— (different from first, second, and third) Class ——— Level ——— Room ———
Assistant Principal ———— NAME	After observation, during next planning period of teacher ———— DATE	1. Meet with teacher to discuss the observation: a) Stress positive aspects of his or her teaching. b) Review improvements noted from other, earlier observation reports. c) Have teacher self-evaluate the lesson before you give your observations. d) Add any additional prescriptive items to action plan. 2. Write up a report summarizing both the good and bad points observed, points of disagreement, and additional items added to the action plan by agreement of the teacher.	

Continued

TO BE DONE

WHO	WHEN	ACTION TO BE TAKEN	NOTES
		3. Give a copy of the report to the teacher and a copy to the principal. 4. Discuss the observation with the principal. 5. Also, you should include negative reactions of the teacher to your critique.	
Principal NAME	Before Holiday break NAME	1. Call a meeting of the team members who have been working with the new teacher. 2. Discuss the observed strengths and weaknesses of the new teacher and how well he or she has taken advice, improved teaching, and carried out aspects of the action plan. 3. Begin to create a staff development program for the teacher to be implemented during the second semester.	
Principal NAME	January DATE	1. Hold a conference with the teacher to discuss his or her progress, particularly in relation to the action plan. 2. Discuss the recommended staff development program. 3. Discuss the various ways in which the staff development program may be implemented: literature, teacher center workshops, additional college courses, etc. 4. Try to finalize plans for the staff development program. 5. Review administrative problems that may have occurred during the first semester.	
Senior Faculty Member NAME	January DATE	1. Sit down with the teacher and discuss how he or she is getting along. 2. Let the teacher know that you are concerned. Be a good listener. Again, offer suggestions if sought by the teacher.	
Librarian NAME	February DATE	1. Reoffer services if not already used. 2. Help set up a library project or assignment with the teacher for his or her class. 3. Discuss new acquisitions that might be of value to the teacher.	

Continued

TO BE DONE			
WHO	**WHEN**	**ACTION TO BE TAKEN**	**NOTES**
A-V Coordinator ——————— NAME	February ——————— DATE	1. Review usage of A-V materials by the teacher. 2. Make suggestions for second-semester use of A-V equipment. 3. Discuss new acquisitions that might be of use to the teacher. 4. Help the teacher arrange for classroom use of materials and equipment.	

Principal
 	
———————
NAME
	March
	
	———————
	DATE
		1. Meet with the teacher to discuss extension of his or her contract.
		2. Discuss teacher's first-year experiences:
		  a) How he or she feels about
		    1) Teaching as a career.
		    2) This school, faculty, students, rules, etc.
		    3) Subjects taught.
		  b) How he or she would evaluate the induction program:
		    1) What was most helpful?
		    2) What was least helpful?
		    3) Was anything disliked?
		    4) What was most liked?
		    5) Was there something that might have helped more?
		    6) Suggestions for improving the program.
		3. Review other areas of concern.
		  a) Areas in which the teacher is still weak.
		  b) Remind the teacher of school policies.
		  c) Encourage the teacher to keep striving for excellence and thank the teacher for past efforts.
		4. If contract will not be extended, explain why, orally and in writing.	

APPENDIX B*
INDUCTION CALENDAR

	Pre-Sch	1st Week	2nd Week	3rd Week	4th Week	5th Week	6th Week	7th Week	8th Week	9th Week	10th Week	11th Week	12th Week	13th Week	Dec.	Jan.	Feb.	Mar.
Principal	II				POI	O									Team II	II		II
Assistant Principal	II												POI	O				
Department Chairperson	II	II	POI	O			(optional) (POI O)					A						
Guidance Counselor		A	A						A									
A-V Coordinator		A	A		A												A	
Activities Director		A	A								A							
Athletic Director		A	A								A							
Student Council Advisor		A	A								A							
Librarian		A	A				A										A	
Senior Faculty Advisor				A												A		

CODE: II = Information interview and discussion
POI = Pre-observation interview and discussion
O = Observation followed by discussion and written report to principal
A = Assistance offer and discussion

*Adapted from the following: Ronald Gagnepain, M.A., "Induction Calendar" (Unpublished research paper, St. Louis University, 1978), p. 20.

SELECTED BIBLIOGRAPHY

Bey, T. M., C. F. Holmer, eds. *Mentoring: Developing Successful Teachers,* Reston, VA: Association of Teacher Educators, 1990.

Brock, B. L., "Profile of the beginning teacher." *Momentum* (1990), pp. 54–57.

Chester, Mitchell D., and Barbara Q. Beaudin, "Efficacy Beliefs of Newly Hired Teachers in Urban Schools," *American Educational Research Journal,* 33, no. 1 (Spring 1996), pp. 233–257.

Cohn, Kathleen C., "Mentor Principals to Ensure Success," *The School Administrator,* 48, no. 3 (March 1991), pp. 40–43.

DeBolt, G. P., ed., *Teacher Induction and Mentoring: School-Based Collaborative Programs.* New York: State University of New York, 1991.

Drummond, R. J., M. L. Grimes, M. S. Terrell, "Beginning Teacher Program: Perceptions of Policy," *Education,* 111, no. 2 (1990), pp. 187–189.

Drury, William R., "Entry-Year Administrator Induction: A State and Local School District Model," *Spectrum: Journal of School Research and Information,* 6, no. 1 (Winter 1988), pp. 8–10.

Emrick, William S., "Implementing a Mentoring and Peer Coaching Program," *Spectrum: Journal of School Research and Information,* 7, no. 3 (Summer 1989), pp. 17–21.

Holdaway, Edward A., Neil A. Johnson, and Eugene W. Ratsoy, "The Value of an Internship Program for Beginning Teachers," *Educational Evaluation and Policy Analysis,* 16, no. 2 (Summer 1994), pp. 205–221.

Johnson, Nancy C., and J. Kenneth Orso, "Teacher Induction Programs," *Spectrum: Journal of School Research and Information,* 6, no. 3 (Summer 1988), pp. 22–24.

Johnston, J. M., and T. L. James, *Leadership and Cooperation Through Mentoring: Rethinking Roles in Teacher Education.* Flagstaff, Ariz.: Association of Teacher Education, 1986.

Metropolitan Life Survey of the American Teacher, *The Second Year: New Teachers' Expectations and Ideals.* New York: Metropolitan Life, 1992.

Odell, Sandra J., *Mentor Teacher Programs.* West Haven, Connecticut: NEA Professional Library, 1990.

Pence, Jean L., "Mentorship Programs for Aspiring and New School Administrators," *Oregon School Study Council Bulletin,* 32, no. 7, 1989.

Playko, Marsha A. and John C. Daresh, "Mentoring Programs for Aspiring Administrators: An Analysis of Benefits to Mentors," *Spectrum: Journal of School Research and Information,* 11, no. 3 (Summer 1993), pp. 12–17.

Reinhartz, Judy, ed., *Teacher Induction.* West Haven, Connecticut: NEA Professional Library, 1990.

Sindelar, Nancy W., "Development of a Teacher Mentorship Program: High Professionalism and Low Cost," *Spectrum: Journal of School Research and Information,* 10, no. 2 (Spring 1992), pp. 13–18.

Stammer, John D., and Gary E. Cooke, "A Decision-Making Model for Promotion, Retention, and Placement at the Elementary Level," *Spectrum: Journal of School Research and Information,* 4, no. 3 (Summer 1986), pp. 43–46.

Strusinski, Marianne, "The Professional Orientation Program in the Dade County Schools," *Spectrum: Journal of School Research and Information,* 11, no. 2 (Spring 1993), pp. 10–16.

Tomlin, Michael E., "The Evolution of a New Teacher," *The Executive Educator,* 15, no. 3 (March 1993), pp. 39–41.

Tranter, William H., "The New Principal," *The Executive Educator,* 14, no. 2 (February 1992), pp. 29–32.

Vienne, Dorothy T., "Mentors with a Mission," *The Executive Educator,* 13, no. 8 (August 1991), pp. 32–34.

6

STAFF DEVELOPMENT

Change is a constant occurrence in contemporary society. Instant communication channels, produced by technological advances, place before student and educator changes in politics, economics, science, and social status from every corner of the world. The mandate of public schools, of course, is to educate the children, adolescents, and young adults of our country in order to help them meet the challenges that tomorrow will bring because of these changes.

As an organization, a school district needs well-qualified administrators, teachers, and support personnel to fulfill this mandate. As the positions and job requirements within a school district become more complex, the importance of staff development programs increases.

Staff development practices have undergone considerable change over the last two decades. Three trends that have contributed to this metamorphosis are: results-driven education, the systems approach to school and school district organization, and constructivism. As a practice, results-driven staff development is concerned with changing the behavior and/or attitudes of teachers, administrators, and staff members rather than being concerned with the number of participants in such programs. The systems approach to administration recognizes the interrelatedness of all components in a given school and ultimately in a school district. Thus, an innovation in elementary school instructional techniques could have ramifications for the counseling program and for the curriculum committee in a school. Across the district an innovation in an elementary school could affect the program in that district's middle school and eventually, the high school instructional program.

Finally, constructivism sets forth the premise that learners build knowledge structures in their minds rather than having the knowledged received and imprinted in their minds by a teacher. The implication for staff development is that teachers, administrators, and staff members could be engaged in such activities as action research and mentoring programs in addition to the more traditional milieu through which programs are delivered.[1]

---

[1]Dennis Sparks, "A Paradigm Shift in Staff Development," *Education Week,* 16 March 1994, p. 42.

It is literally impossible today for any individual to take on a job or enter a profession and remain in it for forty or so years with his or her skills basically unchanged. Therefore, staff development is not only desirable but also an activity to which each school system must commit human and fiscal resources if it is to maintain a skilled and knowledgeable staff.

ADULT LEARNING

Adult learning usually consists of two processes, training and education. Training is the process of learning a sequence of programmed behaviors.[2] Typists, custodians, cooks, and maintenance personnel thus can be trained because their job-related activities are capable of being broken down and analyzed in order to determine the best way to perform certain tasks. In this connotation training is the application of knowledge that provides employees with a set of procedures that will guide their work-related behaviors.

The emphasis in the training component of a staff development program is on the acquisition of motor skills and on producing simple conditioning methods that will improve an employee's ability to perform his or her job.

Education is the process of helping an individual understand and interpret knowledge.[3] Education emphasizes acquiring sound reasoning processes rather than learning a body of serial facts. Education helps an employee develop a rational approach towards analyzing the relationship between variables and consequently understanding phenomena.

Teachers and administrators have job responsibilities that, in most respects, require education rather than training. Teachers and administrators usually do not perform programmed work. For example, an administrator can be trained in management techniques and procedures. However, an administrator cannot be trained to manage. Speaking about managers in the private sector, Stephen Robbins summarizes the differences between training and education:

> Successful managers have analytical, human, conceptual, and specialized skills. They are able to think and understand. Training, per se, cannot overcome the inability of a manager or potential manager to understand cause-and-effect relations, to synthesize from experience, to visualize relationships, or to think logically. As a result, we suggest that management development must be predominantly an education process rather than a training process![4]

In discussing the distinction between training and education, care must be taken not to assume that all job-related activities of a particular position are either trainable or educable. Teachers and administrators perform some activities that can be enhanced by training because these activities are capable of being programmed. Both teachers and

---

[2]Stephen P. Robbins, *Personnel: The Management of Human Resources,* 2nd ed. (Englewood Cliffs, N.J.: Prentice-Hall, 1982), p. 220.

[3]Robbins, *Personnel, ibid.*

[4]Robbins, *Personnel, ibid.*

administrators need good listening skills and interviewing skills; in today's automated society, they also need skills in using the computer. However, understanding the instructional-learning process and being able to create a learning environment conducive to teaching goes beyond the scope of training and requires education.

This same distinction must also be applied to support personnel. A secretary needs to develop and upgrade skills in using word-processing equipment and in carrying out routine office procedures; these are trainable skills. However, a secretary is often called on to make decisions about setting up and prioritizing appointments for an administrator; this requires an understanding of the importance of each appointment relative to the responsibilities of that administrator. An effective secretary should also have the ability to analyze inquiries and to refer them to the appropriate staff member. Acquiring such abilities goes beyond the scope of training and requires education.

To some, this distinction between training and education may seem to be only an academic exercise; however, it has very practical application. As will be demonstrated later in this chapter, it is extremely important to categorize and analyze the needs of employees in order to establish objectives for the various components of a staff development program. Understanding the type of learning required to meet these needs is essential to an effective program.

The Conditions of Learning

A staff development program centers around creating instructional learning situations. Consequently, those charged with organizing such a program must have a profound understanding of the psychology and conditions required for effective learning.

Numerous theories have been proposed about how learning occurs. In this chapter, I will not elucidate all of the principles described by these theories but rather will present those aspects of learning common to the major theories.

Learning is a change in human capability that can be retained, and which is not simply ascribable to the process of growth. The manifestation of change as described in this definition is the behavior of the learner. The extent to which learning has occurred is measured by comparing those behaviors that were present before the individual was placed in the instructional-learning situation against those behaviors that can be demonstrated after the experience. The desired change is usually an increased skill or capability of more than momentary significance.

Changes in behavior are brought about by four basic learning conditions: stimulus, response, reinforcement, and motivation. A *stimulus* is someone or something that initiates an action. An instructor will stimulate a learner by asking a question. When the learner answers the question, he is making a *response*. If the instructor responds to the learner with, "that is a correct and appropriate answer," the learner is receiving *reinforcement*. Finally, if the learner perceives completion of the course of instruction as a means of obtaining a job, a promotion, a raise in salary, or some other desired goal, the learner is said to have *motivation*. Although this explanation of the four basic components of learning is rather simplistic, it does present the necessary conditions for learning to take place.

Considerations that impinge on these conditions of learning should be mentioned here for the sake of completeness, but they will not be elaborated on to any great extent.

First, a certain amount of planning must precede the instructional learning situation in order to determine the most appropriate learning structure for the subject matter that will be taught. In learning, every new capability builds on a foundation established by previously learned capabilities. Planning specifies and orders these prerequisite capabilities in order that a learning objective can be reached. For example, a staff developing workshop designed to help teachers construct metric system materials for classroom use should be preceded by a seminar explaining the metric system to teachers who are unfamiliar with the system.

Second, the environment of learning must be effectively managed. Those responsible for planning should ask themselves, what is the most appropriate time and setting to carry out instruction? A comfortable and stimulating environment certainly enhances learning; and especially for adult learners, the instruction should take place at a time of day when they are not fatigued. This suggests that certain staff development seminars, workshops, or courses for teachers should be scheduled on days when school is not in session. This also implies that an effective staff development program should provide employees with released time from their regular duties so they can attend during the working day.

Third, instruction must have some practical application for the adult learner. Adults generally can learn more material in less time than children, but they must see that the material can help them in their work. A school bus driver who attends a workshop on managing student behavior must be shown techniques that he or she can actually use with disruptive students riding his or her bus.

Fourth, learning rarely takes place at a constant rate; rather, it fluctuates according to the difficulty of the subject matter or skill to be learned and the ability of the learner. Developing skill at typing is a good example. During the first three months of instruction, the learner becomes familiar with the keyboard and the basic techniques of typing. During the next three months, the individual develops speed, and learning accelerates. After six months of instruction, learning normally slows down because the individual has progressed to the point of technique refinement.

CREATING A STAFF DEVELOPMENT PROGRAM

Experience has taught personnel administrators the folly of approaching staff development merely from the "Let's have a workshop" model. This traditional concept of what was and is still referred to in some school districts as "in-service training" has severe limitations not only in scope but also in effectiveness. Rather, the concept of "staff development" addresses the real needs of educational organizations. The evolution of this approach is mirrored in all of our societal institutions. In the past, changes were thrust upon the schools without giving teachers and administrators an opportunity to prepare for such changes. With the decline in pupil enrollments, there was a greater need for developing existing personnel resources to assume different positions created by change. Also, both the Elementary and Secondary Education Act of 1965 and the Education Professions Development Act of 1968 provided funding for staff development projects. These funds helped to forward the current interest in staff development.

FIGURE 6–1　**A model for a staff development program**

During the last decade, there has been a myriad of research on staff development. Most of this research has centered on identifying those variables that produce effective staff development programs. As a consequence of this research, many models have been created. Some of the most proposed in staff development literature are PET (Program for Effective Teaching); RPTIM (Readiness, Planning, Training, Implementation, Maintenance); CBAM (Concern-Based Adoption Model); and SDSI (Staff Development for School Improvement). A common thread connecting all these models is the goal of producing effective instruction through clinical supervision. As principals evaluate and supervise teachers in order to improve instruction, staff development programs become a vehicle through which teachers can enhance skills and remedy deficiencies.

Commitment to Staff Development

A major reason why some employees perceive staff development activities as ineffective is because these employees receive little support for implementing newly acquired skills and ideas. Other conditions that affect the success of a staff development program include lack of appropriate program organization and lack of supervision during implementation. Clearly, these conditions are symptomatic of a more fundamental problem, the lack of commitment. In any organization this commitment must emanate from the highest level of responsibility down through the various levels of administration to the employees. In order to be effective, the board of education must support the program; the administration must organize and supervise the program; and the employees must participate in program planning.

In delineating the tasks to be performed by the various components of a school district, the board of education must set the stage by creating a positive climate for the program and by providing the necessary fiscal funding and appropriate policies for implementation. The central-office administration, through the director of staff development, is responsible for creating a master plan and for overall management and supervision of the program. Building principals and supervisors are responsible for identifying the knowledge, skills, and abilities that are needed to carry out the goals and objectives of the school district. Teachers and staff members are responsible for participating not only in program planning but also in the programs. Consequently, the success of a staff development program depends on the commitment of each individual within each level of the school district.

Georgea Sparks confirms the importance of commitment as follows:

> . . . the major factor affecting success of the program was administrative support from both principals and superintendents. . . . Simply put, in schools where staff development had the greatest influence on teaching, teachers shared their ideas about instruction and tried out new techniques in their classrooms . . . the major responsibility for planning and implementation is given to the local school staff . . . the most commonly mentioned strength of the program was the opportunity to have responsibility for the staff development and the improved school climate.[5]

Sparks also promotes the concept of *site specific* staff development, an approach that places the responsibility for program development at the local school level. While this concept has merit, the contemporary school faculty is already so burdened with tasks and responsibilities that the idea is very difficult to implement.

School District Goals and Objectives

Educational goals and objectives, taken in the broadest sense, are similar across the country. Schools are concerned about educating children in the basic skills and developing in our children those cultural values that will perpetuate our American heritage. How the various school districts adjust these goals and objectives to their particular situation accounts for the fact that no two staff development programs will be exactly the same.[6]

The genesis of a staff development program, therefore, originates from educational goals and objectives. When these goals and objectives are formulated into written policies of the board of education, a staff development program has the guidance necessary for integrating the individual goals of employees with those of the school district.

[5]Georgea Sparks, "Synthesis of Research on Staff Development for Effective Teaching," *Educational Leadership,* November 1983, p. 66.

[6]See D. R. Davies and C. D. Armistead, *Inservice Education: Current Trends in School Policies and Programs* (Arlington, Va.: National School Public Relations Association, 1975), p. 10.

Needs Assessment

The primary purpose of a staff development program is to increase the knowledge and skills of employees and thereby increase the potential of the school district to attain its goals and objectives. The process of assessing employee needs is essentially the process of determining the discrepancy between the existing and the needed competencies of the staff. This analysis also must consider projected human resource needs. Thus, a staff development program must be concerned not only with the abilities of individuals currently occupying positions but also with the abilities individuals will need to qualify for promotion to positions of more responsibility. The data obtained from the human resource inventories used in the human resource planning process along with the data obtained from needs assessment techniques provide the framework within which program goals and objectives can be established.

Establishing Staff Development Goals and Objectives

Staff development goals and objectives will continually change to meet the continually changing needs of individual staff members and the school district. A predominantly white suburban school district that begins to get an influx of African-American families might consider creating a program for the administrative, teaching, and support staffs on the impact that the mingling of these two distinctive American cultures will have on the functioning of the school district. The purchase of word-processing office equipment will create a need to instruct the office staff on the most effective use of this new equipment.

These examples of changes that affect the operations of a school district should be more broadly formulated into goals and objectives. For example, a staff development goal involving integration might be stated as follows: To prepare the administration, teachers, and staff to effectively address the integration of black students into the school community. Objectives specifying this goal could be formulated as follows:

1. To develop a sense of appreciation for cultural differences on the part of teachers, administrators, and staff members.
2. To develop strategies for pupil behavior management should conflicts arise between students of different cultural heritages.

Such a goal with accompanying objectives provides direction to the next phase in creating a staff development program—designing the program.

Program Design

Designing a program involves more than simply finding a university professor who is interested in giving a workshop on a particular topic. Broadly conceived, program design is a process of matching needs with available resources through an effective delivery method. Therefore, it is obviously unproductive to assign or endorse an activity without considering how this activity helps to meet goals and objectives.

Also, it is unproductive to consider only one method of delivering a staff development program. The National Education Association's Research Division lists nineteen methods used in program delivery:

1. Classes and courses	**11.** Camping
2. Institutes	**12.** Work experience
3. Conferences	**13.** Teacher exchanges
4. Workshops	**14.** Research
5. Staff meetings	**15.** Professional writing
6. Committee work	**16.** Professional association work
7. Professional reading	**17.** Cultural experiences
8. Individual conferences	**18.** Visits and demonstrations
9. Field trips	**19.** Community organization work
10. Travel	

This is certainly not a listing of all the possibilities for designing a staff development program, and it is important to recognize that no one technique will satisfy all individuals, but that different techniques will meet different needs.[7]

A variety of resource people will also enhance a staff development program. Among the most available and knowledgeable persons are teachers, senior staff members, college and university personnel, professional consultants, journal authors, teacher organization representatives, and administrators.

Group-oriented design has proven to be an effective method for delivering staff development programs. In Omaha, Nebraska, this method was used to adapt new mathematics materials to individual student needs. After group meetings were held to identify areas of study, the staff was then divided into teams that specialized in single problem areas. Upon completion of the study, the various teams reported to the entire group, providing suggestions and techniques for individual application of the materials.[8]

Another group-oriented program, implemented in Mamaroneck, New York, centered around behavior modification techniques in the instructional-learning environment. Traditional workshops and seminars were employed to explain the theory of behavior modification and to analyze those behaviors amenable to each technique. Two teams of teachers were then selected to observe groups of children. After the observations were made, these two groups met to present and discuss the results of the observations.

Individualized programs are another alternative to the traditional program design model. Such programs allow the individual maximum creativity in matching personal interests and needs to the goals and objectives of the school district. Teachers who engage in personalized activities usually improve their teaching skills. Selma, Alabama, has implemented an individualized development program that gives teachers an opportunity to

---

[7]See Jay E. Greene, *School Personnel Administration* (Philadelphia: Chilton Book Co., 1971), p. 275.

[8]See D. R. Davies and C. D. Armistead, *Inservice Education: Current Trends in School Policies and Programs* (Arlington, Va.: National School Public Relations Association, 1975), p. 25.

contract in writing each year to carry out certain self-selected activities. These activities include the following:

1. Long-range activities, which could include serving on curriculum research and improvement committees.
2. The development of curriculum materials.
3. Professional writing for journals and conducting research.
4. Professional reading, which must include three books and at least ten articles.
5. Attending conferences and conventions.
6. Professional development through travel.
7. Engaging in community relations activities that include conducting parent discussion groups and initiating community projects.
8. Sponsoring uncompensated student activities.
9. Other activities that have a demonstrated effect on implementing school district goals and objectives.[9]

Program design is an organic process that will continually change to meet the needs of individual staff members and the needs of the school district.

Implementation and Delivery Plan

A critical aspect in all staff development programs is the implementation and delivery phase. The very best of intentions and planning may result in failure unless attention is paid to providing employees with appropriate incentives to participate, unless satisfactory time arrangements are made, and unless ordinary organizational problems are properly handled.

A common practice is to reimburse employees for tuition and fees incurred in attending workshops or taking courses. Many school districts also pay for substitutes in order to facilitate program arrangements.[10] The research on staff development programs generally agrees that incentives should be provided. For example, one study identified the following incentives in order of preference: credit for certificate renewal; reimbursement for expenses incurred for attendance at meetings, workshops, and other qualified programs; college or university credit; and advancement on the salary schedule.[11] Although direct payment in the form of salary increments is a proven incentive, this study indicates that indirect financial aid is more influential in promoting participation in staff development programs.

Time is a valuable commodity to all employees and, thus, it is a key factor in organizing and encouraging employee participation in development programs. There is a growing trend to incorporate staff development programs as part of the working day or, at least, as an extension of the day. Some school districts set aside a number of afternoons each month for development programs; others bring courses and lectures directly to the schools.

---

[9]Davies and Armistead, *Inservice Education,* pp. 21–23.

[10]See Davies and Armistead, *Inservice Education,* p. 36.

[11]See Darrell Jenson, Loren Betz, and Patricia Zignarmi, "Organizing Inservice for Teachers," *NASSP Bulletin,* LXII (April 1978), p. 13.

In Providence, Rhode Island, every school has thirty days of early dismissal each year for staff development programming. A variation of this approach is to release students by subject area so that the teachers in a given discipline can meet for an entire day.

Whatever the arrangement for delivering a staff development program, experience indicates that the least effective time is after a full day of teaching or work. No teacher, administrator, or employee will be able to assimilate new ideas when fatigued. The common practice in business and industry should be established in school districts—namely, that staff development programs should be conducted on "company time."[12]

A final consideration in administering a staff development program is providing the administrative mechanism to handle the ordinary problems that occur in all human interaction. Some specific problems that tend to hinder employee participation include the following:

1. When participants are unclear as to what they hope to achieve.
2. When participants consider past programs as a waste of time.
3. When some programs are so highly structured as to hinder creativity.
4. When the best available individuals are not employed to conduct a given program.
5. When there is no orderly plan for a given program.
6. When the group involved with a specific program is so large that participation is hindered.
7. When there is no acceptable method of evaluation being used for the program.[13]

When administrators do their best to deal with such problems effectively, employees will more readily participate and will be more satisfied with the development programs.

Program Evaluation

Effective evaluation is the final phase in a staff development program. Some school districts see this as a rather complicated task involving multiple applications of statistics; others neglect it entirely. For most programs, a perception-based approach is both appropriate and effective. Participants are asked to rate the instructor or individual conducting the program, the content of the program, how the program was organized, and the time and place of the program presentation.

When a particular program centers on skill or technique acquisition, it is appropriate to conduct a follow-up evaluation after the participants have had the opportunity to implement the techniques or use their new skills. The evaluations are then used in future program planning and also should provide the necessary data to improve the entire staff development program.

Burrello and Orbaugh emphasized the controlling effect of program evaluation as follows:

[12]See Davies and Armstead, *Inservice Education,* p. 36.

[13]John Clinton Moffitt, *In-Service Education for Teachers* (New York: The Center for Applied Research in Education, Inc., 1963), pp. 53–54.

1. The evaluation of in-service education should be a collaborative venture whose primary purpose is to assist with the planning and implementing of programs.
2. The decisions concerning the in-service education program should be based on the findings from continuing program evaluation by program participants and others affected by the program.
3. The evaluation design should address planning, implementation, and dissemination.[14]

Also the director of staff development should evaluate the program to ascertain if the program is helping to achieve the mandate of the school district as outlined in its goals and objectives. This is a much more complicated process than evaluating a specific course or workshop and must involve the perceptions of the board of education, superintendent of schools, other central-office administrators, and building administrators.

STAFF DEVELOPMENT FOR THE INSTRUCTIONAL STAFF

During the first few decades of this century, boards of education were concerned about encouraging teachers to earn a baccalaureate degree. This orientation changed in the 1970s to one that emphasized the remediation of teacher deficiencies. The current thrust is to provide teachers with the opportunity to maintain a favorable outlook on teaching and to improve their effectiveness in the classroom. At times it is necessary for principals to recommend certain staff development programs to teachers who are not performing at the level established by the board of education. Therefore, performance appraisal and staff development are complementary aspects of effective supervision.

The following list summarizes the benefits that a staff development program can offer the teacher:

1. *To update skills and knowledge in a subject area.* The knowledge explosion has created the need to reinterpret and restructure former knowledge. A teacher can no longer assume on the basis of past learning that he or she understands the nuances of a subject area.

2. *To keep abreast of societal demands.* Our society is continually changing. This has presented the teacher with a need to understand and interpret the new demands society is placing on all its institutions and on the school in particular.

3. *To become acquainted with research on the instructional process and on new methods of teaching.* Like other professionals, teachers generally have good intentions of keeping up with the advances that are being made in their field. A shortage of available time often prevents them from carrying out this intention, and a staff development program can meet this need.

4. *To become acquainted with the advances in instructional materials and equipment.* Educational TV, cable TV, and computer-assisted instruction are only a few of

---

[14]Leonard C. Burrello and Tim Orbaugh, "Reducing the Discrepancy between the Known and the Unknown in Inservice Education," *Phi Delta Kappan,* February 1982, p. 366.

the many new innovations that have potential for improving the quality of classroom instruction.

In the process of assessing teacher needs, the following sources of information can be of considerable help in designing a staff development program. First, the teacher needs-assessment survey has been a very effective technique. Most surveys take the form of a checklist containing many areas of possible needs and interests (see Appendix A).

A second source of information is the community survey, which is administered to parents, usually through a school-based organization such as the Parent-Teacher Association. This survey may reveal parental concerns about a wide range of issues such as grading, student groupings, discipline, and drug use by students.

Third, certification requirements vary from state to state and occasionally change. The director of staff development needs to keep all teachers and other certificated employees informed about requirements and should plan appropriate credit courses on both an off-campus and on-campus basis. The human resource master plan also will provide the director with information about the future needs of the district in relation to certain categories of certificated employees.

The final source of information is curricular research. Staff development programs can be planned to correlate with future curriculum changes. Research points to future skills and competencies that can be acquired and gradually introduced to insure an even transition.

The historic report, *A Nation At Risk,* published by the National Commission on Excellence in Education, was the impetus for many states to pass legislation centered on improving the quality of education. Much of this legislation calls for the establishment of professional development committees composed of teachers and other staff members who are charged with the responsibility of assisting the administration in identifying the staff development needs of teachers. Along with the administration these committees are also involved in the creation of staff development delivery systems.

STAFF DEVELOPMENT FOR SCHOOL PRINCIPALS

All administrators wonder from time to time about how they will be able to continue meeting the multiple challenges of their job, but school principals are particularly vulnerable because they are on the front line. James L. Olivero, a member of the Association of California School Administrators, wrote an article for the Bulletin of the American Association of School Administrators entitled "Reducing Battle Fatigue—or: Staff Development for School Principals," which significantly addresses this problem. Much of the material in this section has been gleaned from this article.

Types of Staff Development Programs

Many studies concerning the ever-changing role of the school principal have been conducted over the last fifteen years. These studies have identified the following major areas as appropriate for development programs:

1. *Instructional skills.* To effectively evaluate and supervise the instructional process, which includes providing curriculum leadership and securing instructional resources.

2. *Management skills.* To establish job objectives and be able to assess the needs of the staff. To be able to identify problem areas and to plan towards an effective solution. To be capable of unit budgeting and reviewing priorities in the efficient use of scarce resources.

3. *Human relations abilities.* To establish an open, two-way system of communication between students, parents, teachers, and other members of the community. To develop a method of involving parents, students, and teachers in the school-based decision-making process. To create an atmosphere of trust in the school, which encourages the staff and students to perform to the best of their abilities.

4. *Political and cultural awareness.* To have the ability to identify the leaders within the community and to involve them in school-level decision making. To address with positive techniques the resolution of conflicts between the school and community. To work towards meeting the needs of all clients of the school through school programs.

5. *Leadership skills.* Through a plan of self-development, to keep current with advances in the field of education. To share leadership skills with other professionals and with parents and other publics.

6. *Self-understanding.* To develop a plan of self-improvement through evaluation by school-based publics.

Staff Development Programming for Principals

Two types of programming can meet the development needs of principals. The first is the traditional vehicle, which includes workshops, conferences, and seminars that usually focus on a single topic and attempt to transmit a given body of information on such issues as new legislation or drug abuse.

A growing number of school districts are taking a more personalized approach to staff development for principals. This second type of program emphasizes acquiring skills that either help principals with their job or enhance their personal development.

Programs that emphasize the principal's job could include budget preparation, developing performance objectives, and initiating procedures to improve building maintenance. Programs that emphasize personal growth might address techniques for working with advisory groups, methods of communicating verbally and in writing, stress management, or time management.

Whatever an individual principal identifies as the area of personal need, a prerequisite for success is commitment. Therefore, it is advantageous to write down such personalized programs in a document that includes a personal needs assessment and a plan of action.

Future Directions for the Principal and Staff Development

Dramatic changes have occurred in our society over the last ten years, and they in turn have created a new set of competencies that principals need to acquire. A great many principals were trained and educated before the emergence of such current trends as cultural pluralism, community involvement, special education, student rights, and collective bargaining.

These trends, of course, are by no means the end but rather just the beginning of even more dramatic changes taking place at an accelerated pace. We must be prepared to meet this ongoing challenge in staff development.

Effective staff development for principals can be enhanced if the development programs are

1. Systematic, concrete, and relevant to the principal's job, including not only what the job is but what the job should be.
2. Ongoing and personalized.
3. Flexible and adaptable to change as the need arises.
4. Carried out when the participant is not fatigued because of work.
5. An integral part of the school district's policies and supported by adequate funds.

STAFF DEVELOPMENT FOR CLASSIFIED EMPLOYEES

Employee development programs in some school districts are limited to teachers and administrators. Development programs for classified employees have just recently taken hold on a large scale throughout the United States. Ironically, classified employees working in business and industry were given the opportunity to participate in development programs long before such programs were initiated for executives.

Three methods of development are commonly used for classified employees: on-the-job, off-the-job, and apprenticeship training. Because of the nature of their job responsibilities, classified employee development programs are aimed more at training than education. Nevertheless, there is a growing awareness that secretaries, custodians, bus drivers, and cafeteria workers will perform more efficiently if they are given the opportunity to participate in personal growth activities. Time management and human relations skills are important abilities for all school district employees, particularly with the current emphasis on community involvement in the schools.

Staff development has a definite orientation for classified employees. It is used not only to update skills but also to introduce new employees to the requirements and tasks they will be responsible for performing. Classified employees who are promoted to supervisory positions, in most cases, will learn how to handle their new responsibilities through a staff development program. This is also a nuance of development programs for classified employees.

On-the-Job Training[15]

Most training takes place on the job and in all probability this method is a most effective means of training. Besides being the simplest form of training to organize, it is also least costly to operate. Employees are placed in the actual work situation, which makes them feel immediately productive. They learn by doing, which is the most suitable training method for jobs that are difficult to simulate or that can be learned quickly by performance.

[15]See Robbins, *Personnel,* pp. 207, 208.

A significant drawback to on-the-job training is the possibility of future low productivity because in this setting an individual may never fully develop needed work-related skills when left to work alone.

A modification of on-the-job training is job-instruction training, a more systematic approach to training developed during World War II. This highly effective method consists of the following steps: (1) preparing trainees by telling them about the job, (2) presenting information essential to performing the job, (3) having trainees demonstrate their understanding of the job, and (4) placing trainees in the job on their own and assigning a resource person to assist the trainees if they need help.

Off-the-Job Training[16]

The term *off-the-job* training refers to various kinds of programs, such as lectures, seminars, workshops, case studies, programmed instruction, and simulations. The lecture method is best suited to conveying information such as procedures, methods, and rules. Contrary to common assumptions, lectures can be either highly structured or fairly informal, allowing for a considerable amount of two-way communications.

In the last two decades the business community has substantially increased the use of case studies, programmed instruction, and simulation exercises in training programs. The case study allows the employee to study a particular problem in depth. After analyzing the problem, the individual evaluates alternative courses of action and finally selects one that appears to provide the best potential for solving the problem.

Programmed instruction is a method that can be carried out through manuals and textbooks as well as teaching equipment. This approach condenses the material to be learned into a highly organized and logical sequence. The trainee responds to a question or set of circumstances and is provided with immediate feedback, telling the trainee if the response was right or wrong.

Simulations are the most expensive but also most effective method of training. The trainee is placed in an environment that nearly duplicates the actual work situation. This method has been widely used by airlines to train pilots and by schools in driver education classes. By using computer-based equipment, it is possible to simulate a wide variety of job dimensions without risking mistakes in a real-life situation, which might be dangerous or very costly.

Apprenticeship Training[17]

The oldest form of training is the apprenticeship. By this method, a trainee understudies a master worker for a given period of time or until the trainee acquires the necessary skills. Apprenticeships are common in the skilled trades but have seldom been used in staff development programs. However, the concept is applicable and is gaining in popularity.

---

[16]See Robbins, *Personnel,* pp. 208, 209.

[17]See Robbins, *Personnel,* pp. 207–208.

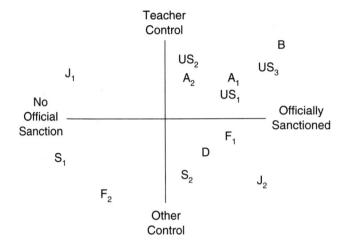

J₁   Japanese Study Circle   S₂   Japanese Institute of Education
J₂   Japanese Education Center   A₁   Australian Education Center
B   British Teacher Center   A₂   Australian Teacher Center
D   Denmark School Center   US₁ U.S. Training Complex
F₁   French Regional Center   US₂ U.S. Informal Teachers' Center
F₂   French Professional Association US₃ U.S. PI 94–482 Teacher Center
S₁   Spanish Private Center

FIGURE 6–2   Teacher centers around the world

Adapted from Vere De Vault, M. Egan, Kathleen Batato, and Lucia Ann Olmstead, "A Comparative View of Teacher Centers," *High School Journal,* LXI (The University of North Carolina Press, January 1978), 162. Copyright 1978.

TEACHER CENTERS AND STAFF DEVELOPMENT

In the early 1980s, there were ninety teacher centers operating in the United States under the U.S. Department of Education's Teacher Center Program (Public Law 94–482). This legislation was a direct outgrowth of the strategy employed by the National Education Association in its efforts to help teachers gain more control over curricular innovations. Teacher centers had long existed throughout the world before their emergence in the United States. Although the orientation of such centers varied considerably, many had evolved as a mechanism to help teachers deal with change. Figure 6–2 summarizes the degree of governance that existed and still exists in some teacher centers around the world. In the early fifties the Japanese Education Centers were founded to help implement post-World War II curricular emphasis on the sciences. These centers are in direct contrast to the Japanese "study circles," which receive little official sanction and no government funds but provide places where teachers can address common interests and problems.

The British teacher centers, which are the most renowned, were developed in the early sixties to help implement the Nuffield Mathematics Program and have governing boards composed predominantly of teachers. These centers now number over five hundred, and have evolved into places where teachers plan and implement their own in-service education.

With the proliferation of teacher-center literature during the last two decades, many different center models have been initiated in the United States. Many were cooperative endeavors that included centers established by local school districts along with universities. Some state-funded teacher centers also emerged, along with federally funded centers established under Title III of the Elementary and Secondary Education Act.

The U.S. Congress, through the provisions of the Education Amendments of 1976 (PL 94–482, Section 153), funded the establishment of local teacher centers that operated in-service programs aimed at improving the classroom skills and techniques of teachers.

Essentially, a teacher center program is concerned with curriculum development and/or in-service education for elementary and secondary teachers carried out in one or more local education agencies. The Teacher Center Policy Board (TCPB) should be composed primarily of practicing elementary and secondary teachers from the area served. Other membership on a policy board may include administrators, board members, or representatives from institutions of higher education—all from the local area to be served.[18]

Teacher centers were founded on the premise that teachers are self-motivating professionals who are capable of determining their own needs and who, through the policies of the governing board, can best deliver a staff development program to meet these needs. Although the premise is undeniably true, there remain a number of concerns that must be outlined. First, federal funding for teacher centers no longer exists. Second, staff development is a need not only for teachers but also for all employees of a school district. Therefore, a board of education should assume the initial responsibility in providing fiscal resources to develop and administer such programs. Third, teacher centers are essentially delivery systems and should be funded with local and state funds if this is determined to be the most effective way to conduct a staff development program. Teachers, like all employees, must be involved in the entire staff development planning process if such programs are going to meet their needs. This is a normal procedure in all effective staff development programs.

Teacher centers have been a worthwhile innovation for those school districts that lacked an effective staff development program, but they should not be considered a panacea for all school districts. With commitment and proper local and state funding, most school districts are capable of providing adequate programs utilizing a more traditional model administered by a director of staff development.

---

[18]See "Congress Enacts NEA Teacher Center Bill," *Today's Education,* LXVI (March-April 1977), p. 74.

SUMMARY

Change is a constant condition of our American way of life. Improved communications place before students and educators changes in politics, economics, and science almost as soon as they occur.

School districts have a mandate to educate the youth of our country. To do so successfully, schools need well-qualified teachers, administrators, and support personnel. No employee will remain qualified in the face of accelerating change without some form of ongoing education and training. This is the impetus behind the recent emphasis on staff development programs.

Adult learning usually consists of two processes, training and education. Training is designed to teach a sequence of programmed behaviors; education seeks to impart understanding and an ability to interpret knowledge. Both types of learning can occur in a staff development program depending on the objectives to be reached.

In all learning environments four basic components must be present to ensure success: stimulus, response, reinforcement, and motivation.

Creating a staff development program consists of six separate but sequential processes: (1) establishing school district goals and objectives, which become the foundation of the program; (2) assessing the needs of the school district employees to determine if there is a discrepancy between the competencies of the staff and the requirements of the organization; (3) establishing staff development goals and objectives; (4) designing a program that will meet the staff development requirements; (5) implementing the designed plan in such a way that effective learning may occur; and (6) evaluating the program to ascertain if it is meeting its objectives, which in turn will affect future program designs.

A staff development program for the instructional staff will focus on updating subject area skills and knowledge in order to improve instruction; outlining societal demands and changes; presenting the findings of research on teaching methods and practices; and updating teachers on the advances in instructional materials and equipment.

In assessing the needs of teachers, four sources of information may be helpful: (1) the teacher needs assessment survey, (2) community surveys, (3) certification information coupled with the human resource master plan, and (4) research and curricular studies.

In the last decade the school principalship has experienced multiple challenges brought on by such trends as cultural pluralism, community involvement, special education, student rights, and collective bargaining. A recent study conducted in California identified the following areas as appropriate for principal development programs: instructional skills, management skills, human relations abilities, political and cultural awareness, leadership skills, and self-understanding.

Besides the traditional models of staff development for principals, which include workshops and seminars, many school districts are taking a more personalized approach directed at helping principals acquire skills that relate simultaneously to their job and their personal development.

Staff development programs have been limited to the professional staff in many school districts. However, all employees can profit from development programs, and classified employees should have the opportunity to increase their skills and to participate in personal growth activities. Newly hired and promoted classified employees can be inducted into the responsibilities of their positions through a staff development program. The three most commonly used methods are on-the-job training, off-the-job training, and apprenticeship training.

An innovation in staff development programming was the emergence of teacher centers, which was a direct result of Public Law 94–482, Section 153. These federally funded centers were locally governed and operated. They aimed at improving the instructional techniques of teachers.

APPENDIX A
NEEDS ASSESSMENT SURVEY

NEEDS ASSESSMENT SURVEY FOR THE INSTRUCTIONAL STAFF

(Directions: Please Check All Items According to Your Degree of Interest. Return This Completed Form to the Administration Office.)

Degree of Interest

	None	Some	Much
1. Methods of Motivating Students	___	___	___
2. Behavioral Objectives	___	___	___
3. Dealing with Individual Differences	___	___	___
4. New Grouping Patterns (Non-Graded School Team Teaching)	___	___	___
5. Teaching Critical Thinking Skills	___	___	___
6. Programmed Learning	___	___	___
7. Designing Independent Projects	___	___	___
8. Work-Study Programs	___	___	___
9. Career Education	___	___	___
10. Using Performance Objectives	___	___	___
11. Advanced Placement	___	___	___
12. Linguistics	___	___	___
13. Teacher Made Tests & Mechanical Scoring	___	___	___
14. Modern Math Workshop	___	___	___
15. Elementary School Science (Experiment & Demonstration)	___	___	___
16. Seminar on Literature	___	___	___
17. Computer Programming (Course of Study)	___	___	___
18. Oral Communication	___	___	___
19. Education for Economic Competencies	___	___	___
20. Developmental Reading	___	___	___
21. English for Junior & Senior High Teachers (Develop a course of study)	___	___	___
22. Audiovisual Aids Workshop (Teachers)	___	___	___
23. Audiovisual Aids Workshops (Teachers' Aides)	___	___	___
24. Black History Workshop	___	___	___
25. Consumer Education in the Secondary Curriculum	___	___	___
26. New Directions in Social Studies	___	___	___
27. Outdoor Education Workshop	___	___	___

Continued

Degree of Interest

	None	Some	Much
28. Ecology Workshop			
29. Minicourses (In your field)			
30. Music for Elementary School Teachers			
31. Seasonal Art Projects for Elementary Classrooms			
32. Public Library Resources			
33. Selection & Evaluation of Audiovisual & other Instructional Media			
34. Spanish for Teachers			
35. Math for 1st and 2nd grade Teachers			
36. Learning Disabilities (Identification & Remediation)			
37. Social Studies for 5th & 6th grade Teachers			
38. Art Workshop			
39. Field Trips			
40. Physical Education Specialists			
41. School Library			
42. Industrial Arts (All purpose)			
43. Pupil Services			
44. Speech Therapy			
45. Driver Training (Rap Sessions)			
46. Learning Center (Elementary)			
47. Teaching English Composition			
48. Modern Economics			
49. Medical Seminar (Nurses)			
50. Math Enrichment (Elementary)			
51. Retirement & Social Security (Teachers of Retirement Age)			
52. New Elementary Math Adoptions (Primary)			
53. New Elementary Math Adoptions (Intermediate)			
54. Early Childhood (Kindergarten Curriculum)			
55. Teachers' Legal Limitations & Liabilities in the School			
56. Learning and Behavior			
57. Behavior and Discipline in the Elementary School			
58. The Open Space School			
59. Language Arts (Elementary)			
60. Elementary Library Facilities			
61. Parent-Teachers Relations			
62. Involving the Child in Social Studies (Elementary)			
63. Involving the Child in Science (Elementary)			
64. Personalizing Math (Elementary)			
65. Music for Secondary School Teachers			
66. Orientations for New Teachers			
67. The Psychology of the Disadvantaged Child			
68. Classroom Management			
69. Behavior Modification			
70. Parliamentary Procedure			
71. Home Economics			
72. Special Education on Elementary Level			
73. Special Education on Secondary Level			
74. Guidance Workshop			
75. Seminar in Your Subject Area			
76. Adolescent Psychology in the Modern World			
77. General Trends in Education			

	Degree of Interest		
	None	Some	Much
78. Newspaper in the Classroom	___	___	___
79. Data Processing Seminar (Student attendance and grade reporting)	___	___	___
80. Teacher-Made Training Aids	___	___	___
81. Rap Sessions in Your Subject Area	___	___	___
82. Creative Classroom (Display & Bulletin Boards)	___	___	___
83. Individualized Reading	___	___	___
84. Techniques of Teaching Slow Children	___	___	___
85. Instruction Materials	___	___	___
86. Instructional Games	___	___	___
87. Physical Education (Elementary)	___	___	___
88. Constructive Seat Work	___	___	___
89. Individualized Teaching & Learning (Elementary)	___	___	___
90. Involving the Child in Language Arts (Elementary)	___	___	___
91. Updating Courses of Study (In your field)	___	___	___
92. Community Resources	___	___	___
93. Effective Questioning	___	___	___
94. Interaction Analysis	___	___	___
95. Metric Measurement (International System)	___	___	___
96. Communications and Drug Abuse Seminar	___	___	___
97. Other Suggestions	___	___	___

Source: Lincoln Intermediate Unit No. 12, New Oxford, Pennsylvania.

SELECTED BIBLIOGRAPHY

Allen, Carol, et al., "Model for Administrator Training, Development Uses Both Theory and Practice," *NASSP Bulletin,* 68 (January 1984), pp. 14–19.

Andrew, Carmen, "Teacher-Directed Inservice Education in Southern Indiana," *Phi Delta Kappan,* 64, no. 7 (March 1983), pp. 504–505.

Black, Susan, "Evaluating Professional Development Programs: The Elmira School District Model," *Spectrum: Journal of School Research and Information,* 7, no. 1 (Winter 1989). pp. 34–40.

Brightman, Harvey J., "Improving Principals' Performance through Training in the Decision Sciences," *Educational Leadership,* 41, 5 (February 1984), pp. 50–56.

Caldwell, Sarah DeJarnette, editor, *Staff Development: A Handbook of Effective Practices.* Oxford, Ohio: National Staff Development Council, 1989.

DeFigio, Nicholas F., Naomi Zigmond, and Paul LeMahieu, "Educators' Views of Educational Problems: Changes Related to a Staff Development Initiative, 1990–1996," *Spectrum: Journal of School Research and Information,* 8, no. 1 (Winter 1990), pp. 39–47.

Edwards, Sara A., and Susan Barnes, "A Research-Based Staff Development Model that Works," *Educational Leadership,* 42, no. 7 (April 1985), pp. 54–57.

Glatthorn, Allan A., and Linda E. Fox. *Quality Teaching through Professional Development.* Thousand Oaks, California: Corwin Press, Inc., 1995.

Goldstein, I. L. *Training and Development in Organizations.* Monterey, California: Brooks-Cole, 1992.

Joyce, Bruce, editor, *Changing School Culture Through Staff Development.* Alexandria, Va.: Association for Supervision and Curriculum Development, 1990.

Lieberman, Ann and Lynne Miller, eds., *Staff Development for Education in the '90s: New Demands, New Realities, New Perspectives.* New York: Teachers College Press, Columbia University, 1991.

Marczely, Bernadette. *Personalizing Professional Growth: Staff Development that Works.* Thousand Oaks, California: Corwin Press, Inc., 1996.

McCarthy, Bernice, "What Format Training Teaches Us About Staff Development," *Educational Leadership,* 42, no. 7 (April 1985), pp. 61–68.

Noe, R. A., "Mentoring Relationships for Employee Development," *Applied Psychology in Business: The Manager's Handbook.* Lexington, Massachusetts: Lexington Press, 1991, pp. 475–482.

Ondrovich, Peggy Chnupa, "Staff Development: Meeting Teachers' Psychological and Professional Needs," *Spectrum: Journal of School Research and Information,* 7, no. 4. (Fall 1989), pp. 22–26.

Richardson, Virginia, ed. *Teacher Change and the Staff Development Process: A Case in Reading Instruction.* New York: Teachers College Press, 1994.

Showers, Beverly, "Teachers Coaching Teachers," *Educational Leadership,* 42, no. 7 (April 1985), pp. 43–49.

Sparks, Georgea, Marsha Nowakowski, Burris Hall, Rudi Alec, and Joseph Imrick, "School Improvement through Staff Development," *Educational Leadership,* 42, no. 6 (March 1985), pp. 59–62.

Strong, Richard W., Harvery R. Silver, J. Robert Hanson, Robert J. Marzano, Pat Wolfe, Tom Dewing, and Wende Brock, "Thoughtful Education: Staff Development for the 1990s," *Educational Leadership,* 47, no. 5 (February 1990), pp. 25–30.

Wexley, K. N., and G. P. Latham. *Developing and Training Human Resources in Organizations.* Glenview, Illinois: Scott Foresman, Inc., 1991.

Wideen, Marvin F. and Ian Andrews, *Staff Development for School Improvement: A Focus on the Teacher.* New York, N.Y.: The Falmer Press, 1987.

7

APPRAISAL

The appraisal of teachers' performance is as old as the education profession. However, for the most part, only three stages of historical development in American education during this century were concerned with the formal evaluation of teachers. During the 1920s, the efforts were primarily centered around analyzing if a given teaching style correlated with the philosophy and psychology of William James or John Dewey. The second stage was more concerned with ascribing certain personality traits as being related to excellence in teaching. The final stage, which appeared in the 1960s and persisted through the 1970s, emphasized generic teaching behaviors that would be effective in all instructional settings. The research in this area coined such catch words as *structured* and *task-oriented* when speaking about the types of teacher behavior that produced effective student outcomes.

In 1976 the National Institute of Education, in a request for proposals, called for a new approach to the definition of effective teacher training. This signaled the growth of a movement to license teachers on the basis of competencies and performance rather than on the completion of a teacher education program at an accredited college or university. Obviously, such an approach is predicated on a preconceived notion of what constitutes effective teaching.

The last two decades have ushered in a dramatic change in the entire concept of evaluation. Parents and taxpayers have been demanding more accountability at all levels of performance.[1] Also, school board members are subject to this trend towards accountability which has developed to the point that school employees, parents, and even organizations such as the National Education Association support specific candidates in school board elections because of their dissatisfaction with the policies of particular board members.

The "systems" approach to management, which has been used extensively by industry and received a big boost in the early 1960s when Robert S. McNamara advocated its

[1]See Gregg W. Downey, "How to Get Rid of Your Bad Teachers and Help Your Good Ones Get Better," *American School Board Journal* (June 1978), p. 23.

181

use in the U.S. Department of Defense, shifted the emphasis away from the traditional concept of teacher evaluation to the broader concept of employee appraisal management. Appraisal by objectives has become the touchstone phrase for the 1990s. This implies that an employee can he effectively evaluated only within the context of attaining certain preestablished objectives. Establishing these objectives is part of the overall process of determining the organizational objectives of the school district.

Because of the integral relationship between all employees and because one employee's performance can affect the performance of other employees, all personnel should be evaluated. This begins with the evaluation of the superintendent of schools by the board of education and proceeds down through the chain of command, with each administrator evaluating those employees reporting to him. This process applies not only to the professional staff but also to classified employees. The performance of bus drivers, custodians, and secretaries should be evaluated by their immediate supervisors.

This chapter is concerned with establishing an effective process for appraising the performance of individual employees. Although each position within a school district has a unique character, the following are universal reasons for appraisal, applicable to all school districts and all positions:

1. Appraisal fosters the self-development of each employee.
2. Appraisal helps to identify a variety of tasks that an employee is capable of performing.
3. Appraisal helps to identify staff development needs.
4. Appraisal helps to improve performance.
5. Appraisal helps to determine if an employee should be retained in the school district and how large a salary increase he or she should be given.
6. Appraisal helps to determine the placement, transfer, or promotion of an employee.

While parents and taxpayers are demanding increased accountability in employee performance, employees also are demanding accountability in the appraisal methods and techniques used in their evaluations. Administrators and supervisors are being asked to defend their evaluations and the procedures they used in making them. Consequently, it is extremely important to develop a consistent benchmark in establishing an appraisal process.

In the business and industrial community, that benchmark is the "job description" under which an individual was employed. Thus, an employee is evaluated in relation to his job description, which is the only defensible criterion against which performance should be measured.[2] Although this does not mean that a given job position will remain unchanged, it does imply that a revised job description may be needed if a job has undergone considerable modification. While job descriptions are seldom used as a component of evaluation in education, such use is a necessary prerequisite to establishing an effective appraisal process.

[2]See Stephen P. Robbins, *Personnel: The Management of Human Resources,* 2nd ed. (Englewood Cliffs, N.J.: Prentice-Hall, 1982), pp. 318–319.

A significant distinction must be made at this point to avoid confusion. This chapter is addressing the appraisal process from a central-office perspective with emphasis on the development of procedures, on the use of instruments and methods, and on the legal considerations of the process. It is not concerned with supervision as a task of the principal and other administrators. Supervision addresses the human interaction between teachers and administrators, an interaction which is required of the principal in fulfilling his role as the instructional leader within a particular school.

DEVELOPING AN APPRAISAL PROCESS

The ultimate goal of all school districts is to educate children and adolescents. How this is accomplished depends upon a multitude of subordinate goals and objectives. It is not only organizationally appropriate but also legally wise for a school board to establish a policy statement on employee appraisal, which will serve as one of these supportive goals. Such a policy gives direction to the various administrative divisions of the school district in their development of organizational objectives. A policy statement might read:

> Recognizing that quality education for the children and adolescents of this school district depends on the level of teacher, administrator, and staff member performance, the board of education directs the superintendent of schools to develop and implement a process for employee appraisal.
>
> This process must address as its first priority the impartial and objective evaluation of individual employees, in relation to the requirements of their positions within the school district. A second priority is to analyze how these positions help to actualize and support the instructional goals and objectives of this school board.

In meeting the mandate of this policy, each organizational division within the school district is responsible for developing divisional objectives.[3] The three major divisions in most school districts are personnel, instruction, and support services. Following the organizational structure outlined in Chapter 1, the assistant superintendents for personnel, administrative services, secondary education, elementary education, and instructional services must develop divisional objectives. In the personnel division objectives might center on improving recruitment techniques, human resource planning methods, or interviewing procedures.

The administrative services division could establish objectives in business management aimed at constructing a more effective investment schedule. The transportation component of this division might work on fuel-efficient bus routing, which would free up funds to improve other areas in the organization.

---

[3]See the American Association of School Administrators, *How to Evaluate Administrative and Supervisory Personnel,* Volume IX, AASA Executive Handbook Series (Arlington, Va.: The Association, 1977), p. 50.

It is certainly obvious that this procedure of developing objectives may reach a level of refinement within a division that would reach down to component objectives developed by directors (director of federal programs, director of special education, director of pupil personnel services, and so on). This is a legitimate procedure, which in fact is followed in some school districts and in private business and industry. However, individual school districts may not need this level of refinement and divisional objectives could be sufficient—the assumption being employed in this chapter.

After divisional objectives have been established by the appropriate assistant superintendents, all employees in that division are responsible for developing personal objectives that support the divisional objectives.

An assistant superintendent for secondary education might see a need to be present more often in the schools to observe operations firsthand. This would constitute a personal objective to be accomplished over a given period of time. A high school teacher of American history might develop an objective aimed at using more audiovisual techniques in lesson presentations. A custodian might attempt to reorganize his floor waxing schedule to make better use of work time when students are not in school. This constitutes an objective for the custodian.

The next step in the appraisal development process is to decide on formal evaluation procedures. These procedures should be in written form and made available to the entire staff. A concern often voiced by employees is that they were not adequately informed about the appraisal process. Because evaluation procedures are applicable to all school district employees, a common practice is to incorporate them into the board of education policy manual that is distributed to all employees when they are hired. Other school districts have employee handbooks that outline working conditions and specify the procedures and forms used in the appraisal process.

Developing the actual procedures is a task that is best performed by involving employee representatives who both evaluate and will be evaluated. This committee approach produces a sense of involvement and accountability that will help to defend appraisal procedures in the face of possible criticism.

It is appropriate to divide the employees of the school district into two groups, professional and classified, when organizing the appraisal development committees. The work situations of these two groups are significantly different and consequently may necessitate different appraisal procedures. It is more defensible to have committee members elected by the employees they represent than to have them appointed. If a school district's employees belong to unions or professional associations, it would be appropriate to have these organizations appoint representatives to serve on the committees.

The number of committee members will vary depending on the size of the school district, the number of employees represented, and the number of unions and associations active in the district. However, the most important consideration is that the committee be composed of an odd number of members such as three, five, seven, or nine, which will avoid the possibility of deadlocked decisions.

Of course, the procedures will be tailored to the needs of the individual school district. However, the following questions should be addressed in every set of procedures:

1. Who, by position, has the primary responsibility for making evaluations? (Examples: assistant superintendent for elementary education, principals, director of transportation, director of food service.)

2. Who is evaluated by these designated positions? (Examples: assistant superintendent for secondary education evaluates secondary school principals; building principals evaluate teachers; director of maintenance evaluates carpenters.)

3. In what settings will formal evaluations take place? (Examples: a teacher will be evaluated in the classroom when he or she is teaching a lesson; a principal will be evaluated in how he or she conducts a staff meeting.)

4. On how many occasions will formal evaluations occur? (Examples: tenured teachers will be evaluated on one formal occasion each year; probationary teachers will be evaluated at a minimum on two formal occasions.)

5. In what setting will the results of formal evaluations be communicated to the person evaluated? (Examples: in a conference immediately after the evaluation in the teacher's classroom; in a conference held in the principal's office at the end of each semester.)

6. If an employee disagrees with his evaluation, what grievance procedure should be available? (Examples: written rebuttal may be attached to the evaluation form; appeal may be made to the superintendent.)

7. What effect will evaluation have on salary increase? (Examples: a teacher with an excellent rating may receive a double step on the salary schedule; an employee may receive a merit increase in addition to a step increase on the salary schedule.)

Appendix A, *Teacher Evaluation Policies and Procedures,* presents a typical set of such procedures that speak to most of the questions. In analyzing these procedures, it is important to realize that appraisal of all employees is a continual and ongoing process. However, it is just as important to have "formal" evaluations when an employee can demonstrate his performance capabilities. Formal evaluation is applicable to situations that involve interaction between an individual and a defined group. Teachers are subject to this process because of their interaction with students. Principals can be evaluated in this manner on how effectively they handle staff meetings. Bus drivers can be formally evaluated when transporting children to and from school.

Other employees perform jobs that are more appropriately evaluated on a continuing basis but not on a formal occasion. Cooks, custodians, and administrators can be evaluated on results obtained. This implies that the substance of the evaluation was obtained outside a formal setting but that the evaluation is communicated to the employee in a formal setting.

The final step in the appraisal process is analysis of the results that have been obtained through employee evaluations to determine if division objectives are being met. If objectives have not been reached, and if they are still relevant to implementing the objectives and goals of the school board, the divisional objectives should be retargeted. This suggests that the employee objectives apparently did not support the divisional objectives and should be realigned to support them. If both the divisional and employee objectives have been realized, new objectives can be identified that will further the goals of the organization and

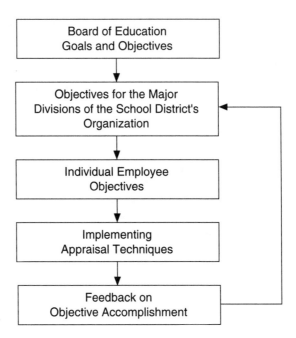

**FIGURE 7–1   Model for developing an
employee appraisal process**

the development of individual employees. Figure 7–1 is a schematic representation of the appraisal process.

There are a number of popular evaluation techniques that have not been addressed in this section, such as self-evaluation, peer evaluation, and student evaluation. These techniques are aimed more at personal growth and do not directly affect the appraisal process from a central-office perspective. They are referred to more properly as supervisory techniques.

The Construction of Evaluation Instruments

As with the development of appraisal procedures, evaluation instruments should be constructed by the committee process. Many management consulting firms have developed appraisal forms that are easily adapted to the requirements of a given school district. However, the construction of appraisal forms is not a difficult task, particularly with the many prototypes available for the asking from neighboring school districts.

The basic format of an evaluation instrument has certain theoretical overtones. Most authors recognize two basic categories, trait forms and result forms. In the trait approach the employee is rated against a predetermined list of traits in order to ascertain his level of performance. The results method compares the employee's performance against objectives that were developed by the employee and agreed to by his or her supervisor. In this latter method the employee has the responsibility for documenting how the objectives were reached.[4]

This author believes that the most appropriate method of evaluating performance is to use a trait instrument to ascertain overall performance and to target objectives to specify needed improvement in performance. The results method also helps to ascertain if employee objectives are supporting divisional and school board objectives. Employee objectives can be developed easily if overall performance has been measured. While the simultaneous use of trait instruments and objectives is not a common practice, the exclusive use of one or the other has never proven in experience to be superior. Appendices B, D, and E represent various trait formats that have wide use in educational organizations.

Job descriptions play an important role in constructing appraisal instruments and in the developing of objectives. The job requirements of a position are the legal parameters within which appraisal must be confined. An employee performs job requirements to an acceptable, unacceptable, or superior level. To require an employee to assume responsibilities that are not within his or her job description and to evaluate how he or she carries out these responsibilities is poor management. The dismissal of an employee because he or she did not perform responsibilities omitted from the job description, will not hold up in court.

Employee Discipline

The term *discipline* is often used with a negative connotation. However, the term itself refers to a condition in an organization created by employees conducting themselves according to the rules and regulations of the organization and conducting themselves in a socially accepted manner. Most individuals are self-disciplined and have little difficulty in following rules and regulations. Also, fellow employees can exert significant pressure on people who violate socially accepted norms. Using inappropriate language is a typical example of conduct offensive to most people.

There are two areas of misconduct that call for some action on the part of management: excessive absence from work and inappropriate on-the-job behavior. Absenteeism has become a major issue in private business and industry, costing consumers literally millions of dollars. School districts are no exception to the rule. Many theories have been proposed for this change in work ethic. However, the cause is usually rooted in the person who must take responsibility for his or her actions.

"Inappropriate on-the-job behavior" is meant to cover a variety of offenses such as carelessness, failure to use safety devices, fighting, alcohol and drug abuse. There are a number of variables that affect the seriousness of absenteeism and inappropriate on-the-job behavior. The administration must consider the nature of the problem, the duration of the problem, the frequency of the problem, the employee's work history, and other extenuating factors. However, it is clear to all practicing administrators that a response must be made that will correct the problem.

---

[4]See James Lewis, Jr., *Appraising Teacher Performance* (New York: Parker Publishing Company, 1973), pp. 25–28.

It is commonly accepted in the business and industrial communities that the response of management to such problems must be corrective rather than punitive; and the action taken must be progressive if it is to withstand the test of "due process." For example, if a custodian is tardy for work two times within a given week, the custodial supervisor should give that custodian a verbal warning. If the custodian is late the following week, the supervisor should then present the custodian with a written warning. If the tardiness continues for a third week, the custodian should be suspended from work for a week without pay. If the inappropriate behavior continues after the suspension period, the supervisor must continue with progressive discipline involving demotion, a pay cut, and finally, dismissal.

In terminating the employment of a person, it is critical for the supervisor and a designated staff member from the personnel department to carefully review the documentation of the reasons for the termination with the school district's attorney for assurance that defensible and appropriate procedures were followed. In preparing for the meeting at which the employee will be informed that his or her employment with the school district is being terminated, the individual's supervisor and a personnel staff member should have completed all the necessary reports and documents along with obtaining the individual's final paycheck. It is always important to have two people present at the meeting who will be representing the school district, usually the person's supervisor and a staff member from the personnel department. This provides a witness to the proceedings which may be important in the event of a lawsuit filed against the school district by the fired employee. It may be helpful to role-play what will take place at the meeting, including the anticipated reaction of the person to be fired.

Selection of the time and place of the meeting is important because the objective is to conduct the meeting in the most pleasant way possible for the person being fired and in the least disruptive way possible to other employees. For example, Monday afternoon may be the most appropriate time to have the meeting because the fired person will be able to use the rest of the week to search for another job, whereas Friday afternoon might result in intensifying the persons' anger during the weekend. Immediately after the meeting, district property should be returned and after the individual collects his or her personal property, the fired person should be escorted out of the building by either the supervisor or the personnel staff member.

At the meeting the following should take place: present the reasons why the person's employment is being terminated; make clear that the decision is final; allow the person to briefly respond; advise the employee of the school district's appeal process; and discuss severance and vacation pay along with information about fringe benefits such as COBRA.[5]

In a school district with a collective negotiated master agreement, such a progressive disciplinary process should be clearly outlined in the agreement.

This type of disciplinary process is very effective with classified personnel such as custodians, cooks, and bus drivers, but it is not very useful with teachers and adminis-

---

[5]Allen Fishman, "Firing Someone the Right Way Can Avoid Legal Hassles," *St. Louis Business Journal,* 20–26 July 1992, p. 13.

trators. Therefore, the following section deals with the due process that is more appropriately applied to certificated staff members. Both processes, however, may lead to the same outcome, termination of employment. It is important to keep in mind that a progressive discipline process does not supersede the appraisal process. Rather, it is a method of dealing with problems that cannot wait to be dealt with through the normal appraisal process.

DEVELOPING TERMINATION PROCEDURES

A universally accepted purpose for evaluating an individual's performance is to make a determination concerning the desirability of retaining that person as an employee of the school district. A decision to dismiss an employee, of course, is extremely difficult to make because of the importance of employment to a person's welfare and also because of the effects such a decision has on the employee's dependents.

Employment counselors have seen the devastating financial and psychological effects that "getting fired" has on a person's life. In fact, the trauma usually centers on the individual's self-concept. Feelings of inadequacy, failure, self-contempt, and anger are common to people who have their employment terminated. Although most individuals are able to cope with such a situation, others never fully recover from such an experience. Consequently, it is not only good personnel management but also a humane responsibility for school district administrators to develop termination procedures that are objective and fair, and that incorporate a due process that gives an employee the opportunity to modify or defend his behavior. Appendix E, *Missouri State Statutes Governing Revocation of License, Contract Management, and Termination Procedures* presents a model that will be used here to explicate the nuances of due process and the grounds for terminating employment. Although these statutes pertain specifically to teachers, the concepts explained are applicable to other categories of employees.

Grounds for Terminating the Employment of Tenured Teachers (Statute 168.114)

A tenured teacher may have his or her employment terminated for one or more of the following causes: Physical or mental condition unfitting him or her to instruct or associate with children; immoral conduct; insubordination, inefficiency, or incompetency in the line of duty; willful or persistent violation of, or failure to obey, the state laws pertaining to schools; willful or persistent violation of the published policies and procedures of the school board; excessive or unreasonable absence from work; conviction of a felony or a crime involving moral turpitude.

The first cause listed must be understood within the context of the Rehabilitation Act of 1973. A handicap does not constitute a physical condition that may in any way be construed as unfitting an individual from associating with children or students. In fact, the prevalent interpretation of the law is that an aide must be hired to assist an employee if the employee's handicap interferes with the instruction or supervision of children. The only possible physical condition that would prevent an employee from associating with children is the contracting of a contagious disease. This would be a potential cause for dismissal only if the individual refused to get medical treatment and insisted on working while he or she was contagious. Emotional illness that produces dangerous or bizarre behavior is also a potential cause for dismissal if the employee refuses to receive medical treatment and insists on working while ill. In both cases, documentation from a physician is necessary to proceed with the termination process. Of course, the school district is responsible for all expenses incurred in securing the expert opinion of the physician.

Immoral conduct must be judged within the context of local standards but also must be reasonable and consistent with recent court decisions. A number of significant court cases have been reviewed and form the foundation for the following principles that should be used in judging employee conduct. First, the health of the pupil-teacher relationship is the criterion for judging employee behavior. A teacher or other employee who establishes a relationship with a student that goes beyond friendship and is exhibited in some form of "dating" is unacceptable. Second, illegal sexual acts are cause for immediate suspension. If an employee is convicted of performing such an act, his employment with the district must be terminated. Suspension is a justifiable practice while investigating allegations of sexual misconduct, if the employee receives his or her salary during this period. Third, private nonconventional sexual life styles are not a cause for employee dismissal. Such practices as wife swapping, homosexuality, and cohabitation outside of matrimony may be unacceptable to the majority of people in the community, but such practices do not inherently affect an individual's performance in the workplace. These and other practices are displayed publicly on television and in other media, which to an extent has nullified their impact on students. Fourth, if an employee advocates nonconventional sexual life styles at school, the employee has placed himself or herself in a position where termination is possible, because such life styles are in direct conflict with local standards.

Insubordination in the line of duty is always a cause for dismissal. Although the interpretation of what constitutes insubordination may appear to be self-evident, insubordination has restricted application. Employees can be insubordinate only if they refuse to comply with a directive of their supervisor that is clearly within their job expertise. If a principal asks a teacher to supervise the children on the playground during the teacher's preparation time and the teacher refuses, the teacher is insubordinate because teachers have the job-related responsibility of supervising children. On the other hand, if the principal were to direct a custodian to supervise the children on the playground and he refused, the custodian would not be guilty of insubordination because this is not within his occupational expertise. Nor would it be insubordination if a teacher refused to fill-in for the principal's secretary, who was absent from work because of illness. The teacher was not hired to perform secretarial functions and may refuse this directive. The manner in which an employee responds to a directive does not usually constitute insubordination if the employee performs the task. Thus, if a teacher responds in a sharp tone to the principal when assigned to playground duty, but obeys the directive, the teacher is not guilty of insubordination.

Inefficiency is relatively easy to document. It usually refers to the inability of an individual to manage those tasks that are integral to a job responsibility. A teacher who never takes class attendance or who cannot account for the equipment, books, or materials assigned to his or her class is obviously inefficient. A principal who is always late in turning in building budgets or other reports also falls into this category.

Incompetency is perhaps the most difficult cause to document in terminating an employee. It also is directly related to the formal evaluation process. If a tenured teacher is performing in an incompetent manner, it means that he or she is hindering the instructional-learning process. The evaluations made by the principal must clearly indicate that major deficiencies have been identified and that objectives to remedy these deficiencies have not been met.

Claiming willful or persistent violation of state school laws or board of education policies and procedures as a cause for termination presupposes that school district employees have been informed of these. An effective method of notifying employees about these laws, policies, and procedures is through the publication and distribution of a handbook or manual that clearly outlines the employee's responsibilities.

Excessive or unreasonable absence from work is a relative circumstance that can be substantiated only through a policy defining what is meant by *excessive* or *unreasonable*. Local school boards probably will rely on patterns of absences in making their determination. Five consecutive days per month over a year's span, for example, could be considered excessive if the employee is not suffering from a chronic physical condition that interferes with attendance at work.

Conviction of a felony is obviously a reason to terminate the employment of an individual. The conviction for a crime involving moral turpitude, however, requires some explanation. Prostitution is usually classified as a misdemeanor, but because it involves morally offensive conduct according to most community standards, it is a reason to terminate a tenured teacher. The selling of pornography or a conviction for the use or sale of drugs also falls within the definition of moral turpitude.

In 1989 Congress passed the Drug-Free Workplace Act, which gives employers the choice of rehabilitating or dismissing staff members working in federal grant programs who are convicted of drug abuse offenses in the workplace. This law and federal administrative regulations require school districts to maintain a drug-free work environment by explicitly prohibiting employees from manufacturing, distributing, dispensing, possessing, or using unlawful drugs in the workplace. In addition schools must also provide a drug-free awareness program, which must include a description of the dangers of drug abuse, notification of the new requirements and penalties for violations, and information on available employee assistance programs. Employees must inform their supervisor within five days of a criminal conviction for a workplace drug crime. Job applicants must inform a potential employer of prior workplace drug conviction.

It is becoming common practice for school districts to give a second chance to persons convicted of a workplace drug offense by offering them the services of a drug rehabilitation program. This also points up the growing necessity of employee assistance programs as a voluntary fringe benefit for all employees.

This law also gives school district administrators the right to require persons to be tested for drugs when there is reason to suspect that these individuals are using or are under the influence of drugs on school premises or at school functions.[6]

Notification of Charges Against a Tenured Teacher (Statute 168.116)

After a behavior has been identified that could result in the termination of an employee, the next step in a due process is notification. This is a formal procedure of serving the employee with written charges specifying the alleged grounds that, if not corrected, will eventuate in dismissal. It must be kept in mind that notification with an opportunity to correct behavior is applicable only to charges arising out of incompetency, inefficiency, or insubordination in the line of duty. Physical or mental conditions as described above, immoral conduct, violation of school laws or board of education policies and procedures, excessive absences, and conviction of a felony or crime involving moral turpitude require a hearing before termination of employment, but they obviously do not require a period of time to correct the behavior. The behavior has already gone beyond what is rectifiable in an educational setting. A hearing is required, however, to determine if the facts substantiate the allegation.

Notification of charges, an extremely formal process, must not be confused with evaluation procedures that permit an employee the right to disagree with a written evaluation. As a normal course of action, employees may attach a written rebuttal to the evaluation instrument, setting forth points of disagreement and including any documentation to support their position.

Time periods are an essential component of the notification process. Three time periods are specified in these statutes: a thirty-day period during which time the employee has an opportunity to modify his behavior; a twenty-day period before a hearing is held, which allows the employee time to gather evidence supporting his or her position; and a ten-day period after service on the teacher of a hearing during which time he or she must respond to the notification that he or she wishes to have the hearing. If the employee does not wish to have a hearing on the charges, the board of education may terminate his or her employment with the school district by a majority vote of the board members.

This statute also sets forth another common practice in termination proceedings. The teacher may be suspended with pay after notice of a hearing until the board of education makes a determination concerning the employment of the teacher.

Termination Hearing on Charges Against a Tenured Teacher (Statute 168.118)

This statute outlines a procedure that must be followed in conducting a hearing that might eventuate in the dismissal of a tenured teacher. Once again, these statutes present a model that is applicable to all termination proceedings.

---

[6]Staff, "The Administrative Angle on Policy Implementation," *National School Boards Association,* no. 2 (June 1989), p. 1.

1. The hearing shall be held in a public forum. There is a distinction between a public hearing and a hearing held in public. At a public hearing, those in attendance are usually allowed to address those conducting the hearing according to preestablished procedures; at a hearing held in a public forum, only those representing the party making the allegation and those representing the party against whom the allegation is made are allowed to speak and participate in the hearing.

2. Both parties may be represented by an attorney, who may cross-examine witnesses.

3. The testimony given at a hearing shall be under oath. Government agencies such as school districts are usually allowed the privilege of administering oaths in official proceedings. Normally, the president or secretary of the board of education is the official so empowered.

4. The board of education may subpoena witnesses and documentary evidence requested by the teacher. As with the power to administer oaths, school districts usually have subpoena rights and may limit the number of witnesses called on behalf of the teacher or school district administrators.

5. The proceedings at the hearing should be recorded by a stenographer employed by the school district. A tape recording of the hearing is usually acceptable in lieu of a stenographer. A transcript of the proceedings must be made available not only to the school board but also to the teacher. The transcript of a hearing held in public should be open to public inspection.

6. Except for the fee paid to the attorney representing the teacher, all expenses for conducting the hearing should be paid by the school district.

7. The decision by the board of education should be reached within a preestablished time period to ensure fair treatment to the employee.

The board of education is exercising judicial authority in conducting the hearing and reaching a decision on the possible dismissal of a tenured teacher. This is a unique circumstance because the school board acts in two capacities: prosecution, in the sense that the charges are brought against the employee in the name of the school board; and judicial, because the school board renders the decision. In this respect the board of education is reviewing its own action. Consequently, it is extremely important to demonstrate, as much as possible, impartiality in the hearing structure. The evidence should be presented by an attorney representing the building principal and other line administrators because these administrators have the responsibility for evaluating and reviewing employee performance.

The room should be arranged to clearly delineate the functions that will be exercised at the hearing. The board of education will occupy a central place in the room seated at a table. A second table with a chair could be set up perhaps ten to fifteen feet in front of and facing the board members where witnesses will give testimony. To either side of the board table and facing each other should be two tables: seated at one, the teacher and his or her attorney; and at the other, the appropriate administrator with the school district's attorney. Those in attendance should be seated in a manner that clearly indicates that they are observers and not participants in the proceedings.

Another mechanism sometimes used in lieu of a formal hearing when discussing the possible termination of an employee is an executive session board meeting. Most states have statutes permitting government bodies to hold such private meetings at which public attendance is excluded. If a teacher or any employee is confronted with documentary evidence that could possibly result in his or her termination and if that employee had been given notice that his or her behavior must be modified, it may be possible to invite the employee to discuss his or her lack of improvement at an executive session of the school board. If the employee resigns in the face of the documentation, the expense and potential embarrassment of a public hearing are avoided.

Figure 7–2, *Evaluation of a Permanent Teacher,* schematically represents the relationship between the statutes elucidated in this section concerning the termination of a tenured teacher.

Appeal by a Tenured Teacher to a Termination Decision Issued by the Board of Education (Statute 168.120)

Because school districts are state government agencies, appeal from the decision of a school board is made to the state circuit court, which is the court of original jurisdiction in state civil and criminal matters. In most states this appeal must be made usually within a set period of time. All evidence, documentation, records, and the transcript of the hearing probably will be requested by the court. Of course, the employee has the right to appeal the decision of the circuit court, as in all civil cases, through to a court of appeals and supreme court if there is a justifiable reason.

Termination Procedures for Probationary Teachers (Statute 168.126)

A distinction must be made from the very beginning of this section between terminating the employment of a probationary teacher and not renewing a probationary teacher's contract. In the latter situation no formal due process is necessary; the employer–employee relationship simply ceases to exist with the expiration of the contract. This may occur if a probationary teacher is not performing at a level acceptable to the administration. A probationary teacher may have difficulty interacting with the students, staff, or parents in the school district or may be teaching at a minimal level. It is not only to the district's benefit but also to the teacher's benefit not to renew the contract since the teacher might be more successful in another school district. Not renewing a contract presupposes that evaluations have been made by the teacher's principal, that deficiencies have been pointed out, and that advice and help have been offered on how to improve performance or correct the stated deficiencies. If such a process has occurred, nonrenewal of the teacher's contract is justified.

This statute refers to terminating the employment of a probationary teacher before his or her contract expires. As with all other school district employees, the teacher must be given a written statement setting forth the allegations along with a reasonable time period to correct deficiencies and improve performance. If such corrections or improvements are not made within the specified time, the employee may be dismissed by action of the board of education.

Grounds and Procedure for Revocation of a Teacher's License to Teach (Statute 168.071)

A final formal procedure must be briefly alluded to when discussing termination procedures. A teacher's license to teach may be revoked if it can be proven that he or she has

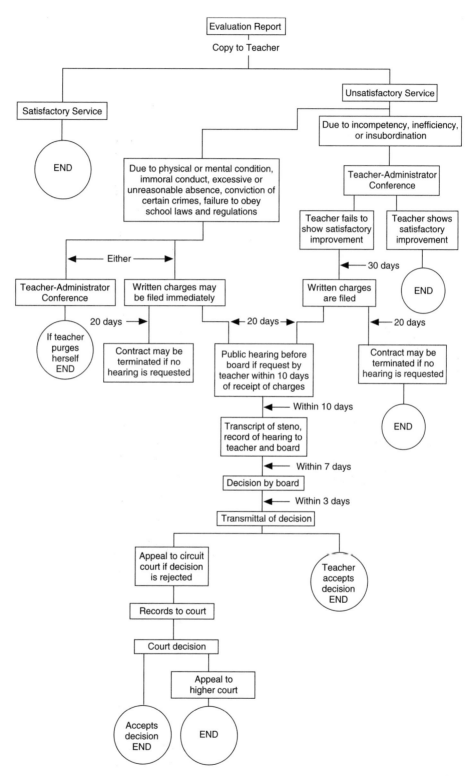

FIGURE 7-2 **Evaluation of a permanent teacher**

exhibited incompetency, cruelty, immorality, drunkenness, neglect of duty, or the annulling of a written contract with the board of education. As in the statute dealing with the termination of a tenured teacher, the reasons for revocation of a teacher's license have a very narrow interpretation.

Incompetency means that the teacher seriously hinders the instructional-learning process. A chronic mental illness or sociopathic behavior that has been diagnosed by a psychiatrist are examples of incompetency that could result in revocation of a teacher's license.

Cruelty refers not only to physical but also to mental or emotional abuse of children. The conditions that constitute cruelty may be summarized as follows: Any act that is meant to injure or bring serious ridicule and embarrassment to a child is abusive and cruel.

Of course, immorality is an extremely sensitive accusation. For practical considerations, this cause is commonly interpreted to mean that an individual has been convicted of a serious sexual offense or a crime involving moral turpitude. The examples provided earlier in this chapter are applicable to immorality as a cause for revocation of a teacher's license.

Drunkenness as a cause for revocation of an individual's license is usually interpreted to mean that the employee is either intoxicated or drinks alcoholic beverages while working. This cause is further strengthened by the fact that drinking alcoholic beverages in a government building such as a school is a misdemeanor in most states. A complicating factor is how drunkenness relates to the issue of alcoholism. Because alcoholism is considered to be a disease by the medical profession, the same considerations should be afforded the alcoholic as are granted to other employees with a medical problem. These considerations usually involve granting sick leave to an employee receiving medical treatment or reassigning the employee to a position with limited responsibilities during treatment. If an employee is not a diagnosed alcoholic and if he or she persists in drinking alcoholic beverages at work or continuously arrives at school intoxicated, license revocation is in the best interest of a school district's clientele, the children.

Neglect of duty presupposes that an employee has been informed about the responsibilities that are integral to his or her position with the school district. This is usually accomplished through written job descriptions or in policy manuals and handbooks specifying these responsibilities. Neglect of duty as a cause for revoking a teacher's license requires that the teacher be given an opportunity to rectify his or her behavior. Thus, evaluations that set forth the employee's deficiencies are necessary to such a situation. It also must be remembered that revocation of license is extremely serious and the neglect of duty, in like manner, must be extremely serious and chronic. A teacher who leaves young children unattended on a field trip—behavior that could result in an injury to a child—and who continues such irresponsible behavior after being informed of the danger by the principal has exhibited a lack of understanding that seriously affects his or her ability to supervise children. This is a reason not only to terminate the employment of the individual but also to safeguard against this teacher's potential employment with another school district by proceeding to have his or her license revoked.

Annulling of a written contract with the board of education is an improperly worded statement in this statute. Annulment means that both parties have agreed to the dissolution of the contract and the governing board has formally approved the dissolution. As cause for revocation of license, however, this aspect of the statute refers to the breaking of a contract by a teacher. Sometimes a teacher or other employee is offered a position with another school district or in private business and industry. If that teacher neglects to request a contract annulment from the school board and assumes another position, the board of education may proceed to have his or her license revoked. Most school boards are not resistant to annulling a contract except in those cases when the education of the students would be seriously affected. A teacher who tenders a resignation the day before the opening of school in September may not receive a contract annulment until a suitable replacement is obtained.

It should be clearly understood that the board of education does not have the authority to revoke a license; rather, the board may follow a statutory procedure that could eventuate in the revocation of a teacher's license. The state board of education, which issues teaching licenses, has the sole authority to revoke them.

Finally, revocation of a teacher's license is usually irreversible unless the statutory procedures were neglected or the evidence was faulty. It is, therefore, a very serious matter that should be initiated only if the education or health and safety of children will be significantly jeopardized not only now but also in future situations. Terminating the employment of an individual obviously removes him or her from injuring the children presently in his or her care. Revocation of license prevents the teacher from bringing such injury to children in another school district where he or she could be employed. A classic example involves the teacher who is convicted of child molestation and subsequently is fired from his position but who manages to get hired in another school district and commits a similar crime because his license was not revoked.

Humane Considerations in the Termination Process

The procedures described in this section may appear to overemphasize the legal and negative side of the appraisal process. It is, however, an aspect of appraisal that is seldom addressed and that is extremely important. Confusion over appropriate and fair termination procedures could result in a school district being saddled with an employee who hinders the instructional-learning process or who, in fact, may place children in an unsafe situation.

The educational welfare of children is the primary responsibility of a school district. The hiring, retaining, developing, and terminating of personnel should be guided by this mandate. However, employees also have rights that must be taken into consideration when developing appraisal procedures and dealing with employee evaluation. Due process is one right that has long been a fundamental principle in English common law and is basic to the legal procedures of American democracy.[7]

Chapter 6, *Staff Development,* makes the point that a legitimate objective of a staff development program is helping teachers and other employees to overcome deficiencies that affect their job performance. In like manner, Chapter 5, *Placement and Induction,* further provides guidelines for the transfer and placement of personnel to improve their performance.

---

[7]See the American Association of School Administrators, *Teacher Tenure Ain't the Problem* (Arlington, Va.: The Association, 1973), p. 24.

Humane personnel management presupposes that all alternatives have been exhausted in helping employees improve their performance or remove deficiencies before the process of termination is initiated.

SUMMARY

There are three historical stages of development in American education during this century concerning the evaluation of teachers. In the 1920s, efforts were primarily centered around analyzing if a given teaching style correlated with the philosophy and psychology of William James and John Dewey. The second stage was concerned with ascribing certain personality traits as being related to excellence in teaching. In the 1960s, the final stage emphasized generic teaching behaviors.

The last five years have ushered in a dramatic change in evaluation procedures. The traditional concept of teacher evaluation has been replaced by the broader concept of appraisal management. By this approach an employee is evaluated within the context of attaining certain preestablished objectives.

The reasons that justify the establishment and implementation of an appraisal process for all school district employees include the following: to foster self-development, to identify a variety of tasks which an employee is capable of performing, to identify staff development needs, to improve employee performance, to determine if an employee should be retained and what his salary increase should be, and to help in the proper placement or promotion of an employee.

A significant aspect of an appraisal process is measuring an employee's performance against his job responsibilities as outlined in his job description.

In developing an appraisal process, the board of education should establish a policy on employee appraisal that will give direction to the various divisions within a school district. These divisions are responsible for developing objectives aimed at implementing the goals of the school board. Each employee is then responsible for developing personal objectives that further the divisional objectives. Consequently, employee performance is measured against the degree to which each individual has attained his or her objectives. Feedback data is then available to analyze if divisional objectives have been reached. The actual appraisal procedures for implementing this process are best developed by involving representatives of the employees who will be evaluated.

As with the development of appraisal procedures, evaluation instruments are more appropriately constructed by the committee process. There are two basic categories of evaluation instruments: trait forms and result forms. The trait approach rates an employee against a predetermined list of traits to ascertain overall performance. The results approach involves comparing an employee's performance against objectives that were developed by the employee and agreed to by his or her supervisor. Using both types of instruments helps to identify areas where improvement is needed.

Termination procedures, an aspect of the appraisal process that is seldom addressed, are extremely important. Because "getting fired" has such a devastating effect on the financial and emotional welfare of an individual, termination procedures must be fair and objective. Most states have statutory provisions outlining the due process that must be afforded teachers before termination. Such legislation, while applying to the professional staff, also provides a model for boards of education in establishing similar procedures for all employees. The educational welfare of students is the primary concern of a school district, but employees also have rights that must be taken into consideration when developing appraisal procedures and dealing with employee dismissal.

APPENDIX A*
TEACHER EVALUATION POLICIES AND PROCEDURES

Professional Evaluation

   I. Philosophy and Policy—The performance of all certified personnel in the Valley Park School District shall be periodically evaluated. Evaluation shall be thorough, fair and objective. It shall be designed to improve instruction and to assist the professional staff in the growth and development of professional abilities, as well as to identify areas of strengths and weakness.

  II. Goals of Evaluation
    1. Improvement of instruction
    2. Fairness in tenure decisions
    3. Foster community relations
    4. Improvement in staff supervision
    5. Aid in gauging the quality of instruction
    6. Encourage professional improvement and growth through constant self-evaluation

 III. Rules of Procedure
    1. The building principal or supervisor has the primary responsibility for evaluation and shall be responsible for making recommendations concerning teachers to the superintendent.
    2. The teacher has a responsibility for continuous self-appraisal in relation to his or her areas of professional competence through discussion with the principal or supervisor.
    3. Evaluation is always functioning. It will occur through teacher–principal contacts, classroom visitations, teacher meetings, casual informal contacts, etc. This should not constitute any threat to effective principal–teacher relationships; no teacher need feel that he or she must be on his or her guard, watch his or her step or be wary of confiding in his or her principal, because each individual must be evaluated for and on the basis of what he or she really is, and is really doing, not on the basis of how well he or she can conceal reality. The professional knows what he or she is doing and why. The professional should not only welcome evaluation, but should seek it out to guarantee and substantiate his or her own self-evaluation and to resolve differences if there are any discovered.
      a. Probationary teacher's formal evaluation shall occur at least three times each year. The first evaluation of probationary teachers will be completed by November 1, the second by January 15, the third by March 1.
      b. Permanent teacher's formal evaluation shall occur at least one time each year, before March 1.
    4. Minimum formal evaluation shall occur as follows:
      a. The evaluator will visit the teacher's classroom informally a number of times throughout the year.
      b. Each classroom visitation should be recorded and included in the teacher's evaluation file as a record.

Professional Evaluation, Valley Park School District. St. Louis County, Missouri, 1981.

   c. All conferences and recommendations to the teacher shall be recorded with copies to the teacher. Both teacher and evaluator will sign these reports.
   d. The teacher should take the initiative to request spot visits by the principal over and above those indicated whenever the teacher feels that it will assist the principal in the evaluative process.
   e. The principal will maintain a cumulative evaluation file of all pertinent data relating to each teacher. This file shall be available for the teacher's examination and use.
   f. Prior to the date of the formal evaluation report, the principal or supervisor will schedule a formal evaluative interview with each teacher.
   g. In the evaluative interview the evaluator and teacher will discuss classroom visits and compare the completed instruments. Any significant differences should be thoroughly analyzed and resolved if possible.
   h. In the case of traveling or special teachers each principal to whom the individual is assigned shall be responsible for at least one classroom visitation. Reports on this visit shall be discussed with the teacher and recorded. The formal evaluative conference will be conducted in the manner described above by each building principal. The final evaluative report and recommendation may be prepared either jointly or individually by the principals concerned.
   i. The formal evaluation in March shall contain recommendations concerning reemployment and tenure.
   j. If a teacher is not satisfied with a given evaluation, he or she may submit in writing to the superintendent a rebuttal, which will be reviewed and will be placed in the teacher's personnel folder. A copy of the rebuttal should be submitted to the building principal. A conference may be scheduled with the superintendent by the teacher to discuss the evaluation.
   k. The individual teacher's evaluation file shall be open to no one except the teacher, administrative personnel, and the Board of Education meeting in executive session.
5. Training of Evaluators—An in-service program for training of personnel responsible for evaluation will be provided. Provision will be made to have annual training sessions. In addition constant efforts are to be made by the school district personnel to keep current on methods of improvement of instruction, learning theories and methods.
6. Record Keeping—It shall be the responsibility of the personnel office to keep necessary records required by the tenure law and the teacher evaluation procedure. The superintendent will provide the principal with necessary information concerning the tenure law at the beginning of the school year. Other information will be provided as needed. All records concerning teacher evaluation are confidential records and should be dealt with accordingly.
7. Evaluation in each of the evaluative categories will be determined during the interview conference between the evaluator and the teacher. The composite evaluation will be determined in accordance with the explanation attached.

Personal Traits

• Maintains adequate physical vitality.
• Is punctual.
• Is well-groomed.
• Maintains appropriate emotional control.
• Is conscientious.
• Fulfills responsibilities without constant supervision.
• Makes practical common sense judgments.
• Uses tact.
• Can act in original situations without directions.

- Is cooperative and a good team worker.
- Is receptive to constructive criticism and suggestion.
- Is self-confident.
- Is reasonable in self-evaluation.
- Is able to meet people on a courteous level of mutual self-respect.

Executive Traits and Classroom Management
- Completes necessary paper work promptly and accurately.
- Arranges to have materials at hand when needed.
- Evaluates materials and keeps only applicable materials to meet curriculum objectives.
- Recognizes each student as an individual within the framework of the school program.
- Assumes the responsibility for discipline unless unusual factors are involved.
- Makes authority understood and accepted in a gracious manner.
- Transmits enthusiasm for the subject.
- Assumes responsibility for appropriate evaluation of assignments.
- Maintains a neat, clean classroom conducive to learning.
- Is willing to use professional resource people within the school system.
- Is in control of classroom at all times.

Teaching Power
- Selects and organizes material with definite objectives compatible with the curriculum guides that are adapted to pupil needs, interests and capacities.
- Has prepared unit lesson plans based on specific objectives.
- Is aware of the importance of proper motivation.
- Uses student experiences to enrich and give meaning to content.
- Uses a variety of techniques and innovations to reach desirable goals.
- Uses student responses to aid his teaching.
- Accepts his responsibility to improve attitudes, work habits and skills.
- Uses grammatically correct, precise English.
- Uses a well modulated voice.
- Evaluates instruction regularly and reteaches when necessary.
- Shows imagination in adapting materials for classroom use.
- Displays materials that stimulate students' desire to learn.
- Can present ideas in a clear and concise manner.

Professional Responsibility
- Develops a relationship with students which is warm and inspiring and yet professional.
- Adheres to the NEA *Code of Ethics of the Education Profession.*
- Is proud to be a teacher and lets this pride show.
- Supports the profession, regarding this as a privilege to be able to participate in activities which improve the profession.
- Takes personal responsibility for individual professional growth.
- Contributes to the advancement of education by working effectively on committees, by assuming individual responsibility for improvement of schools.
- Understands and follows school policies and procedures.
- Respects group decisions.

- Respects and is discreet in using professional information.
- Can explain an educational point of view clearly and convincingly.
- Maintains a spirit of mutual respect in teacher–student, teacher–teacher, principal–teacher, and parent–teacher relationships.

Scholarship
- Works to develop a mastery of his chosen field of specialization.
- Maintains a continuing spirit of learning and understanding.
- Knows the psychology of learning, learning theories, and is aware of new trends in the field.
- Surveys recent educational periodicals and reads information pertinent to his work.

Community Relations
- Is informed about local school problems.
- Is aware of the strengths and the problems of the Valley Park School community.
- Realizes that the adequate support of free public schools in the community is based upon a general understanding of and respect for the educational program.
- Speaks and acts in community contacts to promote the general understanding of and respect for the educational program, distinguishing between personal opinion and district policy.

Explanation of Composite Evaluation for Use in the Valley Park School District

Professional Staff Evaluation

Superior   An individual receiving this evaluation is truly outstanding. He or she meets all the criteria under each evaluative category.

Strong   An individual receiving this evaluation is a very definite asset to the children of the school district. He or she meets a large majority of the criteria under each evaluative category, and receives a similar composite rating. This person is expected to recognize his or her determined weaknesses and to compensate by exercising strengths. Weaknesses are corrected or minimized.

Average   An individual receiving this evaluation is fulfilling assigned tasks at a satisfactory level. He or she meets a majority of the criteria under each evaluative category and receives a similar composite rating. This person will be expected to show an affinity for correcting or minimizing the obvious weaknesses isolated during the evaluative process.

Unsatisfactory   An individual receiving this evaluation is not adequately fulfilling assigned tasks. He or she does not meet the criteria under each evaluative category deemed necessary for continued employment in the Valley Park School District.

No Data   Information is not available or does not apply to the position.

APPENDIX B*
TEACHER EVALUATION REPORT FORMS
AND PERFORMANCE INDICATORS

LINDBERGH SCHOOL DISTRICT

4900 So. Lindbergh Blvd.
St. Louis, MO 63126

TEACHER EVALUATION REPORT

Teacher _____ School _____ Year _____

Subject or grade _____ Years in system _____

Status of Teacher ( ) Probationary ( ) Tenured

Philosophy   Evaluation is a means of improving the quality of instruction.

Purposes

1. To improve the quality of teaching and service to students.
2. To enable the teacher to recognize her/his role in the total school program.
3. To assist the teacher in achieving the established goals of the curriculum.
4. To help the teacher identify her/his strengths and weaknesses as a personal guide for her/his improvement.
5. To provide assistance to the teacher to help correct weaknesses.
6. To recognize the teacher's special talents and to encourage and facilitate their utilization.
7. To serve as a guide for renewed employment, termination of employment, promotion, assignment, and unrequested leave for tenured teachers.
8. To protect the teacher from dismissal without just cause.
9. To protect the teaching profession from unethical and incompetent personnel.

Implementation

The evaluation is to be made by the building principal, grade principal. assistant principal, or acting principal.

If a teacher does not agree with an evaluation, she/he may request an additional evaluation to be made by another administrator of her/his choice.

Evaluation of a probationary (non-tenured) teacher's services will be made semi-annually during the probationary period with one of the evaluations completed during the first semester, and both completed before April 1. Each evaluation must be preceded by at least one classroom visit.

Evaluation of a permanent (tenured) teacher's services will be made every year with the evaluation completed before April 1. Each evaluation must be preceded by at least one classroom visit.

Continued

---

*Lindbergh School District, St. Louis, Missouri, 1985.

Definition of terms

1. *Superior:* Consistently exceptional.
2. *Strong:* Usually surpasses standards of Lindbergh School District.
3. *Average:* Generally meets standards of Lindbergh School District.
4. *Improvement needed:* Occasionally does not meet standards of Lindbergh School District.
5. *Unsatisfactory:* Does not measure up to standards of Lindbergh School District.

NOTE: The space at the end of this form marked "Principal's Comments" may be utilized to record the observations of the teacher's exceptional performances and/or to record the principal's recommendations for improvement.

The space at the end of this form marked "Teacher's Comments" may be utilized by the teacher to record any comment or comments which she/he wishes to make.

	Superior	Strong	Average	I-N	Unsatis-factory
I. TEACHING PERFORMANCE	**1**	**2**	**3**	**4**	**5**
A. Plans and organizes carefully					
1. Lesson is well planned					
2. Sets definite goals including student participation					
3. Makes clear, specific assignments					
4. Is familiar with appropriate guide and adapts to the recommendations therein					
5. Provides for individual and group instruction					
B. Is skillful in questioning and explaining					
1. Asks thought provoking questions					
2. Gives clear explanation of subject matter					
3. Exposes students to varying points of view					
4. Is aware of both verbal and non-verbal acceptance or rejection of student's ideas, and uses this skill positively					
C. Stimulates learning through innovative activities and resources					
1. Encourages class discussion, pupil questions and pupil demonstrations					
2. Uses a variety of teaching aids and resources					
D. Displays knowledge of and enthusiasm for subject matter taught					
E. Provides a classroom atmosphere conducive to good learning					
1. Maintains a healthy and flexible environment					
2. Observes the care of instructional material and equipment					

Continued

	Superior	Strong	Average	I-N	Unsatis-factory

F. Keeps adequate and accurate records
  1. Records sufficient quantitative and qualitative data on which to base pupil progress reports

G. Has wholesome relationship with pupils
  1. Knows and works with pupils as individuals
  2. Encourages relationships that are mutually respectful and friendly
  3. Uses positive language with students which is devoid of sarcasm

H. Initiates and preserves classroom and general school management and discipline
  1. Rules of pupil conduct have been developed and teacher requires observance of these rules
  2. Rules of safety have been developed and teacher requires observance of these rules

II. PROFESSIONAL QUALITIES

A. Recognition and acceptance of out-of-class responsibilities
  1. Participates in the general and necessary school activities
  2. Sometimes volunteers for the "extra" duties
  3. Serves on school committees

B. Intra-school relationship
  1. Cooperates effectively and pleasantly with colleagues, administration and non-professional personnel

C. Public relations
  1. Cooperates effectively and pleasantly with parents
  2. Practices good relationships between school and community

D. Professional growth and vision
  1. Accepts constructive criticism
  2. Participates in conferences, workshops and study
  3. Tries new methods and materials

E. Utilization of staff services
  1. Makes proper use of available special services

F. Understands the growth patterns and behaviors of students at various stages of development and copes satisfactorily with situations as they occur

G. Ethical behavior
  1. Protects professional use of confidential data

Continued

DEFINITION OF TERMS FOR PERSONAL QUALITIES

S - Satisfactory: meets or surpasses standard for Lindbergh School District teachers.

I - Improvement needed: does not measure up to standards Lindbergh School District teachers meet.

III. PERSONAL QUALITIES

	S	I

A. Health and vigor
1. Has a good and reasonable attendance record
2. Is cheerful
3. Displays a sense of humor

B. Speech
1. Is articulate
2. Can be heard and understood by all pupils in the room
3. Speaks on the level of pupils' understanding

C. Grooming and appropriateness of dress
1. Practices habits of good grooming

D. Promptness in meeting obligations
1. Reports to classes on time
2. Performs assigned tasks properly
3. Completes reports on time

A copy of the written evaluation will be submitted to the teacher at the time of the conference following the observation(s). The final evaluation report form is to be signed and retained by the principal, and a copy is to be retained by the teacher. In the event the teacher feels the evaluation was incomplete, inaccurate, or unjust, she/he may put the objections in writing and have them attached to the evaluation report to be placed in her/his personal files. Teacher's signature acknowledges that the conference has taken place.

DATE OF OBSERVATION(S) _____

TIME OF OBSERVATION(S) _____

LENGTH OF OBSERVATION(S) _____

DATE EVALUATION MADE _____

PRINCIPAL'S SIGNATURE _____

TEACHER'S SIGNATURE _____

PRINCIPAL'S COMMENTS

TEACHER COMMENTS

Performance Indicators

Indicators for the evaluation items in the Teacher Evaluation Report were developed by the administrators in the Lindbergh School District. The indicators are representative of the kinds of teacher-learning techniques the evaluator will be looking for when observing a teacher in a classroom situation. It is expected that each teacher will perform the skill as listed but that the final evaluation will be based on the degree of performance.

I. TEACHING PERFORMANCE
   A. *Plans and organizes carefully*
      1. *Lesson is well-planned*
         a. Written plans are available and followed by classroom teacher.
         b. Lesson includes preview, statement of objective, and review.
         c. Lesson fits within an alloted time frame.
         d. Lesson follows a logical sequence.
         e. Lesson meets the needs of the student group.
         f. Long- and short-range goals are clearly defined.
         g. Lesson indicates the teacher has used the concept of diagnosis and prescription.
         h. Lesson is flexible to permit spontaneous teaching.
         i. Plans and procedures are provided.
         j. Materials and equipment are readily available.
      2. *Sets definite goals including student participation,*
         a. Long- and short-range goals are clearly defined.
         b. Students are involved in the goal-setting process when appropriate.
      3. *Makes clear, specific assignment*
         a. Reasonable and clear assignments are given in written form.
         b. Adequate time is given for clarification and discussion of assignment.
      4. *Is familiar with appropriate guide and adapts to the recommendation therein*
         a. Lesson reflects thorough knowledge of curriculum guide.
         b. Long-range planning for coverage of objectives in curriculum guide is indicated.
      5. *Provides for individual and group instruction*
         a. Lesson provides for individual instruction.
         b. Lesson provides for group instruction.
         c. Type of instruction is suited to lesson presented.
   B. *Is skillful in questioning and explaining*
      1. *Asks thought-provoking questions*
         a. Asks questions requiring more than a one-word answer.
         b. Questions stimulate critical and divergent thinking.
         c. Written questions are thought provoking.
         d. Questions asked stimulate a response from students.
      2. *Gives clear explanation of subject matter*
         a. Obtains response indicating understanding before continuing further explanation.
         b. Presents ideas in a logical sequence.
         c. Consistently uses correct grammar and vocabulary suited to student.
         d. Presents accurate and complete content information.
      3. *Exposes students to varying points of view*
         a. Establishes a background of general information on the topic before presenting varying points of view.

b. Presents varying points of view consistent with curriculum.

c. Elicits from students their points of view.

4. *Is aware of both verbal and nonverbal acceptance or rejection of students' ideas, and uses this skill positively*

a. Does not show rejection through verbal or physical expression.

b. Does not allow peer-rejection.

c. Praises, elicits, and responds to student questions and answers before proceeding.

C. *Stimulates learning through innovative activities and resources,*

1. *Encourages class discussion, pupil questions, and pupil demonstrations*

a. Listens patiently to students' comments, questions, and answers.

b. Questions are asked according to students' ability to answer correctly.

c. Gives each student an opportunity to participate.

2. *Uses a variety of teaching aids and resources*

a. Looks for and uses models, manipulative materials, films,, outside speeches, worksheets, records, etc.

b. Materials and resources are appropriate for the lesson.

c. Displays materials that are coordinated with the lesson.

D. *Displays knowledge of and enthusiasm for subject matter taught*

1. *Displays knowledge of subject matter taught*

a. Displays knowledge of content of textbook(s).

b. Demonstrates competence and familiarity with subject matter.

c. Has comprehensive knowledge of related disciplines and uses it when appropriate.

d. Answers students' questions readily and thoroughly.

e. Probes for knowledge of content presented (encourages questions and activities that are designed to stimulate critical thinking).

f. Goes beyond the textbook to enhance the content (may be observed by use of films, resource persons, reference materials,, charts, etc.).

2. *Enthusiasm*

a. Students respond positively to the teacher (Do the students appear interested? Are they listening to the teacher? Are they awake? Are they talking to other students? Do they appear bored?).

b. Interest and enthusiasm are evidenced from the teacher's presentation.

c. Responds positively to the students, both verbally and visually.

d. Elicits enthusiastic response from the students, to the questions and answers.

e. Uses techniques that engender enthusiasm in students (a change of pace, voice inflections, body movement).

E. *Provides a classroom atmosphere conducive to good learning,*

1. *Maintains a healthy and flexible environment*

a. Sets the tone for students to feel free to ask and to respond to questions (students are not intimidated).

b. Classroom atmosphere is controlled but not dominated by the teacher (students interact with the environment).

c. Differing views and values are allowed to be discussed.

d. Positive interpersonal relationships are easily observed.

e. Uses humor in proper perspective.

f. Room reflects students' work.

2. *Observes the care of instructional material and equipment,*

a. Equipment in use is carefully supervised.

b. Equipment or material not in use is properly stored.

    c. Equipment is properly maintained and/or reported to the office for repair.

    d. Desks are devoid of writing and graffiti.

    e. Promotes respect for instructional materials and equipment.

F. *Keeps adequate and accurate records*

    1. *Records sufficient quantitative and qualitative data on which to base pupil progress reports*

        a. Records a number of written assignments, test scores,, daily grades, and exam grades in the grade book (indicators of each student's performance).

        b. Quality of data recorded shows relationship between the objectives and grades.

        c. Daily attendance is correctly recorded.

G. *Has wholesome relationship with pupils*

    1. *Knows and works with pupils as individuals*

        a. Individual strengths and weaknesses of each student have been identified.

        b. Knows and calls each student by name.

        c. Listens carefully and politely to each student.

        d. Encourages student ideas and concentrates on their response.

        e. Students do not hesitate to ask for clarification.

        f. Students appear to be an active part of the class.

        g. Creative responses are encouraged.

    2. *Encourages relationships that are mutually respectful and friendly*

        a. Encourages positive behavior by maintaining complete control of self.

        b. Words and actions are positive.

        c. Exhibits qualities of warmth towards students.

        d. Elicits student responses.

        e. Sets an example of respect.

        f. Is sensitive to students' moods.

        g. Behavior is consistent with all students and situations.

        h. Handling of misconduct centers on the conduct or behavior,, not the student.

        i. Requires student attention and gives attention in return.

    3. *Uses positive language with students that is devoid of sarcasm*

        a. Praises and elicits responses from students.

        b. Sarcasm is not used.

        c. Is positive in actions, voice tones, and movements.

        d. Tone of voice is moderate and even.

H. *Initiates and preserves classroom and general school management and discipline*

    1. *Rules of pupil conduct have been developed and teacher requires observance of these rules*

        a. Classroom incidents handled so as not to interrupt entire class.

        b. Pupils are aware of rules and regulations.

        c. Students understand and follow room routine readily without teacher's direction.

        d. Demonstrates behavior that is achievement oriented or businesslike.

        e. Is consistent and fair in expectations of behavior.

        f. Students enter room quietly and take seats.

        g. Students ask and receive permission to change patterns.

    2. *Rules of safety have been developed and teacher requires observance of these rules*

        a. Classroom behavior shows a concern for safety.

        b. Safety procedures are properly posted and followed.

        c. Horseplay is not tolerated.

        d. Plays an active and positive role in the supervision of halls, restrooms, lunchrooms, and pre/post class time as well as at assemblies.

        e. Classroom is free of hazards.

II. PROFESSIONAL QUALITIES
   A. *Recognition and acceptance of out-of-class responsibilities,*
      1. *Participates in the general and necessary school activities,*
         a. Performs assigned duties consistently.
         b. Follows the school time schedule.
         c. Attends and participates in school-related activities.
         d. Participates in assigned meetings.
      2. *Sometimes volunteers for the "extra" duties,*
         a. Accepts responsibilities other than those considered general or necessary.
         b. Initiates volunteer services to the overall school program.
      3. *Serves on school committees*
         a. Serves on district and/or school committees.
         b. Attends school and/or district committee meetings.
         c. Participates in school and/or district level committees.
   B. *Intra-school relationship*
      1. *Cooperates effectively and pleasantly with colleagues,, administration, and nonprofessional personnel*
         a. Relationships with other professionals indicate acceptance of differing views or values.
         b. Practices relationships that are mutually respectful and friendly.
         c. Shares ideas, materials, and methods.
         d. Informs appropriate personnel of school-related matters.
         e. Cooperates fairly and works well with all school personnel.
         f. Is effective in providing a climate that encourages communication between self and professional colleagues.
   C. *Public relations*
      1. *Cooperates effectively and pleasantly with parents,*
         a. Maintains good communication with parents.
         b. Keeps best interest of student in mind.
         c. Provides a climate that opens up communication between the teacher and parent.
      2. *Practices good relationship between school and community*
         a. Enhances school involvement with communities.
         b. Encourages community involvement and attendance in school situations.
   D. *Professional growth and vision*
      1. *Accepts constructive criticism*
         a. Asks positive questions.
         b. Responds pleasantly to criticism.
      2. *Participates in conferences, workshops, and studies,*
         a. Is engaged in activities that promote professional growth.
         b. Engages in professional activities that are not required.
      3. *Tries new methods and materials*
         a. Uses new methods and materials at appropriate times.
         b. Modifies materials when needed.
         c. Understands new techniques before using.
   E. *Utilization of staff services*
      1. *Makes proper use of available special services*
         a. Makes use of and cooperates with district service personnel (guidance, library, supervisory, specialists, as well as classified staff members).
         b. Makes student recommendations and referrals to appropriate staff members as needed.

F. *Understands the growth patterns and behaviors of students at various stages of development and copes satisfactorily with situations as they occur*
  a. Uses a variety of techniques to achieve desired work and skills, and adjusts the techniques to the age and maturity of the student.
  b. Does not expect identical behavior from all students, but allows for individual differences.
  c. Is understanding and sympathetic to students with special learning and behavior problems.

G. *Ethical behavior*
  1. *Protects professional use of confidential data*
    a. Confidential information concerning students and their parents and staff members is not discussed in the lounge, cafeteria, or in the classroom.
    b. Respects confidential information.
  2. *Supports the teaching profession*
    a. Has a positive attitude toward teaching.
    b. Uses positive statements regarding teaching, students,, school, and profession.

III. PERSONAL QUALITIES
  A. *Health and vigor*
    1. *Has a good and reasonable attendance record*
      a. Absences are infrequent and justifiable.
      b. Places emphasis on assigned duties.
      c. Except in cases of extreme illness, is present at school and is prepared.
    2. *Is cheerful*
      a. Allows occasional humorous interruptions.
      b. Can relax and joke with students.
      c. Laughs with, not at, others.
    3. *Displays a sense of humor*
      a. Smiles easily.
      b. Has a friendly attitude.
  B. *Speech*
    1. *Is articulate*
      a. Consistently uses appropriate grammar.
      b. Communicates clearly.
    2. *Can be heard and understood by all pupils in the room,*
      a. Consistently uses appropriate tone of voice.
      b. Is easy to hear and understand.
    3. *Speaks on the level of pupils' understanding*
      a. Uses appropriate vocabulary and examples according to student's level of under-standing.
  C. *Grooming and appropriateness of dress*
    1. *Practices habits of good grooming*
      a. Is clean and neat.
      b. Clothes are appropriate for job task.
      c. Dress adds to rather than detracts from classroom performance.
  D. *Promptness in meeting obligations*
    1. *Reports to classes on time*
      a. Arrives at classroom before students.
      b. Classroom is open and in readiness prior to student arrival.

       c. Classroom preparations do not interfere with obligations.

       d. Arrives in the building at the required time.

    2. *Performs assigned tasks properly*

       a. Tasks are completed on time.

       b. Tasks are completed to letter and in spirit of the assignment.

  3. *Completes reports on time*

       a. Does not have to be reminded of reports that are due.

       b. Completes reports according to expectations of administrator.

LINDBERGH SCHOOL DISTRICT

4900 So. Lindbergh Blvd.
St. Louis, MO 63126

SHORT CLASSROOM VISIT FORM

The purpose of this form is to record data that will be pertinent in the overall evaluation of the teacher. The form will be used in conjunction with the Teacher Evaluation Report.

TEACHER _____ DATE OF VISIT _____

LENGTH OF VISIT _____ PERIOD _____

1. Did the lesson appear to be well planned? _____
   Topic being discussed _____

2. Was enthusiasm evidenced in the teacher's presentation? _____
   _____

3. Class reaction to the lesson _____
   Were the students involved? _____ Did they appear to be interested in the lesson?
   _____

4. Describe the type of interactions between the teacher and students, and students with students _____

5. Was there any unusual activity taking place? _____

6. Was there anything unusual about the physical appearance of the room? _____
   _____

7. Were personal qualities positive? _____
   _____

                      (speech, dress, grooming)

Principal's suggestions, comments _____

_____

_____

                            _____

                                Principal's Signature

APPENDIX C*

Administrator Evaluation Report

ADMINISTRATOR _____ YEAR _____
POSITION _____ SCHOOL _____
YEARS IN LINDBERGH ADMINISTRATION _____

Purposes:

Evaluation is to ensure that the administrator displays adequate management skills and leadership among the students, staff, and community. The evaluation process will assure that the administrator has goals appropriate to his level of responsibility and in line with overall school system goals. This process will aid the administrator in the improvement of his performance and provide a basis for merit pay adjustment.

Implementation:

1. The Superintendent will evaluate all building principals.
2. Evaluation of grade principals and assistant principals will be made by the building principal. The Superintendent will review these evaluations and confer with the principal prior to the formal evaluation.
3. The Evaluator will receive appropriate input from all Central Office Administrators prior to completing the evaluation.
4. Administrators will be evaluated on the standards and expectations of Lindbergh School District.
5. The evaluation will be made on a scale of one to nine ranging from improvement needed to consistently outstanding.
6. The overall rating will not be adversely affected by items marked not applicable.
7. The formal evaluation will take place following the close of the school year.

ADMINISTRATIVE SKILLS	Consistently Outstanding							Needs Improvement	NA
1. Has implemented procedures for budget preparation and accounting methods for monitoring the budget									
2. Has implemented a plan for the effective cleaning and maintenance of the facility									
3. Has implemented a process for inventorying, acquiring, and replacing of equipment									
4. Has implemented safety and energy conservation procedures									
5. Has established procedures for the use of student, teacher, and parent feedback									

Continued

*Lindebergh School District, St. Louis, Missouri, 1985.

ADMINISTRATIVE SKILLS	Consistently Outstanding							Needs Improvement	NA

6. Has developed and follows procedures for administrative scheduling and reporting

7. Has completed written communications accurately and on schedule

Total points _____ ÷ _____ number of items marked = _____ average marking.

INSTRUCTIONAL LEADERSHIP	Consistently Outstanding							Needs Improvement	NA

1. Has demonstrated knowledge of curricular issues in various subject areas

2. Has assisted classroom teacher in the implementation of the curriculum

3. Has evaluated the instructional program and used the results to plan program improvements

4. Has knowledge of good teaching methods and assists teachers to improve diagnostic skills and teaching strategies

5. Has carried out procedures to evaluate and maintain a building climate conducive to learning

Total points _____ ÷ _____ number of items marked = _____ average marking.

SUPERVISION	Consistently Outstanding							Needs Improvement	NA

1. Has coordinated the work of special and support personnel with the programs of the school

2. Has conducted a program of faculty and staff supervision that includes periodic visits, conferences and evaluation of all personnel

3. Has carried out a procedure for the orientation and supervision of all new personnel

Continued

SUPERVISION	Consistently Outstanding				Needs Improvement	NA
4. Has developed and implemented procedures to maintain effective school discipline						
5. Has maintained a system of supervision of all after school activities						

Total points _____ ÷ _____ number of items marked = _____ average marking.

SCHOOL AND COMMUNITY	Consistently Outstanding				Needs Improvement	NA
1. Has promoted good relationships between the school and community through positive interpretation and implementation of district policy						
2. Has conducted a comprehensive and effective system of communication with the students of the school						
3. Has conducted a comprehensive and effective system of communication with the parents of the school						
4. Has coordinated and maintained a volunteer program in the school						
5. Has participated in various civic, service, and community groups and community functions to help assure public knowledge and understanding of the school program						
6. Has provided support and guidance to P.T.O., Mothers' Club, and other parent groups						

Total points _____ ÷ _____ number of items marked = _____ average marking.

PERSONAL QUALITIES	Consistently Outstanding				Needs Improvement	NA
1. Has exhibited professional growth through in-service activities, conferences and conventions, membership in and participation in professional organizations, and continuing formal education						
2. Has displayed appropriate decision making skills by recognizing problems, evaluating facts, and implementing decisions						

Continued

PERSONAL QUALITIES	Consistently Outstanding						Needs Improvement	NA
3. Has displayed good personal relationships with administration, faculty, staff, parents, and students								
4. Has evidenced personal and professional ethics in all relationships								
5. Has shown sustained effort and enthusiasm in the quality and quantity of work accomplished								

Total points _____ ÷ _____ number of items marked = _____ average marking.

Building Priorities:

Each building priority is rated separately on a combination of the following criteria:

1. Building priorities are identified with input from teachers, students, and/or parents.
2. The design to meet each priority is clearly written with definitive steps and a timetable.
3. Periodic review of progress towards accomplishing each priority is carried out, and necessary adjustments are made during the year.

	Consistently Outstanding							Needs Improvement	NA
Priority I									
Priority II									
Priority III									
Priority IV									
Priority V									
Priority VI									
Priority VII									

Total points _____ ÷ _____ number of items marked = _____ average marking.

4. Accomplishment of building priorities involves participation and input from the school faculty and other affected groups when appropriate.
5. Each priority is completed according to the timetable and definitive steps in the original written design. Deviations from that design are stated and explained.

Rating System:

1. The *average marking* in each category is multiplied by the percentage weight given that area.
2. The weighted scores for each area are added. The sum will fall in a range from one to nine. The total score will be carried out to the third decimal place.
3. The sum of the weighted scores is applied directly to the merit portion of the administrators' salary schedule.

Continued

	Average Marking		Percentage Weight	Weighted Score
Administrative Skills	_____	X	.10	_____
Instructional Leadership	_____	X	.20	_____
Supervision	_____	X	.20	_____
School and Community	_____	X	.10	_____
Personal Qualities	_____	X	.10	_____
Building Priorities	_____	X	.30	_____
			Total	_____

EVALUATOR'S COMMENTS:

ADMINISTRATOR'S COMMENTS:

Evaluator's Signature _____ Date _____
Administratator's Signature _____ Date _____

APPENDIX D*
RATING SCALE TO EVALUATE ADMINISTRATOR PERFORMANCE

RATING SHEET
Administrator Evaluation Form

Instructions: Place an x on numbered line for each item. Leave item blank if you have no opinion.

	Negative				Positive		
	1	**2**	**3**	**4**	**5**	**6**	**7**
1. Maintains an open, positive working relationship with:							
A. Parents							
B. Staff							
C. Pupils							
D. Non-teaching staff							
E. Other administrators							
2. Is supportive of the classroom concerns of teachers							

Continued

*Thomas S. Butera, "Principal, Know Thyself," *NASSP Bulletin,* 60 (September 1976), p. 85.

	Negative				Positive		
	1	2	3	4	5	6	7
3. Is understanding of the personal concerns of teachers							
4. Takes definite steps to aid teachers' professional growth							
5. Evaluates teachers in objective manner							
6. Takes time to praise teachers							
7. Is open to suggestions and ideas							
8. Allows teachers to try new ideas							
9. Encourages new ideas							
10. Is able to mediate differences among staff							
11. Plans and executes inservice programs for staff							
12. Displays knowledge of curriculum							
13. Displays knowledge of new methods and materials							
14. Displays knowledge of budget and business procedures							
15. Delegates work to right people							
16. Helps establish a positive guiding climate							
17. Helps create and maintain high morale							
18. Is flexible							
19. Has knowledge of characteristics of this age group student							
20. Has general knowledge of the students in this building							
21. Treats students with respect							
22. Helps develop student control and responsible discipline							
23. Is aware of "what's going on" in building							
24. Makes commitments to educational beliefs							
25. Is respected by staff							
26. Is respected by students							
27. Availability							
28. Personality							
29. Appearance							
30. Visibility							

Using the items listed above as a guide, please use the remaining portion of this form to make any suggestions you feel would aid in improving this administrator's performance. You might indicate what you feel are some of his strongest assets and then some areas that need improvement.

APPENDIX E*
PERFORMANCE APPRAISAL—CUSTODIAL, LANDSCAPE, MAINTENANCE

Employee's Name _____

Position _____

Location _____ School Year _____

Instructions:

The Supervisor is to complete this form by placing the number of the rating on each item in the space provided. If an item is rated 1 or 2 then a statement is to be written in the comment area clarifying what needs to be done to improve. A form is to be completed at the end of three months on new employees and a second evaluation is to be completed by June 1 of each year. One copy of the form is to be given to the employee and a second copy is to be sent to the Personnel Department to be placed in the employee's file.

I. *Quality of Work*   Rating _____
   Indicators: Neatness, accuracy, consistency of quality.
   5. Exceptionally neat and accurate. Practically no mistakes.
   4. Usually accurate. Very neat. Seldom necessary to check work.
   3. Acceptable. Usually neat. Occasional errors—some supervision required.
   2. Acceptable work if closely supervised.
   1. Unacceptable work. Too many errors.

   Comment: _____
   _____

II. *Job Knowledge*   Rating _____
   Indicators: Experience, special training, education.
   5. Well informed on all phases of the job.
   4. Knowledge is thorough enough to perform without assistance.
   3. Knows job fairly well.
   2. Requires assistance frequently.
   1. Inadequate knowledge.

   Comment: _____
   _____

III. *Quantity of Work*   Rating _____
   Indicators: Amount of work required under normal conditions.
   5. Exceptional quantity. Rapid worker. Usually good production.
   4. Good volume—will do more than is expected.
   3. Average volume—does what is expected.
   2. Does not always complete expected amount of work.
   1. Slow Worker. Frequently does not complete duties.

   Comment: _____
   _____

Continued

*Lindbergh School District, St. Louis, Missouri, 1985.

IV. *Dependability*   Rating _____
   Indicators: Tasks are completed on time.
   5. Work is always completed on time.
   4. Work is almost always completed on time.
   3. Work is usually completed on time.
   2. Work is completed on time only under close supervision.
   1. Work is rarely completed on time.

   Comment: _____
   _____

V. *Initiative*   Rating _____
   Indicators: Develops new ideas, develops efficient ways of doing jobs, takes charge
   when something needs to be done, is self-reliant.
   5. Highly motivated and contributes new ideas frequently. Does other jobs without
      being told.
   4. Very resourceful. Can work on own. Occasionally contributes new ideas and
      methods. Does small jobs without being told.
   3. Does job very well. Will do other jobs when told to.
   2. Rarely volunteers to help in other area. Usually waits for instructions.
   1. Needs constant supervision. Not motivated. Displays little interest in improving.
      Does only what is told to do.

   Comment: _____
   _____

VI. *Cooperation and Relationship with Others*   Rating _____
   Indicators: How employee works with co-workers, supervisors, subordinates,
   parents, teachers, students, visitors.
   5. Goes out of the way to cooperate with others. Always has a positive attitude.
      Takes and gives instructions easily.
   4. Gets along well with others. Does not complain about others. Good attitude.
   3. Satisfactory relationship with others and only occasionally complains.
   2. Shows reluctance to cooperate and complains often.
   1. Very poor cooperation. Does not follow instructions. Complains often.

   Comment: _____
   _____

VII. *Ability to Learn*   Rating _____
   Indicators: Speed of understanding new routines, ability to understand explanations,
   how well instructions are carried out, ability to retain knowledge.
   5. Exceptional ability to learn assigned work and adjust to now conditions.
   4. Learns rapidly. Follows instructions well. Retains instructions.
   3. Usually understands instructions and masters new ideas reasonably well.
   2. Requires extra instruction. Necessary to repeat instructions.
   1. Very slow to understand instructions. Cannot remember instructions. Very slow
      to master new ideas.

   Comment: _____
   _____

Continued

VIII. *Attendance*   Rating _____
   Indicators: Number of days of absenteeism, number of tardies (consider the reasons for absenteeisms).
   5. Less than three days absent and less than three days tardy.
   4. Three or four days absent and less than three days tardy.
   3. Five or six days absent and less than five days tardy.
   2. Seven or eight days absent and less than seven days tardy.
   1. Nine or more days absent and more than six days tardy.

   Comment: _____

   _____

IX. *Appearance*   Rating _____
   Indicators: Cleanliness, appropriate dress (uniforms where applicable).
   5. Always neat and clean and appropriately dressed.
   4. Almost always neat and clean and appropriately dressed.
   3. Usually neat and clean and appropriately dressed.
   2. Usually neat and clean but not appropriately dressed.
   1. Often not neat and clean and often carelessly dressed.

   Comment: _____

   _____

Directions for Overall Evaluation

1. Add the ratings for all nine categories   _____
2. Divide by nine   _____
3. Circle the category that corresponds to the average.

4.6–5.0	Doing an excellent job.
3.6–4.5	Doing a very good job.
2.6–3.5	Doing a satisfactory job.
1.6–2.5	Work needs to be improved.
1.0–1.5	Work is unacceptable.

Employee Comments: _____

_____

_____

_____

_____

_____   _____
Signature of Supervisor   Signature of Employee

_____   _____
Date   Date

Employee's signature indicates the employee has had this form reviewed with him/her. The signature does not indicate agreement. An employee may appeal the decision of the supervisor to the next line supervisor. The decision of the superintendent is final.

APPENDIX F*
MISSOURI STATE STATUTES GOVERNING REVOCATION OF LICENSE, CONTRACT MANAGEMENT, AND TERMINATION PROCEDURES

168.071. Grounds for Revocation of License—Procedure—Appeal.

A certificate of license to teach may be revoked by the authority which issued the certificate upon satisfactory proof of incompetency, cruelty, immorality, drunkenness, neglect of duty, or the annulling of a written contract with the local board of education without the consent of the majority of the members of the board which is a party to the contract. All charges must be preferred in writing. They shall be signed by the chief administrative officer of the district or by the president of the board when so authorized by a majority of the board. The charges must be sworn to by the party or parties making the accusation, and filed with the respective certificating authority. The teacher must be given due notice of not less than ten days, and an opportunity to be heard, together with witnesses. The complaint must plainly and fully specify what incompetency, immorality, neglect of duty or other charges are made against the teacher, and if after a hearing the certificate is revoked, the teacher may appeal to the circuit court at any time within ten days thereafter by filing an affidavit and giving bond as is now required before magistrates. On appeal, the judge of the circuit court shall, with or without a jury at the option either of the teacher or the person making the complaint, try the matter de novo, affirming or denying the action of the certificating authority, and shall tax the cost against the appellant if the judgment of the certificating authority is affirmed. If the court disaffirms the judgment, then it shall assess the costs of the whole proceedings against the district making the complaint.

168.106. Indefinite Contract, What Affects

The contract between a school district and a permanent teacher shall be known as an indefinite contract and shall continue in effect for an indefinite period, subject only to:

(1) Compulsory or optional retirement when the teacher reaches the age of retirement provided by law, or regulation established by the local board of education;
(2) Modification by a succeeding indefinite contract or contracts in the manner hereinafter provided;
(3) The death of the teacher;
(4) Resignation of the teacher with the written consent of the school board;
(5) Termination by the board of education after a hearing as hereinafter provided; and
(6) The revocation of the teacher's certificate.

168.114. Board May Terminate, Grounds For

1. An indefinite contract with a permanent teacher shall not be terminated by the board of education of a school district except for one or more of the following cases:

The Public School Laws of Missouri. Department of Elementary and Secondary Education, Jefferson, Missouri: The Department, 1979, pp. 104–116.

(1) Physical or mental condition unfitting him to instruct or associate with children;

(2) Immoral conduct;

(3) Incompetency, inefficiency or insubordination in the line of duty;

(4) Willful or persistent violation of, or failure to obey the school laws of the state or the published regulations of the board of education of the school district employing him;

(5) Excessive or unreasonable absence from performance of duties; or

(6) Conviction of a felony or a crime involving moral turpitude.

2. In determining the professional competency of or efficiency of a permanent teacher, consideration should be given to regular and special evaluation reports prepared in accordance with the policy of the employing school district and to any written standards of performance which may have been adopted by the school board.

168.116. Termination By Board—Notice—Charges

1. The indefinite contract of a permanent teacher may not be terminated by the board of education until after service upon the teacher of written charges specifying with particularity the grounds alleged to exist for termination of such contract, notice of a hearing on charges and a hearing by the board of education of charges if requested by the teacher.

2. At least thirty days before service of notice of charges of incompetency, inefficiency, or insubordination in line of duty, the teacher shall be given by the school board or the superintendent of schools warning in writing stating specifically the causes which, if not removed, may result in charges. Thereafter, both the superintendent, or his designated representative, and the teacher shall meet and confer in an effort to resolve the matter.

3. Notice of a hearing on charges, together with a copy of charges, shall be served on the permanent teacher at least twenty days prior to the date of the hearing. The notice and copy of the charges may be served upon the teacher by certified mail with personal delivery addressed to him or her at his or her last known address. If the teacher or his agent does not within ten days after receipt of the notice request a hearing on the charges, the board of education, by a majority vote, may order the contract of the teacher terminated. If a hearing is requested by either the teacher or the board of education, it shall take place not less than twenty nor more than thirty days after notice of a hearing has been furnished the permanent teacher.

4. On the filing of charges in accordance with this section, the board of education may suspend the teacher from active performance of duty until a decision is rendered by the board of education but the teacher's salary shall be continued during such suspension. If a decision to terminate a teacher's employment by the board of education is appealed, and the decision is reversed, the teacher shall be paid his salary lost during the pending of the appeal.

168.118. Termination Hearing, Procedure, Costs

If a hearing is requested on the termination of an indefinite contract it shall be conducted by the board of education in accordance with the following provisions:

1. The hearing shall be public.

2. Both the teacher and the person filing charges may be represented by counsel who may cross-examine witnesses.

3. Testimony at hearings shall be on oath or affirmation administered by the president of the board of education, who for the purpose of hearings held under section 168.102 or 168.130 shall have the authority to administer oaths.

4. The school board shall have the power to subpoena witnesses and documentary evidence as provided in section 536.077 RSMo and shall do so on its own motion or at the request of the teacher against whom charges have been made. The school board shall hear testimony of all witnesses named by the teacher; however, the school board may limit the number of witnesses to be subpoenaed on behalf of the teacher to not more than ten.

5. The board of education shall employ a stenographer who shall make a full record of the proceedings of the hearing and who shall furnish, within ten days after the conclusion thereof, the board of education and the teacher, at no cost to the teacher, with a copy of the transcript of the record, which shall be certified by the stenographer to be complete and correct. The transcript shall not be open to public inspection, unless the hearing on the termination of the contract was an open hearing or if an appeal from the decision of the board is taken by the teacher.

6. All costs of the hearing shall be paid by the school board except the cost of counsel for the teacher.

7. The decision of the board of education resulting in the demotion of a permanent teacher or the termination of an indefinite contract shall be by a majority vote of the members of the board of education and the decision shall be made within seven days after the transcript is furnished them. A written copy of the decision shall be furnished the teacher within three days thereafter.

168. 120. Appeal By Teacher, Procedure

1. The teacher shall have the right to appeal from the decision of the board of education to the circuit court of the county where the employing school district is located. The appeal shall be taken within fifteen days after service of a copy of the decision of the board of education upon the teacher, and if an appeal is not taken within the time, then the decision of the board of education shall become final.

2. The appeal may be taken by filing notice of appeal with the board of education, whereupon the board of education, under its certificate, shall forward to the court all documents and papers on file in the matter, together with a transcript of the evidence, the findings and the decision of the board of education, which shall thereupon become the record of the cause. Such appeal shall be heard as provided in chapter 536, RSMo.

3. Appeals from the circuit court shall be allowed in the same manner as in civil actions, except that the original transcript prepared and filed in the circuit court by the board of education, together with a transcript of the proceedings held in the circuit court, shall constitute the transcript on appeal in the appellate court. The board of education shall make available, to the parties, copies of any transcript prepared and filed by it in the circuit court and upon final determination of the cause in the appellate court the original record of the board of education filed as a part of the transcript on appeal shall be certified back to the board of education by the appellate court. In all appeals from the board of education or circuit court the costs thereof shall be assessed against the losing party as provided by law in civil cases. All appeals to the circuit court and appellate courts shall have precedence over all cases except election contests.

4. If the circuit court finds for the teacher, he shall be restored to permanent teaching status and shall receive compensation for the period during which he had been suspended from work, and such other relief as may be granted by the court.

168.126. Probationary Teachers, How Terminated—Reemployed, How

1. A board of education at a regular or special meeting may contract with and employ by a majority vote legally qualified probationary teachers for the school district. The contract shall be made by order of the board; shall specify the number of months school is to be taught and the wages per month to be paid; shall be signed by the probationary teacher and the president of the board and attested by the secretary of the board. The board shall not employ one of its members as a teacher; nor shall any person be employed as a teacher who is related within the fourth degree to any board member, either by consanguinity or affinity, where the vote of the board member is necessary to the selection of the person.

2. If in the opinion of the board of education any probationary teacher has been doing unsatisfactory work, the board of education through its authorized administrative representative, shall provide the teacher with a written statement definitely setting forth his alleged incompetency and specifying the nature thereof, in order to furnish the teacher an opportunity to correct his fault and overcome his incompetency. If improvement satisfactory to the board of education has not been made within ninety days of the receipt of the notification, the board of education may terminate the employment of the probationary teacher immediately or at the end of the school year. Any motion to terminate the employment of a probationary teacher shall include only one person and must be approved by a majority of the members of the board of education. A tie vote thereon constitutes termination. On or before the fifteenth day of April but not before April 1 in each school year, the board of education shall notify a probationary teacher who will not be retained by the school district of the termination of his employment.

3. Any probationary teacher who is not notified of the termination of his employment shall be deemed to have been appointed for the next school year, under the terms of the contract for the preceding year. A probationary teacher who is informed of reelection by written notice of tender of contract on or before the fifteenth day of April but not before April 1 shall within fifteen days thereafter present to the employing board of education a written acceptance or rejection of the employment tendered, and failure of such teacher to present the acceptance within such time constitutes a rejection of the board's offer. A contract between a probationary teacher and a board of education may be terminated or modified at any time by the mutual consent of the parties thereto.

SELECTED BIBLIOGRAPHY

Association of Teacher Educators, *Assessing Teachers.* Reston, Va: The Association, 1988.

Beebe, Robert J., "Planning Ahead for Professional Dismissals," *Spectrum: Journal of School Research and Information,* 3, no. 2 (Spring 1985), pp. 15–19.

Bridges, Edwin, *Managing the Incompetent Teacher.* Eugene, Oreg.: ERIC Clearinghouse on Educational Management, 1990.

Buttram, Joan L., and Bruce L. Wilson, "Promising Trends in Teacher Evaluation," *Educational Leadership,* 44, no. 7 (April 1987), pp. 4–7.

Darling-Hammond, Linda and Jason Millman, eds., *The New Handbook of Teacher Evaluation: Assessing Elementary and Secondary School Teachers.* Newbury Park, California: Sage Publications, 1990.

Educational Research Service Staff, "Educator Opinions About Teacher Evaluation," *Spectrum: Journal of School Research and Information,* 6, no. 1 (Winter 1988), pp. 43–46.

Educational Research Service Staff, *Evaluating Administrative Performance.* Arlington, Va.: Educational Research Service, 1985.

Educational Research Service Staff, *Teacher Evaluation: Practices and Procedures Report,* Arlington, Va.: Educational Research Service, 1988.

Guskey, Thomas R., ed. *High Stakes Performance Assessment: Perspectives on Kentucky's Educational Reform.* Thousand Oaks, California: Corwin Press, Inc., 1994.

Harrison, William C., "Principal Evaluation: Administrators' Perceptions," *Spectrum: Journal of School Research and Information,* 6, no. 4 (Fall 1988), pp. 3–9.

Hinkin, T. R., and C. A. Schriesheim, "Relationships Between Subordinate Perceptions of Supervisor Influence Tactics and Attributed bases of Supervisory Power," *Human Relations,* 43 (1990), pp. 221–237.

Joint Committee on Standards for Educational Evaluation, *The Personnel Evaluation Standards: How to Assess Systems for Evaluating Educators.* Newbury Park, Calif.: Sage Publications, 1989.

Manning, Renfro C., *The Teacher Evaluation Handbook.* Englewood Cliffs, N.J.: Prentice-Hall, 1989.

Matlock, John, "Solving the Problem of Problem Employees," *The Executive Educator,* 14, no. 10 (October 1992), pp. 39–41.

Meyer, C. "What's the Difference Between Authentic and Performance Assessment?, *Educational Leadership,* 49, no. 8 (1992), pp. 39–41.

National Association of Elementary School Principals, *Effective Teachers: Effective Evaluation in America's Elementary and Middle Schools.* Alexandria, Va.: The Association, 1988.

O'Neil, I. Riley and David R. Adamson, "When Teachers Falter," *The Executive Educator,* 15, no. 1 (February 1993), pp. 25–32.

Pekoe Jr., Lawrence C., "Expert Evaluation," *The Executive Educator,* 13, no. 10 (October 1991), pp. 39–40.

Peterson, Kenneth D. *Teacher Evaluation: A Comprehensive Guide to New Directions and Practices.* Thousand Oaks, California: Corwin Press, Inc., 1995.

Rossow, Lawrence F. and Jerry Parkinson, *The Law of Teacher Evaluation.* Topeka, Kansas: National Organization on Legal Problems of Education, 1991.

Schiller, Robert E., and Joseph P. McGarry. "Improving an Administrator Evaluation Program: A Case Study," *Spectrum: Journal of School Research and Information,* 4, no. 2 (Spring 1986), pp. 26–31.

Stein, Andrea R., "The Supervision Quandary," *The Executive Educator,* 14, no. 4 (April 1992), pp. 33–35.

Sternberg, Robert J., and Joseph A. Horvath, "A Prototype View of Expert Teaching," *Educational Research,* 24, no. 6 (August/September 1995), pp. 9–17.

Stoner, Candy L., "Terminating the Tenured," *School and College Product News* (October 1986), pp. 43–48.

Strange, James H., *Evaluating Professional Support Personnel in Education.* Thousand Oaks, California: Corwin Press, Inc., 1991.

Swanson, David B., Geoffrey R. Norman, and Robert L. Linn, "Performance-Based Assessment: Lessons from the Health Professions," *Educational Research,* 24, no. 5 (June/July 1995), pp. 5–11.

Vogt, Craig G., "Developing a Teacher Evaluation System," *Spectrum: Journal of School Research and Information,* 2, no. 1 (Winter 1984), pp. 41–46.

8

REWARDS

Before engaging in any activity, every human being consciously or subconsciously asks the same question, "What will I get out of this?" Psychologists have recognized for a long time that satisfaction of needs is the motivation behind all actions. This satisfaction or reward might be money, a promotion, recognition, acceptance, receipt of information, or the feeling that comes from doing a good job.

This self-interest motive often carries a negative connotation, yet it is a reality of life. People act in ways that they perceive to be in their own best interests. Whether a given act is truly in an individual's best interest is irrelevant; what counts is that he or she believes it to be so. Even if an action appears to be irrational, such as handing in a resignation because of a minor misunderstanding at work, to the individual resigning, the act may be totally in keeping with what he or she believes to be in his or her best interest.

From an administrative standpoint, a manager can develop a unique rewards system if he or she understands what his or her employees believe to be in their best interest. Not all individuals value the same type of rewards. Consequently, a rewards program must be flexible enough to meet the expectations of individual employees. It is also necessary to structure a rewards program in such a way that people will realize they are acting in their own best interest when they are acting in the best interest of the school district. This exemplifies the importance of rewards in an "expectancy model." As a result of this model, several things become clear.[1]

1. Rewards must be linked to behaviors that the school system classifies as desirable.
2. The employee should recognize that good job performance is compatible with self-interest.

---

[1]Stephen P. Robbins, *Personnel: The Management of Human Resources,* 2nd ed. (Englewood Cliffs, N.J.: Prentice-Hall, 1982), p. 349. (Some major concepts elucidated in this chapter have also been patterned after Robbins' work, pp. 349–387.)

3. The employee should recognize that the rewards system also will satisfy his own needs.

4. Administrators must analyze and interpret the needs of the employees.

The fourth statement requires further explanation. In recommending that administrators analyze and interpret employees' needs, the major question that arises is, How can this best be accomplished?

The most obvious way of learning about an individual's needs is to ask the person. However, some people do not always understand their own needs and self-interests; others find it difficult to put such needs into words. The most immediate way for an administrator to learn about employees' needs is to observe and develop an awareness of employee behaviors. Behavior is usually a stronger indicator than the verbal utterances of employees. Unfortunately, developing skill in interpreting behavior takes time and practice. The only reliable method of determining needs is through social scientific research aimed at determining patterns of needs, quantified and analyzed through statistical applications. A number of consulting firms are capable of providing this service, and some packaged programs are available that can be administered by staff employees.

VARIABLES AFFECTING REWARDS

The main purpose for establishing a rewards policy is to attract and retain qualified employees who will provide the type of service expected by the public. It is essential that employees understand the rewards structure and have confidence in the objectivity by which the system is implemented. Five major variables must be taken into consideration by the administration in constructing and recommending a rewards policy to the board of education for approval: performance, effort, seniority, skills, and job requirements. It is not important how appropriations are allocated for the rewards system; whether through board approval of the budget or collectively negotiated with employee unions, these variables are necessary to the policy.

Performance

The evaluation of performance is concerned with a basic question, Did you get the job done? Rewarding individuals requires criteria that define performance. The task of constructing valid and reliable criteria for evaluating performance was treated in Chapter 7. The importance of using performance as a basis for rewarding employees is critical to all effective rewards systems.

Effort

School districts have required teachers to consider the effort put forth by students as a determinant in evaluating student performance. Even if effort does not directly influence a grade, some method is usually employed to indicate whether a given student is putting forth his or her best effort. It is ironic, therefore, that school districts have long neglected using the degree of effort put forth by employees as a component in their rewards systems. Yet, without such an orientation, a school district will fall prey to rewarding quantity rather than quality and the end rather than the means. Also, there are some situations in which an outcome is difficult to evaluate and effort becomes a primary determinant of rewards. One such instance is cited by Stephen Robbins. A major eastern university was attempting to increase its research efforts and had designated the objective of obtaining grants or funded research as a critical benchmark towards that end. All faculty members were informed that rewards for the coming year would be based on performance in obtaining grants. Approximately 20 percent of the faculty made grant applications; however, after the first year of the program none were approved. When the time came for performance evaluation and the distribution of rewards, the dean chose to give the majority of the funds available for pay raises to those faculty members who had applied for grants. Performance, defined in terms of obtaining funded research grants, was zero, so the dean chose to allocate rewards based on effort.[2]

This discussion is obviously concerned with a topic much debated in education: merit pay. There is no one best method for rewarding performance with money; however, the following comments will help to clarify this issue.

A merit pay system will be ineffective unless it has the following components:

1. Effective teacher evaluation procedures.
2. Training programs for management and supervisory personnel who will implement the plan.
3. School board and management commitment to the plan in time and resources.
4. Staff involvement in developing the program.
5. Teacher acceptance and satisfaction.
6. Adequate financing.
7. Rewards for all who meet the criteria.
8. Plausible, fair and equitable performance criteria.
9. Valid and verifiable measures of results.
10. Objectivity and consistency in applying assessment measures.
11. Increased student learning promoted.[3]

Seniority

Length of time in a particular position plays a significant role in the allocation of rewards in the public sector. The civil service system of the United States is the best example of how seniority operates in a rewards program. The master salary schedule approach used by many school districts, incorporating channels for credentials and an incremental dollar amount for years of service, testifies to the influence of seniority in rewards systems. In business and industry, seniority has some impact on the rewards systems collectively

---

[2]See Robbins, *Personnel,* p. 365.

[3]Glen H. Tecker, *Merit, Measurement, and Money: Establishing Teacher Performance Evaluation and Incentive Programs* (Alexandria Va.: National School Boards Association, 1985), p. 14.

bargained by unions. However, for management positions, seniority has little or no effect upon rewards.

The reason that seniority has been used by educational organizations to determine financial rewards is because it can be applied so easily. A principal may evaluate a given teacher's performance either higher or lower than another teacher's performance; but if both teachers perform within the limits of what is considered satisfactory, both will get the same salary increase if they both have served the same number of years in the school system. This relieves the principal from recommending to the superintendent different dollar amount rewards for each teacher based on his or her evaluation of their performance.

Nevertheless, seniority is a variable to be incorporated into a rewards system because the basic purpose of establishing a rewards policy is to attract and retain qualified employees. A rewards system is ineffective when its sole criterion for rewarding employees is seniority.

The necessity of retaining some form of seniority in a compensation plan that also rewards performance has led to the establishment of what is commonly referred to as "career ladders." Two of the more frequently discussed programs are the Charlotte-Mecklenburg Schools Career Development Plan and the Tennessee Better Schools Program. The objective of these two and most other programs is to encourage teachers to direct their careers along a path that will lead to refined skills and higher levels of responsibilities. For example, a person entering the education profession as an apprentice teacher must have met the following requirements:

a. Completed a teacher education program offered through an approved college or university.
b. Attained a Bachelor's degree.
c. Successfully completed student teaching.
d. Successfully passed the National Teacher's Examination.

This apprentice teacher could progress to subsequent higher levels of designation such as "professional teacher," "senior teacher," and finally "master teacher." The path to these levels requires additional education and the assuming of more and more responsibilities. For example, a master teacher could be expected to serve as a curriculum specialist, seminar presenter in a staff development program, or a resource person to apprentice teachers. Each level of attainment could be rewarded with perhaps a more lucrative salary schedule. A bonus upon attaining each successive level would be another method of rewarding those reaching such levels. Exhibit 8–1 shows the career paths for teachers in Tennessee.

Skills

A common practice in organizations, particularly in the private sector, is allocating rewards based on the skills of employees. Those who possess the most advanced skills receive the highest compensation. When an individual is hired by an organization, his or her skill level is usually a major consideration in determining the amount of compensation to be received.

EXHIBIT 8–1   Career Paths for Teachers

Apprentice Teacher

Entry Routes:

- Completion of a teacher training program and recommendation by an approved institution of higher education
- Trade shop personnel who meet appropriate standards

Qualifications/Requirements:

- Student teaching
- Successful completion of the National Teacher's Examination
- Bachelor's degree
        or
- Employment standards required for trade shop personnel

Certificate:

- Three-year
- Nonrenewable

Contract/State Salary:

- Regular school term of 200 days
- State salary schedule based on training and experience

Professional Teacher

Entry Routes:

- Three (3) years as an apprentice teacher
- A currently certified teacher with three (3) or more years of experience who wishes to enter the new career paths

Qualifications/Requirements:

- Knowledge of subject matter
- Acceptable student achievement
- Participation in professional growth activities
- Observation by evaluating team/teacher interview

Certificate:

- Five-year
- Renewable

Contract/State Salary:

- Regular school term of 200 days
- State salary schedule based on training and experience *plus* state incentive pay supplement of $1,000

Continued

EXHIBIT 8–1   *Continued*

Senior Teacher

Entry Routes:

- Three (3) to five (5) years as a professional teacher
- A currently certified teacher who has eight (8) or more years of appropriate experience

Qualifications/Requirements:

- Acceptable student achievement
- Participation in professional growth activities
- Observation by evaluation team/teacher interview
- Exceptional classroom practice
- Evaluations by local supervisors and administrators

Certificate:

- Five-year
- Renewable

Contract/State Salary:

- Contract for 10 months (200 days)—*current teachers only*—state salary schedule based on training and experience *plus* state incentive pay supplement of $2,000
- Contract for 11 months (220 days)—state salary schedule based on training and experience *plus* state incentive pay supplement of $4,000

Master Teacher

Entry Routes:

- Five (5) years as a senior teacher
- A currently certified teacher who has twelve (12) or more years of appropriate experience

Qualifications/Requirements:

- Acceptable student achievement
- Participation in professional growth activities
- Observation by evaluation team/teacher interview
- Classroom effectiveness
- Capability and willingness to assume additional duties
- Evaluations by local supervisors and administrators
- Skill in supervising, evaluating, and improving the performance of other teachers

Certificate:

- Five-year
- Renewable

Contract/State Salary:

- Contract for 10 months (200 days)—*current teachers only*—state salary schedule based on training and experience *plus* state incentive pay supplement of $3,000

Source: Tennessee Better Schools Program (Tennessee: Master Teacher–Master Administrator Act, 1983), p. 3.

Competition, therefore, to hire individuals with certain skills becomes an element in the rewards package. The standard as to what constitutes a desirable skill is imposed from either the human resource requirements of the organization or from the occupational category itself. If the board of education has mandated having a career education program in the secondary schools, individuals possessing the experience and educational qualifications necessary for implementing such a program have skills that will demand a quality rewards package. Career education professionals are rather scarce throughout the United States, and thus the occupational category itself further demands an attractive rewards package.

Job Requirements

The complexity and responsibility of a job are often criteria by which rewards are distributed. A job that is difficult to perform because of stress, unpleasant working conditions, or level of responsibility must also offer higher rewards to attract capable individuals. A major determinant of job difficulty is the degree of discretion a job requires. The greater the discretion, the greater need for good judgment and, consequently, the greater need for commensurate rewards.

Any good rewards system must recognize effort, seniority, skills, and job requirements; performance, however, must also be given a primary emphasis. Quality individuals are attracted to school districts that reward performance, which in turn affects the quality of education offered by a school district.

TYPES OF REWARDS

If rewards are to motivate performance, employees must recognize the relationship between performance and rewards. Most school districts have traditionally used nonperformance criteria, such as seniority-based salary schedules, for allocating rewards. However, this chapter views rewards primarily as a payoff for performance. This concept is in keeping with the outcry for accountability and, if properly applied, might be the only realistic approach to improving the quality of education. For too long, teachers and other employees of school districts have been placed apart from the rest of mankind by taxpayers who believe that they should be more dedicated to service than concerned about making a living. Teachers and other public employees have fought this long-held belief by engaging in unionism and collective negotiations for wages and fringe benefits. A reasonable rewards system that recognizes quality performance and that is objectively administered could help remedy some of the dissatisfaction voiced by school district employees.

The most obvious kinds of rewards are wages and fringe benefits. However, a truly effective rewards system must be multifaceted, incorporating both intrinsic and extrinsic aspects. Although modern school districts employ people in many different occupational categories, many of the possible rewards are applicable only to particular job positions. For example, teachers, administrators, bus drivers, and custodians would receive a salary; administrators, in addition, would have greater job discretion; and custodians could receive overtime pay. Figure 8–1 summarizes many possible types of rewards.

STRUCTURE OF REWARDS

FIGURE 8–1   **Structure of rewards**

Intrinsic rewards are rewards that the employee receives from doing the job itself. The employee's satisfaction on the job is usually increased by the following: participation in the decision-making process, greater job discretion, increased responsibility, more challenging tasks, opportunities for personal growth, and diversity of activities.

Extrinsic rewards are divided into direct and indirect compensation. Direct compensation is considered taxable income by the Internal Revenue Service during the period in which it is received. The most common forms of direct compensation are salary, overtime pay, holiday pay, and merit pay for performance. Direct compensation is also the part of a rewards system that generates the most controversy and disgruntlement among employees. Industrial psychologists have long contended that rate of pay is not the most important determinant of job satisfaction. However, it is an indispensable part of every rewards package and, because of its importance, is treated at length under a separate title in this chapter.

Indirect compensation usually includes protection programs, pay for time away from work, and services. There is a widespread attitude among personnel administrators who view indirect compensation as that which helps to retain individuals in an organization rather than motivating them to greater performance. Direct compensation is considered the stimulus to better performance. Because of the complexity and importance of indirect compensation, more frequently referred to as *fringe benefits,* this also is treated under a separate heading in this chapter.

Nonfinancial rewards have begun to appear in some school districts. These rewards may either motivate an employee to greater performance or help to retain his or her services. The limits to the kind and extent of nonfinancial rewards are established only by the creativity of those responsible for establishing a rewards program. Nonfinancial rewards, however, are effective only if they meet the needs of specific employees. What one person considers desirable might seem superfluous to another. For example, a very status-conscious employee might be motivated by a job title, a reserved parking place, the services of a private secretary, or a paneled and carpeted office. Another individual might value working without close supervision as a reward that could both motivate performance and retain his or her services. The significant point is that organizations can use a variety of nonfinancial rewards as part of a total program and that these rewards may be more appreciated by certain individuals than direct or indirect forms of compensation.

DIRECT COMPENSATION: SALARY AND WAGE ADMINISTRATION

The basic philosophy underlying pay systems in school districts is compensation for services rendered. However, the subjective nature of administrative judgments, of collectively bargained agreements, of state and federal pay guidelines, and of salary rates in the public and private sectors have a definite influence on actual wage programs. To ensure external and internal wage comparability, a school district must continually gather data on the wage and salary policies of other school districts and also of public and private employers in the community and region. Most organizations are cooperative in sharing information-concerning salary programs because they too understand that their systems are influenced by others. Surveys by telephone and letter, governmental publications, and literature published by employee organizations and unions are also valuable resources in gathering information.

Because the principle of compensation for services rendered is somewhat elusive, the following guidelines should help a school district in developing a salary and wage policy aimed at fair treatment for all employees.[4]

- *Equitable Salary System.* All salary systems must recognize the skills required in various positions. Therefore, every position must be evaluated to determine its importance in relation to other positions. All positions are then arranged in order of their relative value, with the position of greatest value and responsibility at the top. This establishes a gradation classification system that serves as a basis for the uniform administration of salaries and wages.
- *Comparability.* The salary system must be competitive with other school districts and, as much as possible, with other public agencies and private industry.
- *Position Evaluation.* The relative value for every position should be established cooperatively through a salary committee composed of employees and administrators.

[4]Charles W. Foster, ed., *Wage and Salary Administration: A Handbook for School Business Officials* (Chicago: Research Corporation of the Association of School Business Officials, 1969), pp. 7–8.

- *Performance Incentives.* The primary focus of a rewards program is improvement of performance. Because salary is a major component of a rewards program, the salary system should be constructed so as to encourage employees to improve performance and assume greater responsibility. This, of course, requires that the district establish a uniform and fair method of appraising an individual's performance and a suitable personnel records system to maintain performance evaluations.
- *Salary Review.* Salary schedules must be reviewed annually to ascertain if they are competitive with other school districts and keeping pace with the increases received by employees in other public agencies and in the private sector.

The Effects of Salary on Motivation

An interesting question central to all pay systems is, "Does money stimulate an employee to put forth more effort?" The answer to this question is closely related to individual needs because money in itself is rarely an end but rather a means to "purchasing an end." A $2,000 raise for an employee making $20,000 a year would help that individual maintain his standard of living in the face of ordinary inflation. That same raise would considerably improve the standard of living for an individual earning $10,000 a year, but it would have much less effect on the life style of someone earning $40,000 per year. From this perspective money does have a potential to motivate if an individual is seeking to maintain or improve his standard of living. We rarely find a person who is not concerned when his life style deteriorates because salary increases have not been keeping pace with inflation.

A study based on the responses of 157 professionals in an electronics company further supports the position that each dollar of merit increase had a value to the employee.[5] This research suggests that money is important to employees, regardless of the job level in the organization or the amount of salary that the individual earns. In addition, money has a great deal of symbolic value in our society, even though it has varying degrees of importance to individuals having different backgrounds and experiences.

If money is to motivate an individual within an organization to greater performance, it must be very clear that such performance is indeed rewarded with more money. The behavior that is thus rewarded will be repeated, and the behaviors that are not rewarded with money will not be repeated. This, of course, is not the modus operandi of most school systems in the United States. The common position has been one of emphasizing intrinsic motivation. Teachers and other school district employees are expected to perform to the best of their abilities because of the importance of educating children and because of the status afforded to these individuals. The accountability movement, with taxpayers demanding a return on their dollar from school district employees by way of increased student performance, and the number of teacher strikes for higher wages should dispel the myth that the performance of any group of employees in any organization, public or private, is unaffected by money.

---

[5]See Brian A. Giles and Gerald V. Barrett, "Utility of Merit Increases," *Journal of Applied Psychology,* 55, no. 2 (April 1971), pp. 103–109.

In addition to this experientially proven conclusion, statistical data support the position that money increases intrinsic motivation under the following two conditions: (1) monetary rewards must closely follow performance so as to be reinforcing, and (2) the employee must perceive the monetary rewards as being related to work behavior.[6]

A reasonable conclusion concerning the relationship of money to motivation is that money definitely affects performance under certain circumstances. Unfortunately, most school districts use a seniority-based salary schedule, which does not reward performance but rather rewards an individual's survival for another year.

Public Disclosure of Salaries

Because school districts are public agencies, salary schedules and budget information are disclosed not only to school district employees but also to the general public and at times to the news media. However, many school districts consider the salaries of individual employees to be confidential. This situation brings up a number of concerns. First, in public agencies supported by tax money, the public would seem to have a right to know how tax money is being spent and for what. Second, secrecy regarding salaries sometimes leads to misperceptions, which in turn may lead to the dissatisfaction of employees with their pay.

An open salary policy may also affect management effectiveness. If pay information became common knowledge among employees, individuals could compare their salaries, and inequities in the pay system would soon become apparent. Of course, there also would be petty complaints and misperceived inequities. However, an open pay system would demonstrate that the administration has confidence in the management of the pay system and this may increase the trust individual employees have in the school district's administration.

Although very few statistical data are available on the preferences of employees concerning an open salary policy, experience suggests that most Americans are sensitive about their wages and would probably prefer to have their salaries undisclosed.

The Equal Employment Opportunity Commission has experienced an increasing number of cases alleging that women are being paid less than men for doing comparable work. This, of course, is contrary to the provisions of the Equal Pay Act of 1963. In like manner, school districts receiving federal funds must disclose wage and salary information to demonstrate commitment to the principles of affirmative action. An interesting addendum to the increased activities of federal agencies with regard to salary information is the decision by the National Labor Relations Board against Blue Cross–Blue Shield of Alabama, which stated that the company's attempt to prohibit discussion of pay during working hours was an infringement of the constitutional rights of employees.[7]

---

[6]See Fred Luthans, Mark Martinko and Tom Kess, "An Analysis of the Impact of Contingency Monetary Rewards on Intrinsic Motivation," *Proceedings of the 19th Annual Midwest Academy of Management* (St. Louis, 1976), pp. 209–221.

[7]See Lawrence Stassin, "Keep Your Eyes Off My Paycheck," *New York Times,* June 3, 1976, p. F10.

Compensation Packaging

Because individual employees have individual needs, no compensation program will satisfy everyone. A number of corporations, recognizing this fact, have developed compensation programs that allow each employee to choose a combination of rewards most attractive to that person. Thus, employees are informed that their compensation is X dollars, and they then choose a mix of salary, life insurance, annuities, or any other benefit suited to their particular situation and offered by the corporation. The concept underlying this approach is that an employee will be motivated towards higher performance if such performance carries a dollar value that can then be "spent" by the individual for rewards tailored to meet his or her needs.

Although it is difficult to generalize, younger employees appear to be more concerned with salary and educational reimbursement programs than with life insurance and retirement plans. Married employees are usually more concerned about life insurance and medical programs than single individuals; older employees are justifiably interested in retirement benefits.

With this type of compensation packaging, a considerable amount of information must be made available to employees for them to have adequate data on which to base decisions. This will obviously increase the administrative costs of the compensation programs. However, the potential benefit in terms of increased performance and the retention of employees could significantly offset the additional costs.

Equity of Pay and Performance

In any organization employees tend to compare what they get from their job with what they must put into it. At the same time they are comparing what they make in wages with what co-workers make and how productive their co-workers are. The inevitable outcome of this comparison process is that an individual will see his or her compensation as either equal or unequal to that of fellow employees. Those who feel inequality exists will view themselves as under-rewarded or over-rewarded.

Three variables can color an employee's perception.[8] The first variable, usually termed the "other" category, includes colleagues, friends, and neighbors. With information received from these individuals and from newspapers and other communication media, the employee compares his or her pay to that of others. The "system" category is the second variable and includes organizational pay policies, pay procedures, and administration of the pay system. The final category is the "self," which refers to the input–output ratio unique to the individual. This category is also influenced by past jobs and current family role commitments.

An employee who perceives an inequality may choose one or more of the following alternatives: distort his or her own inputs or outputs or those of others; attempt to induce others to match his or her inputs or outputs; change his or her own inputs or outputs; choose a different frame of reference for comparing pay; or quit the job.[9] Administrators must realize that employees are not only concerned about the absolute amount of money they

---

[8]See Paul S. Goodman, "An Examination of Referents Used in the Evaluation of Pay," *Organizational Behavior and Human Performance,* 12, no. 2 (October 1974), 170–195.

[9]See Robbins, *Personnel,* p. 358.

are paid but also with the relationship of that dollar amount to what others are paid. When an inequality is perceived, tension is created. The implication for personnel administrators is very clear. Employees are motivated not only by their absolute rewards but also by the relativity of rewards. Where employees perceive inequality, quality of performance may diminish, absenteeism may increase, and resignations may even rise.

Employee Relations in Salary Management

Employees who believe they are unfairly compensated will certainly create a morale problem for the administration. However, low wages alone will not necessarily create a morale problem if employees believe the administration and board of education are doing everything possible to improve wages. Therefore, how salary decisions are presented to the employees is of great importance. The method, of course, will vary with each individual school district because of local traditions and the number of employees.[10] However, most presentation plans must be formulated with a sensitivity to the process used in making salary decisions. The two most commonly used processes are briefly explained here.

In the first process, the administration analyzes the fiscal condition of the school district; formulates a recommendation that appears reasonable; receives approval from the board of education; and, finally, informs the school district employees of the decision. This method is the most efficient in terms of time spent by the administration, but it is also the most vulnerable in terms of good staff morale because it is basically a "take it or leave it" approach. Although this method is traditional in education, it is also highly suspect even in those school districts where it is used successfully because it has all the markings of a benevolent dictatorship.

In the second process, which is the more defensible, administration and employee representatives work together to develop a mutually acceptable salary and wage package. In over half the states this process is mandated in varying degrees by state collective negotiations legislation. However, the process is certainly valid even in those states that prohibit collective negotiations by public school employees. Where such a prohibition exists, salary decisions remain with the board of education, but the task of formulating a recommendation becomes a mutual concern of both administrators and employees.

This collaborative process is not without its drawbacks. It can be very time consuming, and the administration may disagree with the proposals presented by the employee representatives. Chapter 9 discusses in detail the process of collective negotiations as practiced in public school districts.

Whatever process is used, the administration must ultimately present the salary plan and the decision of the board of education to the school district employees. A significant advantage of the bilateral model is that the employees through their representatives have some knowledge of the administration's position. The sensitive nature of salary and wage decisions cannot be overemphasized. Wages affect an individual's ability to support his or her family and maintain an adequate standard of living; a paycheck represents security in

---

[10]See John W. Boyle, "Techniques for Consultation and Presentation," in *Wage and Salary Administration: A Handbook for School Business Officials,* Charles W. Foster, ed. (Chicago: Research Corporation of the Association of School Business Officials, 1960), pp. 39–40.

a highly materialistic society. Therefore, effective communication is essential in explaining policies and decisions.

There are four basic principles that, if followed, will maximize the effectiveness of presenting salary and wage decisions to the employees: (1) the board of education must place top priority on paying adequate wages when it draws up and approves the school district's budget; (2) the administration must make complete disclosure of the fiscal condition of the school district; (3) the administration must avoid presenting too many technical details of the financial conditions, which could give the semblance of a "snow job"; and (4) the administration should prepare a position statement to distribute to all employees and to the news media. This document may take various forms, but at a minimum it should contain the decision on salary and wages, the process used in reaching the decision, facts about the financial condition of the school district, and data about wages in comparable school districts and the business community.

It is also effective in minimizing confusion and misrepresentation to invite employees to call a designated office, which will be responsible for answering questions about the salary and wage document. The most obvious central-office component to take this responsibility, of course, is the business and finance office. However, those districts that maintain a public relations office would more properly place this responsibility with the director of community relations.

A final yet very important point should be made concerning employee relations in salary management. The building principal is often the last person to be informed about central office and board of education decisions, but he or she is usually the first person contacted by teachers and other building level employees when they have questions. Therefore, it is both good administrative procedure and good public relations to inform the principals first about salary decisions. This will also help principals identify themselves as members of the school district's administrative team.

Collecting Community Wage Data

A defensible technique in developing cooperation is to establish salary parameters compatible with wages paid by other government agencies and by business and industry in the community served by the school system. In metropolitan areas, this would include more than the immediate vicinity; salaries in the surrounding area would probably give a better indication of the adequacy of salary levels within the district. Thus a school district located in suburban Chicago should be concerned with the wages paid by private business and industry, municipal governments, and other school districts in the entire metropolitan Chicago area.

If salaries are to be competitive and comparable enough to sustain a reasonable standard of living for school district employees, they must be relative to the salaries received by other individuals living in the same community. Another reason for seeking salary data from other employers in the area is because these corporations and their employees support the school district through taxation; and school district salaries must not be out of proportion with the wages paid and received by these constituents.

A source of information on salaries and wages paid in the community to individuals with occupations similar to noninstructional employees of a school district is the employment agency. Although the quality of such agencies varies, both private and public employment agencies usually have valuable data on wages. The civil service commissions of state and municipal governments also have readily available information on salary systems used in their respective jurisdictions.

The most effective way to gather data on salaries and wages is through a survey. Such a technique has the advantage of clarity and precision. If the survey instrument is accompanied by a cover letter explaining its purpose, most agencies and corporations will cooperate with the school district by supplying the data because they usually view this type of cooperation as a public service.

The following guidelines are applicable to wage and salary surveys for noninstructional positions and should be valuable to those school districts using this technique for the first time.[11]

1. The material for the survey must be obtained on a confidential basis. All summaries must be prepared in a manner that preserves the anonymity of each firm or school asked to participate. Also, let it be known that the data in the summary will be restricted to confidential management use, and that no publicity will be given to the data or the survey.
2. Every effort must he made to make this an objective, unbiased survey. Statistical techniques should be used to select a sample of firms that would produce an unbiased representation, since it is too expensive to survey all the firms in a given locality.
3. Request wage rates that are the averages for each occupation. Use straight-time day work rates for regularly employed full-time employees and show as an equivalent forty-hour week rate.
4. The occupations should be grouped into two general categories—craft and clerical. The occupations selected for the survey will cover such a wide range of experiences and skills that they cannot be considered typical of any one firm or group of firms. Rather, the intent is to represent occupations found widely throughout industry in general, as well as certain special occupations of particular interest. If a single occupation is reported by fewer than three firms, the occupation should be eliminated from the summary to preserve the confidential nature of the information.
5. The job descriptions to be used in the survey should provide for the "slotting" of jobs (see Exhibit 8–2)
6. Samples of other craft occupations
   Mechanic
   Sheet Metal Worker
   Electrician
   Plumber
   Carpenter
7. Samples of clerical occupations
   Bookkeeping—Machine Operator
   Accounting Clerk
   Payroll Clerk
   Secretary
   Stenographer
   Switchboard Operator Receptionist

[11]Foster, *Wage and Salary Administration,* pp. 10–12, with modifications.

EXHIBIT 8–2   Sample Job Description

JANITOR, PORTER, OR CLEANER

Cleans and keeps in an orderly condition, factory working area and washrooms, or premises of an office, apartment house, school building, or commercial establishment. Duties involve a combination of the following:

Sweeping, mopping, or scrubbing, and polishing floors; removing trash and other refuse; dusting equipment, furniture, or fixtures; polishing metal fixtures or trimmings; providing supplies and minor maintenance services; cleaning lavatories, showers, and restrooms. Workers who specialize in window washing are excluded.

Surveys dealing with instructional and administrative positions generally follow these guidelines, substituting appropriate position titles, salary, and job descriptions.

The practice of keeping school district wage and salary rates comparable to the wages paid in the community is becoming imperative not only because of the teacher shortage in some fields but also because more and more school district employees are attracted to jobs in business and industry. This, of course, is particularly true of craft and clerical positions because of the ease of transferring from public to private sector employment. Secretaries, electricians, cooks, and bus drivers are sometimes "in training" with public school districts until an appropriate job becomes available in business or industry. Thus, the principle of like pay for public employees for like work in corporations and other organizations is becoming a necessary personnel policy. Such a policy not only helps a school district to be competitive with the private sector for quality employees but also helps a school district retain its employees and reduces the expense involved with high turnover.

The salary rates being offered in the private sector are also attracting instructional and administrative personnel. Mathematics, industrial arts, and science teachers are finding many more opportunities in business and industry than ever before. This trend is also reaching into the liberal arts disciplines as corporations recognize that they can train an individual for almost any job if that person is motivated and has a basic college education. Inflation has motivated many teachers to seek employment in the private sector and in jobs where the rewards systems recognize performance.

Thus, collecting data about salaries and wages is extremely important. Although school districts individually gather information through the survey method, many cooperative ventures also have emerged with most or all of the school districts in a metropolitan area jointly sponsoring salary and wage surveys.

The following techniques for establishing the survey purpose, preparing the schedule, and tabulating the data should prove valuable to school districts planning to use this method.[12]

---

[12]Foster, *Wage and Sale Administration,* pp. 13–14.

1. Collect basic factual data to provide a basis for establishing the rates of pay for employees in the school district.
2. Determine the degree and amount of wage movement that occurs in the community within a given period of time.
3. Determine wage relationships among categories within the school district.
4. Collect data on basic working conditions such as the length of the work week, general pay practices, overtime practices, prerequisites, etc.

Prepare the schedule or questionnaire so that the following are taken into consideration:

5. Include only those technical terms commonly used in the pertinent industries and/or schools.
6. or by implication.
7. Define the processes, equipment, or terms specific to the benchmark job.
8. Prepare detailed guide notes which clearly define in both negative and positive terms what the survey field person should be looking for and what he or she should avoid in job comparisons.
9. Consider the desirability of obtaining organization charts which indicate the relationship between the benchmark job and other related jobs.
10. For accuracy in the results of the survey, computerized data processing must be used.
11. Consultation with data processing personnel at the time the survey is being constructed will facilitate the proper tabulation of the data.
12. Preparation of the report can easily be made from the data processing tabulation runs.

Salary and Wage Review

Since approximately 80 percent of most school districts' budgets is spent on wages, salary planning and review is an essential part of the entire compensation process. Two methods are commonly used by school systems to review compensation programs: continual salary review and annual review.

A continual salary review system is usually tied into a cost of living index. Government agencies use a number of indicators to determine inflation rates, with the Consumer Price Index being the most commonly used. A major problem with such a measure is the fact that this is an average; the actual cost of living in a community may be higher or lower than the average reported.

Under a continual salary review system, adjustments are automatically made on salary schedules as the selected cost of living indicator changes, necessitating a change in the hourly rates for classified employees and the contracts for administrative and instructional personnel. Such a system does not of itself reward performance; it merely adjusts the basic salary of all employees. Merit increases, therefore, are not addressed by the continual review process.

The annual salary review process functions from a much different perspective. Salary schedules are adjusted annually in relation to the prevailing wages in other school districts and businesses in the community. The adjustment may or may not be in keeping with a recognized cost of living indicator; rather its major focus is on the local community as the appropriate measure. The concern of the annual salary review process is that wages in other school districts and businesses in the community, which continually change, may steal away the more talented employees. As with the continual salary review process, the annual review method does not of itself reward performance. Therefore, merit increases must be viewed as a separate component of the compensation program.

The decision of a school district as to what method best meets the needs of the employees must be tempered with the constraints of the budget. There are two significant differences between public sector and private sector financing: first, school districts are financed primarily by tax revenue, which is usually not received on a consistent monthly basis but rather as taxes are collected; second, in most states, taxes can be raised to meet higher costs only by voter approval, whereas in the private sector, the price of an item can be raised at any time to offset costs. These financial considerations would make the continual salary review process difficult to implement in a school district.

Salary Schedule Construction

In the public sector and particularly in the civil service systems of the state and federal governments, salary schedules are divided into a number of grades, each of which has several step rates. The use of salary schedules can have three distinct advantages.[13] First, recruitment of personnel can be more effective because a potential employee may be offered a step above the minimum in the grade—often a necessary inducement to hire the most qualified applicant. Second, an employee will be able to see potential salary increases, assuming satisfactory performance. Finally, with multiple steps within a grade system, an employee may receive step increases for meritorious performance.

A major question in establishing such an approach is deciding on the appropriate number of steps to be included within a grade. If the steps are numerous and small, employees will be unhappy because salary increases will be small. If the steps are large and few, an employee will reach the maximum within a grade in a relatively short time and consequently will have no place to progress to over the long term.

A realistic approach, therefore, could be a compromise setting up six or seven steps within each grade, with each representing a certain percentage increment. Each grade may be further improved by adding longevity steps to the top and expressing these in even dollar amounts rather than percentages. For example, a salary schedule could grant an employee a longevity increase for every two years of service after reaching the last step within a grade.

Each position in the school district is assigned to one of the salary ranges, and each employee is assigned to one of the steps. As new people are hired, they are placed within the range assigned to that position and on a step negotiated with the administration. Advancement from one step to another is based on performance. Consequently, an employee who is performing unsatisfactorily could remain on the same step until termination or

---

[13]Cyrus Knutson, "Development of a Master Salary Schedule," in Foster, *Wage and Salary Administration,* p. 15.

resignation. An employee performing satisfactorily could receive a step advancement that would represent a certain percentage salary increase. A meritorious employee could be granted a two- or three-step advancement.

Some school districts have initiated a policy of placing a new employee on the first step for a probationary period, then advancing the employee as he or she demonstrates satisfactory performance. For example, an employee might be moved to the second step after six months. This method is usually effective only with classified employees who, unlike teachers, are not working under an individual contract.

Advancement from one salary range to another is usually based on either a promotion or an increase in educational qualifications. A teacher who becomes an assistant principal will usually advance to the salary range established for the assistant principalship. In like manner, a teacher who receives a master's degree would be advanced to the salary range established for teachers with master's degrees. This same process is applicable to classified employees. A custodian who is promoted to a head custodial position with supervisory responsibilities over the other custodians in a building would be placed on the appropriate salary level. It is important to note that advancement to a higher salary grade will not necessarily result in a higher wage for an employee. For example, step 5 of the bachelor's degree teacher salary range may be higher than step 1 of the master's degree salary range. Consequently, when moving employees to a higher grade, it is important to place them on a step that will ensure an increase in wages for having upgraded their academic qualifications or for taking on greater responsibilities.

While the types of salary ranges will vary from one school district to another, a few examples of common designations are:

ADMINISTRATIVE	INSTRUCTIONAL	CLASSIFIED
Central Office Director (Example: Director of Federal Programs)	Bachelor's degree	Custodian
	Bachelor's degree plus 30 graduate hours	Head Custodian
Secondary School Principal	Master's degree	Maintenance Employee
Secondary School Assistant Principal	Master's degree plus 30 graduate hours	Maintenance Supervisor
Elementary School Principal	Doctoral degree	
Elementary School Assistant Principal		

Each of these designations would have a salary range with multiple steps.

Exhibit 8–3 is an example of the type of teacher salary schedule to be found in most school districts. There are five categories that correspond to the academic requirement necessary for placement in each category. The categories progress from the "Bachelor's Degree" level on through to the "Doctoral Degree" level. The steps in each category are listed down the left side of the schedule. Those teachers in Category 1 could receive a step increase with satisfactory performance up through ten steps. At that point they would not receive a step increase until they acquired fifteen graduate hours of additional education in their subject area and thus would move to Step 11 in Category 2. Therefore, this method

EXHIBIT 8–3 Salary Schedule

Step	Bachelor's Degree Category 1	Bachelor's Degree plus 15 graduate hours Category 2	Master's Degree plus 2 years experience Category 3	Master's Degree plus 15 graduate hours Category 4	Doctoral Degree plus 3 years experience Category 5
1	21,000.00	21,945.00		22,890.00	
2	21,945.00	22,890.00		24,255.00	
3	22,890.00	23,835.00	24,307.50	25,620.00	
4	23,835.00	24,780.00	25,252.50	26,985.00	27,930.00
5	24,780.00	25,725.00	26,197.50	28,350.00	29,295.00
6	25,725.00	26,670.00	27,142.50	29,715.00	30,660.00
7	26,670.00	27,615.00	28,087.50	31,080.00	32,025.00
8	27,615.00	28,560.00	29,032.50	32,445.00	33,390.00
9	28,560.00	29,506.00	29,977.50	33,810.00	34,755.00
10	29,505.00	30,450.00	30,922.50	35,175.00	36,120.00
11		31,395.00	31,867.50	36,540.00	37,485.00
12			32,812.50	37,905.00	38,850.00
13				39,270.00	40,215.00
14					42,000.00
15					43,365.00
16					44,730.00
17					46,095.00
18					47,460.00
19					48,825.00
20					50,190.00

encourages teachers to upgrade their knowledge and skills. Such is the case with all categories. There are two categories that have experience requirements in addition to the academic ones. The "Master's Degree" level also requires two years of successful teaching experience; the "Doctoral Degree" level requires three years. Thus, if a person pursued his master's degree or doctoral degree on a full-time basis without experience in teaching, upon employment he would be placed in the preceding category until completing the successful teaching requirement.

Exhibit 8–4 indicates the percent of increase between categories and steps. Such a salary schedule is commonly referred to as an "index" system. The designation "incremental" system refers to those salary schedules that have an equal dollar amount between steps, such as $500 between Step 1 and Step 2; also, $500 between Step 2 and 3, etc.

Multiple Salary Ranges

There will probably be multiple salary ranges in most school districts for administrative and instructional positions. These ranges are necessary to recognize the various levels of academic preparation and responsibility. A secondary school principal with a master's degree, usually a minimum academic qualification, should not receive as much compensation as a secondary school principal with a doctorate. Thus, when a salary

EXHIBIT 8–4   Indices

STEP	INDEX	INDEX	INDEX	INDEX	INDEX
1	1.0000	1.0450		1.0900	
2	1.0450	1.0900		1.1550	
3	1.0900	1.1350	1.1575	1.2200	
4	1.1350	1.1800	1.2025	1.2850	1.3300
5	1.1800	1.2250	1.2475	1.3500	1.3950
6	1.2250	1.2700	1.2925	1.4150	1.4600
7	1.2700	1.3150	1.3375	1.4800	1.5250
8	1.3150	1.3600	1.3825	1.5450	1.5900
9	1.3600	1.4050	1.4275	1.6100	1.6550
10	1.4050	1.4500	1.4725	1.6750	1.7200
11		1.4950	1.5175	1.7400	1.7850
12			1.5625	1.8050	1.8500
13				1.8700	1.9150
14					2.0000
15					2.0650
16					2.1300
17					2.1950
18					2.2600
19					2.3250
20					2.3900

plan has multiple ranges, it is usually designated as a "salary schedule." The teachers' salary schedule would usually have a range for each of the following: bachelor's degree, bachelor's degree plus thirty graduate hours, master's degree, master's degree plus thirty graduate hours, and doctorate. Consequently, it is common to find multiple salary schedules with multiple ranges in most school systems. For these professional positions, it is relatively easy to identify appropriate ranges, which is not the case with classified positions.

For classified employees, it is necessary to designate job families based on similarity in duties and responsibilities and similarity in qualifications. From time to time, it might be necessary to reevaluate a position to determine if these criteria are still applicable. An example of a family of jobs with similar responsibilities, duties, and qualifications is the designation, "secretarial-clerical." Not all school district secretaries and clerical personnel have exactly the same working conditions. Therefore, a salary schedule for this designation could be constructed with ranges established to discriminate between the various working conditions. The highest range could be reserved for executive secretaries working for the superintendent and assistant superintendents. Another range would be assigned to building secretarial positions and the lowest range to clerk-typist positions.

A job family for classified transportation supervisory personnel could include ranges for transportation supervisor, mechanic foreman, and dispatcher, with salary ranges appropriate to these designations.

Establishing Base Salaries

There are two processes that can be used to establish the basic wage for each salary schedule range. The preceding discussion of types of salary ranges illustrates the various methods used to calculate step increases but provides no indication of base salaries.

The first process centers on gathering salary data from other school districts and from the business-industrial community. There is little difficulty in analyzing the data in relation to administrative and teaching positions. Classified positions, on the other hand, present a more challenging situation because of the multitude of job categories with responsibilities unique to the individual organization.

A successful method of setting classified salaries is by designating certain jobs as benchmark positions. The following four-step process exemplifies how the benchmark positions are used to set the salaries of other positions in a job family.

- Step 1. Through the procedures of job description and analysis, classes of noninstructional positions can be determined. These classes are grouped into broad job families as follows:

  Clerical: Clerk-Typist, Senior Clerk, Accounting Clerk, School Secretary, Administrative Secretary, Superintendent's Secretary.
  Maintenance and Operations: Custodian, Gardener, Head Custodian, Maintenance Person, Maintenance Supervisor.

- Step 2. Benchmark positions are selected which can be compared reliably with prevailing rates for comparable jobs in local industry and other public agencies. In this hypothetical example, the benchmarks chosen could be Clerk-Typist and Custodian.
- Step 3. Salary survey data are applied to the benchmark positions. The best fitting ranges on the master salary schedule, using the survey statistics of central tendency (mean and median) and dispersion (interquartile range), are selected for the benchmark positions.
- Step 4. The alignment of other positions is determined according to their skill relationships, using for each position the predetermined benchmark position as a reference point.[14]

The second process involves gathering data from individual employees within the organization concerning the extent of their responsibilities, the tasks they perform, and their qualifications. The data can be analyzed and used to establish salaries as part of the annual review process. The data also provide a vehicle for reevaluating jobs to ascertain if they are properly assigned to the appropriate salary schedule and in the correct range. Appendix A illustrates an employee questionnaire that can be used for this position analysis; it also contains samples of job evaluation forms. The use of this questionnaire and the evaluation forms is predicated on a procedure that utilizes a salary review committee.

---

[14]Richard Maxfield, "Application of Classes Within the Classified Service to the Master Salary Schedule," in Foster, *Wage and Salary Administration.* p. 26.

In most situations where this procedure is used, the salary review committee is composed of administrators, supervisors, teachers, and noninstructional personnel who are not directly employed in the job categories being evaluated but who have a knowledge of the working conditions involved. This gives credibility and objectivity to the process. A committee of three or five people is optimal for the evaluation task. Thus, if a secondary school principal's position is being evaluated, the committee could be composed of one or two elementary school principals, one or two secondary school teachers, and the assistant superintendent for secondary education. In like manner, if a building-level secretarial position is being evaluated, the committee could be composed of one or two central-office executive secretaries, one or two clerk-typists, and the director of staff development.

Each committee member studies the questionnaire completed by the employee and his or her supervisor. Using a scale of one to five with five indicating the highest requirement, each person evaluates the position in terms of the factors indicated on the evaluation form. Finally, a tally sheet summarizing the evaluations is completed. From these data, the assistant superintendent for personnel or another central office administrator can establish the salary range appropriate to the position.

Payroll Deductions

Making deductions from an employee's salary is such a common practice that most individuals take it for granted. Yet it has significant consequences because of legal and personal considerations. Therefore, the board of education should have a comprehensive payroll deduction policy covering such areas as the minimum and maximum amounts that may be deducted; the number and types of deductions authorized; deduction procedures; the opening and closing dates for entering deductions on the payroll records.

No payroll deduction should be initiated without written authorization from the employee unless authorized by law or the courts. John Ramsey has put together the following list of payroll deductions, which describes not only the commonly accepted categories but also information about procedures (see Exhibit 8–5).

Pay Periods

The complexity and size of modern school districts has raised a question for education that has been answered in the private sector for many years. Should salaries be paid on a monthly, semimonthly, biweekly, or weekly schedule? School districts no longer employ just a few people in simple jobs, and their payrolls can no longer be managed by a hand-worked method. The complexity of multiple deductions for extensive employee classifications has mandated computerization of payroll management, and this in turn has increased the importance of deadlines.

The basic principles for determining pay periods are the type of work done by the employee, the amount earned, and the cost to the school district.

Different classifications of employees have different expectations about how often they should be paid. Custodians, bus drivers, and cafeteria workers are more accustomed to being paid on a weekly basis in the business community, and such employees will

EXHIBIT 8–5   Categories of Payroll Deductions

I. **Income Tax Deductions.** Government income tax legislation requires each employee to execute a certificate of exemptions to be used as a basis for calculating income tax deductions. In most instances the certificate will provide the following information:

a) *Full Name*—It is recommended that it be typed or printed for legibility. In the case of married women, use first name, maiden name and last name.

b) *Employee Account Number*—This is needed for identification on payroll tax returns as well as for employee record cards. All employees should be required to show their account card and also to copy the name as it appears on the card. The existing U.S. Income Tax Regulations require a Social Security (FICA) Account Number for all employees subject to withholding taxes. If an employee has not filed an account number, he or she should be advised to fill out an application form and send it to the nearest district office of the U.S. Social Security Administration. Forms to obtain lost account cards are also available at the same office.

c) *Home Address*—Print or type this information, including City, State or Province and other identifying postal information.

d) *Claim for Withholding Exemptions*—The school district must allow exemptions to each employee on the basis of the withholding certificate. If an employee fails to furnish a certificate, the school district is required to withhold tax as if the employee had claimed no withholding exemptions. A certificate filed by a new employee is to be made effective upon the first payment of salary. Once filed with the school district, a withholding exemption certificate will remain in effect until an amended certificate is furnished.

The following classifications of exemption are usually considered:

a) *Single*—This refers to persons not married and who desire to claim an exemption. A mark, number or other designation is made on the form for this claim of exemption.

b) *Married*—This classification allows one exemption each for husband and wife if not claimed on another certificate. If claim is made for both exemptions, then an indication is inserted on the certificate; if one of the exemptions is claimed, or no exemptions are claimed, this is also indicated on the form.

c) *Other Exemptions*—This classification covers such exemptions as:
   1) Age (over 65).
   2) Blindness.
   3) Other relatives who qualify as dependents.

Employees may file an amended exemption certificate, increasing the number of exemptions, at any time. Normally the deductions are reflected in the next payment of wages.

School districts will usually find it convenient to determine the amount of income tax required to be withheld from wage bracket tables. Government agencies provide these tables free of charge—commercial tax tables may also be purchased from office supply houses, professional accountants' organizations and suppliers of tax services. Tax tables are available for various pay periods, i.e., weekly, biweekly, semimonthly, monthly, daily or miscellaneous periods.

In addition to making payroll withholding as specified by Internal Revenue Service tax tables, a percentage method may be used. Additional amounts may be withheld under

Continued

EXHIBIT 8–5 *Continued*

a written agreement between the school district and the employee. This agreement will be effective for such periods as may be mutually agreed upon.

The school district usually is assigned a reporting number for purposes of transmitting and accounting for payroll taxes deducted. Returns are usually rendered monthly or quarterly; and an annual reconciliation is required.

Some cities or local government units require collection of an occupational license or payroll tax. The law serves as the basis for the deduction and no authorizing action is required of the employee. In most instances, this tax is based on a percentage of gross salary, with no provision for exemptions.

The same employer reporting is required as mentioned above.

II. **Retirement Deductions.** These deductions usually come under one of three classifications—a government retirement plan for all employees, a program specifically limited to certificated or non-certificated personnel, or a commercial underwriting program. Some school districts may permit certificated employees to participate in all three plans or only one plan. This is usually determined by the school board or a governing board or by law. Deductions are usually based on a fixed percentage of gross salary.

III. **Court-Ordered Deductions.** The problems of deductions relative to garnishments, bankruptcies, levies, and other deductions of this nature are sometimes vexing to school districts. Employees should be encouraged to keep their personal financial affairs in sufficient order to prevent this type of action. . . . Of course, the employee should be given every opportunity to rectify the situation if it is an oversight or an honest error on the debtor's part.

In determining this deduction, care must be taken to note the following important information:

a) Name of Plaintiff or Debtor.
b) Date of garnishment served and received by school district.
c) Amount of garnishment.
d) Court costs—advisable to verify with Court.
e) Amount of pay due as of date of garnishment.
f) Number of days permitted to answer the garnishment.

A copy of the garnishment or order should be sent to the employee for his information. It is possible that a form entitled "Release" may be obtained by the employee which will alter the sum of money to be deducted from his salary. In no instance should the school district accept the word of the plaintiff's or defendant's attorney, or the debtor, relative to reduction in the principal amount of the debt unless a written form is furnished by the Court responsible for the original garnishment order.

At this time, it is appropriate to stress these four points:

a) Recover the amount required by the Court up to the date of the garnishment. If the salary earned is not sufficient to take care of indebtedness, there is a possibility that a subsequent garnishment will be initiated.
b) File with Court the necessary answer, within the specified time permitted. Deduction check should be made payable to the Court.
c) Always advise employee of the garnishment and give him or her every opportunity to clear the matter up prior to actual deduction.
d) Establish a policy relative to number of garnishments permitted and acquaint all employees of the policy requirements.

Continued

EXHIBIT 8–5   *Continued*

IV. **Miscellaneous Deductions.** The preceding paragraphs have dealt with deductions that are mandatory in nature and which are based on government regulations or court orders. Reference has been made to the control of deductions through an approved policy of the school district. In this connection, surveys of other school district deduction policies may be made to assist in development of the individual district policy.

The deductions discussed in the ensuing paragraphs are on a voluntary basis, and are usually identified as fringe benefits. The types of deductions are varied in scope. However, only a few will he presented in this chapter, to be used for guidance and direction.

a) *Health, Accident, and Hospital Plans*—These deductions are based on a predetermined premium made by the underwriting company. Rates are based on the type of coverage desired by the employee—the more coverage desired, the higher the premium. A part of the premium may or may not be paid by the school district depending upon the policy of the board along with applicable state laws. Some school districts may pay all of the premiums. In most instances, an application form is required of the employee in which personal information as well as family health history is indicated. A deduction authorization should also be signed by the employee and may or may not be included as a part of the application form. Group insurance certificates or individual policies are usually issued to the employee and confirm the coverage authorized on the deduction form.

b) *Life Insurance Plans*—These deductions generally follow the same outline as the plan for health, accident, and hospitalization. Many retirement plans now include life insurance as a part of their comprehensive program.

c) *Employment Association Dues*—Deductions for association dues are becoming increasingly popular among school districts. These include such deductions as local unit, state or province association dues which may be paid in one or more installments out of the salary of the employee. Many associations also provide for other deductions as a part of their overall program. This could include a life insurance program, disability income protection, and personal liability insurance.

d) *Credit Union*—This is becoming a more popular deduction for school district employees. The Credit Union has as its major purpose the encouragement of savings as well as the providing of a source of financial assistance. It is suggested that the deduction authorization form be worded in such a way that the deduction amount will not he identified as to whether it is a savings or a loan payment. The Treasurer of the Credit Union should determine the monthly amount to be paid or the savings desired and secure the signed authorization for payroll records. Many Credit Unions pay for deduction service on the basis of the number of accounts serviced.

e) *Community Fund Contributions*—Considerable pressure is exerted on the school districts to participate in various solicitations for the welfare of the underprivileged in the community. Many localities have combined all the campaigns into one, on an annual basis. It is emphasized that every attempt be made to combine these appeals into one amount for deduction purposes. A signed deduction form should be obtained which would indicate the amount to be deducted, and the period covered.

Source: John L. Ramsey, "Payroll Deductions," in Foster, *Wage and Salary Administration,* pp. 47–51. Modified foor this presentation.

expect a weekly check when working for a school district. These employees usually need their money more often than skilled employees, administrators, and teachers, whose wages are higher. Skilled employees such as plumbers, electricians, and carpenters generally receive higher wages than unskilled workers and are more accustomed to being paid on a monthly or biweekly basis. Finally, professional employees such as administrators and teachers are usually paid on a monthly basis; they normally have individual contracts for a set dollar amount, which is divided into equal payments. Some school districts by policy allow teachers to be paid in either nine or twelve payments, at the discretion of the individual teachers. Some building principals, in like manner, work ten months and are given the option of receiving their salary in ten or twelve monthly payments.

The size of the school district will determine the complexity of the payroll process. In larger school systems, of course, more people are employed, which usually increases the number of job classifications having different payroll periods. This will demand more computerization as well as deadlines and specific procedures for handling the payroll. More payroll personnel specialists and equipment will be needed, which will increase the school district's cost in managing the payroll process.

In conclusion, the importance of the payroll process to the school system is unquestioned. "It is essential that each person, as soon as he is employed, knows just how much he will earn, what deductions will be made, what retirement benefits he will receive, how often he will be paid, and when. Good payroll administration can do more to establish good morale in the school system than any other single factor."[15]

Principles for Presenting Recommendations to the School Board

It is assumed that all salary recommendations presented to the board of education will be based on sound wage and salary practices. The previous sections in this chapter outline defensible procedures which, if followed, will place the administration in such a position. The next objective, then, is to present the recommendations in a manner that will evoke favorable approval by the school board.

Dr. W. E. Campbell had identified three factors that will affect the presentation of salary recommendations: fiscal condition of the school district; the administrative organization of the school district; and the unions and associations to which the various categories of employees belong.[16]

The Fiscal Condition of the School District

In the present economy, salary recommendations almost always call for an increase, and in some cases a substantial increase, in wages. Salary appropriations account for 80 percent

---

[15]Thomas E. Smith, "Pay Periods and Discussion of Monthly, Semi-monthly, Bi-Weekly and Weekly Pay Periods," in Foster, *Wage and Salary Administration,* p. 45.

[16]W. E. Campbell, "Presentation of Salary Recommendations to the Board and the Community," in Foster, *Wage and Salary Administration,* pp. 59–62.

of school district budgets. Clearly, an increase in salaries will create one of the following situations: less money will be available for other categories of school operations; the school district will have enough revenue and/or balances to accommodate the salary increases; or the board of education will have to find additional sources of revenue to meet the increases. In most states additional revenue can be obtained only through a tax levy increase which, of course, requires voter approval. Inflation has generally created scarcity for most school districts. Therefore, a board of education may be unable to approve a recommendation if the cost is unrealistically high.

The Administrative Organization of the School District

Usually, only two administrative structures affect salary recommendations. If a school district does not engage in collective bargaining, the superintendent of schools, with the advice of the school business administrator, is directly responsible for making the salary recommendations. However, if the school district engages in collective bargaining, the board will be asked to ratify a master contract, which will normally have major sections devoted to salary and wages. The chief negotiator for the school district, with input from the superintendent of schools, will have negotiated within preestablished fiscal considerations. In this latter situation, the salary recommendations along with working conditions and fringe benefits, which also have a dollar value, must be evaluated by the board.

Employee Unions and Associations

The American Federation of Teachers, the National Education Association, and many unions representing noninstructional personnel have official positions on salary and wage policies. Most of these unions and associations seek comparability with the private sector and negotiate for their membership along this line. Within the last ten years these organizations have come to realize that, because of the large numbers of people they represent, they have a great deal of political influence. This influence has had an effect on the election not only of school board members but also of state legislators and even national candidates. An endorsement by a national labor or teacher organization such as the National Education Association is much sought after by all presidential candidates.

Salary Recommendation Procedures

The procedure for presentation of salary schedules to the Board, of course, will vary with the particular needs of the locality. Campbell has put together a set of procedures that can act as a guide to the superintendent of schools in formulating salary recommendations to the board of education. Following are his suggestions for adaptation to local needs.

  1. Be sure that the recommendations are sound, that they have the backing of the staff, and that the employees themselves are reasonably satisfied. On these bases the administrator should have full confidence in his recommendations.

  2. Prepare as much supporting data as needed to verify the soundness of the recommendations. Present schedules from comparable school systems and from private enterprise. Provide information relative to previous increases and show whether the recommendations will keep the non-instructional personnel at a desirable rate of increase in comparison with the increase granted the professional personnel.

3. Try to make recommendations as part of a package deal for all employees. Salary increases for teachers are generally favored in the community, even though funds may not always be available to pay as well as the public sentiment indicates. A factor especially in favor of the package deal is that the funds necessary to meet the salaries of the non-instructional personnel will represent a relatively small proportion of the total salary needs of the school system.

4. Secure when needed the services of a consulting firm to compile data regarding prevailing rates in the community. A consulting firm can also be of assistance in establishing classifications of employees and in writing job descriptions.

5. Emphasize the importance of the non-instructional personnel to the educational program. Show how instruction can be improved by having capable, well-paid employees to drive the busses, to provide the food services, to maintain the buildings and grounds, to care for and clean the physical facilities, to furnish the needed classroom materials at the appropriate time, and so on.

6. Appeal to the business side of the board members by showing the need for capable people to care for the Board's property—to protect its investment. School buildings now require services beyond the level of the ordinary custodian. Efficiency reduces waste and breakdown and produces savings in time and funds.

7. Bring about realization on the part of the Board of the value of the non-instructional employees to community life and their influence on how the community may view the schools. The non-instructional personnel are more likely to live in the immediate community than are the professional personnel. Employees satisfied with their salary schedules are more likely to be proud of their work and should be more likely to perform at a level of work efficiency which will benefit the school system and have beneficial effects in the community.

8. Emphasize the business and financial aspects of the school system to the community. The school system may be operating the largest bus system in the community. It may be selling more meals than the largest restaurant or possibly more than all the restaurants combined. Its program of maintenance and operation of buildings and grounds may be the largest in the community. Its total expenditures in the community for goods and contractual services may be among the highest in dollar volume in the community.[17]

Small Business Job Protection Act of 1996[18]

This legislation is commonly referred to as the "Minimum Wage Law" because the intent of the legislation was to increase the take-home wages of employees. The passage and signing into law of this act attracted much attention in the news media. When President Clinton signed the bill in August, 1996, the ceremony featured minimum-wage workers and their children, labor union officials, Congressional leaders, and Vice President Al Gore. To sign the bill, President Clinton used the desk of President Franklin Roosevelt's Labor Secretary, Francis Perkins.

---

[17]Campbell, *Presentation of Salary Recommendations,* pp. 62–63. Modified for this presentation.

[18]Small Business Job Protection Act of 1996, H.R. 3448, 104th Cong., 2nd Session, (1996).

The minimum wage was increased in two stages, $.50 per hour on October 1, 1996, which raised the total to $4.75; and on September 1, 1997, the minimum-wage was increased by $.40 per hour to $5.15. The new law impacted approximately 10 million workers who received an increase in their pay checks. However, individual states can raise the minimum wage to even higher levels. At the time the bill was signed into law, California, Montana, Oregon, and Missouri had plans to place before their respective voters a wage law that would increase the minimum above the federal mandate. Further, cities may increase the minimum wage beyond federal and state levels. Denver, for example, had an initiative that would increase the minimum wage to $7.15 by 1999.

Because the new law was opposed by many small businesses, Congress included approximately 9 billion dollars in tax breaks for businesses which will take effect over the next seven years. For example, in the year of purchase the total cost of new equipment that a small business can claim for tax exemption was raised from $17,500 to $25,000.

The new law also included the establishment of a "training wage" of $4.25 per hour for employees under twenty years of age for the first ninety day of employment. In addition, homemakers can contribute $2,000 per year to an individual retirement account. Other employer benefits included: a simplified pension plan for companies with one hundred or fewer employees; reinstatement of the $5,250 exemption for employer-provided, graduate-level tuition until June, 1996 and undergraduate tuition through May, 1997. While the "tax exemption" provisions and a few other sections do not pertain to school districts, it is important to be aware of these because future public debate will be impacted by the contents of the entire law.

A major implication for school districts, of course, is that budgets must be adjusted to account for the required increase in wages. Custodians, cafeteria workers, and bus drivers are probably the employees most affected by the new law.

Conclusions

A few final comments are appropriate at the end of this section on salary and wage administration. First, executive salaries are usually negotiated on a personal basis and do not fall within the limits of a salary schedule. The executive positions in school districts are relatively few and commonly pertain to the superintendency and associate or assistant superintendencies.

Second, it is extremely important to consider each salary schedule as a separate entity. In some school systems increases to teacher salary schedules are reflected in an additional percentage increase being applied to administrator schedules. This, of course, defeats the integrity of the salary schedule objective, which is to reward performance within salary limits that are competitive with other school districts and businesses in the community. This can only be done by analyzing each individual salary schedule.

When collective bargaining is involved, such a tied-in procedure also violates the distinction between management and employees. If an administrative salary schedule is affected by an increase to the teacher salary schedule resulting from collective negotiations, the administrators are in actuality being represented by the teachers' bargaining agent.

Third, extra pay for extra duty, which is the common language applied to overtime pay for instructional personnel and overtime pay for classified employees, should be determined by the same procedure used to establish regular salary and wages. The rewards of performance and competitiveness are also primary considerations in overtime compensation.

Fourth, this chapter was written from the viewpoint that salary and wage increases are rewards for performance and are not simply rewards for seniority with the school district. Many districts have developed salary schedules with channels reflecting academic preparation (bachelor's degree, master's degree, and so on) and steps reflecting seniority in the school district. The salary schedules recommended in this chapter provide for ranges reflecting job classification with step increases based on performance.

The practices in most public school districts are not in keeping with the principles set forth in this chapter, which essentially recommend establishing competitive compensation programs that will attract quality personnel. Allan Ornstein's predictions are even more ominous:

> These data and projections pose a grave threat to the teaching profession, affecting entry standards, job performance, and teacher morale. The bleak prospect will put tremendous pressure on teacher organizations to resort to strikes for improved salaries. Strikes, in turn, will pit teachers against the public. Departments and colleges of education will not escape unscathed. Fewer students—especially the academically talented—will seek careers in teaching. Unless we can convince the public that education is a wise investment, the future looks grim indeed.[19]

INDIRECT COMPENSATION: FRINGE BENEFIT ADMINISTRATION

Fringe benefits may be defined as benefits available to all employees resulting from a direct fiscal expenditure. Because fringe benefits are available to all employees and are not contingent upon performance, such services are not motivators but are more properly considered maintenance factors. Nevertheless, fringe benefits are commonly considered to be an important part of an effective compensation program. Retirement programs, medical and hospitalization insurance, and life insurance are only a few of the many fringe benefits offered to employees in school systems. Because these services are essential in our society, the quality of these and other fringe benefit programs can have a significant effect on the ability of a school district to attract and retain good employees. Conversely, absenteeism and employee turnover, which are signs of employee dissatisfaction, can possibly be kept to a tolerable level with good fringe benefit and salary programs.

High employee turnover across the nation costs school districts millions of dollars each year. Recruiting, and hiring new employees, which creates direct expenditures of money, should be minimized to a reasonable turnover rate. This factor, however, does not begin to address the problem of meeting the primary objective of the school district to educate students when there is a continual flow of new employees.

Absenteeism costs corporations in the United States an average of $20 billion each year. Although figures on the cost of absenteeism to public education are not readily available, millions of dollars would be a conservative estimate. A substitute teacher must be hired whenever a teacher is absent. The students are still present and the task of teaching these students cannot be passed on to another of the district's regular teachers, nor can it wait until the absent teacher returns.

[19]Allan C. Ornstein, "Teacher Salaries: Past, Present, Future," *Phi Delta Kappan* (June 1980), p. 679.

The key factor in addressing high employee turnover and absenteeism is to establish a positive approach. Attracting individuals with excellent credentials and a desire for excellence in performance, from the outset, will ultimately correct high turnover and absenteeism. Quality fringe benefits attract quality candidates for positions and will maintain employee commitment to the school district.

Types of Fringe Benefits

Inflation continually eats away at real salaries and wages, which is the reason for the rapid growth in wages over the last ten-year period. This same period has also produced a significant increase in fringe benefits offered to employees of public school districts. The prediction made by John Sullivan in 1972 has come to pass.[20] The cost of fringe benefits in the United States has risen to approximately 35 percent of total salary and wages paid to employees.

School districts across the country are experiencing severe financial problems. With financial problems continuing to spread, school districts have found that fringe benefit enrichment is an alternative when large wage and salary increases are not feasible. As more school districts develop elaborate fringe benefit programs, greater pressure has been placed on competing school districts to develop similar programs to attract and keep employees.

There is also a growing recognition that fringe benefits are nontaxable, which has been another major stimulus towards their expansion. If a teacher wants a certain amount of life insurance, there are two advantages in having it purchased by the school district. First, the premium will be lower because the school district will be purchasing a large degree of protection. Second, the teacher would pay the premium for the insurance out of his or her net pay, which is the dollar amount left over after paying taxes. If the school district pays the premium, the teacher has more wages left to pay for other needs and, therefore, this becomes an attractive fringe benefit.

Benefits Required by Law

Certain benefits must be provided by the school district: social security premiums, state retirement insurance, unemployment compensation, and workers' compensation. These benefits provide the employee with financial security and protection at retirement or termination; or when an injury occurs in the workplace; and they provide survivors' benefits to dependents in the event of the employee's death.

The social security program usually covers classified employees. Instructional and administrative personnel are normally included in state retirement programs. Social security is the major source of income for U.S. retirees. This program is financed by the contributions of employees, which are matched by the employer and computed as a percentage of the employee's earnings. Survivors' benefits for the dependents of a deceased employee and disability benefits for an employee who is unable to be gainfully employed are provided through the social security administration.

The Social Security Act is an important aspect of the United States government's attempt to care for and protect the aged by ensuring for them a minimal standard of living. Although social security is often referred to as an insurance program, this is a misnomer. Rather, it is

---

[20]John F. Sullivan, "Indirect Compensation: The Years Ahead," *California Management Review,* (Winter 1972), p. 73.

a transfer program of a trust fund from one generation to another. We, the currently employed, pay a social security tax that is used to support yesterday's retired workers, dependents, and the disabled. It is important for personnel administrators to be cognizant of the fact that social security benefits and the program itself are subject to legislation. Thus, changes are certain to occur and must be continually monitored to ensure that adequate budgetary appropriations are available to meet the demands of these potential changes.

Unemployment compensation laws in most states provide benefits to individuals who are without a job. To qualify for these benefits, a person must usually submit an application to the State Employment Agency for unemployment benefits and register with that agency for available work with a willingness to accept suitable employment offered through the agency. In addition, the person must have worked a minimum number of weeks before becoming unemployed.

Unemployment benefits are derived from a tax levied against employers calculated on a percentage of the employer's total salary payroll. Benefits received by unemployed workers are calculated from the individual's previous wage rate plus the length of previous employment. Unemployment benefits are provided on a limited basis, typically for a twenty-six week period.

Unemployment compensation also serves the total economy of our nation because it provides a stability in spending power during periods of high unemployment, as when a recession occurs.

Workers' compensation programs provide benefits to individuals injured or disabled while engaged in a job-related activity. Benefits paid to employees for injuries are based on schedules for minimum and maximum payments, depending on the type of injury sustained. For example, the loss of a hand is compensated with a higher dollar amount than the loss of a finger. In like manner, disability payments are calculated based on the individual's current salary, future earnings, and financial responsibilities.

The funds for workers' compensation programs are borne entirely by the employer. While the programs are mandated by state laws, the method of obtaining workers' compensation insurance is usually left to the discretion of the employer, who may buy such protection from public or private agencies or provide the protection through a self-insuring program. Like social security and unemployment insurance, workers' compensation is subject to the legislative process. Thus, requirements and benefits will certainly change with the passage of time.

Where mandated by state laws, retirement programs for administrators and teachers generally follow the prescriptions of these other protection programs. Contributions are calculated on the basis of an employee's wages and are usually matched by the school district. Benefits based on contributions are paid upon retirement, with survivors benefits being available for the dependents of deceased employees.

In 1986 the United States Congress passed the Consolidated Omnibus Budget Reconciliation Act (COBRA). This federal law requires school districts that provide group health plans for their employees and their dependents to offer an extension of the coverage on a temporary basis under certain conditions when coverage would usually end. An employee covered by the group health plan is eligible for continuation of coverage if his or her employment with the district is terminated except in cases of gross misconduct, if he or she is laid off for economic reasons, or if he or she is reduced to part-time employment and thereby would usually lose coverage.

Family members of an employee are entitled to continued coverage under the following qualifying events: death of the employee; divorce or legal separation from the employee; medicare becoming the employee's primary health care coverage; termination, layoff, or part-time status of the employee; ceasing to be considered a dependent child under the plan.

There are notification requirements under this law and the employee or family members must pay the premiums for the extended group health plan coverage. Extended coverage may last for eighteen, twenty-nine, or thirty-six months dependent on certain qualifying conditions.

Voluntary Fringe Benefits

This category of benefits may be further divided into insurance programs, time away from the job, and services. Group insurance programs are available for almost every human need. Among the most common are major medical and hospitalization insurance, dental insurance, term life insurance, errors and omissions insurance, and optical insurance. The number of such programs made available to employees depends on the fiscal condition of the school district and the wishes of the employees. A school district is usually restricted by state statute to paying insurance premiums only for employees. Therefore, if an employee wishes to include dependents under such insurance programs, he must pay the additional premium for this coverage.

Under federal law and Internal Revenue Service regulations, school districts can design "cafeteria" fringe benefit plans, which will allow individual employees to choose the benefits that most meet their needs. In addition, if the employee is to bear the cost of some of these programs, the premiums he or she pays can be deducted from his or her gross salary or wages before federal income taxes are levied.

This tax advantage for employees and the opportunity to choose their benefits from a predetermined list are two reasons why such programs are quite desirable. The administrative expense of such a program and the availability of insurance coverage that does not demand a high percentage of participation are problems. For example, a company may offer a dental insurance program to a school district only if there is 60 percent participation by employees.

Federal tax-qualified plans must not be offered to only highly compensated employees. Beginning in 1997, the definition of a *highly compensated employee* was changed to include an employee who was compensated for the preceding year in excess of $80,000 and which placed him or her in the category of the 20-percent highest paid employees. Federal tax-qualified plans are those that are exempt from taxation such as 401(k) salary deferral plans.[21]

A fringe benefit that is often taken for granted by employees but creates an additional expense for a school district is time spent away from work. Therefore, sick leave, vacation time, paid holidays, and sabbatical leave are, in fact, benefits provided at the discretion of the school system. In very large school districts, this amounts to a considerable expenditure.

Corporations have long recognized the value of *services* in a fringe benefit program. Social and recreational events, employee assistance programs, wellness programs, cultural activities, credit unions, company cafeterias, company-provided transportation to and from

---

[21]Newkirk Products, Inc., "Nondiscrimination Provisions," *1996 Tax Law Summary,* 1996, p. 13

work, tuition reimbursements, and child care centers are only a few of the services found in many large corporations.

School systems usually provide much more limited services, but like time away from work such services are seldom recognized by employees as fringe benefits. Those most commonly found in public education are expenses paid for attendance at workshops, professional meetings, and conventions; tuition reimbursement; and free lunches and coffee. In some districts experiencing a decrease in pupil enrollment and, thus, a reduction in staff, career counseling is provided to teachers in order to help them prepare for jobs outside education. In large school districts, central-office administrators are usually provided with district-owned automobiles to use when engaged in school business, or they receive mileage reimbursement.

Fringe benefits are certainly an important component of all compensation programs, and they are becoming even more important as alternatives to large salary and wage increases.

Managed Health Care

Health care costs continue to increase at an alarming rate. If this trend continues, by the year 2000, health care expenditures will consume approximately 16 percent of the gross national product. An alternative approach to traditional insurance programs which is meant to maintain a high quality of care but at a lower cost and in a more efficient manner is *managed health care.*

Basically, managed health care coordinates services around the patient and thereby, produces a more efficient delivery system. In order to accomplish this, school districts must employ *case management specialists* who have the job responsibility of evaluating cases that require extensive and/or expensive medical treatment. As an alternative to hiring case management specialists, a school district can contract with a company specializing in *third party health care administration.* These case managers or third party administrators work with patients and physicians in order to identify alternatives that are medically sound yet cost effective. A common example is developing a plan that incorporates out-patient care after sufficient in-patient hospital care rather than a prolonged hospital stay. Such specialists should also develop employee programs that encourage healthy lifestyles and the prevention of illness. It would probably be cost effective for a school district to offer mammograms or diabetes testing at a nominal cost to employees.

There are various levels of managed health care. *Utilization management* attempts to control the cost of a school district's health benefit plan. This is best accomplished through *catastrophic case management* and *utilization review.* When an employee suffers a catastrophic illness, the case manager begins the process of assisting the patient and his or her physicians to access the best treatment at the lowest cost. This could include care in a rehabilitation center, nursing home, extended care facility, or out-patient services in the patient's home. The case manager will help negotiate rates with these various facilities.

Utilization review usually includes the reviewing of all in-patient admissions, out-patient surgical procedures, in-patient substance cases, and in-patient psychiatric care. The purpose is to ascertain if such services are medically sound. In addition, before a claim is paid, the case manager will review the charges for accuracy.

An alternative to hiring case management specialists or contracting with a third party health care administrator, is for a school district to join a *managed care network.* Physicians who are members of the network have agreed to certain fee guidelines and medical facilities that belong to the network have agreed to a certain quality of service and fee guidelines. The network provides the school district with the efficient processing of paperwork and also with cost information that will help the school district in its financial planning.

There are various types of networks. One type is called a *preferred provider organization* or PPO. Both hospitals and physicians belong to such a network. Physicians treat patients in their own offices. If a school district employee chooses a physician or hospital outside the network, most PPOs will pay a much smaller percentage of the bill. Hospitals and physicians outside the network cannot be monitored to insure quality care and cost containment.

A second type is a *health maintenance organization* or HMO. In this arrangement, each patient is provided with a network primary care physician who controls access within the network to care for the employee and his or her dependents. A prepaid fixed monthly fee for all services is another important feature of the HMO. Typically, HMO's are organized around four models: group, staff, individual practice, and point-of-service. In the group model, a group or groups of physicians provide care to patients at one or more locations. In the staff model, physicians are actually employed by an HMO and provide services at one or more locations. In the individual practice association model, an HMO contracts with physicians who practice out of their own offices. In the point-of-service model, an HMO allows school district employees to chose physicians outside the network but the employee will pay a higher percentage of the cost.

Many PPOs and HMOs have prescription drug plans whereby certain pharmacies within a network offer medication at a reduced cost. This kind of network can also be found outside of PPOs and HMOs.

Health Insurance Portability and Accountability Act of 1996[22]

There was little media coverage of this bill until August 21, 1996 when it was signed into law by President Bill Clinton. The new law addresses the needs of approximately 25 million Americans who are denied health insurance coverage because of an illness or who cannot change jobs because they, their spouse, or their dependents would be denied insurance coverage because of a preexisting medical condition such as diabetes. The law becomes effective at the beginning of a new plan year after July 1, 1997. The following are major provisions of the new law:

- Immediate coverage for the employee, spouse, and dependents by the new employer if the employee, spouse, and dependents were covered by the previous employer's health care plan for twelve months or eighteen months if they enter the new employer's plan late.
- Immediate coverage for pregnancy, newborns, and children placed in the employee's home pending adoption.
- The new employer can deny coverage for up to one year for a preexisting condition, if the employee, spouse, and dependents were not covered by the previous employer for twelve or eighteen months respectively. If there was a break in the previous coverage for more than sixty-three days, the waiting period could start over again.

[22]Health Insurance Portability and Accountability Act of 1996, H.R. 3103, 104th Cong., 2nd Session (1996).

- Employers can limit a new employee, spouse, and dependents to the same coverage they had with the previous employer even if other employees have additional coverage.
- The health care plan with the new employer could exclude coverage for certain illnesses and could place a cap on benefit coverage
- Local and state government health care plans may exempt themselves from this law.
- Employers can make premium adjustments to their plans or increase copayments and deductibles in order to offset high claims experience as long as these modifications are applicable to all employees.
- If the new employer does not provide a health care plan, the state in which the school district is located is responsible for providing unrestricted access to a choice of individual health-insurance policies to those individuals, their spouses and dependents who were covered by a group health care plan for at least eighteen months with a previous employer.

The new law does not address the needs of people who are uninsured because they cannot afford to pay insurance premiums. Additionally, individuals who have insurance for long-term care can receive a tax deduction for the cost of the premium and the cost of the care. Finally, the new law authorized a pilot program, *medical savings accounts,* as an alternative to conventional health insurance policies for self-employed people and for employees of small companies.

The new law also required medical plans to cover illnesses arising from genetic defects. Further, accidents which are caused through participation in recreation activities or hobbies such as skiing must now be covered by health care plans.

School districts must now require their insurance companies to delete provisions from insurance policies that discriminate against employees, employee spouses, and their dependents because of preexisting medical conditions. Small school districts could also be eligible for medical savings accounts.

Medical Savings Accounts[23]

The Health Insurance Portability and Accountability Act of 1996 established a pilot Medical Saving Accounts (MSAs) program which is an attempt to control the rising cost of health care. The program began in 1997 and will continue through the year 2000. After the year 2000, employees of school districts which have already established MSAs may continue with this program. In order to qualify, a school district must provide a health care plan with a large deductible and must meet the "small employer" designation. Under this approach, employees can choose the physicians, hospitals, and treatment options they want. Major illnesses are paid for by school districts' insurance companies while money withdrawn from the Medical Savings Accounts is used to pay for minor health-care costs. Health insurance coverage with a high-deductible creates a much lower costing premium than coverage with a low deductible. A high-deductible plan is one with an annual deductible of at least $1,500 but not more than $2,250 for single coverage or for family coverage with at least a $3,000 but no more than a $4,500 deductible.

Thus, the employer could purchase high-deductible health care insurance and would establish MSAs for each employee. The amount of money saved by the district could then

[23]Newkirk Products, Inc.,"Health Care-Related Provisions," *1996 Tax Law Summary, 1996,* pp. 1–3.

be placed in each employee's medical savings account. Also, the employee can authorize the employer to deduct a certain amount of money from his or her payroll check before taxes are assessed which would be placed in the medical savings account to pay for depended spouse and/or children health care costs that are minor. If and when the deductible is reached, the health insurance company will pay for the incurred cost.

A small school district is one with no more than fifty employees during the preceding or second preceding year. An employer may continue to establish an MSA for new employees or employees who previously did not have an MSA until the year following the first year when a school district has two hundred employees. After reaching this plateau, no new MSAs may be established.

The medical savings account is under the control of the employee and each year additional contributions could be made to MSAs from the employee through the employer for his or her dependent coverage. The account should be interest bearing and unspent funds can grow from the contributions and interest. The employee could make withdrawals for nonmedical purposes but such withdrawals would be taxed and penalized.

It is estimated that only five to ten percent of employees would reach the deductible each year. Former employees on Medicare have an option of receiving health insurance and a large contribution to a medical savings account from Medicare funds.

The advantages of MSAs are considerable. Among the most obvious are:

National reduction of health-care costs
Increased savings for employers
Increased saving for employees
Retirement savings for health and non-health expenses
Patients' control of health care choice
Health care coverage for people and their dependents between jobs (portability)

Procuring Health Care and Related Insurance[24]

In large school districts, the process for procuring fringe benefit insurance is usually the responsibility of the purchasing and procurement departments along with significant involvement of the director of employee benefits who reports to the assistant superintendent for personnel. In medium-size districts, an assistant superintendent may be assigned this responsibility; while in small school districts, the superintendent of schools will probably implement the procurement process. Of course, many school districts hire an insurance consultant or broker, who will not be permitted to place a bid, to help in developing the bid specifications and may also oversee the bidding process including the analysis of the bids.

The health care industry has been experiencing a period of significant change and modification; Exhibit 8–6 sets forth categories of coverage in a typical health care program which must be considered when developing such a program. Further, Exhibit 8–7 presents a glossary of health care terms and acronyms that should be helpful in understanding the vocabulary of the health care industry.

[24]William T. Rebore, Ronald W. Rebore, *Financial and Business Administration in Public Education* (Needham Heights, MA: Allyn & Bacon, 1993), pp. 271–278.

EXHIBIT 8–6   Categories of Coverage in a Typical Health Care Program

Physician and Hospital Selection
Annual Deductible
Copayment
Preventive Care
   Routine Physical
   Gynecological Exams
   Eye Exams
   Immunizations
   Well-Baby and Pediatric Care
   Pediatric Dental Exams
Health Education
Home Care
Physician Care
Diagnostic Services (including X-ray and laboratory tests)
Surgery
   Outpatient
   Consultations and Second Opinions
Physical Medicine and Occupational Therapy
Hospital Services
Maternity Care
   Prenatal Care
   Postnatal Care
   Delivery
Mental Health Benefits
   Outpatient
   Inpatient
Chemical Dependency Benefits
   Outpatient
   Inpatient
Emergency Care
Prescription Drugs and Medications
Away From Home Care
Maximum Out-of-pocket Costs to the Employee
Maximum Cost Paid in Claims for the Employee

The Insurance Agent and Broker

An insurance policy is a legal contract between an insurance company and the school district. The provisions of insurance policies are usually developed by a third party, an insurance agent or broker. The majority of insurance companies do business under the American Agency System whereby insurance companies contract with individuals within a given territory. This individual is referred to as an agent because he or she is authorized to issue policies, collect premiums, and solicit renewals. Independent agents represent several insurance companies, while exclusive agents only represent a single company.

EXHIBIT 8–7   Glossary of Health Care Terms and Acronyms

ASO	Administrative Service Organization. This refers to a third party administrator under contract to a school district responsible for monitoring and processing claims when a school district is self-insured.
COBRA	Consolidated Omnibus Budget Reconciliation Act of 1986. Federal law which permits employees, their spouses and their dependents to continue health care coverage through the school district's group insurance programs under certain conditions when the employee is no longer employed by the district.
Catastrophic Case Management	When an employee, or his or her spouse, his or her dependent suffers a catastrophic illness and under the managed care approach, a case manager assists the patient and his or her physician to access the best treatment at the lowest cost.
HMO	Health Maintenance Organization. In this approach to health care management, health insurance and the delivery of health care are combined. Physicians receive a salary for providing services or through a contract, the physicians receive a fixed per-patient payment regardless of the number of visits.
Indemnity Health Care Plan	Traditional health care insurance plan which allows the employee, employee spouse, and dependents to choose any physician and hospital to receive services.
IPA	Independent Practice Association. Groups or networks of physicians by which physicians can remain independent while contracting with HMO's.
Managed Health Care	An approach to coordinating services around the patient and thereby, producing a more efficient health care delivery system which also will be more cost-effective.
Out-of-Network	If an employee, his or her spouse, or dependent accesses the services of a physician or hospital that is not under contract to an HMO or a PPO, the health care plan pays a smaller portion of the costs that result from receiving the services.
POS	Point of Service. This refers to an HMO plan which permits a member to access health care services outside the HMO. However, the HMO plan usually imposes a high deductible for such services and further, will pay a much smaller portion of the cost after the deductible is reached.
PPO	Preferred Provider Organization. This term is used to refer to individual health care professionals, hospitals, health care organizations, or groups of health care organizations that provide services to employees, their spouses or dependents at an agreed upon discount.
Primary Care Physician	The health care professional who acts as a gatekeeper by being the person through whom all referrals are made in order for the patient to receive health care services.

Insurance brokers are not under contract to any specific insurance company and they act on a free-lance basis. Thus, brokers buy insurance coverage for clients. The broker can purchase insurance directly from an insurance company or may place business through an insurance agent. The major difference, therefore, between an agent and a broker lies in the fact that the agent may act on behalf of the company. If an agent states that the school district is covered by an insurance policy even before the policy is issued, then it is covered. Whereas, a broker must receive written verification from an insurance company.

Selecting Insurance Companies

There are literally thousands of insurance companies selling some form of health care and related insurance in the United States. Companies differ significantly due to their financial capacity to assure timely and accurate processing and payment of claims. In addition, third party management companies which process claims for school districts that are self-insured also vary depending on their fiscal solvency and performance.

Thus, when bids are received from health care and related services insurance companies or third-party management companies, it is essential to check their performance and financial solvency with well established rating firms. Among the nationally recognized rating firms are A.M. Best of Oldwick (New Jersey), Duff & Phelps of Chicago, Moody's of New York, and Standard & Poor's of New York. These firms use a letter grade which they award to insurance provider companies based on each company's performance and viability. A.M. Best awards a top range of A++ to a low grade of F; Duff & Phelps uses AAA to CCC; Moody awards range from a top of AAA to a low grade of C, Standard & Poor's uses AAA to R. School districts can directly contact at least one of these rating firms with the list of insurance companies that have submitted a bid. The rating firms may charge the school district a fee for their services. Insurance companies desiring a rating must pay an annual fee to the rating firms; thus, many insurance companies may not request a rating from all the rating companies. Consequently, school districts should request in the bidding process that the insurance companies identify the firm or firms by whom they are rated.

The specifications in the request for proposals bid package should be written in such a way that the school district can select a single company to provide all of the lines of health care and related insurance or a group of companies with each providing a different benefit. In selecting one or more health care and related insurance companies or third party companies, the following criteria should constitute the minimum required: successful experience in providing coverage or management in at least two other school districts with an equal number of employees and similar benefits; written references from other school districts stating that claims were accurately and promptly processed; useful communication literature for employees concerning the coverage and claims process; evidence that the school district will be required to provide only reasonable administrative assistance; affordable premiums for the district and the employees; and evidence that the insurance companies or management companies will use accurate and appropriate data in establishing future premiums.

Of course, there is a direct relationship between the premium that a school district will pay for health care and related insurance and the claims experience of the group of employees covered by the insurance. When the sum of money paid in claims is high, premiums are correspondingly higher. Most insurance companies are "for profit" and therefore, the premium will include a profit for the company. Premiums will also include not only enough money to pay claims but also to build up a reserve which will be used for cash flow purposes. In addition, the premium will include a reserve to pay outstanding claims if the school district takes bids and awards a contract to a different insurance company

There is a significant financial advantage to the school district if the health care and related insurance lines have a deductible which must be paid by the employee before the district's insurance program incurs a claim. There is a direct relationship between the amount of the premium paid by the district and the size of the deductible. For example, if an employee must pay the first $250 in medical costs, the cost of premium paid by the district will be less then if the employee had to pay only the first $100. The reason for this is obvious, a claim is incurred after the $100 rather than after $250.

There are several reasons why a school district should require a deductible for all premium related fringe benefits. The most important reasons are:

- Deductibles encourage employees to retain some responsibility for controlling costs.
- Deductibles avoid nuisance claims.
- Deductibles help to preserve a competitive market for the district's insurance program.
- Deductibles help to reduce administrative costs.

A *copayment* is an alternative to deductibles which would also be a financial benefit to a school district if it were incorporated into the district's health care and related insurance program. For example, a district's program could require a $10 copayment for an office visit to a physician; the insurance program would pay the remainder of the cost for the visit. The copayment approach is more commonly used for prescription drugs and medications. Like deductibles, the copayments would encourage employees to be more responsible in controlling health costs.

Even if a school district has self-funded health care and related insurance programs, deductibles and copayments can bring about the same advantages cited above. The single most important reason why a school district would create a self-funded health care and related benefits program is to save money. There are two ways that a school district can save money if it uses a self-funded approach: first, the premium set aside by the district will not include a profit; second, the money budgeted from the district's revenue for health care and related benefits can be invested and the interest will help to reduce the cost of the benefits programs during periods of time without large claims.

Self-funding, however, will require a school district to purchase 'stop loss' insurance. The purpose of stop loss insurance is to pay a portion of the cost of claims arising from catastrophic illnesses which would significantly deplete the pool of money set aside to pay claims. Insurance should be purchased for individual claims after a certain amount has been paid through the district's self-funded programs and for claims in the aggregate after a certain amount has been paid. For example, the birth of a premature baby will result in a costly hospital bill. Stop loss insurance could pay for that portion of the hospital bill which exceeded $100,000 or any other limit set by the school district. In like manner, stop loss insurance could pay for claims from all employees taken together that exceed $3,000,000. The cost of the premium for stop loss insurance depends on the amount of money which the school district pays in claims. Obviously, the more money the school district pays in claims, the less the district will pay in premiums for stop loss insurance.

In those school districts where employee benefits are bargained collectively, these issues will be affected by the master agreement. If a school district and its employees do not bargain collectively or do not include these benefits in the negotiations, it is very important for the superintendent to establish an employee advisory committee. This committee should be charged with reviewing the district's health care and related programs, making suggestions for improvements in benefits, making suggestions for containing costs, reviewing specifications for bidding benefit insurance, reviewing the analysis of bids, and for annually making recommendations to the assistant superintendent for personnel through the director of employee benefits.

Health Risks in the Workplace

A major issue facing many school districts across the nation, is the rising cost of workers' compensation. In the early years of this century, workers who were injured on the job had to pay for their own medical treatment and probably received no wages during the recovery period. If a worker was seriously injured with an extensive recovery period, he or she most likely would not have a job even when able to return to work. Around 1910 individual states began to adopt various systems of workers' compensation. This approach required employers to compensate workers injured on the job regardless of who was at fault. In return the workers were not allowed to sue their employers. The system has been beneficial not only for workers but also for employers.[25]

However, medical costs associated with workers' compensation has risen approximately 11 percent per year over the last ten years. Today employers pay approximately 60 billion dollars each year for workers' compensation which is approximately $500 per employee.

There are probably three major reasons for this dramatic rise in cost. First, in trying to contain general health-care costs, employers have initiated cost cutting measures such as higher deductibles, copayments, case management, utilization reviews, and the establishment of health maintenance and preferred provider organizations. While containing costs in general health care, employees are now utilizing workers' compensation to receive the same level of benefits prior to initiating the cost cutting measures. Workers' compensation usually pays the total cost of medical treatment. Second, the original "no fault" approach has deteriorated into a massive legal bureaucracy where lawyers and judges have become the central figures in workers' compensation cases. Finally, the nature of the workplace has dramatically changed with the effect of producing more complicated injuries. In addition there has emerged a new category of injuries termed "cumulative trauma," which is associated with repetitive work such as using a computer and thus, being exposed to a video display terminal for long periods of time. Psychological and mental stress is also a form of cumulative trauma.[26]

For school district employees, there are three major categories of health risks. School facility environmental risks are the first. These include: radon gas, lead in the drinking water,

[25]Greg Steinmetz, "States Take On the Job of Holding Down Medical Costs of Workers' Compensation," *Wall Street Journal,* 3 March 1993, sec. B, p. B1.

[26]Michael S. Pritula, "Workers' Comp: Tranquilizing a Benefit Gone Mad," *Wall Street Journal,* 13 January 1992, sec. A, p. A16.

asbestos in floor tile and other building materials, tobacco smoke, fungi, mold and spores, pesticides, cleaning materials, etc.[27] The second category is violence. Today, teachers and staff members are working with students who have a history of committing violent acts. The emergence of gangs is a contributing factor to the increasing number of violent acts committed against teachers and staff members. Finally, there is the risk of contracting infectious disease that comes with working with children. For special education teachers who work with children who are multiply impaired or physically impaired there is the risk of back injuries because many of these children must be lifted from one position to another.

Because fringe benefit management is a component of the personnel function and because workers' compensation is such a complicated and expensive fringe benefit, more and more school districts have established the position of risk manager. This position usually reports to the assistant superintendent for personnel. The responsibilities of this position include identifying and evaluating the school district's exposure to risks. It is possible to seek assistance from the school district's insurance agent or broker or underwriter to help the risk manager conduct an audit in order to ascertain the exposure of the district to injuries on the job. When these risks are identified, the next step is to minimize or eliminate the potential risk.[28] For example, if a school has a problem with gangs, the most appropriate method of dealing with this issue is to develop a comprehensive security program. This plan might include the hiring of security guards; the development of a gang prevention/self-esteem curricula; targeting at-risk students for special prevention programs; increased job opportunities, and drug education; strengthening extracurricular and recreational programs, etc.[29] The development of the strategy which will eventuate into such a security program becomes the responsibility of the assistant superintendents comprising the superintendent's cabinet.

A second example of a method for minimizing or eliminating risk is a comprehensive staff development program. For example, maintenance and custodial staff members are consistently utilizing potentially dangerous equipment and hazardous chemicals. The manufacturer's sales representative or distributor of cleaning chemicals is usually available to train employees in the proper use of equipment and supplies.

Finally, if it is impossible to eliminate or significantly minimize a risk, it will be necessary to develop procedures which will ensure that the workers' compensation program is effective in meeting the needs of the employees.

SUMMARY

Psychologists have long recognized that satisfaction of needs is the primary motivation behind all human actions. In satisfying their needs, individuals will act in ways that they

[27]Cathryn Ehrhardt, "Environmental Policy—a Priority for Schools in the 90's," *Updating School Board Policies,* 20, no. 8 (September 1989), pp. 2–3.

[28]William T. Rebore and Ronald W. Rebore, *Financial and Business Administration in Public Education* (Needham Heights: Allyn & Bacon, 1993), pp. 272–273.

[29]Cathryn Ehrhardt, "Gangs, Cults, and Hate Groups: Where Does Rebellion End and Trouble Begin? *Updating School Board Policies,* 21, no. 4 (April/May 1990), p. 3.

perceive to be in their own best interest. A manager who understands human motivation and what employees believe to be in their best interests is able to develop a unique rewards system.

School district administrators should attempt to utilize an "expectancy model" as the vehicle for developing a rewards system. With this model, rewards are linked to employee behaviors that both meet the objectives of the school district and satisfy the needs of the employees.

Five variables must be taken into consideration in a rewards program: employee performance, employee effort, seniority, employee skills, and job requirements. The rewarding of performance, however, must be the primary objective of a rewards program.

An effective program must include both intrinsic and extrinsic rewards. Intrinsic rewards are those that pertain to the quality of the job situation; they may include participation in the decision-making process, increased responsibility, and greater job discretion. Extrinsic rewards are divided into direct and indirect compensation. Direct compensation is commonly referred to as salary or wages; indirect compensation is frequently referred to as fringe benefits. Nonfinancial rewards have begun to appear in some school districts and are limited only by the imagination of the administration. They are tailored to meet the needs of individual employees. For example, a very status-conscious employee might consider the services of a private secretary and a reserved parking place as a reward for exceptional performance.

Direct compensation, salary and wages, can be effectively administered only if the following principles are incorporated into the pay policy: Skills required in various positions must be recognized; salaries must be competitive; the primary focus of salary increases must be improved performance; and salary schedules must be reviewed annually.

An important question central to all pay policies is, "Does money motivate?" A reasonable conclusion, supported by experience and research, is that money does affect performance if it is clear that performance is rewarded by a salary increase.

There are a number of other issues in salary and wages management that must command the attention of personnel administrators. These issues will have an effect on pay policy development and include public disclosure of salaries, compensation packaging, equity of pay and performance, techniques for collecting community wage data, methods of making salary recommendations to the school board, payroll deductions, employee reactions to salary decisions, appropriate pay periods, annual wage review, and salary schedule construction.

Indirect compensation, or fringe benefits, may be defined as benefits available to all employees that help a school district to attract and retain good employees. Certain fringe benefits are required by law. These include social security, state retirement programs, unemployment insurance, and workers' compensation.

Federal law requires school districts that provide group health plans for their employees and their dependents to offer an extension of the coverage on a temporary basis under certain conditions when coverage would usually end.

Voluntary fringe benefits may be divided into insurance programs, time away from the job, and services. Group insurance programs are available for almost every human need and include medical and hospitalization insurance, dental insurance, term life insurance, errors and omissions insurance, and optical insurance.

A fringe benefit often taken for granted by employees is time away from the job—including sick leave, vacation time, paid holidays, and sabbatical leave. In like manner, certain services offered by school districts are in reality fringe benefits. These include expenses paid for attendance at workshops, professional meetings, and conventions; tuition reimbursement; and free lunches and coffee. Central-office administrators are usually given use of a school district automobile or receive mileage compensation. In districts experiencing decreasing enrollments, teachers are being offered career counseling services in order to help them look for a job outside education.

Health care costs continue to increase at an alarming rate. An alternative approach to the traditional insurance programs which is meant to maintain a high quality of care but at a lower cost and in a more efficient manner is managed health care. Many school districts hire case management specialists who have the job responsibility of helping to contain costs while still providing quality health care to employees of the school district. Two alternatives to this approach are for a district to contract with a third-party health care administration company or to join a managed health care network.

A major issue facing many school districts across the nation, is the rising cost of workers' compensation. For school district employees, there are three major categories of health risks: environmental risks; the risk of violence; and the risks such as contracting infectious disease that come from working with children. Many school districts have created the position of risk manager. The responsibilities of this position include identifying risks and then developing a plan to minimize risks.

The director of employee benefits supervises the staff in the fringe benefits department. Of course, the director reports to the assistant superintendent for personnel.

Fringe benefits, as an alternative to large salary and wage increases will continue to play a significant role in compensating employees.

APPENDIX A*
POSITION DESCRIPTION QUESTIONNAIRE

Instructions to Employee

1. Please read through the entire questionnaire carefully to familiarize yourself with all questions asked.
2. Once you have read the questionnaire, then answer each question as carefully and completely as possible.

   If additional space is needed to answer any question, please indicate "over" and use back side of the sheet.

   If the question asked does not apply to your position, please write "does not apply" or "not applicable" in the space provided. Only in this way can we be certain you have considered each question and can you be certain you have not missed an important question,

*Source: *Wage and Salary Administration: A Handbook for School Business Officials,* Charles W. Foster, ed. (Chicago: Research Corporation of the Association of School Business Officials, 1960), pp. 65–77.

3. When you have completed the questionnaire, return it to your department head or supervisor.

You are urged to use care and deliberation in the completion of the questionnaire. The information you provide in your replies will be one of a number of means used to develop an official description of your position.

When this questionnaire has been completed and reviewed by your supervisor or department head, it should be forwarded to the Director of Personnel. After a description has been written, the job evaluation committee of the school system will evaluate the position and recommend assignment to the appropriate salary classification.

Position Description Questionnaire

I. GENERAL INFORMATION

1. Your full name: _____ Date: _____
               (First)   (Middle or Maiden)   (Last)

2. Title of your position: _____
  When appointed to this position: _____
                                  (Date)

3. To your knowledge, is this position ever referred to by another title? If so, what title or titles are used? _____
_____

4. To which major division is your position assigned? (e.g., Division of Business Administration, Division of School Administration, Division of Instruction, etc.) _____
_____

5. To which specific unit (office, department, school) is your position assigned? _____
_____

6. Regular daily hours of work: From _____ to _____

7. What is the position title and name of your immediate supervisor? (i.e., the person or persons who assign work to you regularly and to whom you report.)
               TITLE   NAME
  _____   _____

8. If your immediate supervisor is someone other than your department head, what is the title and name of your department head? (If same person, write "same.")
               TITLE   NAME
  _____   _____

9. What are the position titles and names of the persons whom you supervise directly? (i.e., the persons to whom you give work assignments and from whom you receive reports on work progress. If no one, write "none.")

Continued

TITLES	DEPT. OR DIVISION	NAMES
_____	_____	_____
_____	_____	_____

10. What employees do you regularly train or instruct on the job?

	FREQUENCY			ONLY NEW EMPLOYEES
POSITION TITLE	WEEKLY	MONTHLY	SEVERAL TIMES A YEAR	JOIN DEPARTMENT
_____	_____	_____	_____	_____

11. To what position, or positions, within the school system would a person normally consider a logical promotion from your position?

_____

12. What jobs or positions within the school system do you feel have responsibilities about equal to yours?

_____   _____

_____   _____

13. What position in the department, bureau, section or office to which you are now assigned is the next more responsible position?

_____

II. ASSIGNED FUNCTIONS AND RESPONSIBILITIES

1. What is the basic function or purpose of your position? (e.g., to provide typing assistance to the _____ department; to receive all persons entering building and direct them to desired office; to direct and coordinate the instructional program, etc.)

_____

_____

2. What regular duties or assigned responsibilities do you perform in your position? (Please list all of the duties you can think of, and be as specific as possible, e.g., clean windows, prepare purchase requisitions, conduct staff conferences, etc.) Indicate frequency of performance by code letters as follows:

    Daily or several times weekly   Code "D"
    Weekly   Code "W"
    Monthly   Code "M"
    Occasionally during the year   Code "Y"

DUTIES	CODE
_____	_____

3. What machines requiring special skills do you use in your work?

	FREQUENCY (CHECK ONE)	
CONTINUOUSLY	FREQUENTLY	OCCASIONALLY
_____	_____	_____
_____	_____	_____

Continued

4. What special non-machine skills do you use in your work? (e.g., shorthand, bookkeeping, creative writing, higher mathematics, etc.)

FREQUENCY (CHECK ONE)

	CONTINUOUSLY	FREQUENTLY	OCCASIONALLY
_____	_____	_____	_____
_____	_____	_____	_____

5. What grade level of education did you complete? (check one)

8th grade (or below)	_____	1 yr. college	_____
9th grade	_____	2 yrs. college	_____
10th grade	_____	3 yrs. college	_____
11th grade	_____	4 yrs. college	_____
12th grade	_____	5 yrs. college	_____
or equivalent to above grade		6 yrs. college	_____
checked in special courses	_____	7 yrs. or more college	_____

Up to
1 year special courses after high school   _____
2 years special courses after high school   _____
3 years special courses after high school   _____
4 years special courses after high school   _____

6. If you have completed a college or university program, what degree(s) did you earn and in what major subject area?

_____

_____

7. Have you taken other courses, not covered above, to enable you to qualify for your present position or another position in the school system? (Please explain type of course, length, etc.)

_____

_____

8. Is accuracy or working within close precision limits a requirement of your job? _____
YES OR NO

If yes, which of the following would best describe the effect of errors you might make?

____ Errors would be corrected early and would not be significant.

____ Errors might involve small losses of money. Corrections can be made with minor inconvenience to other employees or supervisor.

____ Errors might involve significant losses of money or would cause considerable delay, confusion or bad public relations. Can be corrected but with loss of time and expense.

____ Errors would seriously hamper financial operations of school systems or involve loss of prestige of School Board. Difficult and costly to correct.

III. DETAILS CONCERNING RESPONSIBILITIES

1. For what specific activities, programs and/or services do you have responsibilities for formulating objectives and goals? (Please list.)

_____

_____

Continued

2. What is the extent of your responsibilities for objectives? (e.g., formulate and recommend to department head; recommend to School Board; establish, etc.)

   _____

   _____

3. Which of the following statements best describes your responsibilities relative to objectives and goals for your program or service? (check one)

   _____ None

   _____ My opinions are sometimes requested.

   _____ My opinions are regularly requested.

   _____ Formulate and recommend objectives to supervisor or department head.

   _____ Formulate objectives for department, program or service and recommend to division head.

   _____ Formulate objectives for division and recommend to Superintendent.

   _____ Formulate objectives for school system.

   _____ Other (Specify) _____

4. For which specific programs and/or services do you have responsibilities for analyzing requirements and whose requirements are analyzed for each? (e.g., purchasing and warehousing for all schools and services.)

5. For which departments, programs and/or services are you responsible for planning the organization, staffing, facilities or finance? (List and describe your planning responsibilities.)

6. For which specific programs and/or services do you have responsibilities for evaluating effectiveness and results?

7. Which of the following statements best describes your responsibilities for evaluating the results of programs and/or services? (check one)

   _____ None

   _____ Opinions may be requested.

   _____ Opinions are regularly requested.

   _____ Participate in evaluation regularly with supervisor or department head.

   _____ Responsible for evaluation.

   _____ Other (Specify)_____

8. For which specific activities, programs and services do you have responsibility for developing and evaluating plans of organization? _____

   _____

9. Approximately how many staff members are included in plans of organization which you develop and evaluate? _____

   _____

10. If you have supervisory responsibilities, what is the nature of the tasks performed by the majority of the persons you directly or indirectly supervise?

    _____ Repetitive tasks.

    _____ Semiroutine tasks of moderate complexity but not of a highly professional or technical nature.

Continued

_____ Activities of a highly technical or professional nature.
_____ Other (Specify)_____

11. For what specific activities, programs and/or services do you have staff recruitment and/or selection responsibilities?

_____
_____

12. What type of responsibility do you have for facilities planning? (e.g., recommending amounts and layouts of space) _____
_____

13. What responsibility do you have for supervising the use of facilities and equipment? (e.g., supervising one office and office machines; supervising carpenter shop, saws, joiners, etc.)

_____
_____

14. What responsibilities do you have for supervising the care and maintenance of buildings or equipment? _____
_____

15. What kind of financial planning responsibilities do you have and for what programs or services? (e.g., estimating current costs, formulating budget, financial projection, etc.)

_____
_____
_____

16. What is total amount of annual budgets for which you have planning responsibility?
_____ None
_____ Less than $100,000.
_____ $100,000 to $499,000.
_____ $500,000 to $999,000.
_____ $1,000,000 or over.
_____ Please explain: _____
_____

17. What responsibilities do you have for evaluating the management of finances; for which programs and/or services? (e.g., evaluating expenditures for maintenance or repairs; analyzing program costs, etc.)

_____
_____
_____

18. What is the total amount of annual expenditures for which you are responsible to evaluate financial management?

_____ None
_____ Less than $100,000.
_____ $100,000 to $499,000.
_____ $500,000 to $999,000.
_____ $1,000,000 or over.
_____ Please explain: _____
_____

Continued

19. In performing your job, in what ways do you come into contact with the public, employees in other departments, other department heads, etc.? (Briefly describe.)

20. How would you characterize your contacts with the public, employees and others, as you have described them? (Check one.)

    ____ Little or no contact.

    ____ Requires only good manners/no pertinent communication.

    ____ Regular and frequent contact. Manner and attitude are important, but giving and receiving information is not a principal requirement.

    ____ Includes giving and receiving information. Requires ability to handle varied face-to-face situations.

    ____ A predominant feature of the job, necessitating a high degree of tact, courtesy and ability to work effectively with individuals and groups.

21. What responsibilities do you have for planning the external relations (including public relations) of your service, department or program? (Please specify to the extent that you contribute to planning, are responsible for planning, or otherwise.)

    ———————————————————————————————————————

    ———————————————————————————————————————

22. With regard to all of your planning responsibilities, for what period of time are you usually concerned in making plans?

    ____ Current academic or fiscal year.

    ____ Current and next academic or fiscal years.

    ____ Current and next 4 academic or fiscal years.

    ____ Current and next 5 to 9 academic or fiscal years.

    ____ Current and next 10 or more academic or fiscal years.

IV. OTHER INFORMATION

1. Are there any other aspects of your responsibilities that are unusual and should be taken into account in evaluating your position?

    ———————————————————————————————————————

    ———————————————————————————————————————

2. Are there any unique requirements not identified above that should be taken into account in establishing the qualifications of a person to fill the position you now occupy?

    ———————————————————————————————————————

    ———————————————————————————————————————

3. How would you characterize general working conditions necessitated by the nature of your job?

    ____ Work in normal temperatures, clean, comfortable surroundings–normal office conditions.

    ____ A few disagreeable conditions exist such as noise, congestion, drafts.

    ____ Several disagreeable conditions accompany the job such as: abnormal temperatures, humidity, excess noise, and dirt, offensive odors and fumes, etc.

4. Are there any personal hazards related to your job? (e.g., work on high ladders, use sharp knives, electricity, etc.)

    ———————————————————————————————————————

    ———————————————————————————————————————

Continued

V. DEPARTMENT HEAD OR SUPERVISOR'S SECTION

(To be completed by immediate supervisor or department head.)

1. I have read the staff members' responses to the attached questionnaire and believe they accurately reflect the duties, responsibilities and characteristics of the position with the following exceptions: _____

   _____

   _____

2. I believe the minimum educational requirement for this position should be: (List grade completion such as 8th grade, 2–3 years high school, high school graduation, A.B. degree, doctor's degree, etc. Be realistic.) _____

   _____

   _____

3. Which one of the following statements do you feel accurately describes the general work schedule of this position?

   _____ Normal work schedule. Some gaps in the work cycle.
   _____ Little or no pressure.
   _____ Steadily paced with occasional pressure.
   _____ Frequent pressure of work with almost constant accumulation of tasks.
   _____ Very high and unusual pressure created by important decisions or frequent emergency situations.

   _____
   (Signature, Supervisor or Department Head)

SCORE SHEET

JOB EVALUATION COMMITTEE NO. 1
OFFICE, CLERICAL AND MANUAL POSITIONS

Job Title _____ Department _____

Factors:

Technical Demands	_____
Experience	_____
Complexity	_____
Accuracy	_____
Supervision and Training	_____
Independent Action	_____
Contacts	_____
Mental Effort	_____
Physical Effort	_____
Working Conditions	_____
Total	_____

Date: _____   _____
                                   (Signature of Committee Member)

JOB EVALUATION COMMITTEE NO. 1

OFFICE, CLERICAL AND MANUAL POSITIONS

TALLY SHEET

Job Title _____

Department _____ Date _____

Committee / Factors	Technical Demands	Experience	Complexity	Accuracy	Supervision and Training	Independent Action	Contacts	Mental Effort	Physical Effort	Working Conditions	TOTAL

SCORE SHEET

JOB EVALUATION COMMITTEE NO. 2
ADMINISTRATIVE AND PROFESSIONAL POSITIONS

Job Title _____ Department _____

Factors:

Planning Responsibilities	_____
Professional and Technical Demands	_____
Supervision	_____
Staffing	_____
Facilities	_____
Finance	_____
External Relations	_____
Evaluating Responsibilities	_____
Total	_____

Date: _____   _____

(Signature of Committee Member)

JOB EVALUATION COMMITTEE NO. 2

ADMINISTRATIVE AND PROFESSIONAL POSITIONS

TALLY SHEET

Job Title _____

Department _____ Date _____

Factors Committee	Planning Responsibilities	Professional and Technical Demands	Supervision	Staffing	Facilities	Finance	External Relations	Evaluating Responsibilities	TOTAL

SELECTED BIBLIOGRAPHY

Abel, Gene B., "School District Health Care Expenses: Moderating the Escalating Rate of Growth," *School Business Affairs,* 57, no. 12 (December 1991), pp. 26–28.

Andrews, Hans, *Merit in Education.* Stillwater, Okla.: New Forums Press, 1988.

Brandt, Richard M., *Incentive Pay and Career Ladders for Teachers.* Albany, New York: University of New York Press, 1990.

Clapp, Beecher E., "Climb the Tennessee Ladder," *The Executive Educator,* 7, no. 1 (January 1985), pp. 21–22.

Conley, S., and A. R. Ogden. "Linking Teacher Compensation to Teacher Career Development: A Strategic Examination." *Educational Evaluation and Policy Analysis,* 17, no. 2 (1995), pp. 219–238.

Dickson, Lou Ann S., Mary Walton, and Virginia Guy, "Teacher Attitudes Toward a Career Ladder," *Spectrum: Journal of School Research and Information,* 10, no. 2 (Spring 1992), pp. 27–34.

Educational Research Service Staff, "Changes in Salaries and Wages for Public School Employees," *Spectrum: Journal of School Research and Information,* 11, no. 2 (Spring 1993), pp. 44–47.

Educational Research Service Staff, "Fringe Benefits: The Impact of Rising Costs and Increased Benefits on School Budgets," *Spectrum: Journal of School Research and Information,* 6, no. 4 (Fall 1988), pp. 24–26.

Educational Research Service Staff, *Methods of Scheduling Salaries for Teachers,* 3rd ed. Arlington, Va.: The Service, 1987.

Educational Research Service Staff, *Methods of Scheduling Salaries for Principals,* 3rd ed. Arlington, Va.: The Service, 1987.

Edwards, Jr. Clarence M., and John J. English, "Incentive Pay Encourages Teachers to Improve," *The American School Board Journal,* 173, no. 4 (April 1986), pp. 48–50.

Firestone, William A., "Merit Pay and Job Enlargement as Reforms: Incentives, Implementation, and Teacher Response," *Evaluation and Policy Analysis,* 13, no. 3 (1991), pp. 269–288.

Firestone, William A., "Redesigning Teacher Salary Systems for Educational Reform," *American Educational Research Journal,* 31, no. 3 (Fall 1994), pp. 549–574.

Hatry, Harry P., John M. Greiner, and Brenda G. Ashford. *Issues and Case Studies in Teacher Incentive Plans,* 2nd ed. Lanham, Maryland: University Press of America, Inc., 1994.

Jenkins, G. D., G. E. Ledford, N. Gupta, D. H. Doty. *Skill-Based Pay: Practices, Payoffs, Pitfalls, and Prescriptions.* Scottsdale, Arizona: American Compensation Association, 1992.

Kelley, Carolyn, and Allan Odden. *Reinventing Teacher Compensation Systems.* Madison, Wisconsin: Consortium for Policy Research in Education, 1995.

Kohut, Jr., S., and D. J. Wright, "Merit Pay Movement 1980's Style," *Educational Horizons,* 62, no. 2 (1984), pp. 52–54.

Martini, Jr., Gilbert R., "Wellness Programs: Preventive Medicine to Reduce Health Care Costs," *School Business Affairs,* 57, no. 6 (June 1991), pp. 8–12.

McIntyre, K. E., "The Merits and Demerits of Merit Pay," *National Association of Secondary School Principals Bulletin,* 68, no. 469 (1984), pp. 100–104.

Mohrman, Jr., Allan M., Susan Albers Mohrman, and Allan R. Odden, "Aligning Teacher Compensation with Systemic School Reform: Skill-Based Pay and Group-Based Performance Rewards," *Educational Evaluation and Policy Analysis,* 18, no. 1 (Spring 1996), pp. 51–71.

Natale, Jo Anna, "Shopping for Health Benefits," *The American School Board Journal,* 179, no. 1 (January 1992), pp. 38–40.

National Education Association, "Merit Pay: Promises and Facts," *Learning* (May 1984), pp. 17–19.

Odden, Allan, and Carolyn Kelley. *Paying Teachers for What They Know and Do: New and Smarter Compensation Strategies to Improve Schools.* Thousand Oaks, California: Corwin Press, Inc., 1996.

Southern Regional Education Board, *Paying for Performance—Important Questions and Answers.* Atlanta, Ga.: The Board, 1990.

Tecker, Glenn H., *Merit, Measurement, and Money: Establishing Teacher Performance Evaluation and Incentive Programs.* Alexandria, Va.: National School Boards Association, 1985.

U.S. Department of Education, *Teacher Incentive Programs in the Public Schools.* Washington, D.C.: Office of Educational Research and Improvement, 1989.

U.S. Department of Education, *Teacher Salaries—Are They Competitive?* Washington, D.C.: OERI/Education Information Branch, 1993.

9

COLLECTIVE NEGOTIATIONS

Collective negotiations has become an accepted part of American education. The first significant collective bargaining contract was negotiated in 1962 with the teachers in New York City. Since that time many state legislatures have enacted collective bargaining laws. Personnel considerations such as salaries, fringe benefits, and working conditions constitute the major negotiable items. Membership in teacher organizations has stabilized and consequently, because of dues, so have the fiscal resources of these organizations. Because personnel expenditures constitute approximately 80 per cent of school budgets, virtually every aspect of education has been influenced either directly or indirectly by the phenomenon of collective negotiations.

Experience indicates that the underlying consideration in collective negotiations is participation in the decision-making process. Teachers and administrators want to have input concerning the priorities established by boards of education when these affect their salaries, benefits, and working conditions.[1] It is a natural evolution in our democratic society that individuals continually look for more significant ways to participate in governance, whether in the political sphere or in our employing institutions.

It is important for teachers, administrators, and school board members to take a positive attitude toward negotiations.[2] Approaching negotiations as a process to resolve differences will establish a "win, win" atmosphere, wherein both the teachers and school district representatives gain something from conflict resolution.[3]

Furthermore, as a process, collective bargaining is working successfully in both the private and public sectors. This chapter deals with the major components of the collective negotiations process as it operates in education.

The terms *collective bargaining* and *collective negotiations* have been used with various shades of meaning when referring to this process in public education. To avoid

---

[1]Robert M. Cooper, *Management and Labor: Must They Be Adversaries?* (Memphis, Tenn.: Southwestern, 1982), p. ix.

[2]Lewis T. Kohler, ed., *Negotiations and the Manager in Public Education* (Park Ridge, Ill.: ASBO, 1980), p. 1.

[3]Theodore J. Kouralski, "Organizational Climate, Conflict, and Collective Bargaining," *Contemporary Education,* 54, no. 1 (1982), p, 34.

confusion and because the "process" is invariable, these terms are used interchangeably by this author.

There has been much discussion as to whether the National Education Association and the American Federation of Teachers are labor unions or professional associations. This distinction appears to be functional in nature. If representatives of an organized group bargain collectively over salaries, fringe benefits, and working conditions for their membership with management, the group is in essence a labor union. Therefore, the terms *labor union* and *professional association* will also be used interchangeably in this chapter when referring to the involvement these groups have in the negotiations process. The above definition holds true for administrator associations when they engage in collective negotiations, which appears to be a coming trend in public education.

HISTORICAL PERSPECTIVES

Collective Bargaining in the Private Sector

Collective actions by employees have a history going back to the medieval guilds. These actions have always been influenced by the economic, political, and social conditions of the times. Such influences are even stronger today because the technology of the news media makes possible daily updating on economic, political, and social trends.

Four major congressional acts provide legal guidelines for collective bargaining in the private sector: the Norris-LaGuardia Act of 1932, the National Labor Relations Act of 1935 (Wagner Act), the Labor-Management Relations Act of 1947 (Taft-Hartley Act), and the Labor-Management Reporting and Disclosure Act of 1959 (Landrum-Griffin Act).

The Norris-LaGuardia Act was the first general public policy position on labor unionization. The Act supported the concept that workers have a right to organize, if they so desire, into unions. Particularly, the act restricted the U.S. courts from issuing injunctions that would restrict labor activities. It also outlawed the yellow-dog contract, an agreement that employers required employees to sign as a condition of employment stating that they were not members of a union and would not join a union as long as they worked for that company.

The Wagner Act is perhaps the most important piece of labor legislation. This act guaranteed workers the right to organize and join labor unions for the purpose of collective bargaining with employers. The Wagner Act also prohibited employers from engaging in the following unfair labor practices: (1) interfering with or coercing employees in exercising their rights to join labor unions and bargain collectively; (2) interfering with the formation or administration of any labor union; (3) discriminating against an employee because of union activity; (4) discharging or discriminating against an employee who filed charges or gave testimony under this act; and (5) refusing to bargain with the representatives chosen by the employees. The National Labor Relations Board (NLRB) was established and given the responsibility for conducting elections to determine union representation and for applying this law against the stated unfair labor practices.

The Taft-Hartley Act was passed to amend the Wagner Act and to prevent unfair labor practices by unions. It sought to protect a worker's right not to join a union and to protect employers from mistreatment by unions. The Taft-Hartley Act specifically outlawed the closed shop; allowed the federal government to seek an injunction preventing work stoppages for eighty days in a strike defined as injurious to the national welfare; prohibited the use of union funds in connection with national elections; required union officers to swear that they are not members of the Communist party; required unions to file financial statements with their membership and the U.S. Department of Labor; allowed the states to pass right-to-work laws; and made it illegal for any collective agreement to contain a clause requiring compulsory union membership.

The Taft-Hartley Act also prohibits unions from engaging in the following unfair labor practices:

1. Refusing to bargain collectively with an employer.

2. Causing an employer to discriminate against an employee who was refused membership in a union or expelled from a union.

3. Engaging in secondary boycotts, which is exerting pressure on an employer not directly involved in a dispute.

4. Causing an employer to pay for services that were not rendered.

5. Engaging in a conflict between two or more unions over the fight to perform certain types of work.

6. Charging excessive or discriminating initiation fees.

The Landrum-Griffin Act was passed as a result of internal corruption in some unions. This act contains a bill of rights for union members, including freedom of speech at union meetings, secret ballot on proposed dues increases, and protection against improper disciplinary action. It also established the conditions to be observed in electing union officers.

The Landrum-Griffin Act, in addition, contained the following amendments to the Taft-Hartley Act:

1. Repealed the requirement that union officials take a non-Communist oath.

2. Gave states authority over cases outside the jurisdiction of the NLRB.

3. Prohibited picketing by a union when a rival union has been recognized to represent employees or an NLRB election has taken place within twelve months.

4. Guaranteed the right of a striker to vote in union representative elections for twelve months.

5. Prohibited agreements by which employees seek to bring economic pressure on another employer by refusing to handle, sell, use, or transport his products.

6. Authorized union shops in the construction industry and required membership after seven days of employment rather than the traditional thirty days.

Collective Negotiations in the Federal Government

In 1962 President John Kennedy issued Executive Order 10988, which affirmed the right of federal employees to join labor unions and bargain collectively. It required federal agency heads to bargain in good faith, defined unfair labor practices, and established a code of conduct for labor organizations. However, it prohibited the union shop and banned strikes by federal employees.

In 1968 a presidential committee reviewed employee–management relations in the federal service and recommended improvements to the provisions of E.O. 10988. As a consequence, President Richard Nixon issued E.O. 11491 in 1969 to supersede the previous directive.

The objectives of E.O. 11491 are to standardize procedures among federal agencies and to bring federal labor relations more in line with the private sector. It gives the assistant secretary of labor the authority to determine appropriate bargaining units, to oversee recognition procedures, to rule on unfair labor practices, and to enforce the standards of conduct on labor organizations. E.O. 11491 also established the Federal Labor Relations Council, which has the responsibility to supervise the implementation of this executive order; to handle appeals from the decisions of the assistant secretary of labor; and to rule on questionable issues.

Collective Negotiations in Local and State Governments

Although some professional organizations, including the National Education Association, support passage of a federal teacher collective bargaining law, most educators see this as a state issue. In fact, public school employees are working for a state agency operating at the local level, the school district.

Over three-fourths of the states have permissive or mandatory statutes governing the rights of public school employees to organize, negotiate, exercise sanctions, and strike. There are, of course, substantial differences between these state laws. In a number of states, legislation covers all public employees; in others, a specific law covers only school employees.

Model Board of Education Policy on Collective Negotiations

The following is a sample policy on collective negotiations.

> The board of education believes that collaborative decision making is the most effective way to govern a school system. If school district employees have the right to share in the decision-making process affecting salaries, fringe benefits, and working conditions, they become more responsive and better disposed to exchanging ideas and information concerning operations with administrators. Accordingly, management becomes more efficient.
>
> The board of education further declares that harmonious and cooperative relations between itself and school district employees protect the patrons and children of the school district by assuring the orderly operation of the schools.
>
> This position of the board is to be effectuated by:
>
> 1. Recognizing the right of all school district employees to organize for the purpose of collective negotiations.
> 2. Authorizing the director of employee relations to negotiate with the duly elected employee representatives on matters relating to salaries, fringe benefits, and working conditions.

3. Requiring the director of employee relations to establish administrative procedures for the effective implementation of the negotiations process. This is
to be accomplished under the supervision of the assistant superintendent for
personnel who, in turn, is directly responsible to the superintendent of
schools.

Upon successful completion of the negotiations process, the board of education will enter into written agreements with the employee organizations.

Emanating from this board of education policy is the following definition for negotiation: Collective negotiations is the process by which representatives of the school board
meet with representatives of the school district employees in order to make proposals and
counterproposals for the purpose of mutually agreeing on salaries, fringe benefits, and
working conditions covering a specific period of time.

RECOGNITION AND BARGAINING UNIT DETERMINATION

This section is concerned with answering the basic question, Who represents whom? In
labor history most of the violence that occurred in the private sector centered around this
query. Unions fought each other for the right to represent workers against management.
The prize was power. In education the prize is still the same, but the contest is usually non-
violent.

Recognition is defined as the acceptance by an employer of some group or organization as the authorized representative of two or more employees for the purpose of collective negotiations. Without recognition each teacher is left to make his or her own
arrangements with the school board, which is the antithesis of collective negotiations.

There are two basic types of representation in education—multiple and exclusive.
Multiple representation does not occur in many school districts because of the inherent
problems when two or more organizations or unions represent a specific bargaining unit.
In New York City prior to the collective negotiations elections in 1961, ninety-three organizations were accorded equal representational rights by the board of education.[4] Although
this situation was extreme, there are communities in which more than one organization
claims the right to represent a segment of the professional staff.

In multiple representation, recognition is usually granted by the board of education on
the basis of organizational membership. This recognition is operationalized by one of the
following methods: the board meets with representatives of each union separately, the
board meets in joint sessions with equal numbers of representatives from each union, or
the board meets in joint sessions with representatives of the unions proportionally determined. For example, if union A has 500 members and union B has 250 members, A is entitled to twice as many representatives on the negotiating team as B.

[4]Myron Lieberman and Michael H. Moskow, *Collective Negotiations for Teachers* (Chicago: Rand McNally &
Co., 1966), p. 92.

Exclusive recognition occurs when a single union represents all members of a bargaining unit. The technical designation for the union in this role is *bargaining agent*. The bargaining unit consists of all the employees whose salaries, fringe benefits, and working conditions are negotiated by the bargaining agent. The paramount importance of exclusive recognition is that the employer cannot negotiate with anyone in the unit except through the designated bargaining agent.

Exclusive recognition is the most accepted form in education for three basic reasons: first, it is supported by both the National Education Association and the American Federation of Teachers; second, exclusive recognition is mandated by law for the public sector in many states and widely accepted in most communities even in the absence of state legislation; and finally, private business and industry witnesses to the fact that this is the most effective form of recognition.

Recognition procedures take various forms in education. The three most commonly used are membership lists, authorization cards, and elections. If a union can demonstrate that it has 51 percent membership of the employees in a bargaining unit or if 51 percent of the employees in a unit present their signatures on a card authorizing a certain union to represent them, the board may recognize this union as the exclusive bargaining agent.

A more common practice is the "representation election," which also is necessary in the absence of membership lists or authorization cards that signify majority support. Most school boards prefer an election as a requisite to recognizing a union as exclusive bargaining agent for a number of reasons. Some teachers who join a union may not want that union to represent them in negotiations. Teachers join certain unions for social, professional, or other reasons that have nothing to do with negotiations. In some cases, a teacher may be a member of more than one teacher union.

The representation election poses several questions that must be addressed by both the school board and the unions seeking recognition:

- Who conducts the election?
- Who will pay the costs for the election?
- What are the ground rules for electioneering?
- Who is eligible to vote?
- Who will certify the results?
- What will be the duration of the certification?

There are no correct answers to these questions. Rather, they must be answered within a framework that will take into consideration the variables affecting local situations. A cardinal principle is that the board and unions must maintain credibility and, therefore, a third party is often requested to intervene in finding a workable answer to these questions. The Federal Mediation and Conciliation Service or the League of Women Voters are examples of two independent agencies with the public image necessary to act as the appropriate third party. In many of the states with collective bargaining laws, recognition procedures and bargaining unit determination are mandated by state legislation. This discussion thus pertains to those states without legislation and to those states where the law allows latitude on these issues. Some states have public employee relations boards that will conduct the elections and make a determination on who belongs to the bargaining unit.

It is now necessary to more closely define the term *bargaining unit.* School districts not only employ teachers of many different subjects and levels but they also employ a wide variety of specialists, such as psychologists, nurses, social workers, and attendance officers. In addition, there are noncertificated employees: cooks, custodians, bus drivers, maintenance workers, secretaries, and clerks.

To have collective negotiations there must be a determination on what specific category of employees is represented by the bargaining agent who wins the representation election. In practice this determination must occur as part of the recognition process, because only those employees in a given bargaining unit will be allowed to vote on which union will represent them. The definition most commonly accepted states that the bargaining unit is composed of all those employees who are covered by the negotiated agreement or master contract.

The fundamental criterion for determining who belongs to the bargaining unit is formulated on the "community of interest" principle.[5] Although it may sound elusive, the principle is not difficult to implement. Employees have a community of interest if they share skills, functions, educational levels, and working conditions. Elementary-school teachers of all levels, secondary-school teachers of all subjects, and guidance counselors clearly have a community of interest and should belong to the same bargaining unit. Clerks and secretaries on the other hand could not be effectively represented by such a unit and should constitute a separate unit by themselves. It is conceivable that a medium to large size school district might have the following units bargaining separately with the representatives of the school board:

1. Certificated educators exclusive of supervisors and administrators.
2. Building level administrators.
3. Subject matter coordinators.
4. Secretaries and clerks.
5. Cooks and cafeteria workers.
6. Bus drivers.
7. Custodians.
8. Maintenance workers.

Each of these bargaining units would have a separate agreement or master contract, specifying salaries, fringe benefits, and working conditions, that could be quite different from the others.

Besides community of interest, there are two additional considerations determining a bargaining unit. Size of the group is important; an extremely small unit of five or ten employees will have little impact acting alone. In this case employees would have a more strategic base from which to bargain if they combined with other categories of employees. In a small school district, for example, there might be two bargaining units: a certificated employees' unit including teachers, nurses, psychologists, etc.; and a noncertificated employees' unit including cooks, custodians, maintenance personnel, secretaries, etc.

A final consideration in determining bargaining units is effective school administration. An unreasonably large number of units would be unworkable. For example, if guidance

[5]Lieberman and Moskow, *Collective Negotiations,* p. 129.

counselors, classroom teachers, speech therapists, music teachers, physical education teachers, and safety education teachers were each covered by different agreements specifying different working conditions, a building principal would have a difficult job of supervising the staff.

Two other issues have surfaced in recent years that will have an influence on future negotiations—the agency shop and administrator bargaining units. *Agency shop* is a term borrowed from industry and is used when referring to a question of equity: An employee who is a member of a given bargaining unit may not be a dues-paying member of the union that is the bargaining agent. If the negotiated agreement with the school board includes an agency shop clause, such an employee would be required to pay a fee, usually the equivalent of dues, to the union. Although the employee would not be allowed to participate in internal union affairs, he or she would be allowed to participate in such unit activities as attending meetings called by the negotiating team and voting on ratification of an agreement.

A growing number of educational administrators, particularly building principals, are organizing into unions and negotiating with school boards. Phyllis Byers, chief negotiator for the St. Paul Minnesota School District, outlined for the newly formed organization of school board negotiators at Miami in 1979 the reasons why administrators are turning to collective negotiations. Such reasons include decreasing autonomy and power, loss of esteem, economic anxiety, and contagion (teachers are getting theirs, we should too!). It appears that this trend will continue during the next two decades, and school board representatives will be negotiating with increasing numbers of administrator bargaining units.

THE SCOPE OF NEGOTIATIONS

Scope of negotiations refers to those matters that are negotiable. In some school districts, negotiations are limited to salaries; in other districts literally hundreds of items are discussed.

Negotiations must not be limited to unimportant matters, or the process will be considered a failure by teachers. What constitutes an important item, of course, is dictated by local circumstances. A school board might be willing to negotiate only on salaries and refuse to consider such items as a grievance procedure or reduction-in-force policy. Experience indicates that some of these nonmonetary items are just as important to teachers as salaries. Therefore, it is extremely important to place only mandatory limitations on the scope of negotiations. These limitations refer to items that are illegal by reason of state and federal constitutions, state and federal laws, or those items that are contrary to the policies of a given State Board of Education.

Most state laws on collective negotiations stipulate that negotiations must be confined to "working conditions." However, this phrase usually refers to salaries, fringe benefits, and working conditions. The meaning of *salary* is self-evident, but there is some confusion over what is meant by the terms *fringe benefit* and *working condition.*

A fringe benefit may be defined as a service made available to employees as a direct result of a fiscal expenditure by the school district. Such services might include major medical insurance, hospitalization insurance, pension benefits, sick pay, dental insurance, and professional liability insurance.

Working conditions pertain to the quality of the employment situation. Teaching for a particular school district might be more desirable than teaching in other districts located in the same geographic area because that district has desirable policies concerning class size, duty-free lunch periods, preparation periods, sabbatical leave, etc.

A major concern in defining the scope of negotiations for a particular situation centers around the concept of educational policy. School boards are required by state law to set educational policy. Although many teachers are deeply interested in educational policy and believe that they should be consulted in formulating such policy, it is commonly understood that such policy is not subject to negotiations.

The following are examples of policy issues:

1. Should the school district provide a foreign language program in the elementary grades?
2. Should statistics be offered in the high school mathematics program?
3. Should extracurricular activities be sponsored or supported by district funds?

The obvious problem is that virtually all educational policy decisions have implications affecting working conditions. For example, funds expended to introduce a foreign language program in the elementary grades could leave less money available to lower class size. Therefore, it is often impossible to decide issues pertaining to policy apart from those pertaining to working conditions.

Lieberman and Moskow make an observation about the scope of negotiations that summarizes and clarifies this aspect of the process:

> Finally, it must be remembered that the scope of negotiations is itself negotiated or at least affected by the process of negotiations.
>
> When the parties meet to negotiate, there is no formula which prescribes what is negotiable. Good administration does not eliminate the need for negotiations, but the scope of negotiations is likely to include those matters which have been administered in an inequitable manner. The relative strength of the parties may affect the scope of negotiations much more than academic versions of what progressive school administrators or organization leaders should negotiate. Legal, personal, political, economic, and organizational factors may have some impact on the scope of negotiations as well as on the resolution of items actually negotiated. In other words, the process of negotiations inevitably affects its scope and vice versa.[6]

THE BARGAINING PROCESS

The Negotiating Team

The purpose of this section is to analyze those factors that influence the "at-the-table" process of negotiations. The first issue that must be addressed is the composition of the

[6]Lieberman and Moskow, *Collective Negotiations*, p. 247.

school board's negotiating team. There is no universally accepted practice in forming a negotiating team; however, the size of a school district appears to have a significant influence on the makeup of the team. In small school districts, a committee of school board members usually negotiates directly with a team of teachers. In medium to large districts, the assistant superintendent for personnel along with other central-office and/or building-level administrators might be designated by the superintendent to negotiate with the teachers union. In some large districts, a chief negotiator is employed on a full-time or ad hoc basis.

In keeping with the model presented in Chapter 1, this author believes that medium to large school districts should employ a director of employee relations who has responsibility for managing the entire process of collective negotiations and who acts as the chief negotiator on the board's team.

The size of the team is relative, but it should have an odd number of members to avoid a deadlock in making strategy decisions. Therefore, a team of three, five, or seven members would be appropriate. Experience also dictates that a team composed of more than seven members impedes decision making.

Membership on the team may be by job description, appointment, or election. This author prefers a team of five members. The chairperson and chief negotiator, of course, is the director of employee relations, by virtue of job position. Additional membership on the team should include building-level principals, because they are the first-line supervisors who will be managing the master agreement. Also, many principals have been critical of school boards for "negotiating away" their authority. On a five-member team, one principal from each level (elementary school, junior or middle school, high school) elected by the other principals would give the team high credibility among building administrators. The final member of the team should have some specific expertise and knowledge of the district's financial condition. Thus, the assistant superintendent for administrative services or the business manager would be an appropriate appointee.

This team must function as an entity over the entire academic year. As will be pointed out later in this section, the development of strategies and the construction of proposal packages cannot be accomplished only during a few months of the year. Although a major portion of work will fall to the director of employee relations, the team will be required to expend a great deal of time. In fact, it is desirable for the teachers' and board's teams to meet routinely throughout the year to discuss mutual concerns and goals.[7] Such meetings will hopefully create a sense of trust that will facilitate the negotiations sessions.[8] Consequently, it is advisable to provide those principals who serve on the team with some compensation such as a stipend or with additional administrative assistance in their buildings.

The negotiating team for the teachers, of course, is composed of teachers. Sometimes the officers of the local association or union act as the team; in other situations a negotiating team is appointed by the union officers or elected by the teachers. If the local is affiliated with a national union, experts in the bargaining process are made available to advise union officers.

---

[7]Ildiko Knott, "Collective Bargaining Can Enhance the Quality of Worklife," *Community and Junior College Journal* (December/January 1983–84), p. 20.

[8]Unions, Employers Try New Paths to Labor Peace," *U.S. News and World Report,* 10 March 1984, p. 74.

A final issue concerning the board's negotiating team must be addressed. What if the building administrators organize, form a bargaining unit, and elect a bargaining agent to represent them concerning salaries, fringe benefits, and working conditions? This, of course, is the current trend, especially in large urban school districts. In this case the same structure for the board's negotiating team may be maintained with the substitution of assistant superintendents for principals. Because each bargaining unit negotiates a separate master agreement, which reflects salaries, fringe benefits and working conditions for employees in a given job category, it is not inconsistent with good administration for principals on the one hand to negotiate for the board and on the other hand against the board.

Developing Strategies

The negotiating team is responsible for the entire bargaining process, which must begin with strategy development. The quality of this planning will determine the effectiveness of the negotiations sessions.[9] This entails two activities, assessing the needs of the school district and establishing goals for negotiations.

Needs assessment may take various forms, but certain tasks must be completed:

1. Review the current master agreement to determine if its provisions meet the goals of the district and if they allow for effective administration.

2. Study the previous negotiating sessions to determine if the ground rules provide for effective negotiations.

3. Analyze the formal grievances filed by both the union and administration.

4. Study the arbitration decisions rendered on these grievances.

5. Meet with school district administrators to gather input concerning the provisions of the current master agreement.

6. Meet informally with the union to ascertain their concerns over the current agreement.

7. Confer with the board of education and superintendent to learn their concerns and to establish fiscal parameters.

From this information the team sets the goals and objectives for negotiations, which are formulated into operational language in the proposal package.

Setting the Ground Rules

With the advice and consent of the negotiating team, the chairperson should meet with the union negotiators to determine rules for the "at-the-table" process.

Key points that must be determined include

- The time and place for the sessions.
- The number of participants who will sit at the table.
- The role of each participant.

[9]Kohler, *Negotiations and the Manager in Public Education*, p. 1.

- The manner in which each side will present its proposals.
- The target date for completing negotiations.
- The kinds of school district data that will be needed by each side.
- The conditions governing caucuses.
- The provisions for recording the sessions.
- The method to be used in recording counterproposals and agreements.
- The policy on press releases.
- The types of impasse procedures that will be employed and when.
- The format for the written agreement.
- The procedure for agreement approval by the school board and union membership.
- The procedure that will be used in publishing the ratified agreement.

At-the-Table Sessions

There are two objectives for being "at the table." First, through making proposals and counterproposals, the negotiating teams should be able to ascertain what issues are critically important to each side. Second, each team should be able to assess the other side's bargaining power. This is the ability to get the other team to agree on an item or the entire proposal package based on your terms. Viewed schematically, this means:

$$\text{Bargaining power of the school board} = \frac{\text{Teachers' cost of disagreeing with the terms of the school board}}{\text{Teachers' cost of agreeing with the terms of the school board}}$$

$$\text{Bargaining power of the teachers} = \frac{\text{School board's cost of disagreeing with the terms of the teachers}}{\text{School board's cost of agreeing with the terms of the teachers}[10]}$$

Political pressures, negotiating skill, and psychological elements are important sources of bargaining power. Although it is impossible to measure bargaining power exactly, it is apparent that, at some time, the overall advantages of agreement outweigh the overall disadvantages of agreement. During the bargaining sessions, it is very important to keep the board and entire administrative staff informed as to the progress being made. If this is not effectively accomplished, rumors may adversely affect the bargaining power of the board's team.

When an agreement is reached by the negotiating teams, ratification by the respective governing bodies is the final step in the process. The board's team meets with the superintendent and board of education to explain and recommend the agreement. In like manner, the union's team meets with the bargaining unit membership to explain and recommend the agreement. Formal ratification occurs when a majority of school board members vote to

---

[10]Adapted from Neil W. Chamberlain, *The Labor Sector* (New York: McGraw-Hill Book Co., 1965), p. 248.

accept the agreement and when a majority of the bargaining unit membership similarly votes approval.

Because negotiating is an art rather than a science, it is extremely difficult to develop a formula for success. Nevertheless, a number of practical hints may be in order. The following are recommendations made to local boards of education by the Ohio School Board Association.

- KEEP CALM—DON'T LOSE CONTROL OF YOURSELF. Negotiation sessions can be exasperating. The temptation may come to get angry and fight back when intemperate accusations are made or when "the straw that broke the camel's back" is hurled on the table.
- AVOID "OFF THE RECORD" COMMENTS. Actually nothing is "off the record." Innocently made remarks have a way of coming back to haunt their author. Be careful to say only what you are willing to have quoted.
- DON'T BE OVERCANDID. Inexperienced negotiators may, with the best of intentions, desire to "lay the cards on the table face up." This may be done in the mistaken notion that everybody fully understands the other and utter frankness is desired. Complete candor doesn't always serve the best interests of productive negotiations. This is not a plea for duplicity; rather, it is a recommendation for prudent and discriminating utterances.
- BE LONG ON LISTENING. Usually a good listener makes a good negotiator. It is wise to let your "adversaries" do the talking—at least in the beginning.
- DON'T BE AFRAID OF A "LITTLE HEAT." Discussions sometimes generate quite a bit of "heat." Don't be afraid of it. It never hurts to let the "opposition" sound off even when you may be tempted to hit back.
- WATCH THE VOICE LEVEL. A wise practice is to keep the pitch of the voice down even though the temptation may be strong to let it rise under the excitement of emotional stress.
- KEEP FLEXIBLE. One of the skills of good negotiators is the ability to shift position a bit if a positive gain can thus be accomplished. An obstinate adherence to one position or point of view, regardless of the ultimate consequences of that rigidity, may be more of a deterrent than an advantage.
- REFRAIN FROM A FLAT "NO." Especially in the earlier stages of a negotiation it is best to avoid giving a flat "no" answer to a proposition. It doesn't help to work yourself into a box by being totally negative "too early in the game."
- GIVE TO GET. Negotiation is the art of giving and getting. Concede a point to gain a concession. This is the name of the game.
- WORK ON THE EASIER ITEMS FIRST. Settle those things first about which there is the least controversy. Leave the tougher items until later in order to avoid an early deadlock.
- RESPECT YOUR ADVERSARY. Respect those who are seated on the opposite side of the table. Assume that their motives are as sincere as your own, at least until proven otherwise.
- BE PATIENT. If necessary, be willing to sit out tiresome tirades. Time has a way of being on the side of the patient negotiator.

- AVOID WAVING "RED FLAGS." There are some statements that irritate teachers and merely heighten their antipathies. Find out what these are and avoid their use. Needless waving of "red flags" only infuriates.
- LET THE OTHER SIDE "WIN SOME VICTORIES." Each team has to win some victories. A "shut out" may be a hollow gain in negotiation.
- NEGOTIATION IS A "WAY OF LIFE." Obvious resentment of the fact that negotiation is here to stay weakens the effectiveness of the negotiator. The better part of wisdom is to adjust to it and become better prepared to use it as a tool of interstaff relations.

Third-Party Negotiations

In recent years, some parents and other school district patrons have been clamoring for an active involvement in collective negotiations. Proponents of this position have eagerly sought an extension of the sunshine laws to require negotiations sessions to be open to the public. Other forms include: trilateral negotiations, by which a citizen group becomes an equal participant with the board's team and union's team in the negotiating process; public response to proposals before an agreement is reached; and public referendum, by which proposals are voted on by the citizens of the school district. There are other variations on this theme. However, the ultimate objective is the same: citizen participation in the bargaining process.

Collective negotiations demands refined skills of those sitting at the table. Citizens generally do not possess these skills. Furthermore, a third party will bring confusion and can interfere with the employment relationship between the board and employees. In addition, school board members have been elected to represent the interests of parents, students, and district patrons. Third-party involvement seeks to usurp this responsibility.[11]

IMPASSE PROCEDURES

It is extremely difficult to define the term *impasse*. Negotiators often have trouble knowing when an impasse has been reached. However, for this discussion, an impasse will be considered as a persistent disagreement that continues after normal negotiation procedures have been exhausted.

Impasse must be expected to occur from time to time, even when both parties are negotiating in good faith. There are, unfortunately, no procedures that are guaranteed to resolve an impasse. Some procedures have been more successful than others, and the objective of this section is to outline these procedures. Also, it must be kept in mind that improperly used impasse procedures can aggravate rather than resolve a disagreement. Therefore, a working knowledge of procedures is essential to all participants in the negotiating process.

Twenty-two of the states that have passed collective negotiations laws also have established public employee relations boards. Each board is charged with implementing the

---

[11]Ronald W. Rebore, *Educational Administration: A Management Approach* (Englewood Cliffs, N.J.: Prentice-Hall, 1985), p. 213.

law and, in most cases, with administering impasse procedures, including mediation, fact finding, and arbitration.

Mediation

Mediation is usually the first procedure used when an impasse has been reached. The negotiators for both labor and management must agree on the need for third-party assistance. The role of the mediator is advisory, and consequently, the mediator has no authority to dictate a settlement. Some mediators use the tactic of first meeting with both parties separately and thereby attempt to ascertain what concessions each party might be willing to make in order to reach an agreement. This procedure has been most effective when one or both parties consider making concessions to be a sign of weakness. Meeting jointly with both parties is helpful, particularly in assessing the actual status of negotiations and in obtaining agreement from the parties on the importance assigned to each unresolved issue. Most mediators will use a combination of separate and joint meetings to facilitate an agreement.

Mediators usually refrain from recommending a settlement until they are sure that their recommendations will be acceptable to both parties. Up until the time of recommendation, the mediator acts only as a clarifier of issues and through the process attempts to defuse the antagonism between the parties, which is frequently the cause of the impasse.

A mediator may be called into a dispute at any time. In some cases the mediator may even practice preventive mediation by making suggestions useful to the parties early in the negotiations.

Because mediation is a voluntary process, in the stages preparatory to the actual negotiations the parties must decide who will mediate and what the mediator's role will be. In approximately one-third of the states, this issue is settled by statute and a formal declaration of "impasse" is all that is required to put the process in motion. Often a master agreement will contain provisions outlining impasse procedures to be followed in negotiating the agreement. When mediator services are not provided by a governmental agency, the fee for a private mediator is borne equally by both parties to the dispute.

Fact Finding

Fact finding is the procedure by which an individual or a panel holds hearings to review evidence and make recommendations for settling the dispute. Like mediation, the fact-finding process is either governed by a state statute, provided for in a master agreement, or established by both parties before negotiations begin.

The formal hearing is usually open to the public. Parties having a vested interest in the dispute are given the opportunity to offer evidence and arguments in their own behalf. Fact finders are sometimes requested by both parties to mediate the dispute and avoid the formal hearings.

The fact-finding report and recommendations are usually made public. The process is voluntary, and the parties may reject all or part of the report. To a certain extent the action of the parties will depend on the public's reactions, which in turn depend partly on the prestige of the fact finders.

Arbitration

Arbitration is the process by which the parties submit their dispute to an impartial third person or panel of persons that issues an award the parties are required to accept. Arbitration can be either compulsory or voluntary. Compulsory arbitration must be established by statute; nineteen states have such legislation. The National Education Association supports the use of this process and believes that it will curtail long and costly strikes.[12]

The voluntary use of arbitration has gained some acceptance in the public sector for handling grievances arising from the interpretation of master agreements. The American Federation of Teachers supports the use of arbitration for this purpose but opposes it for contract negotiations, believing that the latter use will result in fewer benefits for teachers.[13]

The Federal Mediation and Conciliation Service

The Federal Mediation and Conciliation Service (FMCS) works annually to resolve disagreements arising out of collective negotiations in the public sector, which amounted to approximately 8 percent of the agency's caseload. The Federal Mediation and Conciliation Service is an independent agency of the federal government created by Congress in 1974 with a director appointed by the President of the United States. The primary purpose of the FMCS is to promote labor–management peace. To more effectively carry out this mission, the agency has established regional offices and field offices staffed by professional mediators.

Federal labor laws do not cover employees of state and local governments. However, if state legislatures fail to establish mediation services for public employees, the FMCS may voluntarily enter a dispute. The FMCS also has an Office of Arbitration Services in Washington. This office maintains a roster of arbitrators located in all parts of the country. On request FMCS will furnish a randomly selected list of arbitrators from which the parties to a dispute may choose a mutually acceptable arbitrator to hear the dispute and make a decision.

In summary, it is too difficult to promote one impasse procedure as the most effective approach to handling all persistent disputes that arise at the bargaining table or in grievances over master agreement interpretation. It is more appropriate to think in terms of sequence. Mediation should be utilized first, followed by fact-finding, and then, where it is permitted by law, arbitration. This sequence places the responsibility for resolving the dispute first on the parties themselves. Experience teaches that better and more effective agreements are reached when the parties can resolve their own disputes. Yet, when disputes cannot be resolved and when it is mandated by law, arbitration curtails strikes, which always have a devastating effect on school districts.

WORK STOPPAGE STRATEGIES

The Scope of Strikes

Nothing is more disruptive to a school district than a strike. As board members, administrators, teachers, and support personnel engage in heated and public argument, schisms

---

[12]National School Public Relations Association, *Education U.S.A.,* 21 (January 22, 1979), p. 153.

[13]*Education U.S.A.,* p. 156.

occur that often last for years. Community groups also become divided over who is right and who is wrong. The American Association of School Administrators (AASA) consistently opposes the strike as a weapon when negotiations reach an impasse. The AASA also supports the position that the administrative team has the responsibility to keep the schools open; to protect students who report to school; to protect school property; and to maintain communications with parents, teachers, and the public.

Strikes by public school employees are illegal or, at least, limited by most state laws. However, this has not prevented strikes from occurring each year in many states. The news media daily remind us of the magnitude of this issue. There is also no indication that strikes will go away as school employees, administrators, and teachers become more proficient in the negotiations process.

Ten to fifteen years ago most teachers felt that striking was not in keeping with their professional status. This thinking has vanished, and the personal traumas once associated with this type of action also are gone. Today teachers strike over many issues, including recognition of their unions, salary increases, curriculum control, reduction in force, and lack of community support. Teachers also have honored strikes by non-teaching personnel and have attempted to get their unions to support them in their work stoppages.

School Employee Strike Tactics

A strike by school employees is usually the result of failure at the bargaining table. The objective of all strikes is to gain as favorable a settlement as possible from the board of education within the shortest period of time.

A few key issues have been used by teacher unions to rally support for a strike. These include the pupil–teacher ratio; planning time, particularly for elementary-school teachers; and, extra pay for extra duty, particularly for secondary-school teachers. With the onslaught of the "Excellence in Education" reform movement, the rallying call of the future will probably deal with job security and compensation issues such as performance evaluation and career ladders.

Teacher unions have almost unlimited resources from their state and national affiliates at their disposal in a strike. In very sensitive strikes, as many as a hundred field staff members may be available to help the local union.

A careful examination of several strikes will verify the following tactics as some of the most commonly used by teacher unions.

1. Inundating the community with the reasons for the strike. Handbills, advertisements in the local press, and news coverage are the main vehicles usually employed.

2. Placing the blame on a specific person such as the superintendent of schools or board president, thus channeling the pressure exerted by parents and the community.

3. Encouraging local and state politicians to become involved in the dispute. School employee groups represent a sizable number of votes.

4. Working diligently to gain support from other unions in the community.

5. Staging a strike in the late spring because this will interfere not only with graduation but also with state aid, which is usually calculated on a certain number of days in attendance before the end of the school year.

Although some strikes do occur spontaneously because of unexpected developments, most teacher strikes are well orchestrated. Teacher unions generally are aware weeks or even months in advance that certain negotiation demands are strike-producing issues.

Administrative Strategies

If a school system finds itself in the middle of a strike without an adequate plan of action, the administration and the board of education have not been paying attention to the tenor of the times or the situation in their own school district. In fact, the superintendent and his or her cabinet should have a carefully developed strike plan even in the most tranquil of school settings.

This strike plan should operate at both the district and building levels. The American Association of School Administrators has developed a series of steps in a plan that can serve as a guide for administrators in establishing their own individual district plans (see Exhibit 9–1).

When the Decision-Making Center mentioned in Exhibit 9–1 is established at the central office, duties are assigned by the superintendent of schools with the advice of his or her cabinet. Central-office administrators are assigned specific tasks to be performed during the strike, which correspond to the provisions of the above stated AASA plan. The director of labor relations could be given the task of notifying staff members of the state law and board policy concerning strikes and the legal ramifications of striking. The director of community relations would have the responsibility of notifying the news media of the times and the place for daily briefings concerning the strike. In like manner, the building principal and, if it is a large school, his or her administrative team are responsible for implementing the building-level provisions.

ADMINISTRATION OF THE MASTER AGREEMENT

The process of collective negotiations is usually ineffective unless the agreements reached are put into writing. Written master agreements are essential because they formalize the basic rights governing the parties to each agreement and reduce controversy over the meaning of what was agreed upon.

Provisions of the Agreement

Most master agreements are extremely detailed and replace board of education policies covering those working conditions negotiated. Certain provisions are included in most agreements and are deemed essential. These are

1. Recognition of the union as the exclusive bargaining agent.
2. A statement of purpose.
3. The duration of the agreement and a method for renegotiating the agreement before the expiration date.
4. Incorporation of a grievance procedure.

EXHIBIT 9–1

Before a Strike

District Level

1. Develop the overall district plan as well as a board policy statement well in advance of an anticipated strike (preferably, when there is absolutely no indication of a strike).
2. Provide as early as possible for the notification of news media, parents, staff, of the likelihood or possibility of a strike.
3. Notify staff members of the applicable state law and school board policy concerning a work stoppage and the legal ramifications of such action.
4. Establish provisions for a Decision-Making Center to have the overall direction of a strike and assign specific responsibilities to those key people in the Center.
5. Make contacts with police, fire, health, telephone and other community/state agencies likely to be needed or contacted during a strike.
6. Prepare a list of names and telephone numbers for the specific individuals in each agency who can be contacted day or night in emergency situations.
7. Provide for "hot line" telephones for citizens and staff members so they may receive strike information.
8. Install a bank of unlisted telephones in the Decision-Making Center to facilitate on-going and continual communications.
9. Obtain, or make provisions to obtain, two-way radio systems for strategic places in the district (or mobile car radios, beeper systems).
10. Develop building strike plans and reporting systems for daily status reports from each building.
11. Notify the news media of the media area and provide the time(s) and place of daily (or more often) briefings concerning the strike.
12. Have the board of education pass the necessary legal resolutions required to deal with the strike (restraining orders, injunctions, picket line restrictions, formal notification to personnel on strike, etc.).
13. Continue to seek a solution to the strike and keep such initiative on the side of the administration and board.

Building Level

1. Develop with each building principal a building Strike Plan in conformance with the overall district plan.
2. Secure back-up personnel for each building principal to act in his or her stead during the work stoppage.
3. Make provision within the building Strike Plan for a daily, early-morning report to the Decision Making Center.
4. Make provision for a daily written report listing the names of staff who reported for duty and the number of pupils in attendance at the building.
5. Make provision for continuity of communications in the event that telephone lines are unusable.
6. Make provision for each building principal to have specific guidelines and authority to close the building when the safety and health of the pupils are threatened, or when it is impossible to carry on an educational program.
7. Make provision for adequate building security (leaving lights on at night, security guards, etc.).

Continued

EXHIBIT 9–1   *Continued*

After a Strike

District Level

1. Notify all groups.
2. Hold briefing session for all administrators and board members.
3. Prepare building principals for the return of teachers.
4. Issue public statement detailing strike settlement to news media.
5. Begin making plans to defuse "anti-climactic" emotions.

Building Level

1. Do not allow striking teachers to return to the classrooms until all substitute teachers are out of the building.
2. Make plans to focus major attention on the educational program and learning environment for students.

---

5. Incorporation of impasse procedures.
6. Description of who is a member of the bargaining unit.
7. A statement concerning dues check-off.
8. A fair practices statement.
9. Salary schedules and guidelines for the duration of the agreements.[14]

As an example of the types of articles and appendices that operationalize these provisions, the "Table of Contents" for the Dade County, Florida, master agreement is reproduced in Appendix A.

The style and format of the master agreement will sometimes be dictated by state statutes; but in the absence of legislation, school boards and unions must look elsewhere for help. In many cases, teacher associations affiliated with national unions have access to model master agreements that can be adapted to local situations. In fact, some models are complete in every detail except for filling in the blanks with the proper data.

Implementing the Master Agreement

It is the responsibility of the administration to implement and interpret the provisions of the agreement. Furthermore, the administration is limited only by the specifics of the master agreement, which is commonly referred to as "management prerogative."

In the day-to-day interpretations of the agreement, it is certainly possible for violations to occur. Most written agreements, therefore, provide for a grievance procedure by which individuals or the union can allege that the master agreement is being violated or misinterpreted.

---

[14]Lloyd W. Ashby, James E. McGinnis, and Thomas E. Pering, *Common Sense in Negotiations in Public Education* (Danville, Ill.: The Interstate Printers and Publishers, 1972), pp. 59–60.

Most grievance procedures contain the following elements:

1. A careful definition of the term *grievance.*
2. The purpose of the grievance procedure.
3. A clause stating that a person alleging a grievance or testifying in a grievance will not face prejudicial treatment by the other party.
4. A clear outline of the appropriate steps to be taken in a grievance and the time allotments between each step.
5. In the case of arbitration, who will bear the costs of arbitration and the qualifications required for an arbitrator.

The grievance procedure used in the Dade County School District is reproduced in Appendix B of this chapter because it is an excellent example of how the above provisions can be put into operation.

Labor–Management Relations Committee

In an attempt to diffuse the adversarial relationship that sometimes exists between the board of education/administration and unions, labor–management committees have been organized in some school districts. The charge to these committees is to work through concerns, problems, and issues before they appear at the table in the next round of negotiations. In a large school district, the director of employee relations will have the responsibility of chairing the board/administration team, which should include first line supervisors. In smaller districts an assistant superintendent or even the superintendent may wish to assume this responsibility. Shop stewards or other representatives of a given union will constitute labor's membership on the committee.

The approach to labor–management committee meetings should be informal with the emphasis on mutual interests and collaboration. Compromise is the key to a successful relationship as is true in at-the-table negotiations. A "win, win" strategy should also prevail, with each party attempting to come away with something that it wants. Whatever is agreed to at these sessions should be put into writing, which, in turn, will help avoid confusion at a later time.

Of course, a labor–management committee should not deal with monetary and fringe benefits issues but, rather, with working conditions. If this committee is to be successful, it must meet throughout the term of the master agreement.

Collaborative Bargaining

In the mid 1980s a movement began with the hope of defusing the hostility that sometimes accompanies collective negotiations. This has resulted in a derivation of the collective negotiations model presented in this chapter.

In collaborative bargaining there are not two teams but just one composed of teachers, board members, and administrators. This team's mission is to problem-solve rather than to engage in bargaining.

The collaborative model was operationalized in the Ashland, Oregon School District in 1986. As part of the process, their team went through a seven-part training program that included: communication skills; problem-solving skills; creative-thinking skills; orientation to collaborative bargaining; the development of group agreements; the development of superordinate goals; and group recorder, convener, and process observer roles.

Superordinate goals, such as "enhancing teaching and learning," are highly valued, attainable, and commonly sought after by the group members. These goals provide the framework within which the various issues are addressed and solved. Consensus is the essence of the decision-making process. Thus, if the district's teacher transfer policy is a concern for the teachers, questions are posed which lead to clarification of the issue. For example, What is the purpose of the teacher transfer policy? When the issue is clarified, the team begins the process of problem-solving which might require a review of the district's budget or other documents that have a bearing on the transfer policy.[15]

Collaborative bargaining usually requires more time than the more traditional model. It can be a very effective approach especially if the traditional model has resulted in overt hostility. However, it is important to approach collaborative bargaining with caution. It is not a panacea and time will reveal its effectiveness as an alternative to the traditional model.

SUMMARY

Collective negotiation has become an accepted part of American education, as evidenced by the fact that over three-fourths of the states have enacted collective negotiations laws affecting teachers. The underlying consideration in collective negotiations is participation in the decision-making process, which is a natural extension of our democratic life style. Teachers and administrators want to have input into the priorities established by school boards when these affect their salaries, fringe benefits, and working conditions.

Collective negotiations may be defined as the process by which representatives of the school board meet with representatives of the school district employees in order to make proposals and counterproposals for the purpose of agreeing on salaries, fringe benefits, and working conditions for a specific period of time. To operationalize this process, it is necessary for the board of education to adopt a policy that will give the administration authority to implement negotiations.

Collective actions by employees have a long history in the private sector, reaching back to the time of the medieval guilds. These actions are directly affected by the economic, political, and social conditions of life. Four major congressional acts provide legal guidelines for collective bargaining in the private sector: the Norris-LaGuardia Act of 1932, the National Labor Relations Act of 1935, the Labor–Management Relations Act of 1947, and the Labor–Management Reporting and Disclosure Act of 1959. Executive Orders 10988 and 11491 affirm the right of federal employees to organize and bargain collectively, but strikes are forbidden.

Public school teachers are state employees working in a local unit, the school district. As such they are not covered by federal legislation but rather by the acts of state legislatures.

[15]John M. Daggett, "Collaborative Bargaining: Ashland, Oregon's Experience," *Updating: School Board Policies,* 22, no. 1 (January/February 1991), pp. 1–4.

There are substantial differences in those state statutes granting collective negotiations rights to teachers.

There are six aspects to the collective negotiations process: recognition and bargaining unit determination, the scope of negotiations, the bargaining process, impasse procedures, work stoppages, and the administration of the master agreement.

Recognition and bargaining unit determination answer the question, Who represents whom? Recognition is the acceptance by an employer of a bargaining agent as the authorized representative of a bargaining unit. There are two types of recognition, multiple and exclusive. Experience indicates that exclusive recognition is the most effective. The three most commonly used recognition procedures are membership lists, authorization cards, and elections. In an election a third party, such as the Federal Mediation and Conciliation Service, should be engaged to handle the mechanics of the election process.

The bargaining unit is composed of all employees to be covered by the negotiated master agreement. The criteria for deciding who belongs to the unit include a community of interest among the members, effective bargaining power, and effective school administration.

The scope of what is negotiable usually includes salaries, fringe benefits, and working conditions. A major problem in defining the scope is the fine line between educational policy, which is the prerogative of the school board, and working conditions, which are negotiable.

The at-the-table bargaining process must begin with the formation of a negotiations team. An odd-numbered team composed of the director of employee relations, building principals, and a central-office fiscal administrator has the greatest potential for being effective. This team is responsible for developing strategies, formulating goals, setting the ground rules, preparing proposals, and participating in negotiating sessions. Once an agreement is reached, the team makes a recommendation to the superintendent and school board members, who formally ratify the agreement.

If there is persistent disagreement at the table after normal negotiations procedures are exhausted, an impasse has been reached. The three procedures usually employed in an impasse are mediation, fact finding, and, where permitted by law, arbitration. Mediation is the voluntary process of bringing in a third party who intervenes for the purpose of ending the disagreement. Fact finding is a procedure by which an individual or panel holds hearings for the purpose of reviewing evidence and making a recommendation for settling the dispute. Arbitration occurs when both sides submit the dispute to an impartial third person or panel that issues an award which the parties are required to accept.

Nothing is more disruptive to a school district than a strike, a tactic that is sometimes used by unions when negotiations reaches an impasse. Although strikes by teachers are illegal in most states, a number of strikes occur each year throughout the country. It is extremely important, therefore, for the administration to develop a strike plan, even in the most tranquil of school settings.

The process of collective negotiations is usually ineffective unless the agreements reached are put in writing, thus formalizing the basic rights governing the parties and reducing potential controversy. It is the responsibility of the administration to implement and interpret the master agreement. Furthermore, the administration is limited only by the specifics of the agreement, which is commonly referred to as "management prerogative."

In the day to day interpretation of the master agreement, it is certainly possible for violations to occur. Most written agreements, therefore, provide for a grievance procedure by which individuals or the union may allege that the agreement is being violated.

In some school districts, labor–management relations committees have been formed for the purpose of working through concerns, problems, and issues before they appear at-the-table when the existing master contract is renegotiated.

An innovative approach to collective negotiations was developed in the mid-1980s called "collaborative bargaining" which had as its purpose the defusing of the hostility that sometimes accompanies the traditional negotiations process. In this process there is one team composed of teachers or other categories of employees reflecting the bargaining unit, administrators, and board members. The goal is to problem-solve issues and the essence of the process is consensus.

APPENDIX A
CONTRACT TABLE OF CONTENTS

Contract Between the Dade County Public Schools and the United Teachers of Dade FEA/United, AFT, Local 1974, AFL-CIO

Article

Continued

APPENDIX B*
GRIEVANCE PROCEDURES

A. Purpose

It is recognized that complaints and grievances may arise between the bargaining agent and the employer or between the employer and any one or more employees concerning the application or interpretation of the wages, hours, terms and conditions of employment as defined in this agreement. The employer and the bargaining agent desire that these grievances and complaints be settled in an orderly, prompt and equitable manner so that the efficiency of the Dade County Public Schools may be maintained and the morale of employees not be impaired. Every effort will be made by the employer, employees and the bargaining agent to settle the grievances at the lowest level of supervision. The initiation or presentation of a grievance by an employee will not adversely affect his standing with the employer. No reprisals of any kind will be made by the Board or its representative or any member of the administration against any party in interest, any Union representative or any other participant in the grievance procedure by reason of such participation. All documents, grievance forms, communications, and records dealing with the processing of a grievance shall

Source: Grievance Procedure from the Contract Between the Dade County Public Schools and the United Teachers of Dade (Miami, Fla.: Dade County Public Schools, 1977), pp. 53–66.

be filed separately from the personnel files of any party in interest, including final disposition, except for and exclusively for awards resulting from arbitration.

B. Definitions

1. *Grievance*—formal allegation by an employee and/or the bargaining agent that there has been a violation, misinterpretation, or misapplication of any of the terms and conditions of employment set forth in this contract, *or its appendices.*

2. *Bargaining agent*—the bargaining agent shall mean the employee organization certified as the exclusive bargaining agent pursuant to 447.009 Florida Statutes Chapter 74.100.

3. *Aggrieved employee*—the aggrieved employee shall mean any full time or part time teacher and such other persons who are members of the bargaining unit as certified pursuant to Section 447.009 Florida Statutes Chapter 74.100.

4. *Party in interest*—a party in interest is any person who might be required to take action or against whom action might be taken in order to resolve the grievance.

5. *Supervising administrator*—the individual having immediate administrative authority over the aggrieved employee(s).

6. *Immediate superintendent*—the area, assistant, or associate superintendent having immediate administrative authority over the supervising administrator.

7. *Days*—as referred to in the time limits herein, days shall mean working days.

8. *Letter of inquiry*—request in writing on proper CDPS form, by the bargaining agent to the Division of Legislative and Employee Relations seeking clarification of Dade County Public Schools Rules, State Law or this agreement.

C. Special Provisions

The time limit set forth herein may be extended and/or modified by mutual agreement, using the stipulated Grievance Form.

In the event a grievance is filed at such time as it cannot be processed through all steps in the grievance procedure by the end of the aggrieved employee's contract year, and, if left unresolved until the beginning of the following year could result in irreparable harm to a party in interest, the time limits set forth herein will be reduced so that the grievance procedure may be exhausted as soon as practicable.

If the employer violates any time limits, the bargaining agent may advance to the next step without waiting for the employer response.

The parties acknowledge that as a principle of interpretation, employees are obligated to work as directed while grievances are pending.

The employer and the bargaining agent shall have the right of free choice in designating representatives for the purpose of resolving grievances. Aggrieved employees, or employees who are called as witnesses, will be allowed released time without loss of pay to process or assist in the processing of a grievance.

The bargaining agent in accordance with its own nondiscriminatory internal rules shall have the sole and exclusive right to determine whether any grievance warrants processing through this procedure. In the event the bargaining agent determines at any step of the grievance procedure that a grievance does not warrant processing, a written notification of that determination, using the stipulated Grievance Form, shall be sent to the Special Counsel for Legislative and Employee Relations and to the employee(s) involved who shall then be free to process it themselves or through legal counsel.

If the bargaining agent has declined to process or further process any grievance presented to it, and if any employee or group of employees desire to process it or further process their own grievance through this procedure, the bargaining agent shall be sent copies of all written communications sent by the employer or the employee(s) involved. Further, nothing herein contained shall be construed to prevent any public employees from representing, at any time, their own grievance in person or by legal counsel to the employer and having such grievance(s) adjusted without the intervention of the bargaining agent, provided however, that the adjustment is not inconsistent with the terms of the collective bargaining agreement then in effect, and provided further that the bargaining agent has been given notice and a reasonable opportunity to be present at any meeting called for the resolution of such grievances.

The bargaining agent shall not be responsible for any costs attendant to the resolution of any grievance it has not processed.

The parties acknowledge that multiple grievances may be combined with mutual agreement of the employer and the union.

One set of School Board rules at each work location shall be made available to Union building representatives for the purpose of reference and information as well as for the purpose of expediting the provisions of this grievance procedure.

The use of tape recorders or other mechanical devices is expressly forbidden.

D. Letter of Inquiry

Either the immediate superintendent or bargaining agent may send a Letter of Inquiry on the stipulated Letter of Inquiry form, to the Special Counsel for the Division of Legislative and Employee Relations for the purpose of seeking a clarification of a Dade County Public Schools rule, state law and/or terms and conditions of employment as set forth in this agreement.

The Division of Legislative and Employee Relations shall respond within ten (10) working days of receipt of the Letter of Inquiry. If the interpretation of the Letter of Inquiry is not satisfactory, a formal grievance may be filed.

E. Implementation

Step 1

1. The grievance shall be filed within thirty (30) days of the alleged violation, misinterpretation or misapplication of the terms and conditions of employment set forth in this agreement.

2. The grievance shall be filed in writing stating the specific article, section and language alleged to have been violated, misinterpreted or misapplied to the supervising administrator of the aggrieved employee(s). It is further understood and agreed that the aggrieved employee(s) shall be granted released time to attend formal proceedings, as

described herein, which are held during working hours. No Dade County Public Schools employees, other than the aggrieved employee(s), shall be granted released time to either represent the aggrieved employee(s) or to observe the proceedings as representatives of the bargaining agent.

3. The supervising administrator shall note the date of receipt of the grievance and shall seek to meet with the aggrieved employee at a mutually agreeable time within five (5) working days of receipt of the grievance.

4. The bargaining agent for the unit shall be advised in writing as to the date of the proposed meeting, and shall have the right to send one (1) observer to the proceeding if the bargaining agent is not involved in the actual representation of the aggrieved employee(s).

5. Within five (5) working days of the meeting, the supervising administrator shall render a decision and shall immediately communicate that decision in writing to the aggrieved and the appropriate immediate superintendent or his designee. Additional copies of the decision shall be sent to the Division of Legislative and Employee Relations, and to the exclusive bargaining agent.

6. The aggrieved employee(s) and/or the bargaining agent may appeal the decision of the supervising administrator within five (5) working days of its rendering.

7. The notice of intent to appeal shall be communicated in writing to the immediate superintendent. Failure to appeal the decision of the supervising administrator within five (5) working days shall constitute acceptance by the aggrieved employee(s) and the bargaining agent of the decision as being a satisfactory resolution of the issue raised.

Step II

1. If the aggrieved employee(s) appeals the decision, the immediate superintendent shall schedule a meeting to take place at a mutually agreeable time not more than ten (10) days after receipt of notice of appeal. The immediate superintendent shall immediately communicate notice of appeal to the Division of Legislative and Employee Relations.

   The exclusive bargaining agent shall be advised in writing as to the date of the proposed meeting and shall have the right to send one (1) observer to the proceedings if the agent is not involved in the actual representation of the aggrieved employee(s).

2. Within ten (10) working days of the meeting, the immediate superintendent shall render a decision and shall immediately communicate that decision in writing to the aggrieved employee(s). Copies of the decision shall be sent to the Division of Legislative and Employee Relations, and to the exclusive bargaining agent. A copy is to be retained by the immediate superintendent.

3. The aggrieved employee(s) may appeal the decision of the immediate superintendent within five (5) working days of its rendering. The notice of intent to appeal shall be communicated in writing to the Special Counsel for Legislative and Employee Relations. Failure to appeal the decision of the immediate superintendent within five (5) working days shall constitute acceptance by the aggrieved employee(s) and the bargaining agent of the decision as being a satisfactory resolution of the issue raised.

Step III

1. If the aggrieved employee(s) appeals the decision, the Superintendent or his designee shall schedule a meeting to take place at a mutually agreeable time not more than twelve (12) days after receipt of notice of appeal.
2. Within twelve (12) working days of the meeting, the Superintendent or his designee shall render a decision and shall immediately communicate that decision in writing to the aggrieved employee(s). Copies of the decision shall be sent to the supervising administrator, the immediate superintendent, and to the exclusive bargaining agent.
3. Failure to appeal the decision rendered in Step III within five (5) working days by notice of intent to submit to arbitration, shall deem the decision at Step III to be final and no further appeal will be pursued.

F. Arbitration

If the employer and the aggrieved employee(s) and/or the bargaining agent fail to resolve the grievance, the grievance may be submitted to final and binding disposition by an impartial neutral mutually selected by the parties. Nothing contained in this Appendix or elsewhere in this agreement shall be construed to permit the Union to file an issue for arbitration unless by mutual consent, that has not been processed through applicable steps of the grievance procedure.

1. Notice of intent to submit the grievance to arbitration shall be communicated in writing to the Special Counsel for Legislative and Employee Relations within live (5) working days of the decision at Step III.

2. Prior to the submission of the appeal to arbitration, the arbitrator may hold a prehearing conference to consider and determine:

   a) the simplification of the issues;
   b) the possibility of obtaining stipulation of facts and documents that will avoid unnecessary proof;
   c) such other matters as may aid in the disposition of the grievance;
   d) matters of jurisdiction or applicability.

3. In the event that an employee desires, on his own behalf, to process his grievance to arbitration, the bargaining agent reserves the right to intervene in the arbitration proceeding up to and including the full right to participation as a party. Should the bargaining agent intervene, it shall bear half the employee's cost.

4. Within ten (10) days after written notice of submission to arbitration, the parties will attempt to agree upon a mutually acceptable arbitrator and obtain a commitment from said arbitrator to serve. If the parties are unable to agree upon an arbitrator or to obtain such a commitment within the specified time, a request for a list of arbitrators may be made to the Federal Mediation and Conciliation Service by either party. The parties will be bound by the rules and procedures of the Federal Mediation and Conciliation Service in the selection of an arbitrator and the holding and conduct of an arbitration hearing.

5. The arbitrator, selected by the parties, or pursuant to the rules of the Federal Mediation and Conciliation Service, will issue a decision not later than twenty (20) days from the date of the close of the hearings, or if oral hearings have been waived, then from the date final statements and proofs are submitted. The arbitrator's decision will be in writing and will set forth findings of fact, reasoning and conclusions on the issue submitted and where permitted by law may include a monetary award. The arbitrator will be without power or authority to make any decision which requires the commission of an act prohibited by law, or which adds to, subtracts from, modifies or alters the terms of this collective bargaining agreement. The decision and award of the arbitrator shall be final and binding.

6. All arbitration costs, including the cost of stenographic reporting of the arbitration hearing if agreed to by the parties, shall be divided equally between the employer and the bargaining agent, or if the bargaining agent has determined not to process the grievance through arbitration, between the employer and the employee(s). Each party will pay the cost of presenting its own case; however, the aggrieved employee(s) or the employee(s) who is called as witness for an arbitration hearing will be allowed released time to process or to assist in the processing of their own grievance, or to testify.

7. It is understood and agreed by the employer, members of the unit, and the bargaining agent, that the resolution of complaints which are grievable or litigable shall be pursued through the grievance procedure until such remedy is exhausted. At that time the employer, the aggrieved employee(s) and/or the bargaining agent may seek other legal remedies as are available.

Refusal to discuss a grievance in good faith shall constitute an Unfair Labor Practice and shall be subject to the penalties provided for in Section 447.017 Florida Statutes 74–100.

8. Both parties agree to negotiate and mutually agree to the rules and procedures which govern arbitration. In the event mutual agreement cannot be reached, the American Arbitration Association will be utilized to process arbitration cases.

APPENDIX C*
GLOSSARY OF TERMS USED IN COLLECTIVE NEGOTIATIONS

Agency Shop:	This term is used when employees who are not members of an employee organization, but who are represented by it during the bargaining process and in the administration of a bargained agreement, are required to pay a service fee to the organization.
Arbitration:	A procedure whereby parties unable to agree on a solution to a problem (i.e., at impasse in contract negotiations or a grievance procedure) will be bound by the decision of a third party.

*Source: Education Commission of the States, *Cuebook II: State Education Collective Bargaining Laws* (Denver, Colo.: The Commission, 1980), pp. 74–78.

Bargaining Unit: A group of employees organized as a single unit and having the right to bargain, through their designated representative(s), with the employer.

Certificated/Certified Employee: As the term applies to education: a teacher, supervisor, principal or other administrator who must hold a state certificate in order to be employed in the profession.

Certification: As the term applies in the recognition process: designation, by an authorized person or agency, of the employee organization representing a bargaining unit as an "exclusive representative" for bargaining purposes.

Community of Interest: As used in determining an appropriate bargaining unit: similar work, interests, salaries, concerns, etc.

Conciliation: See *Mediation.*

Contract: A written agreement on terms and conditions of employment arrived at through the bargaining process. Also *Memorandum of Agreement, Memorandum of Understanding.*

Court Review: The means through which a court of appropriate jurisdiction may consider and rule upon actions or findings of a labor relations board or other involved agency or individual.

Decertification: The withdrawal of authorization as an exclusive representative for an employee organization. May occur when another employee organization successfully challenges the qualifications of the first organization, or as a penalty for violation of law, rule or regulation.

Dues Checkoff: Deduction of employee organization dues from member's paychecks for remission to the organization treasury. Some state laws do not permit this practice; others do. When permitted, the dues deduction procedure often is negotiated as part of the contract between employer and employee bargaining unit.

Employee Organization: A group of similar employees organized for the purpose of bargaining their salaries, wages and terms and conditions of employment with their employer. Most teacher organizations are affiliated with the National Education Association or the American Federation of Teachers. This term is often used interchangeably with *union* in the area of labor relations.

Exclusive Representation: An employee organization has exclusive representation when it is recognized by the employer, for bargaining purposes, as the sole representative of the kinds of employees who are members of the bargaining unit.

Fact-Finding: The process of gathering and analyzing facts, information and testimony to be used as a basis for recommendations for the resolution of a bargaining impasse or grievance charge.

Fair Share Fee: An amount proportionate to members' dues in an employee organization that is paid to the organization by non-members who, nevertheless, are represented in a bargaining unit by the organization. A form of service fee, based on the proportion of dues that is directly related to the services the non-member employee receives from the organization. Often negotiated.

Grievance: An allegation by an employee or by the employee organization that the employer or one of its agents, often in the process of implementing a contract, is guilty of misapplication, misinterpretation or violation of one or more specific provisions of the existent contract.

Impasse: That stage in negotiations at which two parties are unable to achieve agreement on the issues still on the bargaining table. There is an apparent lack of agreement among state laws and among state labor relations personnel as to the point at which impasse occurs, when mediation has failed, or when fact-finding has failed.

Impasse Resolution: A process aimed at resolving disagreements that occur during the bargaining of a contract. Three steps may be involved: mediation, fact-finding, and arbitration. Also known as interest resolution.

Injunctive Relief: An order by a court to perform or cease to perform a specific activity.

Interest Resolution: See *Impasse Resolution.*

Intervention/Intervenor: A challenge to an employee organization's right to be an exclusive representative for a bargaining unit. May be issued by a competing organization or one or more employees. Most state laws limit the times for such intervention to specific points in the establishment of a bargaining relationship, during or after the term of a contract.

Maintenance of Membership: A requirement that employees who are members of an employee organization that has been certified as an exclusive representative remain members during the term of a bargained contract.

Management Rights: Certain rights, privileges, responsibilities and authority requisite to the conduct of an enterprise by its management.

Mediation: That form of impasse resolution (usually implemented first) in which a third party meets with the two parties involved in the dispute, together and/or separately, in order to perform a catalytic function in an effort to help the parties reach an agreement.

Memorandum of Agreement: See *Contract*.

Memorandum of Understanding: See *Contract*.

Middle Management: The term encompasses personnel from supervisors to a level just below top management.

Nonprofessional Employee: Most often, a lower-level employee whose work is routine, the performance of which is not dependent on specialized education at the postsecondary level or equivalent experience.

Organizational Security: See *Union Security*.

Professional Employee: Most often, a higher-level employee whose work is not routine or measurable, the performance of which is dependent on specialized education at the postsecondary level or equivalent experience.

Recognition: The accomplishment of the status, by the employee organization with the employer, of collective bargaining agent for a unit of defined extent.

Representation Election: An election held to identify an appropriate employee organization as the exclusive representative of employees in a defined bargaining unit. The employee organization receiving a majority of votes is the winner.

Scope of Bargaining: Bargainable items—the limits, if any, of the appropriate subject matter for bargaining. If such are not set by law, they are determined by the interaction at the bargaining table. If there is not agreement on the scope of bargaining, decisions may be made by a public employment relations board, other administering agency, individual or by an appropriate court.

Service Fees: A sum of money paid to the bargaining unit by nonmember employees who, nevertheless, are represented by the bargaining unit. Some state laws permit these fees; others do not. Service fees may be equal to a unit member's regular dues; they may be a certain percentage of these dues; they may be equal to that portion of membership dues that is used to cover the expense of negotiating and administering a contract. In some states, non-members represented by a negotiating unit who have valid religious objections to the payment of service fees to an organized bargaining unit may be granted an exemption from the requirement; or their service fee may be remitted to an appropriate charity.

Showing of Support/Interest: Submission of evidence by an employee organization wishing to represent a bargaining unit that it has adequate support/ interest/membership from personnel in the bargaining unit. This may be in the form of signature cards, petition signatures, etc.

Strike: A concerted work stoppage, usually used as an effort at the time of impasse to accomplish a contract on terms acceptable to the union.

Supervisor: An individual who, using independent judgment, directs other employees and has a voice in their employment, reward, discipline, dismissal and grievances.

Union: An employee organization that has as one of its purposes the bargaining of terms and conditions of employment with an employer.

Union Security: A blanket term for rights, granted to a union by law or agreement, that reinforces its position as exclusive representative. Dues deduction and service fees are forms of union security, as are specified periods of time during which the union's standing as exclusive representative may not be challenged.

Union Shop: This term applies when an employee is required under the terms of a bargained agreement to become a member of the bargaining unit within a short time after initial employment in order to retain the job. Membership must be maintained during the term of the bargained agreement. In rare cases, union shops are permitted under state law.

Unit Determination: The process of deciding which employees will be in a proposed bargaining unit. Criteria for determination include community of interest, practicality. In some states, units are specifically defined by law.

Unit Modification: A change in the composition (kinds of employees) of a bargaining unit.

SELECTED BIBLIOGRAPHY

Abel, Gene P., "Equity, Accountability and Teacher Negotiations in the '90s," *School Business Affairs,* 57, no. 5 (May 1991), pp. 30–31.

"Are Unions Moving Towards Professionalism?" Education USA, 27, no. 25 (February 1985), p. 197.

Birnbaum, Robert, James P. Begin, and Bert R. Brown, *Cooperation in Academic Negotiations: A Guide to Mutual Gains Bargaining.* New Brunswick, N.J.: Institute of Management and Labor Relations, Rutgers University, 1985.

Bland, Michael, and Peter Jackson. *Effective Employee Relations.* London: Kogan Page Ltd., 1990.

Coulson, Robert, *Arbitration in the Public Schools.* New York, N.Y.: the American Arbitration Association, 1986.

Decker, Robert H., "Helping the Board of Education & Negotiating Team Understand their Roles in Collective Bargaining," *School Business Affairs,* 57, no. 2 (February 1991), pp. 6–10.

Deering, Thomas E., and Michael A. Deering, "A Collective Bargaining Proposal for Public School Teachers," *Education,* 104 (Spring 1984), pp. 278–280.

Eiler, Edward E., "When Collective Bargaining Isn't Working," *School Business Affairs,* 57, no. 2 (February 1991), pp. 18–21.

ERIC Clearinghouse on Educational Management, *Collective Bargaining and Alternatives,* Eugene, Oreg.: University of Oregon, 1987.

Frombach, John W., "Negotiations—Are You Prepared?" *School Business Affairs,* 57, no. 2 (February 1991), pp. 14–18.

Gerardi, Robert, "Strikes: Some Lessons from a Yankee Past." *Thrust for Educational Leadership,* 14 (September 1984), pp. 27–28.

Glaser, John P. and James W. Tamm, "Better Bargaining," *The Executive Educator,* 13, no. 12 (December 1991), pp. 22–25.

Goldschmidt, Steven M., Bruce Bowers, Max Riley, and Leland E. Stuart, *The Extent and Nature of Educational Policy Bargaining.* Eugene, Oreg.: University of Oregon Center for Educational Policy and Management, 1984.

Herman, Jerry J., "The Two Faces of Collective Bargaining," *School Business Affairs,* 57, no. 2 (February 1991), pp. 10–14.

Illinois Association of School Boards, *Collective Bargaining and the School Board Member.* Springfield, Ill.: The Association, 1985.

Jessup, Dorothy Kerr, *Teachers, Unions, and Change. A Comparative Study.* New York: Praeger Publishers, 1985.

Kerchner, Charles Taylor, *Labor Policy in School Districts: Its Diffusion and Impact on Work Structures.* Eugene, Oreg.: University of Oregon Center for Educational Policy and Management, 1986.

Lieberman, Myron, "Beware These Four Common Fallacies of School System Labor Relations," *The American School Board Journal,* 171 (June 1984), p. 33.

Rauth, Marilyn, "Exploring Heresy in Collective Bargaining and School Restructuring," *Phi Delta Kappan,* 71 (1990), pp. 781–790.

Sharp, William L., *Collective Bargaining in the Public Schools,* Dubuque, Iowa: William C. Brown Communications, Inc., 1993.

Smith, Stuart C., Diana Ball, and Demetri Liontos, *Working Together: The Collaborative Style of Bargaining.* Eugene, Oregon: ERIC Clearinghouse on Educational Management, 1991.

Sommers, Norman L., "Collective Bargaining: Is It Time to Dump Your Hired Gun?" *The American School Board Journal,* 172, no. 5 (May 1985), pp. 29–36.

Streshly, William A., and Todd A. DeMitchell. *Teacher Unions and TQE: Building Quality Labor Relations.* Thousand Oaks, California: Corwin Press, Inc., 1994.

Vidak, Jim, "Take the Sting Out of Negotiations," *The Executive Educator,* 13, no. 3 (March 1991), pp. 24–25.

Wood, Craig R., "In Good Faith: When It Comes to Collective Bargaining, What Are Your Rights and Obligations?" *American School and University,* 57, no. 1 (September 1984), pp. 36–38.

10

LEGAL, ETHICAL, AND POLICY ISSUES IN THE ADMINISTRATION OF HUMAN RESOURCES

This final chapter is concerned with legal, ethical, and policy issues in the administration of human resources. An understanding by current and future personnel managers of contract management and the nuances of litigation has become more important within the last decade because of the ever-increasing societal emphasis on legal rights and responsibilities. Personnel managers are as vulnerable to litigation as teachers and principals. In fact, with the multitude of federal and state laws, regulations, and procedures that impinge on personnel functions, defensibility and accountability must be continuing concerns in the personnel department.

Relevant, concise, and clear personnel policies become the foundation upon which the eight personnel functions rest. Administrative processes and procedures operationalize these policies and provide the internal structure necessary to accomplish the school district's primary mandate, to educate children.

Consequently, this chapter has been written with these issues in mind and should provide direction to all persons concerned with human resource administration including boards of education, superintendents, assistant superintendents, and personnel managers.

CONTRACT MANAGEMENT[1]

Teachers and administrators usually work under the provisions of an individual contract; classified personnel such as secretaries, bus drivers, and custodians are employed at an hourly rate or for an annual salary. In school districts where a master contract has been negotiated by a union, teachers and/or administrators belonging to the bargaining unit do not

[1]An extended treatment of the essential matter in this section may be found in the following reference: Steven Knowles, *Contracts* (Larchmont, N.Y.: Emanuel Law Outlines, Inc., 1993–94 edition).

have individual contracts but rather work under the provisions of the master agreement. There are exceptions to these general statements; however, for all practical purposes these are the alternative methods by which employees are hired to work in a school system.

The question may legitimately be asked, What is the purpose of issuing individual contracts to teachers and administrators? The most accurate response is tradition. As professionals, teachers and administrators are employed to perform a service for which they receive a certain amount of financial compensation. The performance of the service may require a teacher to take student projects home to be graded or may require a teacher to remain after the school day to talk with the parents of a student having problems. The time it takes to perform the service and the amount of work involved are not considerations under the contract method of employment.

Classified employees also are paid to perform a service, but the time and work involved does make a difference in the amount of money received. When such employees are required to work after the regular eight-hour day, they receive overtime pay. If they are required to perform a task not specified by the categories outlined in their job descriptions, they receive additional compensation.

Those professional employees who are covered by the terms of a master agreement have a closer identity to classified employees than to teachers and administrators with individual contracts. Their working conditions are spelled out in the master agreement.

Board of education policies sometimes address working conditions, but these policies are usually not as specific as the terms of a master agreement. Teacher and administrator handbooks also may contain references to working conditions, but these are usually more concerned with internal procedures.

While using individual contracts for teachers and administrators is a matter of tradition, this is mandated by statute in some states. Individual contracts also distinguish an individual's working conditions from those termed "classified." A teacher's or administrator's contract must meet the requirements of general contract law. Because school districts are legal entities with a corporate character, they may sue and be sued; purchase, receive, or sell real and personal property; make contracts and be contracted with. The contracts entered into by a school district must not only conform to contract law but also must conform to state statutes governing contracts and to the precedents established through case law.

A *contract* is an agreement which must possess five basic components in order for it to be valid. The components are: offer and acceptance, competent persons, consideration, legal subject matter, and proper form.

Offer and Acceptance

A valid contract must contain an offer and an acceptance. In the selection process, therefore, it is poor procedure to notify unsuccessful candidates for a position that the job has been filled until after the prospective employee has accepted the offer of employment. If the board of education approves a contract for a specific person to teach high school English, there is no agreement until the contract is executed, which constitutes acceptance.

A few other facts about the legal nature of an agreement must be kept in mind. First, an offer can be accepted only by the person to whom it was made. For example, the husband of a candidate for a teaching position cannot accept the offer for his wife. Second, an offer must be accepted within a reasonable time after it is made. If an individual does not sign and return a contract within a few weeks in the hope that another job offer will be made by a different school district, the board of education may offer the contract to another candidate. Finally, a newspaper advertisement is not an offer of a position but rather an invitation to become a candidate for a job.

Competent Persons

A contract is not valid unless it is entered into by two or more competent persons. This means that the persons have the legal capacity to enter into a contract. As a corporate entity, a school district has the power, through the legal action of the school board, to enter into a contract. Certain classes of individuals, however, have a limited capacity to contract. The most commonly identified classes include minors, mentally ill persons, and individuals who are intoxicated.

If a person was mentally ill or intoxicated at the time of entering into a contract to the extent that he or she did not understand the significance of the action, he or she may have the contract set aside because there was no agreement, which is essential to the validity of every contract.

Consideration

For a contract to be valid, it must be supported by a consideration, which is usually defined as something of value. The type of consideration found in an employment contract is referred to as "a promise for an act." For example, in a teacher's contract the board of education promises to pay an individual $25,000 to teach third grade for one year. The teacher fulfills the act by teaching during the designated time period.

Legal Subject Matter

In all fifty states an individual may teach only if he or she possesses a license to teach issued by the respective state department of education. Consequently, if a board of education enters into a contract with a person who does not possess a license to teach the third grade, such a contract would involve illegal subject matter and would be invalid.

Proper Form

For a contract to be enforceable, it must be in the form required by law. The courts recognize both oral and written contracts. However, most states have statutory provisions that require teachers' and administrators' contracts to be in writing and even specify the proper wording for the contracts.

LITIGATION IN HUMAN RESOURCE MANAGEMENT

Over the last decade, school districts have experienced an increase in litigation partially due to the fact that sovereign immunity has been abrogated by many state legislatures.

Sovereign immunity is the common law principle that protects government officials from lawsuits resulting from the performance of their duties. School districts are governmental subdivisions of the state operating on the local level, and thus, school board members have been protected from such lawsuits. However, more than twenty-eight states have taken away this cloak of immunity, and the 1990s may see most of the remaining states in a similar posture.

The ripple effect from this situation has caused personnel administrators to become more vulnerable to judicial review of their decisions and actions than personnel administrators of a decade ago. Even if personnel administrators act in good faith and with reasonable deliberation, they may find themselves defending their actions in court.

Therefore, it is imperative that all administrators have a rudimentary understanding of the American judicial system and are capable of carrying out their daily responsibilities in such a manner that they can legally defend themselves if they are sued.

The following discussion is meant to provide future personnel administrators with a better understanding of their potential liabilities.

The U.S. Judicial System

There are two systems of law. The first, known as "civil law," is descended from Roman law; the rule of law in this system is established through statutes enacted by a legislative body. The second system, known as "common law," is the basis of law in England. Under this system, the decisions rendered by a court become a guide or precedent to be followed by the court in dealing with future cases. The system of law found in the United States is a mixed system, using both civil and common law principles.

Sources of Law

There are three major sources of law that form the foundation of the American judicial system: constitutions, statutes, and case law.

Constitutions

Constitutions are bodies of precepts that provide the framework within which government carries out its duties. The federal and state constitutions contain provisions that secure the personal, property, and political rights of citizens.

School districts have been continually confronted with constitutional issues, many of which have resulted in lawsuits. Some of these issues have dealt with racial discrimination in hiring practices, due process rights for individuals faced with employment termination, and the privacy right of employees in relation to their personnel records.

Statutes

Statutes, more commonly called "laws," are the enactments of legislative bodies. Thus, the U.S. Congress or a given state legislature may enact a new law or change an old law by the passage of legislation. A statute is subject to review by the respective state or federal court to determine if it is in violation of the precepts set forth in a state constitution and/or the Federal Constitution.

The presumption is that laws enacted by legislative bodies are constitutional, and the burden of proving otherwise is determined only through litigation. Thus, if a state legislature passes a law that allows school administrators the right to terminate tenured teachers without a hearing before the school board, a teacher or group of teachers could initiate a lawsuit asking the state's supreme court to consider the constitutionality of the new law. The basis for the lawsuit might be a provision in the state constitution dealing with the permanent employment status of tenured teachers.

Because public schools are state agencies, the legislature of every state has created statutes governing school districts. School operation, therefore, must be in compliance with such state statutes, and it is the responsibility of the board of education and the superintendent of schools to ensure compliance. Further, the board of education cannot establish policies that are in conflict with state statutes or the acts of the U.S. Congress; in addition, the policies must not be in conflict with either the federal or state constitutions. If a school board, for example, creates a policy prohibiting the employment of handicapped individuals as teachers, this policy would be in violation of federal law—in particular, the Rehabilitation Act of 1973—and probably violates the due process guaranteed by the Fourteenth Amendment to the U.S. Constitution; it might also violate a given state constitutional provision stipulating that all citizens have a right to employment opportunities.

Case Law

The third source, *common law,* is more properly called "case law" because it is derived from court decisions rather than from legislative acts. Past court decisions are considered to be binding on subsequent cases if the material facts are similar. This is the doctrine of "precedent." Lower courts usually adhere to the precedent (rule of law) established by higher courts in the same jurisdiction. The U.S. Supreme Court and state supreme courts can reverse their own previous decisions and thereby change the rule of law. Thus, a state circuit court may apply a rule of law established by a state supreme court as to what constitutes due process in the termination of a tenured teacher. In a later case, the supreme court may redefine what constitutes due process and thus change the rule of law.

There are two additional sources of law that affect education even though they are not primary sources: administrative law and attorney general opinions.

Administrative law has developed through the creation of state and federal boards and commissions charged with administering certain federal and state laws. In carrying out their responsibilities, these boards and commissions establish rules and regulations. For example, school employees are likely to be affected by the regulations of the Social Security Administration, the Employment Security Administration, or the Workers' Compensation Commission. Of course, the actions of these boards and commissions are subject to review by the courts.

A second and frequently initiated legal procedure is the requesting of an opinion from a state attorney general on the interpretation of a certain statute. In the absence of case law, this opinion can be used by educators in addressing legal issues.

Therefore, personnel administrators must continually research professional journals that speak to significant court decisions and legislation. Most state departments of education also notify school administrators concerning recent state court decisions and laws that affect school district personnel practices and policies. The agencies of the federal government are very diligent in notifying school districts across the country about regulations with which they are required to be in compliance.

Major Divisions of Law

There are two broad classifications of law: criminal and civil. Criminal law is concerned with protecting the rights of society; and as such, the state, representing the people, is responsible for prosecuting wrongs committed against society by individuals or corporate entities. Civil law is concerned with protecting the rights that exist between individuals, between an individual and a corporate entity, or between two corporate entities. Most of the litigation that arises out of personnel management, of course, will deal with civil law. Civil law embraces many areas including contracts, wills and estates, corporate law, divorce, and torts. Personnel administrators are most vulnerable in lawsuits dealing with contracts and torts.

The Court Structure

The municipal court structure is of little or no concern to personnel administrators. These courts are usually concerned with enforcing the ordinances of municipal governments, which include housing and building codes and traffic ordinances.

The federal court structure, of course, is divided into three levels: the federal district courts, the courts of appeal, and the U.S. Supreme Court. The district courts are courts of original jurisdiction where all suits involving federal law will be filed. Civil suits that involve agencies of the U.S. government also are heard in the federal district courts. Thus, both the Bakke and Weber cases originated in the respective federal district courts. Both cases were eventually appealed to the U.S. Supreme Court and have become landmark decisions. Personnel administrators should be familiar with the nuances of the federal court system due to the multitude of federal employment laws, which are potential areas of litigation.

The state court structure is analogous to the federal system. The court of original jurisdiction in most states is termed the circuit court and is where all civil lawsuits are filed. Cases involving tenure and contract management will be heard in the circuit court. The decisions of the circuit court may be appealed usually to an appellate court and, finally, to the state supreme court. Once again, it must be stated that personnel administrators should become very familiar with the workings of the state court system because of the high incidence of litigation involving state laws as they relate to personnel management.

There is a distinction in the manner by which certain courts can hear cases that is important for personnel administrators to understand. Certain issues are traditionally tried in "equity" by the state circuit courts and federal district courts. The most familiar to personnel administrators are injunctions. For example, a school district may go to a state circuit court to ask for an injunction directing a group of teachers to leave the picket lines and to return to their classrooms, if there is a state statute prohibiting strikes by teachers.

Obviously, if the parties named in an injunction fail to obey the court order, they are in contempt of court and may be punished by a fine or by jailing.

The Role of the Attorney in Personnel Management

A common misconception about the role that a school district's attorney fulfills in a lawsuit against a school district is that he or she will entirely handle the litigation. An attorney's expertise centers around his or her ability to take the material facts in a case and research the statutes and the precedents of other court cases for the purpose of organizing a reasonable defense. An attorney must begin with what you, the personnel administrator, can offer by way of documentation. The defense will only be as strong as the level of accountability that has been demonstrated through personnel procedures and policies. Consequently, a good test of the workability of procedures and policies is whether they will be a help or a hindrance in a lawsuit.

The Anatomy of a Lawsuit

Although lawsuits do not follow a set pattern, there is enough commonality in litigation to make a few general observations. The plaintiff files a petition with the appropriate court of jurisdiction, setting forth the cause of action, which is the allegation. A summons is then delivered by the court to the defendant, who is required to appear in court on a given date for the purpose of pleading to the petition.

The next step involves clarifying the allegation and the material facts supporting it. This may be accomplished by the taking of depositions, a formal procedure in which the parties to the lawsuit answer questions posed by the respective attorneys. Also, written queries may be required by the attorneys in lieu of or in addition to the depositions.

Then a motion may be filed to dismiss the petition if the material facts do not appear to support the allegation. If the judge does not dismiss the petition, a trial date will be set. In civil cases involving tenure, a contract, or a tort, the defendant usually has the option of a jury trial or may rely on the judge to make a decision.

Who the defendant is in a civil lawsuit is determined by the nature of the petition and the material facts. In a tenure or contract dispute, the board of education as a corporate body is usually the defendant because the board approves all personnel contracts. If it is a tort, an individual, or a group of individuals may be named as the defendant because the petition may allege that a civil wrong has been committed against the plaintiff by one person or a group of persons. In a judgment favoring the plaintiff, damages are assessed in dollar amounts to be paid by the defendant.

Tort Liability in Personnel Administration

There is a tendency to take a shotgun approach in some types of civil lawsuits, particularly torts, when identifying defendants in a litigation. If a student is injured as a consequence of using gymnastics equipment, the teacher might be sued for being negligent in supervising the student or for not properly instructing the student on how to use the equipment. The

Plaintiff Files a Petition

Court Serves a Summons on
the Defendant

Defendant Pleads the Petition

Depositions and/or Written Queries
are Taken by Both Parties

Defendant May File a Motion
for Dismissal or Plaintiff May
Drop the Lawsuit

Trial is Held if the Lawsuit
is Not Dismissed or Dropped

Decision of the Judge or Jury
is Rendered

If the Decision is in Favor of
the Defendant—the Case
is Dismissed

If the Decision is in Favor of
the Plaintiff—a Remedy
is Addressed

Appeal by the Defendant

FIGURE 10–1   Anatomy of a lawsuit

Source: Ronald W. Rebore, *Educational Administration:
A Management Approach* (Englewood Cliffs, N.J.: Prentice-Hall, 1985), p. 69.

building principal might be sued for neglecting to properly evaluate and remove the teacher who allegedly did a poor job of supervising the student. The superintendent might be brought into the lawsuit because he neglected to remove the principal who inadequately supervised the teacher. The board of education might he sued because the members neglected to supervise and monitor the superintendent in his responsibility to evaluate the performance of the principal. This path then follows the chain-of-command in a school district and ensures that the responsible party or parties will be identified by the court.

This same type of situation is applicable to personnel management. A case could be made alleging that a given teacher's references were not properly investigated by the assistant superintendent for personnel, which eventuated in the hiring of an unqualified applicant. It goes without saying that employment situations perhaps carry more vulnerability than those involved with instruction.

Therefore, it is important for personnel managers to be well-informed about tort liability. With this knowledge, they will be able to establish personnel processes and procedures that will accomplish the objectives of the personnel department and also will be easy to defend in court. A tort is a civil wrong, other than a breach of contract, committed against a person or a person's property.

Tort law emanates from common law which is composed of those principles established through court cases that are usually referred to as *precedent.* The acts of legislatures have either broadened or narrowed these common law principles. For example, at common law, an individual wrongfully causing the death of another person incurred no civil liability; the Missouri legislature has enacted a statute that imposes civil liabilities in favor of certain persons, including the surviving spouse and children.

There are two major types of torts: intentional torts and negligence. Intentional torts are further classified as to whether the action interfered with a person or with the person's property. Assault, battery, and defamation are the most common types associated with personal interference; malicious trespassing is the most common interference with respect to property rights.

In personnel management, defamation of character is a potential area of litigation with regard to the giving of references and communicating the contents of an individual's personnel file. Defamation occurs when false information is communicated either by word of mouth (slander) or in writing (libel), brings hatred or ridicule on a person, and produces some type of harm to the person. With regard to the personnel function, the harm produced by defamation might be the loss of an employment opportunity or a job promotion.

To protect against such litigation, established procedures should outline who is responsible for writing references and under what circumstances the contents of an individual's personnel file can be released. Although each situation will vary, the following guidelines should be observed:

1. The employee has a right to review the contents of his or her personnel file in the presence of a personnel administrator.

2. The supervisor of an employee has a right to review the contents of an employee's file in the presence of a personnel administrator.

3. Only official and approved documents may be added to an employee's file (for example, attendance records, payroll records, performance evaluation forms).

4. No document may be removed from an individual's personnel file without notification to the employee, who has the right to question the removal.

5. The contents or partial contents of an employee's personnel file may not be released to other parties without the written permission of the employee (for example, attendance records being requested by a potential employer).

6. Under no circumstances should a personnel administrator discuss over the telephone information in an employee's file.

Negligence is that type of tort that involves some form of injury to another person as a result of conduct that falls below an established standard. It is the duty of an assistant superintendent for personnel and other personnel administrators to establish processes and procedures that do not violate federal and state laws and that accomplish the objectives of the personnel function. Therefore, in the recruitment and selection of new employees, affirmative action procedures must be followed so that the rights of protected groups are not violated. A personnel administrator who neglected to properly initiate or follow such procedures could be guilty of a tort if a minority applicant was denied an opportunity to be interviewed for a position and, as a result, lost a job opportunity. Even though a charge of discrimination would probably be filed in this case with the Equal Employment Opportunity Commission, there is also the possibility of a civil lawsuit being brought against an individual administrator.

In a tort liability lawsuit that involves a question of negligence, the court will apply the principle of the *reasonable person.*[2] This concept has a very specific application and definition. The reasonable person is someone who

1. Possesses average intelligence, normal perception, and memory.

2. Possesses such superior skill and knowledge that the defendant has or purports to have.

3. Possesses the same level of experience that the defendant has.

4. Possesses the same physical attributes that the defendant has.

Thus, the conduct of a personnel administrator involved in a lawsuit is compared against the conduct of a mythical reasonable person. If a reasonable person could have prevented the consequence, the administrator will be found negligent by the jury. The moral of the example is that all administrators should examine their professional responsibilities to determine if their conduct in fulfilling these responsibilities can withstand the test of the reasonable person.

In a civil lawsuit resulting in a judgment favoring the plaintiff, the defendant usually will be required to pay actual damages, which is the amount of money that the injury cost. The loss of a job opportunity has a potential for costing the defendant a considerable

---

[2]Daniel C. Pope, "A Brief for School Site Administrators on Liability Concerns," *School Business Affairs,* 51, no. 12 (December 1985), p. 26.

amount of money, which could conceivably reach into the hundreds of thousands of dollars. If it can be demonstrated in court that the defendant deliberately caused the injury, punitive damages may also be levied. This dollar amount is a punishment for intentionally bringing about a civil wrong. In some cases, punitive damages may equal or supersede the actual damages assessed by the court. A personnel administrator who publicly disagrees with the concept of affirmative action and who tells ethnic jokes to fellow employees might be laying the foundation for the allegation that he or she deliberately neglects to follow affirmative action procedures.

Errors and Omissions Liability Insurance

It should be clear from this presentation that each and every personnel administrator should be protected by errors and omissions liability insurance. Sources for obtaining such coverage include professional organizations and the school district's insurance carrier.

The National Education Association, American Federation of Teachers, and the American Association of School Administrators offer this type of insurance as a part of the regular membership benefits. Many of the large insurance companies will be happy to provide such protection under a group policy for all central-office administrators or for any other group of employees. The members of the board of education also may be included in this coverage and should be covered, particularly in those states where sovereign immunity has been abrogated. Finally, it should be remembered that most errors and omissions liability insurance policies do not cover punitive damages, because this would amount to condoning an act that was deliberately perpetrated.

ETHICAL CONSIDERATIONS IN SCHOOL PERSONNEL MANAGEMENT

Since the Watergate episode, the American people have become increasingly aware of the vulnerability of those who occupy leadership positions in private business, government, churches, and in public education. The news media constantly reveals crimes committed even by those who hold not only leadership positions but also positions of significant trust. A recent article in the *Wall Street Journal* indicated that even some lawyers have exhibited less than exemplary conduct.[3] However, nothing is more disheartening than to read about a clergyman or teacher who sexually abuses a child. These occurrences are easily judged as being immoral or unethical.

The central issue in this treatment is the fact that all people must make decisions on a daily basis where the lines of appropriate behavior are somewhat blurred. The grey area! Personnel administrators are particularly vulnerable because their decisions affect people in that most important area of life, employment. Students are also affected because the quality of their education depends upon the quality of the people employed by a school district.

[3]Richard B. Schmitt, "Ethics Courses for Lawyers Draw Comers," *Wall Street Journal,* 8 July 1993, sec. B, p. 82.

The basis for making ethically sound decisions is usually grounded in religious beliefs or philosophical assumptions. The Judeo-Christian-Islamic tradition sets forth norms of appropriate conduct that are accepted by most U.S. citizens. Many of these religious beliefs and philosophical assumptions are contained in the documents upon which the United States was founded. The philosophical assumptions are commonly understood as proceeding from human reason which is fortified by the natural law.[4]

The American Association of School Personnel Administrators has adopted the *Statement of Ethics for School Administrators* which was developed by the American Association of School Administrators. While this statement is appropriate, it is intended for all categories of administrators and does not go far enough to provide guidance in the many diverse and complicated situations that face contemporary school personnel administrators.

There are three principles which have been gleaned from the above sources and which constitute the foundation upon which the responsibilities in Exhibit 10–1 have been developed.

First, the exercise of these responsibilities in making judgments for decisions, over time, will help an individual to determine the sort of person and personnel professional he or she wants to become. Any given decision usually does not determine an individual's central orientation as a person unless it is a decision of monumental significance such as deliberately committing a felony. Rather, people are constantly in the state of becoming either a better person and professional or a person who gradually loses his or her integrity. Even inappropriate decisions about issues that might appear to be rather insignificant can chip away at the edges surrounding a person's central core of integrity.

Second, the decisions of school personnel administrators have a definite effect upon school districts as institutions. This effect will be either positive or negative depending on the motivation for the decision and its magnitude. For example, an assistant superintendent for personnel who attempts to influence the hiring of a certain person solely because he is his or her friend has made a decision which will have a negative effect on the school district for which he or she is employed. If this type of action is repeated over time, the school district could take on a negative image that will affect morale among other employees and among other educators in the surrounding school districts. In a similar manner, the decisions of personnel administrators will have a positive or negative effect upon the school personnel professional associations in which the administrator is a member or has a position of leadership. Human experience indicates that it is virtually impossible to keep inappropriate actions from becoming common knowledge.

The third principle is taken from the Declaration of Independence. " . . . all men are created equal, . . . they are endowed by their creator with certain unalienable rights, that among these are life, liberty, and the pursuit of happiness." Any action by a school personnel administrator to show preferential treatment to certain people, groups, or companies is contrary to this principle. The personnel administrator has a duty to ensure that such rights are manifested not only in the daily actions of employees but also in the policy and procedural processes of the school district.

---

[4]Milton A. Gonsalves, *Fagother's Right & Reason: Ethics in Theory and Practice,* 9th Ed. (Columbus, Ohio: Merrill Publishing Company, 1989), pp. 124–125.

**EXHIBIT 10–1 Responsibilities For the Ethical Management of the School
Personnel Function**

School districts have a moral and legal obligation to provide children and young adults with the best education possible given the human and financial resources available to them. The quality of education depends on the quality of personnel who directly or indirectly provide the educational service. Consequently, boards of education and superintendents of schools must be diligent in the selection of personnel administrators who will manage the personnel function. Once employed, personnel administrators will be held accountable for the following responsibilities.

*Responsibilities to the School District
and its Staff*

The responsibilities to the school district and its staff are to

- support and implement the policies of the board of education in a positive and effective manner;
- support and implement administrative processes and procedures in a positive and effective manner;
- through appropriate means, pursue changing board polices, administrative processes and procedures that are not consistent with sound practice;
- project a positive image of the school district to the community-at-large and the education community;
- promote the equitable treatment of individuals, groups, and companies;
- help colleagues and subordinates fulfill their obligations and aspirations;
- help subordinates achieve their maximum potential;
- treat colleagues and subordinates with dignity and fairness;
- maintain confidentiality in carrying out the obligations of a school personnel administrator;

- promote adherence to all local, state, and national ordinances and laws.

*Responsibilities to the School
Personnel Profession*

The responsibilities to the school personnel Profession are to

- promote membership in and the activities of school personnel professional associations at the local, state, and national levels;
- accept leadership roles in school personnel professional associations;
- promote research in school personnel administration that will enhance the effectiveness of the profession;
- promote professional development activities that will enhance the performance of school personnel administrators.

*Personal
Responsibilities*

Personal responsibilities are to

- fulfill the obligations of a school personnel administrator in an open manner;
- seek consultation from colleagues or other professionals when faced with an ethical or professional problem for which there appears to be no appropriate solution;
- Continue to grow as a person and as a school personnel professional through attendance at conventions, seminars, conferences, or through university coursework;
- develop the virtues of prudence, honesty, and justice so that your behavior will enhance not only your integrity as a person but also the integrity of the school district in which you work and the school personnel profession that you represent.

Ethical Responsibilities of School Personnel Administrators

The responsibilities set forth in Exhibit 10–1 are grouped under three separate headings: those pertaining to the school district and its staff, those pertaining to the school personnel profession, and those pertaining to the personnel administrator as a person. This approach has been selected over the more traditional approach wherein a list of "don'ts" is presented as a code of ethics. The emphasis here is on carrying out responsibilities which will have a positive effect on the school district, the personnel profession, and the personnel administrator. Also, because each human being is constantly in the state of becoming either a better person or a person of decreasing integrity, just avoiding certain types of actions is not enough to steer the becoming process in a positive direction. Each person must be pro-active! This is the reason why, in this presentation, the ethical administrator is portrayed as a person who seeks to fulfill responsibilities.

Responsibilities to the School District and its Staff

This first group of ten responsibilities clearly addresses the *communal* aspect of public school administration and, in particular, the *communal* aspect of school personnel management. School personnel administrators have obligations to the institution for which they work, the school district. Further, they have obligations to their colleagues and subordinates. Thus, loyalty to the board of education, superintendent of schools, colleagues, and subordinates becomes the vehicle for fulfilling these responsibilities. Sometimes it happens that a certain personnel administrator cannot ethically accept the policies or practices of the school district for which he or she works. If the administrator is unable to effect changes in the policies or practices of the district by using the chain-of-command process, he or she should seek other employment.[5]

Responsibilities to the School Personnel Profession

The next group of responsibilities defines the professional obligations of the personnel administrator. Emphasis is placed on participation in professional associations and working within these associations to enhance the profession. This is particularly important in the areas of research and professional development.

Personal Responsibilities

The final group of responsibilities are concerned with the personal growth of the personnel administrator. This growth is nurtured through professional development activities and the practice of certain virtues. The virtue of honesty should help administrators avoid conflict of interest situations and the virtue of prudence should help them to avoid even the

---

[5]National School Boards Association, "Ethics in Education," *The Administrative Angle on Policy Implementation,* Arlington, Virginia: The Association (December 1992), p. 2.

appearance of such a conflict. Thus, accepting gifts, services, or anything of value because of an act performed or withheld certainly violates the virtue of honesty. Accepting gifts, services, or something of value even though "no strings" were attached violates the virtue of prudence. Honesty is also violated when administrators use their position in a professional association for personal gain.

When an employee receives preferential treatment simply because of friendship with a certain administrator, the virtue of justice is violated.

All people need help at times. Seeking consultation from other professionals when the need arises is viewed here as an obligation. Therefore, to continue an inappropriate practice or to persist in behavior which could bring derision on the school district, the personnel profession, or the administrator is a violation of this obligation.

PERSONNEL POLICY DEVELOPMENT

Chapter 1 enumerated the advantages of having board of education policies. Now that the eight personnel functions have been elucidated in detail, it should be very clear that well-defined personnel policies are absolutely necessary. In fact, creating such policies is a major task of the personnel department. The difference between board of education policies and administrative procedures also should be kept in mind. Policies are usually broad statements of direction; procedures are a sequence of steps to be followed in implementing a policy. In practice, however, there is a fine distinction in some situations between the wording of a policy and the wording of a procedure that makes it operational.

Appendix A presents a set of sample policies adapted from policies collected by the Educational Policies Service of the National School Boards Association. These policies demonstrate a variety of construction models; they also demonstrate the overlapping characteristics of policies and procedures. Of course, EPS/NSBA is an exceptional service that would be of benefit to all school districts.

The index to the personnel policy section of the Educational Policies Service has also been included to show the scope that professional staff personnel manuals should entertain. Included for the same reason is Appendix B, which gives the table of contents for a classified employee personnel manual.

SUMMARY

This chapter is concerned with legal, ethical, and policy issues in personnel administration. These issues have become important within the last decade because of the increased emphasis on legal rights and responsibilities.

Teachers and administrators usually work under the provisions of an individual contract; classified personnel are employed at an hourly rate or for an annual salary. Using individual contracts for teachers and administrators is a matter of tradition which also is mandated by law in some states and which distinguishes a professional employee's working conditions from those of classified employees.

Teachers' and administrators' contracts must meet the requirements of general contract law, state statutes, and the precedents established through case law. A contract is an agreement between two or more competent persons for a legal consideration on a legal subject matter in the form required by law. The five basic components, therefore, to every valid contract are offer and acceptance, competent persons, a consideration, legal subject matter, and proper form.

Over the last decade, school districts have experienced an increase in litigation. In addition, personnel administrators are far more vulnerable today to judicial review of their actions than personnel administrators of a decade ago. It is imperative, therefore, that administrators have a rudimentary understanding of the American judicial system and are capable of making decisions that are legally defensible.

There are basically two systems of law. The first, called a civil law system, attempts to establish all laws in the form of statutes enacted by a legislative body. The second is referred to as a common law system. It is the basic approach used in England and was adopted in theory by most of the states in our country. Under this system the decisions rendered by a court become a precedent to be followed by the court in dealing with future cases. The system of law in the United States is a mixture of both civil and common law.

There are three major sources of law that form the foundation of the American judicial system: constitutions, statutes, and court cases. Constitutions are bodies of precepts that provide the framework within which government carries out its duties. Statutes are the enactments of legislative bodies; they are more commonly called laws. As stated above, common law emanates from the decisions of courts rather than from legislative bodies.

There are two additional sources of law that affect education even though they are not traditionally considered primary sources: administrative law and attorney general opinions.

Administrative law consists of those regulations set forth by agencies established by Congress and state legislatures. In the absence of case law, the state attorney general may be requested to render an opinion on the interpretation of a certain statute.

The two broad classifications of law are criminal and civil. Civil law is concerned with protecting the rights of individuals and corporate entities; criminal law is concerned with protecting the rights of society.

The judicial system is composed of municipal, state, and federal courts. Most states have three categories of courts: circuit courts, courts of appeal, and supreme courts. In like manner, there are three categories of federal courts: district courts, the U.S. Courts of Appeals, and the U.S. Supreme Court.

The U.S. judicial system also preserves the concept of equity. The state circuit and U.S. district courts may handle both law and equity issues. Certain issues are traditionally tried in equity, the most common being injunctions.

Personnel administrators should become familiar with the nuances of the state and federal court systems because of the great number of laws affecting employment and because of the potentiality for tort liability lawsuits.

In personnel management it is also extremely important to understand the role of the attorney. The attorney takes the material facts in a case and researches the statutes or laws and precedents of court cases for the purpose of organizing a reasonable defense. The defense will be only as strong as the level of accountability that has been demonstrated through personnel procedures and policies.

A lawsuit begins with the filing of a petition, setting forth the allegation in the appropriate court of jurisdiction. The next step is to clarify the allegation and the material facts. The final step is the trial.

A tort is a civil wrong, other than a breach of contract, committed against a person or a person's property. The two major types of torts are classified as intentional torts and negligence. Assault, battery, defamation, and trespassing are the most common types of intentional torts. In personnel management, defamation is a potential area of litigation with regard to the giving of references and the communicating of the contents of an individual's personnel file.

Negligence is a tort that involves conduct falling below an established standard that results in some type of injury to another person. Negligence, therefore, implies neglect of a duty. The duty of personnel administrators is to establish processes and procedures that do not violate federal and state laws and that meet the objectives of the personnel department. A personnel administrator who neglected to initiate or follow such procedures could be guilty of a tort if a minority applicant was denied an opportunity to be interviewed for a position and, as a result, lost a job opportunity.

In a civil lawsuit resulting in a judgment favoring the plaintiff, the defendant may be assessed actual damages and even punitive damages if the injury was deliberately perpetrated. Each and every personnel administrator, therefore, should be protected by an errors and omissions liability insurance program.

Since the Watergate episode, people in the United States have become increasingly aware of the vulnerability of those who occupy leadership positions. The central issue is that all people must make decisions on a daily basis when the lines of appropriate behavior are somewhat blurred. Personnel administrators are particularly vulnerable because their decisions affect people in that most important area of life, employment.

The basis for making ethically sound decisions is usually grounded in religious beliefs or philosophical assumptions. There are three principles that have been gleaned from these beliefs and assumptions. First, the exercise of responsibilities in making judgments for decisions, over time, will help an individual to determine the sort of person and personnel professional he or she wants to become. Second, the decisions of school personnel administrators have a definite effect upon school districts as institutions. The third principle comes from the Declaration of Independence, which sets forth that all people are created equal and have certain unalienable rights among which are life, liberty, and the pursuit of happiness.

The ethical responsibilities of school personnel administrators are grouped around the following: responsibilities to the school district and its staff; responsibilities to the school personnel profession; and personal responsibilities.

Personnel policies are the key to effective human resource management. Boards of education should take a deliberate approach to policy development that will ensure defensible personnel operations.

APPENDIX A
AN INDEX OF APPROPRIATE POLICIES
WITH SAMPLE PERSONNEL POLICIES

The policies contained herein are meant to exemplify various policy formats employed by a number of school districts. They have been modeled after actual policies currently in effect in different parts of the United States. The source from which the original policies have been drawn is the Educational Policies Service of the National School Boards Association (EPS/NSBA).

The main purpose of this service is to assist school boards with their responsibility to establish and maintain updated written policies. Further, EPS/NSBA assists school boards in developing those kinds of policies that improve the education process and establish productive relationships between the school board, staff, students, and the public.

Along with an index of policies which outlines the scope of common and professional policies necessary for most school districts, two statements are included concerning personnel policy goals and objectives. Specific policies covering the following dimensions of the personnel function also are included:

- Staff Recruiting and Hiring
- Professional Staff Probation and Tenure
- Professional Staff Hiring
- Evaluation of Professional Staff
- Professional Staff Development Opportunities
- Professional Staff Probation and Tenure (administrators)
- Professional Staff Termination of Employment (administrators)
- Staff Complaints and Grievances
- Professional/Support Staff Employee Assistance Fringe Benefit Program
- Professional Staff Contracts and Compensation Plans
- Personnel Records

The variety in content and style of these policies should provide some insight into the nuance of policy development.

Index of Policies

- Personnel Policies Goals
  - Personnel Policies Priority Objectives
- Equal Opportunity Employment
- Staff Involvement in Decision Making
- Staff Ethics
  - Staff Conflicts of Interest
  - Staff Conduct
- Board–Staff Communications
- Staff Health and Safety
- Staff Participation in Community Activities
- Staff Participation in Political Activities

- Staff–Student Relations
- Staff Gifts and Solicitations
- Smoking on School Premises by Staff Members
- Personnel Records
- Staff Complaints and Grievances

Professional Staff
- Professional Staff Positions
- Professional Staff Contracts and Compensation Plans
    Professional Staff Salary Schedules
        Professional Staff Merit System
    Professional Staff Supplementary Pay Plans
    Professional Staff Fringe Benefits
    Professional Staff Leaves and Absences
    Professional Staff Vacations and Holidays
- Professional Staff Recruiting
    Posting of Professional Staff Vacancies
- Professional Staff Hiring
- Part-Time and Substitute Professional Staff Employment
    Arrangements for Professional Staff Substitutes
- Professional Staff Orientation
- Professional Staff Probation and Tenure
- Professional Staff Seniority
- Professional Staff Assignments and Transfers
- Professional Staff Time Schedules
- Professional Staff Work Load
    Professional Staff Extra Duty
    Professional Staff Meetings
- Professional Staff Development Opportunities
- Professional Staff Visitations and Conferences
- Supervision of Professional Staff
- Evaluation of Professional Staff
- Professional Staff Promotions
- Professional Staff Termination of Employment
    Reduction in Professional Staff Work Force
    Resignation of Professional Staff Members
    Retirement of Professional Staff Members
    Suspension and Dismissal of Professional Staff Members
- Miscellaneous Professional Staff Policies
    Nonschool Employment by Professional Staff Members
        Professional Staff Consulting Activities
        Tutoring for Pay
    Professional Research and Publishing
    Exchange Teaching
    Professional Organizations

Personnel Policies Goals

The personnel employed by the district constitute the most important resource for effectively conducting a quality learning program. Important contributions to a successful education program are made by all staff members. The district's program will function best when it employs highly qualified personnel, conducts appropriate staff development activities, and establishes policies and working conditions which are conducive to high morale and which enable each staff member to make the fullest contribution to district programs and services.

The goals of the district's personnel program shall include the following:

1. To develop and implement those strategies and procedures for personnel recruitment, screening, and selection which will result in employing the best available candidates; i.e., those with highest capabilities, strongest commitment to quality education, and greatest probability of effectively implementing the district's learning program.
2. To develop general deployment strategy for greatest contribution to the learning program, and to utilize it as the primary basis for determining staff assignments.
3. To develop a climate in which optimum staff performance, morale, and satisfaction are produced.
4. To provide positive programs of staff development designed to contribute both to improvement of the learning program and to each staff member's career development aspirations.
5. To provide for a genuine team approach to education, including staff involvement in planning, decision making, and evaluation.
6. To provide attractive compensation and benefits as well as other provisions for staff welfare.
7. To develop and utilize for personnel evaluation positive processes which contribute to the improvement of both staff capabilities and the learning program.

Personnel Policies Priority Objectives

In support of its stated personnel policies goals, the Board endorses the following set of priority objectives:

1. By *(month/year)*, all personnel staff assignments will be reviewed to ensure the most effective utilization possible of staff time and capabilities. To the maximum degree possible, each staff member is to be assigned duties which employ his or her talents to the utmost.
2. By *(month/year)*, job descriptions for all staff positions will be reviewed and updated by all employees and their supervisors. All job descriptions are to integrate program requirements with related positions; itemize specific and realistic job performance responsibilities; and provide for measures of assessing job performance. This objective will be considered successfully achieved when there is a consensus by the employee and his or her immediate supervisor.

3. By *(month/year)*, the superintendent will develop a comprehensive Staff Talent Bank, which will provide access to many special skills, talents, and capabilities that district personnel have at their command and which the district may draw upon from time to time to meet specialized needs. This objective will be considered accomplished when the central office can provide immediate answers to questions such as the following: Which staff members can speak the Navajo language, Spanish, Cantonese? Which are published authors? Which have degrees in law? Which know how to climb a mountain, build a house, ride a horse, quilt a rug, or drive a tractor trailer?

4. By *(month/year)*, procedures and methods for recruiting, screening, selecting, and assigning personnel shall be revised to (a) integrate with program needs, and (b) provide humanistic procedures which meet needs and concerns of applicants and employees as adequately as feasible. Measures of success shall be prepared under the district superintendent's supervision, and shall include increased success in program operation, subjective judgments of program managers and others, and perceptions of applicants and employees.

Staff Recruiting/Hiring

Through its personnel policies, the board of education shall maintain an effective recruitment program designed to attract, secure, and hold the highest qualified personnel for all professional, nonprofessional, and paraprofessional positions. The recruitment program shall be based upon an alertness to candidates who will devote themselves to the education and welfare of the children of this school system.

It is the responsibility of the superintendent and of persons delegated by him to determine the personnel needs of the school district and to locate suitable candidates to recommend for employment to the board. Through effective administration procedures, the superintendent shall recommend to the board the retention of personnel who are motivated to do their best work and to be creative.

No inquiry in regard to religion, creed, race, color, or national origin shall be made of a person proposed for or seeking employment.

It shall be the duty of the superintendent to see that persons nominated for employment shall meet all qualifications established by state statute, the rules and regulations of the state board of education, the commissioner of education, the county superintendent, and policies of the board of education for the type of position for which nomination is made.

Priority shall be given to the best qualified *local* applicant when two or more applicants seem equally qualified for a position.

An employee shall be appointed by the board only upon the recommendation of the superintendent. Should a person nominated by the superintendent be rejected by the board, it shall be the duty of the superintendent to make another nomination.

An estimate of the cost of the recruitment and selection program will be made annually by the superintendent and presented to the board for inclusion in the annual budget.

Professional Staff Probation and Tenure

In accordance with state law, all certificated personnel will be granted tenure upon reemployment after three consecutive years of successful service under contract with the district.

The board will expect thorough and competent evaluations of all personnel before they become candidates for tenure. This requires critical evaluation at four stages:

1. At the time of selection.
2. During the first year when emphasis on self-evaluation will help the teacher decide whether he or she commands the necessary skills to contribute to the profession.
3. During the second year when emphasis is on whether the first year's success can be sustained and developed.
4. During the third year when it must be determined whether the teacher will be a permanent asset to the staff.

If evaluations are regular and thorough, and discussed carefully with teachers, candidates for tenure will be aware of their status. The board wishes no teacher to be taken by surprise if he or she is not reappointed, and will direct that due notice of nonrenewal of contracts be served in accordance with state law.

The contract of employment of a probationary or continuing teacher for a school year will be deemed automatically renewed for the ensuing school year unless, on or before April 15, the board, a member thereof acting on behalf of the board, or the superintendent of the school district gives notice to the teacher of the termination of his or her contract.

The probationary or continuing teacher will indicate acceptance of the contract for the ensuing year by signing and returning the contract or by an acceptance in writing which is delivered to the school board within 30 days after receipt of the contract.

Notice of termination of a contract will be delivered personally to the teacher or sent by registered or certified mail bearing a postmark of on or before April 15, directed to the teacher at his or her place of residence as recorded in the school district records. The notice will include a statement of the reasons for not reemploying the teacher.

All continuing teachers will be issued a contract annually.

The superintendent will present to the board of education, on or before April 1 of each year, lists of appointments, reappointments, and non-reappointments for the following school year. These lists will indicate the following information for each employee:

1. Location of employment.
2. Name and position.
3. Sex.
4. Race.

Professional Staff Hiring

The board of education has the legal responsibility of approving the employment of all employees. While this responsibility cannot be waived, the board assigns to the superintendent the process of recruiting staff members. In carrying out this responsibility, the superintendent will involve various administrative and teaching staff members as needed. All personnel selected for employment must be recommended by the superintendent and approved by the board. To aid in obtaining the best available staff members for our schools, the board adopts the following general criteria to be utilized in the selection process for initial employment.

1. There will be no discrimination in the hiring process due to age, sex, creed, race, color, or national origin.
2. Candidates for high school and middle school positions should have a major or its equivalent—30 semester hours—in the teaching field. Elementary candidates should have a major or its equivalent—30 hours—in elementary education or in the special area to which they will be assigned.
3. Candidates for all teaching positions should have an overall grade-point average of 2.5 (A–4, B–3, C–2, D–1). High school and middle school candidates should have a grade-point average of 2.75 in their teaching field.
4. The highest quality of instruction is enhanced by a staff with a wide variation in educational preparation, background, and previous experience. Concerted efforts will be exerted to maintain this variation in the staff.
5. Candidates for teaching positions should provide evidence of meeting the state requirements for regular certification status. In cases of absolute necessity, holders of provisional or temporary certificates may be employed in regular full-time capacity not to exceed one year.

In addition to the above general criteria, the superintendent will submit to the board for approval specific criteria dealing with each vacancy. These specific criteria will describe those competencies needed for success in the position.

In the event that the specific or general criteria are not being met by a particular candidate being recommended, it shall be the responsibility of the superintendent to point out the deficiencies to the board so that they may act accordingly. Should the board not approve the employment of a candidate being recommended by the superintendent, it shall be the duty of the superintendent to make another recommendation.

The employment of each staff member is not official until the contract is approved by the board and signed by the candidate.

The employment sequence shall be as follows:

1. The verbal offer of employment to the candidate.
2. Verbal acceptance by the candidate.
3. Approval of candidate by board.
4. Contract sent to the candidate.
5. Candidate's acceptance as signified by a signed contract returned to superintendent within 15 days.

Evaluation of Professional Staff

The primary purpose of teacher appraisal will be the development of staff and the improvement of teaching. This appraisal will be an ongoing program, important for beginning teachers, but equally as important for teachers with experience. As teachers appraise their present performance and set goals for future performance, they gain in stature and add stature to their profession.

Appraisal procedures will be designed to help teachers define their areas of greatest strength as well as the areas in which improvement is needed. Plans will be made to capitalize on those strengths. Procedures will be set up to help them improve in areas where help is needed. At later conferences, progress will be noted and plans for further improvement made. The appraisals will not be used for merit rating or merit pay. Staff improvement is the goal.

The regulations, procedures, and instruments for the evaluation of teachers will be developed cooperatively by administrators and the teaching staff.

Professional Staff Development Opportunities

Today's dynamic and rapidly changing society, with its tremendous accumulation of new knowledge and the attending obsolescence in some areas of practice makes it imperative that all staff members be engaged in a continuous program of professional and technical growth in order that they may be qualified to provide a quality educational program for all students being served by this school system.

It is the policy of the school board that a program of staff development be established to provide an opportunity for the continuous professional and technical growth of teachers of this school district.

As a result of the operation of this policy, staff members will become knowledgeable regarding new developments and changes in their specialized fields and will utilize new and improved methods in practice.

The administrative staff will provide leadership in establishing a staff development program, which will assist each staff member to make a maximum contribution to the school district's effort to provide a quality educational program.

Professional Staff Probation and Tenure Administrators

School-level administrators shall be on two years' probation upon entry into this school district. On promotion to a new position, an administrator's probation shall not exceed one year.

A year's probation shall be determined on the basis of a full twelve-month period commencing from the effective date of appointment. The probationary year may be interrupted by any leave approved by the board of education. Approved leaves with full pay will not alter the probationary period. Long-term leaves of absence shall result in the probationary period being altered by the exact number of calendar days absent.

On satisfactory completion of his or her probationary period, an administrator shall have tenure in all positions in the same class and salary range or lower classes and salary ranges. Administrators with tenure shall not be suspended, demoted, discharged, or terminated without due process. However, the foregoing is not intended to interfere with the right of the board to relieve employees from duty for legitimate reasons.

Professional Staff Termination of Employment Administrators

This policy sets forth procedures to be used by the board to nonrenew or immediately terminate the contract of a certified administrator. These procedures are designed to protect the rights of both the employee and the board and to ensure that a spirit of fairness prevails.

Procedures for Nonrenewal of Contract Are as Follows:

A. When it becomes evident to a unit superintendent that an administrative employee is not doing an acceptable job, the unit superintendent will arrange a conference to discuss the problem and try to find a solution to it.

B. Within three days of the conference the unit superintendent will make a report in duplicate outlining the problems as seen by the unit superintendent and by the administrator, and the recommendations for resolving the problem. A copy of this report will be sent to the superintendent of schools.

C. Approximately two weeks after the first conference, a second conference will be held and a report made as outlined in (B) above.

D. At least two weeks and not more than four weeks after the second conference, a third conference will be arranged and a report made as outlined in (B) above.

E. If a solution to the problem is found after one or more meetings, the unit superintendent will notify the administrator in writing that his or her work is now satisfactory and further conferences are not necessary.

F. After the third conference, if the problem has been resolved, the unit superintendent will notify the administrator in writing that his or her work is now satisfactory and further conferences are not necessary. If the problem still exists, the unit superintendent may schedule another conference or may recommend to the superintendent of schools that the administrator's contract not be renewed. (This procedure is to ensure that there will be at least three formal conferences before a recommendation is made not to renew a contract. There may be any number of conferences before a problem is solved or a recommendation is made.)

G. In the event the superintendent of schools decides to recommend to the board that an administrator's contract not be renewed, he or she will give written notice to the administrator of his or her pending action.

H. After an administrator receives written notification of the superintendent's intention to recommend that his or her contract not be renewed, he or she will have ten (10) days to file a written request with the president of the board, with a copy to the superintendent of schools, for a hearing before the board. The hearing before the board will be conducted in accordance with provisions outlined in state statutes.

I. Within ten (10) days of the hearing the school board will render a final decision and the administrator will be notified in accordance with state statutes.

Procedures for Immediate Termination of Contract Are as Follows:

A. Any person serving under annual contract may be placed on probation or suspended for cause with pay by the superintendent of schools, who will report such action to the board at its next meeting for final action. Cause includes, but is not limited to, the following: immorality, conduct unbecoming a professional teacher, insubordination, failure to follow reasonable written regulations and policies, physical or mental disability impairing the performance of duties or any conditions which may require immediate action to protect the safety or welfare of the children.

B. While the board may terminate the employee's contract at any time for cause, such action will not take place prior to the employee's receipt of a notice of the specific charges and an opportunity for a hearing before the board of education in accordance with state law.

Staff Complaints and Grievances

All employees of the board of education shall have the right to appeal the application of policies and administrative decisions affecting them. Each employee shall be assured freedom from restraint, interference, coercion, discrimination or reprisal in presenting his or her appeal with respect to a personal grievance.

All grievances shall be handled expeditiously.

Those grievances that involve a complaint of an employee who has sustained a personal loss, injury, or inconvenience because of a violation, misinterpretation, or misapplication of a contract with a collective bargaining unit of which the employee is a member shall be presented and heard according to the procedures established in the particular contract.

All other grievances shall be handled according to the following procedures, which also outline the general pattern for grievance processing established by the negotiated contracts.

Steps in Grievance Procedure

1. *First level:* Any complainant who has a grievance shall discuss it first with his or her principal/other supervisor.

2. *Second level:* If as a result of the informal discussion, the matter is not resolved, the grievant shall initiate a grievance in writing to his or her principal/other immediate supervisor within five (5) school days, giving the full details of his or her grievance. The principal/other immediate supervisor shall communicate his or her decision to the grievant in writing within three (3) school days of the receipt of the written grievance.

3. *Third level:* If the grievance remains unresolved, the grievant no later than five (5) school days after receipt of the above decision may appeal it to the appropriate department head (superintendent, school business administrator, board secretary). The appeal must be made in writing and must give details as to why the decision was unsatisfactory. The department head shall give his or her decision in writing to the grievant within ten (10) school days.

4. *Fourth level:* If the grievance is not resolved, the grievant may, no later than five (5) school days after receipt of the department head's decision, request a review by the board of education. The request shall be made in writing through the department head, who shall attach all papers relating to the grievance. The board, or a committee thereof, shall review the grievance and shall, at the option of the board, hold a hearing with the grievant and render a decision in writing within forty-five (45) days of receipt of the appeal. If the board decides not to hold a hearing, the grievant shall be notified of this decision no later than thirty (30) days after receipt of the appeal.

Representation

An employee shall have the right to present his or her own grievance or may designate a representative of his or her recognition unit to appear with him or her at any level of the above procedure.

The employee who chooses to have representation shall provide advance notice of such in writing to the superior at the respective procedural level at least two (2) days prior to the hearing on the grievance.

Professional/Supportive Staff Employee Assistance Program Fringe Benefit

The school board, the State Teacher Education Associations, and the State Association of Supporting Services Employees recognize that a wide range of problems not directly related to a job may have an effect on an employee's job performance. The problems may be behavioral or medical in nature and involve physical, mental, or emotional illness, alcohol abuse or alcoholism, and drug abuse or chemical dependency; or may involve marital, family, financial, or legal concerns. Alcoholism and other chemical dependencies are recognized as being progressive illnesses and potentially fatal.

In most instances, employees will overcome such personal problems independently, and the effect on job performance will be negligible. However, employees who have a problem they feel may affect their work performance are encouraged to seek voluntarily information and referral by contacting the director or advisors of the employee assistance program.

All requests for help will be considered as confidential.

The purpose of this policy is to assure employees that if personal problems are or may be the cause of current and/or future unsatisfactory job performance, they will receive an offer of assistance to help resolve such problems in an effective and confidential manner. Specifically,

1. It is agreed that almost any problem can be successfully treated provided it is recognized in its early stages and the assistance of an appropriate medical, psychiatric, counseling, and/or self-help service is sought.
2. This aid will be made available to employees through the employee assistance program.
3. Employees are assured that their job, tenure, future, and reputation will not be jeopardized by using this employee service.
4. It is the responsibility of an employee who is chemically dependent or who abuses drugs or alcohol to seek early intervention, assistance, and treatment.
5. Treatment for alcoholism and other chemical dependencies is covered by the present sick leave policy. Extended leave for treatment can be arranged under accumulated sick leave, annual leave, sick leave banks, or leave without pay on the same basis as for other physical or mental health problems.
6. Efforts will be made to ensure that the disease of alcoholism and/or chemical dependency will receive the same employee benefits and insurance coverages provided for other illnesses under established employee benefit plans.
7. All records pertaining to clients in this program will be maintained with the strictest of confidentiality in accordance with the highest medical and ethical standards and state and federal laws. All records will be segregated from an individual's personnel records.
8. Since employee work performance can be affected by the problems of an employee's spouse and other dependents, the program is available to the families of employees as well.
9. School district retirees may also use the services of the employee assistance program.

Professional Staff Contracts and Compensation Plans

It shall be the general policy of this district to pay salaries commensurate with the duties and responsibilities involved and with regard to prevailing practices in other comparable jurisdictions.

It shall be the policy of the board to establish all salaries and benefits for employees insofar as possible by June 1 and no later than June 30 of each year.

It is the intent of the board of trustees to take into consideration the Area Consumer Price Index in its deliberation of employee salaries.

A. Placement on Schedule

Placement within classification shall be made as accurately as possible. At the time of employment each certificated employee shall submit to the personnel department a complete transcript of college units and verification of all previous experience. Contracts shall not be effective until complete transcripts have been received and approved. It is the responsibility of the employee to provide the personnel department with transcripts. Credit for previous experience will be granted as follows:

1. Regular teaching   Previous verified experience as a full-time regularly credentialed teacher in the public schools shall be recognized for the purpose of placement on the salary schedule on a year-to-year basis. A year for the purposes of this section is defined as 75 percent of the school calendar year.

2. Military service   One year of credit on the salary schedule for each two (2) years of honorable military service shall be granted for a maximum of two (2) years on the salary schedule.

3. Other experience   Participation in Peace Corps, Vista, National Teacher Corps and noncombatant service under the direction of the Selective Service System shall be awarded experience credit in the same manner as military experience.

Experience credit may be rewarded for directly related experience (i.e., business for business education; recreation for P.E.; public library for librarians; teaching, counseling, or nursing in private accredited schools, colleges or universities, etc.) as determined by the superintendent or his or her designated representative.

The employee at all times is responsible for providing verifications and certification as required in this section. This section shall apply only to personnel entering the district following date of adoption.

B. Intern Teachers

In recognition of the district's commitment to the progress of education and the professional development of educators, the board of trustees authorizes the administration to employ intern teachers when such employment shall benefit the educator in training and the school district.

The purpose of the intern teaching program is to provide a program for specially selected young people to become fully credentialed teachers. Close supervision of the interns is provided throughout the year by the vice principal for curriculum, department chairperson, and the supervising instructor from the college or university.

All teacher interns shall be placed on step 1 of column 1 and will be eligible for all benefits in direct proportion to their contracts.

Intern teachers whose contracts are for less than a full-time assignment shall receive a prorated salary equal to the contractual percentage of their assignments.

C. Salary Adjustments for Part-Time Teachers

Salary for less than a full year of service shall be paid to certificated personnel in accordance with state statute, which limits payment of the salary to the ratio of days worked to the total number of working days required of that position for the school year by the board of trustees.

Teachers employed part-time shall receive remuneration equal to the contractual percentage of their assignments.

A certificated employee absent for reasons other than illness, accident, personal necessity, or bereavement shall be paid his regular salary less the amount actually paid the substitute, except as otherwise stipulated herein.

Full salary shall be deducted for all periods of unauthorized absences. Salary adjustments for authorized absences shall follow the leave of absence policy.

D. Increments
In general the board of trustees has followed a policy of providing increments for employees on a yearly basis, based upon the current published salary schedule. However, the board reserves the right to approve a salary schedule prior to July 1 of each school year. This approval may include the granting of increments and the stipulation of any and all salary benefits accruing to employees by virtue of the previous salary schedule. The board further reserves the right to delay the operation of a salary schedule in the event of any emergency.

In general, each certificated employee shall receive the annual salary increase provided that

1. He or she holds a regular teaching credential.
2. He or she has not yet reached the highest step in his or her classification.
3. He or she has fulfilled the staff development education requirements as stipulated in the professional development policy.

E. Minimum Salaries
The minimum salary provision of the salary schedule shall not be less than the minimum salary requirements of the State for certificated employees of the public schools as established by the current law.

F. Horizontal Movement on Salary Schedule
A staff member shall provide written notice to the personnel department of the district of the intention to qualify for horizontal movement on the salary schedule prior to March 1 of the school year preceding the year for which advancement is desired. Staff members shall advance no more than one column a year. The official transcripts from the colleges or universities showing credits earned must reach the personnel department by October 1 of the school year for which horizontal advancement has been requested. An employee who qualifies for horizontal advancement on the salary schedule shall be advanced one column and shall then be advanced one increment step if he or she has not already reached the maximum step in the new column. (An employee shall advance only one step per school year.)

With these exceptions only credits earned for upper division or graduate study in accredited universities and colleges shall be counted for advancement on the salary schedule. Such credits shall be earned in the major or minor areas on the teachers' or counselors' credential or as part of a graduate degree program.

1. Undergraduate credits shall be counted toward advancement on the salary schedule only when prior written approval has been obtained from the personnel department.
2. Credit earned under the professional development policy shall be counted towards advancement on the salary schedule at the rate of one unit for every fifteen hours of class attendance in staff development educational programs conducted by the district. Study

in accredited colleges and universities undertaken for the purpose of fulfilling the requirements of the professional development policy shall be granted credit according to that awarded by the educational institution. The maximum number of credits earned under district sponsored staff development programs that may be applied to the salary schedule advancement shall be 15 units.

3. The credit awarded by the professional growth committee also may be used to qualify for horizontal movement on the salary schedule.

G. Professional Development Required for Vertical Movement on Salary Scale

The professional growth of certificated personnel in the district shall include the acquisition or improvement of skills in the areas of high priority as identified by the board of trustees in its goal-setting process. In order to assure continual professional growth, all certificated staff members are required to complete a minimum of four (4) semester units or the equivalent (one semester unit equals 15 hours) in professional development every three years for this service (professional growth period) to qualify for vertical movement on the salary schedule. Fulfillment of the requirement may be met by any of the options listed below. Professional development activities described in options 3, 4, and 5 require approval of the district's professional growth committee.

1. Successful completion of any course, workshop or similar activity offered by an accredited college or university.
2. Participation in staff development education programs offered by this or other districts.
3. Participation in seminars or workshops sponsored by educationally oriented agencies.
4. Successful completion of an individual professional development program approved in advance.
5. Active participation in professional organizations, conferences and other educational groups related to the individual's teaching area.

The initial professional growth period shall begin on September 1 of the first year of employment for new employees and on September 1, 1990, for current employees of the district.

Personnel Records

The school administration shall maintain a personnel file in the office of the superintendent for each teacher it employs. The personnel file shall include the following sections:

1. *Evaluation section.* The evaluation section shall include all complaints against and commendations of the teacher, written suggestions for corrections and improvements, and evaluation reports made by the administration.
2. *Supplementary section.* The supplementary section shall include teacher certificates, health certificates, academic records, preemployment references, and application forms.

Additions to the Evaluation Section

No complaint, commendation, suggestion, or evaluation may be placed in the evaluation files unless it meets the following requirements:

1. The comment is signed by the person making the complaint, commendation, suggestion or evaluation.
2. The superintendent or teacher's principal has notified the teacher by letter or in person that the comment is available in the superintendent's office for inspection prior to its placement in the teacher's evaluation section.

The teacher may offer a denial or explanation of the complaint, commendation, suggestion, or evaluation, and any such denial or explanation shall become a part of the teacher's evaluation section.

General Access to the Teacher's Personnel File

Access to a teacher's personnel file may be given to the following persons without the consent of the teacher:

1. The superintendent, the teacher's principal, the teacher's supervisor, and a school board member if it relates to his or her duties or responsibilities as a board member.
2. Members of the review panel if the teacher requests a review by the Professional Review Committee.

No other person may have access to a teacher's personnel file except under the following circumstances:

1. When the teacher gives written consent to the release of his or her records. The written consent must specify the records to be released and to whom they are to be released. Each consent to release must be handled separately; blanket permission for release of information shall not be accepted.
2. When subpoenaed under court order.

Teacher's Access to His or Her Personnel File

A teacher may have access to his or her own personnel file at all reasonable times; i.e., during regular office hours. The right to access includes the right to make written objections to any information contained in the file. Each written objection must be signed by the teacher and it shall become part of the personnel file.

Records Management

The superintendent shall be the records manager for teacher personnel files and shall have the overall responsibility for maintaining and preserving the confidentiality of teacher personnel files. The superintendent, however, may designate another official to perform the duties of the records manager. The records manager is responsible for granting or denying access to records on the basis of these regulations.

APPENDIX B
TABLE OF CONTENTS FOR A CLASSIFIED EMPLOYEE PERSONNEL MANUAL

GOODVILLE SCHOOL DISTRICT

Classified Employee Personnel Manual

This manual constitutes the personnel policies and regulations for classified employees of the Goodville School District. Accountability for the implementation and maintenance of this manual is delegated to the Assistant Superintendent for Personnel. The policies contained in this manual may be deleted or amended, and additional policies may be included by action of the Board of Education.

Regulations contained herein may, in like manner, be deleted or amended, and new regulations may be included by administrative memorandum.

Each employee will receive a copy of this manual and every employee is expected to become familiar with its contents.

TABLE OF CONTENTS

SELECTED BIBLIOGRAPHY

Alexander, Kern, and M., David Alexander, *The Law of Schools, Students and Teachers.* St. Paul, Minn.: West Publishing Co., 1984.

Beck, Lynn G., and Joseph Murphy. *Ethics in Educational Leadership Programs: An Expanding Role.* Thousand Oaks, California: Corwin Press, Inc., 1994.

Boothe, James W., Leo H. Bradley, T. Michael Flick, Katherine E. Keough, and Susanne P. Kirk, "Questions of Ethics," *The Executive Educator,* 14, no. 2 (February 1992), pp. 17–24.

Data Research, Inc., *U.S. Supreme Court Education Cases,* 4th edition, Rosemount, Minnesota: Data Research, Inc., 1996, pp. 135–191.

Hogan, John C., *The School, the Courts, and the Public Interest* (2nd ed.). Lexington, Mass.: Lexington Books, 1986.

Horton, Janet Little, and Jeffrey J. Horner, "Termination for Immoral Conduct: Can You Make It Stick?" *Updating School Board Policies,* 15, no. 5 (May 1984), p. 4.

Jones, Thomas, Dorel Semler, eds. *School Law Update—Preventive School Law.* Topeka, Kans.: National Organization on Legal Problems of Education, 1985.

Kalish, Judith and David Perry, "Setting Ethical Standards," *The Executive Educator,* 14, no. 2 (February 1992), pp. 24–27.

Lamorte, Michael, *School Law: Cases and Concepts.* Englewood Cliffs, N.J.. Prentice-Hall, 1981.

McCarthy, Martha M., *Public School Law: Teachers' and Students' Rights.* Rockleigh, N.J.: Allyn and Bacon, 1984.

Menacker, Julius, *School Law: Theoretical and Case Perspectives.* Englewood Cliffs, N.J.: Prentice-Hall, 1987.

National School Boards Association, "Protection Against Personal Injury to Limit Your Liability," *Updating School Board Policies,* 16, no. 5 (May 1985), pp. 1–3.

Sovereign, Kenneth, *Personnel Law.* Englewood Cliffs, N.J.: Prentice-Hall, 1984.

Uerling, Donald F., "Constitutional Due Process and Educational Administration," *Spectrum: Journal of School Research and Information,* 3, no. 3 (Summer 1985), pp. 41–46.

Zirkel, Perry A., and Sharon Nalbone Richardson, *A Digest of Supreme Court Decisions Affecting Education,* 2nd ed. Bloomington, Ind.: Phi Delta Kappa Educational Foundation, 1988, pp. 53–85.

EPILOGUE

This book has covered a lot of material in relatively few pages, describing the various dimensions of the personnel function. The reader who has just finished this book must keep in mind that politics and the human situation in general will affect the processes, procedures, and techniques used in personnel administration. For example, a personnel administrator may recommend the employment of a teacher who is turned down by the board while another is hired with fewer qualifications. A given personnel administrator may never know the reason why this occurred. There are always hidden agendas!

There is no issue more important in our contemporary times than *ethical behavior.* This is true not only for teachers and educational administrators but also for governmental officials, business people, and even the clergy. The media continually focuses on illegal and unethical conduct. While professional educational administrators have always recognized the necessity of being above-board, the climate in contemporary society is such that administrators must be able to demonstrate that their actions are based on a system of ethics. It is for this very reason that I developed the section in Chapter 10 dealing with ethics in school personnel management along with a corresponding set of *responsibilities.* It is vital that every administrator learn to carry out his or her professional responsibilities in such a manner that his or her integrity cannot be questioned. Short-term solutions and arbitrary decisions, therefore, must be judiciously avoided.

Technological advances in the last ten years have presented educational administrators with unique opportunities and significant challenges. Administrators must become competent in the use of technology, or the administration of our schools will slip even further behind the private sector. Not only must administrators learn how to utilize computers to perform administrative tasks such as pupil scheduling, attendance reporting, grade reporting, inventory reporting, and fiscal accounting, but personnel administrators must also learn to use the computer in the management of the various dimensions of the personnel function. Some larger school districts have already installed very sophisticated information-management systems, which make for more efficient and accurate personnel management. Computer technology advances so rapidly that it is impossible to recommend hardware and software in this book.

In order to balance involvement in the new technologies, personnel administrators must become more humanistic. Technology tends to isolate individuals from one another and emphasizes solitary activities. What happens, in essence, is that information collection, storage, and use increase while human interaction decreases. In the final analysis, we will know more but understand less, with an accompanying decrease in human relations skills.

The personnel administrator, therefore, must see the necessity of developing innovative ways to interact with teachers and staff members. Utilizing a collaborative approach to personnel management as set forth in this book will provide such an opportunity.

Thus, personnel administrators of the future must be scrupulously ethical. At the same time, they must understand and make use of technological advances, as well as appreciate the necessity of creating ways to improve human interaction.

INDEX